Dreaming of Freedom in South Africa

For Gill

Dreaming of Freedom in South Africa

Literature between Critique and Utopia

David Johnson

Edinburgh University Press is one of the leading university presses in the UK. We publish academic books and journals in our selected subject areas across the humanities and social sciences, combining cutting-edge scholarship with high editorial and production values to produce academic works of lasting importance. For more information visit our website: edinburghuniversitypress.com

© David Johnson, 2020, 2021

Edinburgh University Press Ltd
The Tun – Holyrood Road
12(2f) Jackson's Entry
Edinburgh EH8 8PJ

First published in hardback by Edinburgh University Press 2020

Typeset in 10/12 Goudy Old Style by
Servis Filmsetting Ltd, Stockport, Cheshire

A CIP record for this book is available from the British Library

ISBN 978 1 4744 3021 0 (hardback)
ISBN 978 1 47443 022 7 (paperback)
ISBN 978 1 4744 3023 4 (webready PDF)
ISBN 978 1 4744 3024 1 (epub)

The right of David Johnson to be identified as the author of this work has been asserted in accordance with the Copyright, Designs and Patents Act 1988, and the Copyright and Related Rights Regulations 2003 (SI No. 2498).

Contents

List of Figures	vi
Acknowledgements	vii
Introduction	1
1 Lineages of Hope and Despair	8
2 The Industrial and Commercial Workers Union (ICU) and the Language of Freedom	41
3 Soviet Freedom in South Africa	71
4 Anti-Stalinist Dreams of Freedom	104
5 Pan-Africanism: Freedom for Africa	133
Conclusion	158
Notes	164
Bibliography	196
Index	214

List of Figures

CHAPTER 2

2.1 Cartoon by J. Scott, 'The African workers receive international recognition through the affiliation of the ICU to the International Federation of Trade Unions. The South African white worker is annoyed at the victory of the blacks', *The Workers' Herald*, 18 March 1927.   67

2.2 Cartoon by J. Scott, 'Coming events. Socialism can only be brought about by unity of all workers, irrespective of colour or creed', *The Workers' Herald*, 14 October 1926.   69

CHAPTER 3

3.1 Cartoon by Edward Roux, 'After Worcester – what?', *The South African Worker*, 16 May, 1930.   80

3.2 Cartoon by Edward Roux, 'South Africa's new constitution', *Umsebenzi*, 7 April 1934.   81

3.3 Cartoon by Edward Roux, '"Yea, though I walk through the valley of the shadow of death"', *The South African Worker*, 30 May 1930.   82

3.4 Cartoon by Edward Roux, '"Religion is the opium of the people" – Marx', *Umsebenzi*, 20 June 1930.   83

3.5 Cartoon by Edward Roux, '"Put in the sickles and reap!"', *The South African Worker*, 22 May 1930.   88

3.6 Cartoon by Edward Roux, 'Tata amapasi ako asiwafuni', *Umsebenzi*, 15 December 1934.   99

Acknowledgements

My first debt is to Jackie Jones at Edinburgh University Press, who contracted the book, and provided wonderful support at every stage of its publication. Ersev Ersoy, James Dale, Nicola Wood, Rebecca Mackenzie, Eliza Wright and Rachel Goodyear displayed great professionalism and efficiency in transforming the typescript into a book, and their efforts are much appreciated. I am immensely grateful to two generous friends, who read and commented on the final drafts of all the chapters in the months of rewriting – Rob Morrell and Glen Thompson. Over the eight-year period of working on the book, Shane Moran read all the earlier drafts, helping to sharpen my arguments. I am indebted to many other people, who gave time and consideration to my work by commenting on individual chapters, or by providing research leads: Emma Barker, Katherine Baxter, Mark Bould, Keith Breckenridge, Richard Brown, Madeline Clements, Caroline Davis, Henry Dee, Allison Drew, Gail Gerhart, Suman Gupta, Zakes Hlatshwayo, Christian Høgsbjerg, Anthony Howell, Peter Kallaway, David Kazanjian, Edmund King, Ole Laursen, Lisa Linton, Tom Lodge, Donna Loftus, Andy Mason, Benita Parry, Leo Podlashuc, Deirdre Pretorius, Anita Rupprecht, Kelwyn Sole, Alex Tickell, Anna Vaninskaya, Tony Voss, Dillon Vrana, Dennis Walder, Nicola Watson and Fiona Wilson. Melanie Geustyn, Najwa Hendrickse and Laddy McKechnie at the National Library of South Africa (Cape Town) were incredibly helpful, as were Gaby Mohale and Zofia Sulej at Historical Papers at the University of the Witwatersrand, Clive Kirkwood at Special Collections at the University of Cape Town and Nick Melia at the Borthwick Institute (University of York). The National Library of South Africa (Cape Town) also kindly and efficiently provided all the images in the book. I am especially indebted to Fundile Majola for translating Mqhayi's *U-Don Jadu* from Xhosa to English. The book was written while working for The Open University, where I have enjoyed unstinting support from my colleagues in the English Department, as well as generous funding from the university's research committee. Many of the chapters started out as talks, and my arguments have been influenced by discussions arising from those hosted by Keith Breckenridge and Cathy Burns at WISER in Johannesburg; by Cathy Bergin, Tom Hickey and Mark

Abel at Brighton University; by Lucien van der Walt and Nicole Ulrich at Rhodes University; by Bashir Abu-Manneh at the University of Kent; and by Bill Nasson at the University of Stellenbosch. Finally, I have been helped in many ways by my friends and family. I would like to record my heartfelt thanks to all of them: Gill and BB Clark, Bronwen Findlay, Bill Freund, Garth Fourie, Jackie Fourie, Anne Hood, Rochelle Kapp, Graham MacPhee, Conor McCarthy, Stephen Regan, Clive Van Onselen and Lyn Van Onselen.

Introduction

A poem written in 1975 by Dennis Brutus (1924–2009) begins by proclaiming, 'My cause is a dream of freedom/ and you must help me make my dream a reality,' and then asks, 'Why should I not dream and hope?/ Is not revolution making reality of hopes?'[1] The poem continues, 'Let us work together that my dream may be fulfilled/ that I may return with my people out of exile/ to live in one democracy in peace,' before concluding with another question, 'Is not my dream a noble one/ worthy to stand beside freedom struggles everywhere?'[2] Addressed to sympathetic interlocutors on behalf of all rebels and dreamers, the poem establishes an inexorable historical narrative: the journey begins with a dream of freedom; it gathers pace as individual rebel-dreamers find each other, and form themselves into a community of resistance; and the journey will assuredly culminate in the dreams being fulfilled, with exiles returning to live in a free, unified and peaceful democracy. In the form of a short poem, Brutus thus compresses competing histories of resistance and myriad dreams of freedom in South Africa into one symbolic tale of collective liberation.

Nineteen years later, Nelson Mandela recast the poem's message as a narrative of national liberation in which the agent of freedom is one political organisation – the African National Congress (ANC). In his 1994 inaugural address as South Africa's president, Mandela declared that the dream of a free South Africa had been realised, a dream shared and fought for by all the nation's races: 'Africans, Coloureds, Whites, Indians, Muslims, Christians, Hindus, Jews – all of them united by a common vision of a better life for the people of South Africa.'[3] Updating the political lexicon of the ANC's founding years, Mandela proclaimed the new South Africa to be 'a constitutional, democratic, political order in which, regardless of colour, gender, religion, political opinion or sexual orientation, the law will provide for the equal protection of all citizens', and further, 'there will be regular, open and free elections [and] a social order which respects completely the culture, language and religious rights of all sections of our society and the fundamental rights of the individual'.[4] Mandela's speech summarises the dominant definition of what freedom in South Africa comprises: a legal order based upon the equal protection of all citizens; a democratic political order with a universal franchise; and a social order respecting all sections of society and protecting individual human rights.

Rereading the words of Brutus and Mandela nearly three decades after the end of formal apartheid, their confidence in the imminence of freedom appears to have been misplaced. An opinion piece in May 2018 by the ANC veteran, Ben Turok (1927–), captures the change in mood:

> Among the problems of corruption, state capture and depletion of the national fiscus left by the years of [President Jacob] Zuma's rule, South Africa has also inherited a loss of faith in leadership and what amounts to a national pessimism . . . Especially in his last years as president, pessimism and cynicism became pervasive as South Africans all over the country came to doubt any prospect of improvement in the economy, our education system, the capability to control crime, and so much else.[5]

Turok's widely shared diagnosis invites a reassessment both of the dream of freedom expressed in Brutus's poem, and the claim that freedom had been achieved in Mandela's speech.[6] Most obviously, the current mood of 'national pessimism' provokes the question as to why the ANC's dream of freedom has foundered. The popular answer is that those who struggled against apartheid were good women and men, and that those now in power (in some cases the same women and men) are greedy and corrupt.

Such a biographical framing of the question, a moral tale of dreams betrayed and a search for the individual culprits, is beyond the scope of this study. The focus falls instead on analysing the content and forms of the dreams of freedom themselves: were there flaws in the original dreams of freedom that prevented their ultimate realisation? Why have certain dreams of freedom been forgotten? And why have dreams of freedom – like Brutus's poem – so often been expressed in literary form?

To answer the first question, the book focuses on the liberal-nationalist dreams of freedom that culminated in the ANC's assumption of power. The significance of this dominant tradition goes beyond the specifics of Southern African history, as the ANC's vision of freedom corresponds with what Immanuel Wallerstein calls 'the ideology of centrist liberalism'.[7] The ANC's long-held commitment to the political model of an equal citizenry within a unitary nation-state is by no means unique; rather, it is a particular variety of centrist liberalism, 'the new geoculture of the modern world system . . . which came in the course of the nineteenth century to dominate mentalities and structures'.[8] The hegemony of centrist liberalism has arisen in symbiosis with the globalisation of capitalist economic relations. In Wallerstein's historical schema, the normative state form of centrist liberalism originates in Europe, and is then copied by colonies like South Africa: 'the first [sphere] was the creation of "liberal states" in the core regions of the world system, in which Great Britain and France became the initial and leading exemplars'.[9] Wallerstein's unabashed Eurocentrism might be confounded by registering the imagination and agency of the tradition of liberal-nationalists dreaming of freedom in South Africa.[10] His critique does, however, introduce a necessary note of caution by identifying centrist liberalism as merely one imperfect answer to 'the great political question of the modern world, [namely] how to reconcile the theoretical embrace of equality and the continuing and increasingly acute polarization of real-life opportunities and satisfactions'.[11] In other words, if centrist liberalism as defined by Wallerstein has failed since the nineteenth century to deliver freedom beyond the narrowest limits, why should the post-1994 South African variety of liberal nationalism be the exception that redeems the entire tradition?

The question as to why certain dreams of freedom have been forgotten takes longer to answer. Accordingly, most of the book focuses upon the four major alternative political traditions and organisations whose dreams of freedom remain unrealised – the Industrial and Commercial Workers' Union (ICU); the Communist Party of South Africa (CPSA); the anti-Stalinist Non-European Unity Movement (NEUM), and the Pan-Africanist Congress (PAC). Aside from failing to exert much direct influence upon the post-apartheid political settlement, these four traditions are also alike in that they imagine forms of freedom beyond the liberal-nationalist script.

Surveying histories of resistance across the centuries and in different continents, the anthropologist James C. Scott discovers that subordinate groups 'have no trouble imagining a total reversal of the existing distribution of status and rewards', and that 'levelling beliefs of religious and secular lineage may be found in most, if not all, highly stratified societies'.[12] However, not all such 'total reversals' or 'levelling beliefs' imagine the same degree of political-economic-social transformation. Following Barrington Moore, Scott distinguishes three 'gradients of radicalism in the interrogation of domination', namely:

> The least radical step is to criticize some of the dominant stratum for having violated the norms by which they claim to rule; the next most radical step is to accuse the entire stratum of failing to observe principles of its rule; and the most radical step is to repudiate the very principles by which the dominant stratum justifies its dominance.[13]

Quite how South Africa's liberal-nationalist tradition of resistance pre-1990 might be categorised in relation to these three gradients is open to debate, not least because it combined unequivocal opposition to the state racism of 'the dominant stratum' as represented by the apartheid state with a more equivocal attitude to the economic exploitation by 'the dominant stratum' as represented by South African and international capital. By contrast, the other four traditions, which have failed to realise their dreams of freedom, fall more squarely within the third gradient, as they repudiate in their different ways 'the very principles by which the dominant stratum justifies its dominance', most obviously in their varieties of anti-nationalism and anti-capitalism.

Intrinsic to the inquiry into the many dreams of freedom is an attempt to understand the competing definitions of 'freedom'. Far from self-evident, the meaning of 'freedom' in South Africa has always been elusive and contested: for Olive Schreiner (1855–1920) and the ANC leader Albert Luthuli (1898–1967), freedom meant equal rights for women and men and the extension of the franchise to all races; for the ICU leaders Clements Kadalie (1896–1951) and A. W. G. Champion (1893–1975), freedom required higher wages, job security and the right of Africans to walk on pavements; for the CPSA's Albert Nzula (1905–1934) and Edward Roux (1903–1966), freedom demanded economic redistribution under the dictatorship of the proletariat; for I. B. Tabata (1909–1990) and Dora Taylor (1899–1976) of the NEUM, socialist freedom had to supersede liberal freedoms in an internationalist permanent revolution; and for Muziwakhe Anton Lembede (1914–1947) of the ANC Youth League and Robert Mangaliso Sobukwe (1924–1978) of the PAC, freedom required psychological liberation from racist ideology and the restoration of African land.

For all the differences in these definitions of freedom, however, they all assume that freedom must extend to the whole of society, that much more than the personal freedom of the individual is at stake. Hannah Arendt made the case for examining such public conceptions of freedom, noting that 'in that darkest of times, both inside and outside Germany the temptation was particularly strong, in the face of a seemingly unendurable reality, to shift from the world and its public space to an interior life'.[14] Acknowledging that such '"inner migration", the flight from the world to concealment, from public life to anonymity' could in certain circumstances be justified, Arendt reserved her admiration for those figures who pursued freedom for the collective rather than for those who chose to 'hole up in the refuge of [their] own psyche'.[15] In such 'dark times', Rosa Luxemburg (1871–1919) was exemplary: 'she was alone . . . in her stress on the absolute necessity of not only individual but public freedom under all circumstances'.[16] The selection of responses here to South Africa's prolonged 'dark times' includes examples of writers who chose to seek freedom via 'inner migration'. The main focus, however, is on the South African versions of Luxemburg – the dissident intellectuals and communities who conceived of freedom in public rather than individual terms.

With respect to the question as to why so many dreams of freedom appear in literary form, I assemble as a first step the many literary texts imagining South African futures. By extending the definition of 'Literature' in line with Raymond Williams's exposition of the term's multiple meanings,[17] the texts considered include not only original novels, plays and poems, but also literary appropriations, reviews, commentaries and criticism, as well as the genres or types of discourse Fredric Jameson characterises as being closely related to literary utopias: 'the manifesto; the constitution; the "mirror for princes"; and the great prophecy, which includes within itself that mode called satire'.[18] Jameson's list of utopian genres reveals a Eurocentric bias, and as such is incomplete. In order therefore to include all articulations of South African dreams of freedom, the inquiry extends to ephemeral and quotidian written forms like speeches, pamphlets, newspaper articles and letters, as well as to oral forms like the *imbongo* [praise poem].[19]

This expanded definition of literature proceeds on the assumption that literature 'often anticipates developments in philosophy and ethics . . . in an undeveloped, unsupported, intuitive form'.[20] But more than simply anticipating in intuitive form social developments as yet unexpressed in philosophy or ethics, literary texts can also serve 'the function of inventing imaginary or formal "solutions" to unresolvable social contradictions'.[21] The literary texts dreaming of freedom in South Africa therefore both anticipate developments hitherto unexpressed in other discourses, and invent imaginary solutions to unresolvable social contradictions. Literary texts that look to the future have an additional capacity to illuminate the past. Reinhart Koselleck has argued that it is impossible to grasp the past exclusively by analysing 'spaces of experience'; in addition, he argues, it is necessary to analyse 'horizons of expectation' – how historical agents imagined their futures.[22] Notwithstanding the generic differences between the primary texts in this study, they all promise access to contingent horizons of expectation at discrete historical moments.

In addition to reading a broad selection of texts, the discussion is extended in two further ways – first, by attending to how critiques of the present foreshadow visions of the future; and secondly, by considering literary utopia's 'shadow',[23] namely dystopias, anti-utopias and critical utopias. It is assumed, following Ernst Bloch, that 'the essential function of utopia is a critique of what is present'.[24] For Bloch, Marxism represents an ideal, as it enacts a dialectic between the warm stream (the 'liberator') and the cold stream (the 'detective'), removing in the process 'the frozen antithesis between sobriety [the cold] and enthusiasm [the warm] by bringing both to something New and causing both to work together within it – for exact anticipation, concrete utopia'.[25] Bloch's formulation of Marxism's complementary cold and warm streams provides a vocabulary for apprehending how South African utopian texts generated both critiques of colonialism/segregation/capitalism/apartheid *and* (often implicit) utopian dreams of a better future society. Not all the South African texts discussed here satisfy Bloch's demanding aesthetic; they do all, however, wrestle with the tension between diagnosing the present (critique) and predicting of the future (utopia).

Prophecies of the future, of course, come in the form of nightmares as well as of dreams. Accordingly, although the principal focus here is on dreams of freedom, the nightmares too are given due attention, heeding Jameson's caveat that the former may amount to little more than 'blueprints for bourgeois comfort', whereas the latter have the potential to 'serve the negative purpose of making us more aware of our mental and ideological imprisonment'.[26] In addition to trying to understand both those texts expressing utopian longings and those issuing dystopian warnings, I also try to account for the moments when no evident prophecies of the future were produced, the moments of silence, of apparent acquiescence. The heroic rebels (preeminently Mandela) and their utopian documents (like the Freedom Charter) have been celebrated.[27] But much less scholarly labour has been directed towards the millions of South Africans who endured (or who did not endure) racial oppression, economic exploitation, and 'mental and ideological imprisonment', but who failed to fight back or to produce any dreams of freedom. Writing in the context dys/utopian science fiction, Ursula Le Guin criticises a tendency within the genre to fetishise heroic resistance at the cost of understanding how most of the time oppressive societies preclude even thinking about freedom: 'if a slave is not Spartacus, he is nobody. This is merciless and unrealistic. Most slaves, most oppressed people, are part of the social order which, by the very terms of their oppression, they have no opportunity even to perceive as capable of being changed'.[28] Translating Le Guin's insight into the terms of this study, four of the five chapters are dedicated to the slaves who were not Spartacus/the South African rebels who were not Mandela, and try to read both their now-forgotten dreams of freedom (however fragmentary or inchoate) *and* their silences in relation to the formidable political, economic and ideological structures of power they confronted.

Tempting as it is to claim that this book covers all instances of dreaming of freedom in South Africa, certain limits must be conceded. First, I have focused principally on secular dreams of freedom, referring only to religious visions of the future insofar as they influence the dreams expressed in the language of literature and politics.[29] Second, in parallel with the broadly defined tradition of literary dreams, there is a tradition of economic and political blueprints, running from Milner's kindergarten to the scenario-planning exemplified by Clem Sunter's high and low roads of the 1980s.[30] Almost certainly more influential in determining the shape of South African society, these too are either discussed in relation to the literary dreams, or remain in the footnotes. And third, my survey ends in the mid-1970s, not because the fifteen years immediately before Mandela's release are uninteresting, but because the literary dreams of this period either repeat with only minor variations the substance of earlier dreams, or they become less 'visionary' and more pragmatic.[31]

The chapter structure follows the sequence of the framing questions, starting with a long chapter on the triumphant liberal-nationalist dreams of freedom led by the ANC and its sympathisers. Stretching from the 1880s to the 1970s, and noting how the dreams in this tradition oscillated between hope and despair, the first chapter considers: the dream-allegories of Schreiner; well-known and neglected novels (S. E. K. Mqhayi's *U-Don Jadu* (1929), Alan Paton's *Cry, the Beloved Country* (1948), Lewis Sowden's *Tomorrow's Comet* (1951) and Karel Schoeman's *Promised Land* (1972)); political manifestoes and programmes (R. F. A. Hoernlé's lectures *South African Native Policy and the Liberal Spirit* (1939) and the ANC's Freedom Charter (1955)); and literary appropriations (Luthuli's quotations from Longfellow in his 1961 Nobel Prize acceptance speech).

The balance of the book focuses on the four alternative traditions of dreaming of freedom. Chapter 2 centres upon the dreams of the ICU in the 1920s, analysing the union's manifestos and programmes; Kadalie's speeches and articles; the letters and journalism of Winifred Holtby (1898–1935), as well as her novel *Mandoa, Mandoa* (1932); Champion's pamphlets and poems; the novel *Wild Deer* (1933) by Ethelreda Lewis (1875–1946); and oral interviews with ICU workers. Chapter 3 deals with the dreams of the CPSA in the 1920s-1930s, juxtaposing policy directives of the Communist International (the Comintern) like the 1928 Native Republic thesis and 1930 New Line; the appropriations of poems by Shelley, Byron and Swinburne in the pages of *The International/Umsebenzi/The South African Worker*; the political journalism of Roux and Albert Nzula; and the poems of James La Guma (1894–1961). Chapter 4 focuses on the dreams of anti-Stalinist organisations the 1940s-1950s, surveying the NEUM's Ten-Point Programme; the journalism and lectures of Ben Kies (1919–1979); Dora Taylor's literary reviews; I. B. Tabata's letters and essays; and the novel *House of Bondage* (1990) by Livingstone Mqotsi (1921–2009). The final chapter discusses the trans-continental dreams of the PAC in the 1950s-1960s, reading the 1959 constitution of the PAC alongside the praise poems of Melikhaya Mbutumu; the novels of Peter Abrahams (1919–2017), Richard Rive (1931–1989), Lauretta Ngcobo (1931–2015) and Bessie Head (1937–1986); and the literary opinions Sobukwe expressed in his reviews and letters, both his likes (Howard Fast's novel *Spartacus*) and his dislikes (Shakespeare's play *Hamlet*). The book concludes by contrasting briefly the dreams of freedom of the 1880s to the 1970s with post-apartheid visions of the future.

    The hope is that by piecing together for the first time this discontinuous and heterogeneous collection of literary dreams and political visions, the received view of South Africa's past might be unsettled. These disparate texts introduce new insights into the horizons of expectation of the many historical agents – collective and individual – who struggled for freedom.

1 Lineages of Hope and Despair

INTRODUCTION

In early 1976, a number of political prisoners on Robben Island secretly wrote essays, which were smuggled out by Mac Maharaj (1935–) on his release at the end of that year. In their essays, Nelson Mandela (1918–2013) of the ANC and Eddie Daniels (1928–2017) of the Liberal Party expressed their confident hopes and dreams of a future South Africa free of racism. For Mandela, 'the issue of the precise social order [post-independence] is secondary as long as we agree that it should be stripped of racial hatred'.[1] Acclaiming the support of the resistance movements in the frontline states, Mandela added that '[w]e cannot resist being optimistic', as internal and external pressures will soon compel the apartheid regime to accede to 'our main demand . . . the total abolition of all forms of white supremacy and the extension of the vote to all South Africans'.[2] Daniels echoed Mandela's sentiments, defining freedom for black South Africans as 'the destruction of all racist laws and practices based on racial discrimination, and their acceptance as full citizens of the country with all the democratic rights that go with it'.[3] Drawing inspiration from the successful freedom struggles in the United States, France, the Soviet Union, China, Algeria, Guinea-Bissau, Mozambique, Angola and Vietnam, Daniels argues that 'four-fifths of [South Africa's] population are opposed to the government [placing] an insupportable strain on it, which will not only crack the "granite" wall but will destroy it'.[4] More concerned than Mandela to spell out 'the precise social order' of a free South Africa, Daniels listed what he described as 'the fundamentals' of freedom: 'the vote, equal opportunities based on employment, equal pay for equal work, the right to belong to and form trade unions, equal educational facilities for all, the right to associate freely with others, and free movement for all South Africans'.[5] Claiming these fundamentals as the guiding principles of the outlawed Liberal Party, Daniels repeated his prediction that they would outlive apartheid:

> [The Liberal Party's] principles of universal adult suffrage, equality before the law, the full respect for human dignity, that is, full democracy to be accorded to

all South African citizens irrespective of race, colour or creed, are indestructible, and these principles and beliefs will still live on long after apartheid has disappeared into the mists of time.[6]

The lineage of Mandela and Daniels's dreams on Robben Island of a free South Africa can be traced back to the 1880s, and this opening chapter accordingly revisits a selection of texts expressing versions of their dream. At least as numerous as these optimistic dreams of freedom are the many nightmarish texts prophesying the betrayal or perversion of the Mandela–Daniels dream of freedom, and these too are discussed.

To periodise these utopian and dystopian texts, they are grouped (with one exception) in relation to the passage of increasingly oppressive rafts of racist legislation: the first group of texts react to the Glen Grey Act of the late nineteenth century; the second to the legislation passed in the decade after the Union of South Africa in 1910; the third to the Hertzog Bills drafted in the 1920s and passed into law in the 1930s; the fourth (exceptionally) to the promises of the Atlantic Charter of 1941; the fifth to the first wave apartheid legislation after 1948; and the final group to the post-Sharpeville laws of the 1960s.

In his attempt to explain the timing of utopian moments in the twentieth century, the historian Jay Winter hypothesises that it has been 'the tendency of many figures, great and small, to dream dreams, to erect new edifices, to imagine futures at precisely the moment when those dreams, structures, and futures were least likely to be realised'.[7] Distinguishing between 'major utopians' like Hitler and Stalin, who 'murdered millions of people in their efforts to transform the world', and the sympathetic tradition of 'minor utopians', who 'configured limited and much less sanguinary plans for partial transformations of the world',[8] Winter's examples include the Second International of 1889, the Beveridge Report of 1942, the Universal Declaration of Human Rights of 1948 and the Prague Spring of 1968. Recognising 'that such moments were almost always short-lived, and were followed by defeat, disillusionment and despair', Winter notes the resilience of utopian thought, and reaffirms the tradition of 'men and women who dared to think differently, to break with convention, to speculate about the unlikely in the search for a better way'.[9] Some of the South African examples of utopian thought examined in this chapter fit Winter's schema: they also appear at unpropitious moments; and they also demonstrate the resilience of figures great and small dreaming their dreams. However, the grim decades when no utopian texts appeared, as well as the dystopian texts shadowing the expressions of hope, suggest that the claims on behalf of South Africa's tradition of minor utopias may need qualifying.

THE 1890S: DREAMING OF THE UNION OF SOUTH AFRICA

Before it was possible to dream of freedom in South Africa, it was necessary to imagine the nation-state of South Africa into existence.[10] The imperial dreams of the youthful Cecil John Rhodes (1853–1902) provide early hints of the plan to unite the small British colonies and independent republics of Southern Africa into a single nation. In his 'Confession of Faith' of 2 June 1877, Rhodes articulated his dream for Africa:

> I contend that we are the finest race in the world and that the more of the world we inhabit the better it is for the human race ... Why should we not form a secret society with but one object, the furtherance of the British Empire and the bringing of the whole uncivilised world under British rule ... What a dream, but yet it is probable, it is possible ... Africa is still lying ready for us; it is our duty to take it.[11]

Rhodes's vision for Africa reiterated the Social Darwinist axioms of imperial ideology: that races compete for ascendancy; that the British race was 'the finest in the world'; that bringing the 'uncivilised world' under British tutelage was a moral duty; and that the entire human race would ultimately benefit from Britain's domination of Africa. His pan-continental dreams acquired a specific geographical focus with the discovery of diamonds in Kimberley in 1868 and of gold on the Witwatersrand in 1886. To fulfil Britain's 'duty' in Southern Africa, he pursued policies to combine the British colonies of the Cape and Natal and the Boer republics of the Orange Free State and the Transvaal into one nation under British rule. In a letter from Matabeleland to Sir William Harcourt in London of 13 May 1896, Rhodes defended his ambitions for the region: 'I would be sorry to think that you thought I was "*capable but not honest*". I have tried to unite S. Africa, and no sordid motive has influenced me.'[12] With the acquisition in 1889 of a charter for his British South Africa Company, Rhodes's dream of a unified state in South Africa extended its northern border from the Limpopo to the Zambesi. As one historian explains, Rhodes 'entertained no doubts that the eventual absorption of the Transvaal was inevitable; Kruger's burghers must give way before the mining age just as must the Ndebele'.[13]

Essential to Rhodes's project of forging a unified South African nation was the support of the Afrikaner Bond, and in particular of its guiding spirit, Jan Hendrik Hofmeyr (1845–1909).[14] First established in 1879 by the Afrikaner republican, Reverend S. J. Du Toit (1847–1911), the Bond came under Hofmeyr's sway after Du Toit's departure to the Transvaal in 1883, and it co-operated with Rhodes in aligning the interests of Cape Afrikaner and British capital up until the Jameson Raid of 1895. Hofmeyr never held the highest political offices himself, but was adept at behind-the-scenes politicking, which prompted the Cape Colony's last prime minister, John X. Merriman (1841–1926), to give him the nickname of '"the Mole – an industrious little animal ... you never see him at work, but every now and then a little mound of earth, thrown up here or there, will testify to his activities"'.[15]

The Rhodes–Hofmeyr alliance was built upon shared interests: both accepted the British Empire as the ultimate guarantor of security and prosperity; both sought maximum profits for the white farmers of the Cape and the mine-owners of Kimberley and the Witwatersrand; and both embraced – in word, if not always in deed – the ideals of Cape liberalism. Their partnership was especially effective in reducing the economic and political status of Africans in Southern Africa. In 1870 the Cape's economy still accommodated a land-owning and food-producing African peasantry.[16] As the demand for African labour on white-owned farms and mines increased, however, Rhodes combined with the Bond in order to promote white economic interests at the expense of Africans' self-sufficiency. In 1894, Rhodes drove through parliament the Native Bill for Africa Act (known as the Glen Grey Act), which imposed a labour tax on African men who did not own land; replaced collective land tenure for Africans with individual property ownership; and created separate district councils for Africans with limited powers.[17] In parallel, the political rights of Africans came under attack, with the constriction of the Cape's qualified franchise for Africans. Rhodes had famously declared, '"Equal rights for every civilised man south of the Zambesi,"' explaining that the franchise should be extended to every man, white or black, '"who has sufficient education to write his name, has some property, or who works. In fact, is not a loafer"'.[18] Rhetoric was undermined by realpolitik, however, as the number of African voters was reduced by two Acts of Parliament: the Parliamentary Registration Act of 1887 (promulgated by Hofmeyr) precluded Africans from qualifying for the franchise via the communal ownership of land; and the Franchise and Ballot Act of 1892 (passed under Rhodes's premiership) introduced a literacy test and raised the property qualification from £25 to £75.[19] Despite the opposition of African leaders like John Tengo Jabavu (1859–1921) and the newly formed South African Native National Congress,[20] these Acts reduced the political rights of the African population in the Cape. Rhodes and Hofmeyr might therefore have dreamed of South Africa as an independent nation under British tutelage,[21] but their dream did not envisage freedom for all. On the contrary, despite Rhodes's mantra of equal rights for all south of the Zambesi, his and Hofmeyr's laws laid the foundations for subsequent South African regimes that denied freedom to the nation's black majority.

The manipulation of the African franchise by Hofmeyr and Rhodes in the 1880s and 1890s provoked South Africa's first utopian short story – *The Great Southern Revolution: A Chapter in the History of the United States of South Africa, 1894–1934* by Jaapie Ahmet De Villiers Smith.[22] Published in 1893, *The Great Southern Revolution* looks back from a happy future in 1934 at the imagined political history of the Cape in the intervening years, mixing together historical figures (like Hofmeyr) and fictional ones (like the MP De Villiers). The story begins in 1890, when (fictional) scientists in New York operated on 'a child born an idiot', opening its skull to give its brain space to grow, and by this means restoring the child 'to mental health and vigour'.[23] At the same time as this medical breakthrough, Cape politics was being unscrupulously manipulated by Hofmeyr, who in 1894 legislated that Africans must have a matriculation certificate in order to vote. The immediate effect was 'to abridge the voting power of the coloured man and to increase the political strength of the white man'.[24] With a reduced number of African voters, Hofmeyr became prime minister, and the Bond consolidated its long-term control of parliament. The Bond's racially biased legislation precipitated the flight of African farm workers from the Colony, and the resulting labour crisis was still unresolved in 1906, when the United States of South Africa (stretching from the Cape to Zambesi) won independence from Britain. A year later, however, Mr De Villiers, a charismatic new MP, proposed a solution – 'The Brain Development Act':

> His proposition was simply this, that every coloured child born after Jan. 1st, 1907, should have its skull opened that its brains might grow and develop, and thus in the future the coloured races would provide any number of intelligent workmen and servants, whose work could be depended on and whose mental powers and wants would prevent their return to idleness ... With persuasive words and real eloquence he pictured the benefits that would accrue to '*ons land*' and '*ons volk*' from this bold and novel proposal.[25]

Once the Bill was passed, white armed forces were initially required to enforce the brain-enlarging operations, but as soon as their positive effects on African children were observed, 'eagerness to have the children pass through this surgical process took the place of distrust of the safety of the operation'.[26] Within a decade, as a result of the operations, no African child was ever 'seen at work, herding or other menial occupation without a book in hand or in the pocket ready for an opportunity to study'.[27] Another decade later, the African youth 'looked, and in truth were, superior to the then ruling race in mind and quickness of understanding',[28] and as ever more attained their matriculation certificates, 'a majority of the voters were of the coloured class in the year 1930'.[29]

When the time for elections came, De Villiers anticipated gratitude from the new bloc of African voters, as 'it was he ... who had been the cause of the enlargement of their brains'.[30] But to his dismay, they saw through his blandishments: 'they had read history carefully and thoroughly ... knew every circumstance in the history of their country and people; [and] determined to undo ... the record of the past three decades'.[31] De Villiers and the Bond were as a result 'ignominiously defeated at the polls', and the new voters elected members of parliament from their own ranks, with the result that '[t]he whole aspect of the Assembly was brown, here and there a white face might be seen, but the general complexion of the new representative body was decidedly coloured'.[32] The new cabinet comprised eminently qualified parliamentarians from the different Southern African tribes, and was led by a gifted prime minister, who 'claimed to have within his veins the blood of seven different nationalities, English, Dutch, German, Hottentot, Zulu, Basuto, and Mozambique [and] appeared to have inherited the genius of all these races'.[33] The new government immediately repealed all racist laws, promoted education and initiated an enlightened economic policy encouraging free trade. The out-numbered 'European' in South Africa was advised to 'form an alliance with the now dominant people, to insure his children of partaking of the greatest blessings which the wit of man had ever bestowed on the human race'.[34] Were the white population to embrace this solution – miscegenation – 'in no dim and distant time, all race distinction would pass away, and the whole grand land of the United States of South Africa be filled with a united, and industrious, and above all, a happy and contented people'.[35]

In ideological terms, *The Great Southern Revolution* therefore travels in thirty years from Social Darwinism to liberal humanism, from narrating a society in which the superiority of the white race is assumed to one in which racial difference is erased by miscegenation. The satirical critique in the opening pages directed at Hofmeyr and the Afrikaner Bond gives way in the conclusion to a vision of a utopian society where education is cherished, the franchise open to the educated members of the electorate, the economy managed on the basis of free trade, and race no longer a significant or divisive social category.

Along with the satirical short story, a second literary genre utilised in order to articulate dreams of freedom in Southern Africa was that of the allegory. According to Olive Schreiner, writing to Ernest Rhys in 1888, 'by throwing a thing into the form of an allegory I can condense five or six pages into one, with no loss, but a great gain to clearness'.[36] Judging by the sales figures, Schreiner's fondness for allegory was shared by her readers: her collection *Dreams* (1890) sold 80,000 copies and appeared in twenty-five editions up to 1930.[37] One of the most popular allegories in the collection was 'Three Dreams in a Desert', which was set in Africa.[38] The unnamed first-person narrator is travelling on horseback across an African plain, and stops beneath a mimosa tree for a sleep (the original title was 'Under a Mimosa Tree'). In the first dream, the traveller-dreamer encounters two great beasts of burden, one stretched out on the desert sand, and the second standing alongside it. Asking 'one standing beside me watching' who the prostrate beast is, the traveller-dreamer is told, '"This is woman; she that bears men in her body,"'[39] and then in an extended question-and-answer sequence, learns the history of 'woman'. In the earliest times, woman 'once wandered free over the rocks with [man]', but during the 'Age-of-dominion-of-muscular-force', man placed his 'burden of subjection on to [her back], and tied it on with the broad band of Inevitable Necessity'.[40] While the traveller-dreamer and man are standing beside woman talking, the band breaks, and the burden rolls to the ground. The break is explained as marking the end of the Age-of-muscular-force, killed by the knife of Mechanical Invention, and the beginning of the Age-of-nervous-force. The new age enables woman to stagger to her feet, but her rise is hindered by man, who fails to understand her needs and to support her. The dream ends with woman's eyes lighting up as she gets to her knees. The traveller-dreamer wakes up to the desert heat, noticing ants running up and down the red sand before falling back to sleep.

In the second and longest of the three dreams, the traveller-dreamer sees a woman in a desert coming to a river with high banks. On the river bank, the woman meets an old man bearing a stick with 'Reason' written on it, and when the old man asks her who she is, and what she wants, she replies, '"I am woman; and I am seeking the land of Freedom."'[41] He tells her that the land of Freedom lies across the river, and that the only way to reach it is '"Down the banks of Labour, through the water of Suffering."'[42] Following his instructions, woman disrobes, and throws off 'the mantle of Ancient-received opinions' and 'the shoes of dependence', leaving her clad in a white garment with 'Truth'[43] written on the breast. The old man (now described as 'Reason') notices for the first time a tiny male child clinging to woman's breast. She begs to carry the child across the river with her, recounting that he had lisped the word 'Passion' to her in the desert, and that she dreamed that in the land of Freedom he might learn to say 'Friendship'. Rejecting her protestations, the old man/Reason insists that she lay the child down, explaining that he will fly across the river and arrive there a man: '"In your breast he cannot thrive; put him down that he may grow."'[44] As she stands fearful and alone at the water's edge, the old man/Reason tells her to listen carefully, and she heeds the feet of thousands following her. He explains the significance of her individual effort to cross over to the land of Freedom: '"Have you seen the locusts how they cross a stream? First one comes down to the water-edge, and it is swept away, and then another comes and then another, and then another, and at last with their bodies piled up a bridge is built and the rest pass over."'[45] Grasping his message, woman asks, '"Over that bridge which shall be built with our bodies, who will pass?"' and the old man/Reason answers, '"*The entire human race*."'[46] The second dream ends with woman turning down the path to the river. Again, the traveller-dreamer wakes up to ants running across the red sand.

The final dream is much the shortest, as the traveller-dreamer sees a land where 'walked brave women and brave men, hand in hand. And they looked into each other's eyes, and they were not afraid'.[47] Questioning a male by-stander in the dream, the traveller-dreamer learns that the dreamscape is heaven; that heaven is on earth; and that heaven lies in the future. Upon waking the third time, the heat of the day has receded, and 'the ants were going slowly home'.[48]

There are continuities running through the three dreams, notably the presence of the male interlocutor who explains and interprets the dreamscape for the traveller-dreamer, but there is also progress: in the first dream, the traveller-dreamer sees woman slumped in the desert and then rise haltingly to her knees; in the second dream, s/he observes woman learn from the old man/reason how through labour and suffering she might cross over the river to freedom; and in the third dream, s/he glimpses woman hand-in-hand with man in heaven. Although the figure of woman is individuated, the journey to freedom depends upon collective endeavour and sacrifice that ultimately rewards '*the entire human race*'. The scale of the sacrifice required is communicated by the image of locusts crossing the river, and the final vision of heaven is not of an individual woman, but of a community of women and men enjoying equality. The progress is captured in the contrast between the single figure of the collapsed and over-burdened woman tied to man in the first dream, and the collective image of fearless women and men holding hands in the third dream.

The allegorical form of 'Three Dreams in the Desert' enabled readers to interpret it less as a dream of freedom specific to its African landscape, and more as a universal journey from patriarchal oppression to gender equality. Schreiner's biographers affirm that *Dreams* 'expressed the aspirations of feminism, whether in terms of the vote or the Co-operative Movement', with the words of 'Three Dreams in the Desert' functioning for suffragettes in Holloway prison as '"a literal description of the pilgrimage of women . . . more like an ABC railway guide to our journey than a figurative parable"'.[49] For British socialists too, Schreiner's allegories had a powerful appeal, with Robert Blatchford's best-selling tract *Merrie England* (1895) listing *Dreams* as essential reading.[50]

To grasp Schreiner's dreams of freedom for South Africa, it is necessary to turn from the allegories to her journalism. In the two decades leading up to Union in

1909, Schreiner set out her political vision for a new South Africa, adding specific content to the universalising idealism of the allegories. The evolutionary logic of 'Three Dreams' is echoed in the itinerary Schreiner set for the nascent South African nation. Like 'woman', who progresses from supine exhaustion to a state of equality, Schreiner anticipates the fragmented individual polities of Southern Africa progressing towards a single unified nation. Schreiner describes the first stages of colonisation in Southern Africa as a benign process: 'so far as the colonists, Dutch and English, have populated the land, our progress, though slow, has been wholesome. [Until the mineral revolution] we were progressing steadily, if slowly, and keeping our national wealth for the people as a whole'.[51] Such progress accorded with Britain's imperial dream 'of planting a free and untrammelled branch of the Anglo-Saxon race upon the land'.[52] Schreiner returned often to the metaphor of the Empire as a tree with ever more branches:

> We [English South Africans], too, have had our vision of Empire. We have seen as in a dream the Empire of England as a great banyan tree; silently with the falling of the dew and the dropping of the rain it has extended itself; its branches have drooped down and rooted themselves in the earth; in it all the fowl of heaven have taken refuge, and under its shade all the beast of the field have lain down to rest.[53]

The metaphor implies that denying the growth of the British Empire would be as unnatural as stopping a tree from growing: 'As no sane man supposes an infant will remain perpetually unweaned, or that a healthy sapling will not ultimately form its own bark, so it is inevitable that all healthy off-shoots from European peoples must ultimately form independent nations.'[54] As the tree must grow and produce healthy off-shoots, so the Empire must grow and produce independent nations. Looking forward from 1900 into the future, Schreiner predicts that – like woman and man holding hands in the third dream – South Africa's different races will overcome their differences, and eighty years hence will harmonise to become 'a great and independent nation'.[55]

The major obstacles preventing the South African nation from fulfilling its destiny are the foreign monopolists and the imperialists. Of the former, Schreiner likens them to locusts. In 'Three Dreams', locusts crossing a river are an inspiration to women struggling collectively to reach freedom, but in Schreiner's journalism, they are likened to the monopolist, 'who comes from a foreign clime, and sweeps bare the virgin land before him like the locust; and like the locust, leaves nothing for his successors but the barren earth'.[56] After the Jameson Raid, Schreiner's antipathy to the monopolists – pre-eminently Rhodes – hardened, as she attacked their determination 'to expend the wealth of South Africa in the purchase of social distinction and in the luxury of old-world life',[57] and their willingness to sacrifice the future of South Africa, which is 'no more to them than the future of the Galapagos Islands. We are a hunting ground to them, a field for extracting wealth, for building up fame and fortune, nothing more'.[58] As regards the imperialists, Schreiner was hostile to *all* empires, arguing that the best forms of political community have always been smaller units: 'What humanity has attained in culture, in virtue, in freedom, in knowledge, and in the fullest development of the individual, it has owed to small, close, natural and spontaneous organisations of men – small tribes, small states, and, oftenest, to mere cities'.[59] With its compulsion to expand, imperialism is therefore anathema, 'a deadly disease which under certain conditions tends to afflict the human race, [which] increases in virulence in proportion as it is extended over more distant spaces and more diverse multitudes, till it becomes at last the death shroud of nations'.[60] Applying these principles to Southern Africa, Schreiner abominates Rhodes's desire to extend the Union of South Africa to the Zambesi, arguing that all attempts to build ever bigger political units should be resisted.[61]

Instead of Rhodes's expanded Union of South Africa, Schreiner imagines a free South Africa evolving, 'not as the result of skilful manipulations analogous to those by which one shrewd speculator out speculates another, but through the gradual growth of a consciousness in the people of South Africa that their interests are one, and that in union lies their strength'.[62] In abstract terms, Schreiner describes her ideal state as follows:

> that state is healthiest and strongest . . . in which every adult citizen, irrespective of sex or position, possesses a vote . . . each individual forming an integral part of the community [and] has their all at stake in the community; that the woman's stake is likely to be as large as the man's, and the poor man's as the rich . . . and that their devotion to its future good and their concern in its health is likely to be equal; that the State gains by giving voice to all its integral parts.[63]

In the specific instance of South Africa, the achievement of such an ideal state lies in the distant future, and is delayed and complicated by 'the native question'. Schreiner is sanguine about the white immigrants to South Africa combining to form a new South African nation: 'From great mixtures of races spring great peoples,' she argues, and the South Africa of the future will be made up principally of English and Afrikaans-speakers, supplemented by the 'oppressed Russian Jew', the 'pale German cobbler', the 'half-starved Irish peasant' and the 'rough Cornish miner'.[64] Unlike in Smith's satirical utopia, however, Schreiner does not countenance the mixing of European and African races. Like the new white South African race made up of 'the blood of all these [European] nationalities', South Africa's 'brave Bantu folk' will combine with other races until it ultimately constitutes 'the great *South African Dark Race*'.[65] The result: 'These two great varieties, dark and light, will form the South African nation of the future, their two streams of life, keeping, it may be, racially distinct for ages, but always interacting side by side and forming our South African nation'.[66]

In the months just before Union, Schreiner looked forward to the day when 'our small, to-day dominant, European element [made up of] the most virile of the northern races, [who have] always loved freedom and justice', would demonstrate wisdom and foresight in reconciling with 'our vast Bantu element [made up of] one of the finest breeds of the African stock'.[67] For Schreiner, the inherited racial hierarchy dictates that responsibility for building a free post-Union South African nation lies with 'the small and for the moment absolutely dominant white aristocracy on whom the weight of social reconstruction rests'.[68] Such responsibility demands in the first instance acknowledging that Southern Africa's economy is built upon cheap black labour, and then striving towards the building of a different and better society in which black workers are included as active citizens sharing in the material wealth of the nation. Failure to meet this challenge, Schreiner warns, will be catastrophic:

> If we [the white minority] see nothing in our dark man but a vast engine of labour; if to us he is not man, but only a tool . . . if, unbound to us by gratitude and sympathy, and alien to us in blood and colour, we reduce this vast mass to the condition of a great, seething ignorant proletariat – then I would rather draw a veil over the future of this land.[69]

Schreiner is silent on what form an alternative non-exploitative economy might look like, and indeed her nostalgia for the pre-monopolist/Rhodes phase of colonialism suggests a preference for a gentler form of capitalism, but her warning at least registers both an awareness of the economic inequalities accompanying the political settlement of Union, and her protest against the hyper-exploitation of black workers.

For all their differences, Rhodes, Smith and Schreiner were alike in assuming that the franchise was a *sine qua non* for freedom. In Rhodes's speeches, the franchise should be extended to all 'non-loafers'; in Smith's story, voting rights for the educated of all races would produce 'a united, industrious, happy and contented people'; and in Schreiner's journalism, the state is healthiest when all adult citizens, 'irrespective of race or sex' have the right to vote. Such expressions of faith in the capacity of the franchise to create a free South Africa echo the priority accorded to the struggle for the vote by those historically excluded from citizenship – male European workers, women and black people. For women, Wallerstein has argued, winning the right to vote in the late nineteenth century was seen as the necessary prelude to achieving all other forms of freedom and equality, a sequence analogous to 'the two-stage theory of Marxism: first the vote, then everything else'.[70] But for Wallerstein, the belief that 'everything else' would inevitably follow on from winning the vote was flawed because notwithstanding 'the rhetorical legitimacy of equality and the concept of citizenship as the basis of collective governance', it was important to register that '[c]itizenship always excluded as much as it included [and the] concept of the citizen preceded and provoked the concept of the alien/ immigrant'.[71] Smith is confident that a happy and prosperous nation will inevitably follow the extension of the franchise, but Schreiner expresses doubts. For Smith, the rights and freedoms associated with citizenship – pre-eminently the right to vote – constituted the *only* possible dream of freedom, whereas for Schreiner, the meaning of freedom had to be stretched beyond the franchise to dreams of women and men living in equality (in her allegories), and to dreams of transcending the material inequalities dividing South Africa's 'light and dark races' (in her journalism).

AFTER UNION: THE SUN NEVER SETS?

The Union of South Africa fell well short of delivering the dreams of Smith and Schreiner. Most obviously, the Union constitution failed to extend the Cape Colony's qualified franchise for Africans to the whole of the new nation. Section 9 of the Constitution of the South African Republic (1858) had declared, 'the people desire to permit no equality between coloured people and the white inhabitants, either in Church or State', and Article 1 of the Constitution of the Orange Free State (1866) had defined 'the Burghers [as] all white persons born in the state'.[72] Rather than repealing these exclusionary provisions, the Union constitution entrenched them, with Sections 35 and 36 of the South Africa Act of 1909 confirming the status quo in the two Boer republics and Natal, and requiring a two-thirds majority in both Houses to change the voting rights of Cape voters 'by reason of his race or colour only'.[73] The racist exclusions enshrined in the Act of Union were reinforced by further legislation restricting Africans' freedom of movement (the Urban Areas Native Pass Act of 1909); their freedom of employment (the Mines and Works Act of 1911); and their freedom to own land (the Land Act of 1913). The standard history of the unification of South Africa describes the Union constitution as a 'compromise' between the contending white constituencies: 'the northerners conceded the maintenance ... of the established franchise rights of the non-Europeans in the Cape Colony, and the southerners conceded the maintenance of the established colour bar in the northern colonies'.[74] What the Union 'compromise' guaranteed was that racial difference remained fundamental to determining citizenship, and that rather than gradually fading away – as per the optimistic pre-Union projections of Smith and Schreiner – racial difference increasingly dictated how the future was imagined.

The first decade after Union produced little in the way of secular fictions of the future, but in the 1920s several significant works appeared. The first was *South Africa in Mars* (1923) by Archibald Lamont (1864–1933). Born in Scotland, Lamont worked as a Presbyterian missionary and teacher in Singapore, publishing two novels, *Bright Celestials* (1894) and *The Heights of Hell* (1903), before emigrating a second time, this time to Natal, where he wrote *South Africa in Mars*. His third novel imagines a printer-journalist from Natal travelling to the planet Mars and conversing with a wide range of famous dead people about South Africa's recent history and immediate prospects. In a discussion at the beginning of the novel with the British statesmen William Gladstone (1809–1898) and Joseph Chamberlain (1836–1914), US president William McKinley (1843–1901), Rhodes, Paul Kruger (1825–1904), John Bright (1811–1889), Li Hung Chang (Li Hongzhang, 1823–1901) and Richard Cobden (1804–1865), the narrator encounters an unwavering consensus among his distinguished interlocutors in favour of free trade. McKinley, 'one of the pioneer Protectionists', is obliged to concede under Kruger's 'fine rapier-thrusts [that] America had gone wrong on economics';[75] Cobden declares to unanimous approval that '"national greed begets international selfishness, and injustice thereupon ensues ... [Woodrow] Wilson's League of Nations means, economically, a restoration of the doctrines of Adam Smith and myself"';[76] and in the case of South Africa,

Rhodes explains that '"[Kruger] agrees with me that unrestricted shipping and free immigration will be the making of South Africa."'[77] Lamont therefore imagines the disappearance of nationalism with its protectionist buttressing, and the triumph of a humane free trade capitalism ensuring the wealth of all nations.

Essential to the free trade regime anticipated in Lamont's novel is a liberal imperialism directed to integrating the colonised into the global capitalist economy: Bright alludes to the '"marvellous growth of the Indian Empire since the application, in recent generations, of liberal principles of government in that land"'.[78] For South Africa, Chamberlain counsels '"government by benevolent despotism as a provisional arrangement to make the Kafir, the Fingo, the Basuto, the Hottentot, the Zulu, also the Indian and Malay races less timid to face the ordeal of work"'.[79] Discussion of the possible strategies for an effective colonial policy for Africa is continued on a boat ride the narrator undertakes on Lake Lucidity with four distinguished Scots: the missionary David Livingstone (1813–1873), the poet Robert Burns (1759–1796), the principal of Lovedale, James Stewart (1831–1905) and evangelist-biologist Henry Drummond (1851–1897). All four echo Schreiner's anti-monopolist sentiments in criticising the greed of white South African capitalists, with Stewart, for example, referring to '"that destructive foe of all native progress – the lust for gold, and all at the expense of the bodies and souls of the black and coloured races"'.[80] Despite never having visited Africa, Burns claims that his '"poems and songs ... have done something to foster that British spirit of accommodation and liberalism"', and that it is precisely this spirit that he believes will prevail in South Africa:

> The British Empire will ultimately triumph in South Africa ... notwithstanding sordid motives that bring us discredit as a nation, because Britons recognise that there is a native question that demands honest treatment. And the British Empire will win against all comers, because Britons, despite their faults, will bring genial and Christian principles and methods, compatible with the interests of world-wide humanity, to bear on its native problems, so as to achieve a practical and final settlement.[81]

Drummond picks up Burns's (imputed) argument, and concludes that the combination of 'British Liberalism' and 'British Imperialism' will be the salvation of Africa: '"I am absolutely convinced that Africa is the land of the future, and that even your Nationalist doctrines will inevitably transform themselves ... into healthy and approved and enlightened elements of a great and progressive body politic."'[82] The novel ends with a well-armed spaceship led by Cromwell and Milton flying off to enforce this vision of Pax Britannica in South Africa.

A second novel to appear in 1923 was George Heaton Nicholls's *Bayete! Hail to the King*. Nicholls (1876–1959) was a sugar-cane farmer, an MP and 'by far one of the most articulate proponents of segregation, and at this time one of the most influential in terms of the political power he achieved'.[83] He completed *Bayete!* in 1913, but because of its contentious political content, was discouraged from publishing it by General Jan Christiaan Smuts (1870–1950). About eight years later, the Afrikaans poet C. J. Langenhoven (1873–1932)[84] advised Nicholls to ignore Smuts's advice, and to publish *Bayete!* because 'if it does awaken the native it will, to more effectual purpose, awaken the Whites'.[85] And so, Nicholls concluded, 'gravely considering, feeling that it may awaken us for a moment from the needless drift . . . I send it forth as a note of warning'.[86] In order to 'awaken' white South Africa, Nicholls produced a plot centred on the rise and fall of Balumbata/Nelson, a charismatic African leader.[87] Nelson is the son of the beautiful Arab-African Nanzela from Central Africa, and the two are captured by Lobengula. After Lobengula's death, Nelson resolves to go to America, where he acquires the white man's knowledge so that he can come back one day to free his people. On his return to South Africa, Nelson's liberation campaign gathers momentum as he uses a mix of tactics, including industrial strike action and a version of *satyagraha* (learned from an Indian character based on Mohandas K. Gandhi). Nelson is aided by the naïve liberal Olive Garth (based on Olive Schreiner), and the novel builds towards a violent revolution, but white rule is saved at the eleventh hour, with Nelson killed in the opening skirmishes of the rebellion, and Olive killed by Zena, Nelson's jealous wife. As Olive lies dying, the character of Grim Collingwood, a surrogate for Nicholls, explains:

> 'Olive, you have never quite understood Nelson. You have seen him only as a native leader in agreement with your views, seeking merely to build up a separate individuality for his own race alongside the separate individuality of the white race. You have always believed that Nelson considered the two races could live side by side, each developing along its own lines, territorially and socially separated but politically equal, mixing only for industrial purposes, each race realising that the one was necessary to the development of the other. That is the orthodox view. It is the Booker Washington view. But it never was Nelson's view . . . It would save such a lot of trouble for us all if we could keep black and white in separate compartments. But Nelson's idea of a separate compartment is a Black Africa . . . He believes that the fifty million Bantu organised can rid the country of white dominance. For him there are no political boundaries. The Bantu of the Congo are as much part of his organisation as the Bantu of the Cape. All his activities have been directed to uniting the various elements.'[88]

Collingwood's explanation distils Nicholls's warning to his white South African readers: you are politically naïve to be taken in by the Christian words of educated Africans claiming to seek equality via peaceful co-existence; what underlies their Christian words is the uncompromising goal of 'Black Africa', a continent purged of white interlopers. The death of the duplicitous Balumbata/Nelson ultimately gives a message of hope to white South Africa: if they learn from the narrow escape evoked in the novel, and exercise greater vigilance, they can and should look forward to a secure, racially segregated future.[89]

Leonard Flemming's satirical short story of 1924, 'And So It Came To Pass', is less hopeful, as it evokes vivid scenes of a future in which Africans oppress their former white overlords.[90] A couple of years before the publication of his short story,

Flemming had written an article recalling enthusiastically his eighteen years as a farmer in the Orange Free State, encouraging potential British emigrants to copy his example: 'you have in South Africa vast tracts of country lying idle for want of men ... The work itself is so big and so fine as to be full of joy [and] your work is going to be of value to those who come after'.[91] No such optimism is evident in 'And So It Came To Pass', although the story's shifts between prophecy and satire break up the atmosphere of paranoia. The narrator is a white South African in hell in 2168, recounting the fate of the entire human race, focusing in particular on his homeland. Tracing the history of the two centuries after the First World War, the narrator relates that not long after seizing power, 'the Native races in [South Africa] made short work of their one-time White rulers'.[92] Under 'the Black monarchy', South African society underwent dramatic changes:

> Courts were abolished, large distilleries erected, nine-tenths of the arable land of the Union was under Kaffir corn ... Dingaan's Day became a day of national mourning with trained weepers in every market place, and a great annual festival appears to have taken place in the Government Buildings, Pretoria, on July 27, the date of the massacre of the last White man in South Africa.[93]

Taking advantage of a dispensation in hell allowing damned individuals 24–hour visits back to Earth, the narrator visits South Africa during this period of its history, discovering further details about post-segregationist South Africa from white survivors working for African employers: English had been replaced as the *lingua franca* by 'Buzuluto, a sort of native Esperanto'; the black monarch was under pressure to replace the death penalty 'with a lingering death'; 'the native police force was kept solely to deal with the descendants of the Whites', with Africans seldom punished; and sheep stealing was rewarded so that 'the old traditional cunning and characteristics of the race should not be entirely lost'.[94] Back in hell, the narrator then explains that African rule itself was not to endure, as the black populace after a short period of stability divided over the issue of education, with the disagreements between the 'Pro and Anti-Education Parties ... culminating in the Great War of the Blacks, in which was used every diabolical means of destruction known to science'.[95] Ultimately, after a period of blood-letting, there was 'not one human being on earth ... as it was in the beginning ...'.[96]

In contrast to the pessimism in Flemming's short story, hope persisted in the political and literary dreams of black South Africans in the 1920s. Both the resolutions of the ANC's annual conference in Bloemfontein in May 1923 and the utopian novel *U-Don Jadu* (1929) by S. E. K. Mqhayi temper their critiques of white rule with expressions of confidence in the ultimate unfolding of an egalitarian future under British patronage. The five-point Bill of Rights endorsed at the 1923 annual congress demanded:

> (1) That the Bantu inhabitants of the Union have, as human beings, the indisputable right to a place of abode in this land of their fathers. (2) That all Africans have, as the sons of this soil, the God-given right to unrestricted

ownership of land in this, the land of their birth. (3) That the Bantu, as well as their coloured brethren, have, as British subjects, the inalienable right to the enjoyment of those British principles of the liberty of the subject, justice and equality of all classes in the eyes of the law that have made Great Britain one of the greatest world powers. (4) That the Bantu have, as the subjects of His Majesty King George, the legal and moral right to claim the application or extension to them of Cecil Rhodes' famous formula of 'equal rights for all civilised men south of the Zambesi', as well as the democratic principles of equality of treatment and equality of citizenship in the land, irrespective of race, class, creed or origin. (5) That the peoples of African descent have, as an integral and inseparable element in the population of the great Dominion of South Africa, and as undisputed contributors to the growth and development of the country, the constitutional right of an equal share in the management and direction of the affairs of this the land of their permanent abode, and to direct representation by members of their own race in all the legislative bodies of the land, otherwise, there can be no taxation without representation.[97]

The equal rights of citizenship claimed for black South Africans derive from a variety of sources: their status as 'human beings', as 'sons of the soil', as 'British subjects', as 'subjects of His Majesty King George', 'as an integral and inseparable element in the population of South Africa' and 'as undisputed contributors to the growth and development of the country'. The assumption driving the document is that Rhodes's promise of 'equal rights for all civilised men south of the Zambesi' may yet be honoured, that the British Empire could yet provide the framework for a unified South Africa free from racial oppression.

Mqhayi's *U-Don Jadu* foregrounds the collective resources of the Xhosa people but, like the 1923 ANC Bill of Rights, expresses the belief that the British Empire will enable and support a new Southern African nation based upon racial equality.[98] Looking back over his life in about 1950, the novel's eponymous narrator recalls the years preceding the rise of the new nation of Mnandi (Sweetness), and then reflects upon his four successful five-year terms as its president. In the opening chapters, U-Don Jadu describes a number of difficult encounters in 1920s South Africa, drawing conclusions in each case instructive to the Xhosa nation. In chapter 2, for example, he sees two ostriches fighting with each other. When they see him, the ostriches forget their differences, and chase him from their field, prompting U-Don Jadu to interpret their behaviour as a lesson to his people: 'they who cannot, even momentarily, set aside their infighting and collectively face the invader nation . . . are always found wanting, and defeated by enemy nations'.[99] In chapter 3, U-Don Jadu is pursued by two large dogs owned by an Afrikaner farmer, but he repels them by pointing his umbrella at them, pretending it is a gun. Once the dogs have been frightened off, the apologetic farmer shoots and kills one of them, and feeds and entertains U-Don Jadu generously. Again, the encounter provides lessons: first, the dogs are like 'his people, who would collectively decide to do something, make moves to execute their plan, but then, with the whole world watching in anticipation, be distracted by an insignificant mole they will mistake for an elephant'; and second, the kindness of the Afrikaner farmer proves 'that no single nation is created cruel'.[100] From these experiences, U-Don Jadu learns to understand both the Xhosa nation's potential (in the encounter with the ostriches) and its weaknesses (in the encounter with the dogs), and he uses this acquired wisdom to guide the new state of Mnandi to prosperity during his twenty years as its president.

In the final chapters of *U-Don Jadu*, personal memoir gives way to utopian exposition, as the novel sets out the constitution of Mnandi and summarises the nation's essential characteristics. Mnandi's rules and regulations combine elements of Xhosa, Christian and British law. In some contexts, Christianity prevails: '[B]ecause Mnandi is a Christian state,' U-Don Jadu explains, 'it is no longer necessary to perform any sacrifices for the ancestors'[101] and Christian temperance is enforced because 'alcohol breeds anarchy [and anyone] found sleeping drunk on the streets must be taken to a mental institution'.[102] In many other contexts, Xhosa law and practice continues to be observed: 'Within amaXhosa, there is a tradition of initiating girls into womanhood [and] this tradition will not be left to die'; 'it will be the responsibility of the Priest and a Magistrate to make sure that a boy is circumcised up to a month after birth'; and 'from the pre-colonial Xhosa social settings, there is no record or mention of prisons [and therefore] within this new state, there will be very little relevance for prisons'.[103] The third constituent element of the Mnandi legal system, British law, exerts its authority via a version of indirect rule. U-Don Jadu explains Mnandi's executive hierarchy: thirty district councils are subordinate to the National Council; the National Council is overseen by the prime minister, who in turn answers to the president. But ultimate power rests with the British monarch: 'the same way the amaXhosa have done throughout their lives, there will be area and local chiefs representing the President, who will mediate on issues of dispute and guide their local subjects on issues of collective morality, on behalf of his Majesty the British King'.[104] The guidance and support provided by Britain, U-Don Jadu records, 'ensured that Mnandi has become something magical, and not the banana republic the black states (of the baSotho, the Swazi and the Tswana) were condemned to remain'.[105]

Mnandi's hybrid amaXhosa/Christian/British legal system enabled the flourishing of an economy based upon small-scale peasant production complemented by indigenous leather and textile industries, and a vigorous trade partnership with Britain. Mnandi's regulations prescribed that 'a man with a garden of about an acre must produce approximately two sacks per year, or harvest produce equivalent to a set amount of money';[106] failure to do so triggered the intervention of the state in order to guarantee efficient food production. The manufacture of cowhides, skins, sheep and goat wool, as well as the planting, weaving, spinning and dying of textiles produced high quality export goods, and young amaXhosa men travelled to Britain to study how to build ships and trains, returning with their new skills to further enrich Mnandi. The franchise was enjoyed by men of all races over the age of twenty; women were offered the vote, but declined, 'because they themselves harboured no such interest, mainly because the workload in their households was just too much'.[107] Mnandi welcomed all non-amaXhosa citizens: 'a variety of nations and races have come to settle in Mnandi from their respective kingdoms ... and those who been here for a year voted without being discriminated against on the basis of their nationalities, race, or religion'.[108] As Mnandi thrived, so its relationship with Britain grew ever stronger, with economic ties reinforced by military co-operation. In peaceful old age, U-Don Jadu rejoiced in how the amaXhosa had recovered 'their glory days, their human dignity, their beauty, strength, intellect, honesty, bravery', and in particular, in the many visitors from faraway lands, 'who come to marvel at this amazingly new nation that has grown and developed in so short a period'.[109]

Lamont and Nicholls provide alternative visions of benevolent white rule: Lamont anticipated the British Empire overseeing a compassionate paternalism governing black South Africans, and the narrow nationalisms of Boer and Briton transcended within a single nation state and thriving in a global regime of free trade capitalism, whereas Nicholls looked forward to a chastened white population presiding over a secure, racially segregated South Africa. In its anticipation of a bloody war between black and white followed by the annihilation of all humanity, Flemming's short story shares the paranoid projections of Nicholls, although the elements of satire hint at the mockery rather than the straightforward endorsement of white fears. Even allowing for an element of irony, however, the bleakness of 'And So It Came To Pass' is at odds with the hopeful visions of the future produced in Lamont's *South Africa in Mars* and Mqhayi's *U-Don Jadu*. Lamont's optimism rests exclusively upon his faith in the British Empire's capacity for beneficent governance in Africa, whereas Mqhayi complements his still-intact trust in British colonial rule with his belief in the collective wisdom of the Xhosa people, and the spiritual guidance afforded by Christian doctrine. Like the ANC's 1923 Bill of Rights, Mqhayi's novel attests to durability of the British-imperial ideology in South Africa, not least because the indigenous-settler versions of white rule emerging in the 1920s threatened an even harsher future. Whereas the 1923 ANC Bill of Rights envisions a unified South Africa with Africans enjoying full citizenship rights, Mqhayi's Mnandi is a separate new Xhosa nation state under British patronage, functioning in parallel with the white South African state.

THE HERTZOG BILLS AND THE MOST INERADICABLE CRAVING OF HUMAN NATURE

In the 1930s, any prospects of a state like Mqhayi's Mnandi emerging receded rapidly, as the Hertzog Bills (first tabled in 1926) were passed into law by the Fusion government in 1936. Contrary to the hopes of the ANC, Lamont and Mqhayi, the new legislation reinforced white domination: the Natives' Representation in Parliament Bill removed the qualified franchise for Africans in the Cape; the Native Trust and Land Bill further restricted the property rights of Africans; and the Natives' Council Bill created a Native Representative Council in which white senators represented black constituencies.[110] The effect was to consolidate the restriction of 6 million Africans to 12 per cent of the land (and the balance to 1.5 million white citizens); remove Africans from the common voters' roll; and allocate three of the 150 seats in parliament to three white representatives of the black populace.

The sense of outrage provoked by the Hertzog Bills among African voters in the Cape is captured in the pamphlet *The Crisis* by H. Selby Msimang (1886–1982), which characterised the legislation as an attempt by the Afrikaner government 'to revenge themselves upon the aborigines for the emancipation of slaves a century ago'.[111] In despair at this betrayal of Great Britain's 'magnanimity and greatness of heart' in freeing the slaves, Msimang argues that 'if we refuse to be made slaves then we should seek emancipation by such means as the dictates of self-preservation may lead us to'.[112] Quoting Smuts, the then Minister of Justice, and placing the quoted words in bold for emphasis, Msimang turns Smuts's words against him as he makes the case for African freedom:

> We have it on the authority of General Smuts, the present Minister of Justice, that **'freedom is the most ineradicable craving of human nature; without it, peace, contentment, happiness, and even manhood itself, is not possible'** [bold in original]. If we feel we are sufficiently human to have the craving for freedom, and feel that we cannot surrender our freedom ... then it behoves us to accept General Hertzog's challenge by declaring our refusal to be made slaves and to suffer him to traffic with our freedom in order to uphold the white man's supremacy.[113]

As to how white domination might be opposed, Msimang is confident that 'if we have the soul to resist the machinations of the oppressor, I know of no power in the world and under the sun to conquer us'.[114] More specifically, he identifies 'two alternatives indicating the way to freedom': the first is to accept the logic of the Hertzog Bills, and 'demand a complete segregation on a fifty-fifty basis as to enable us to establish our own State and government wherein to exercise our political, economic and social independence'; and the second is 'to seize the reins of government and regain all the freedom we have lost since the advent of the white man in this country'.[115] The script for following the second alternative, Msimang argues, is provided by Nicholls's *Bayete!*. Msimang ignores the novel's concluding descriptions of a black uprising soundly defeated, and instead interprets Nicholls's work as a rallying cry for African freedom.[116] The second alternative of a unitary non-racial nation, he argues, 'is the only way [to freedom] short of the creation of two States', and requires the education of the black South African masses, who will 'then ... hope and begin to see visions and to dream the dreams of freedom'.[117] Requoting Smuts's rousing words about freedom, Msimang concludes with the declaration that 'we may live to see, if we have the soul and the righteous determination to do and dare, the history of the overthrow of the Russian Empire by the governed, repeated in our dear Fatherland'.[118]

Whereas Msimang discovered in *Bayete!* a literary description of how freedom might be achieved, R. F. Alfred Hoernlé (1880–1943), the director of the South African Institute of Race Relations (1934–43), identified George Bernard Shaw's play *Heartbreak House* (1919) as an approximation of 1930s South Africa.[119] In his Phelps-Stokes lectures, *South African Native Policy and the Liberal Spirit* (1939), Hoernlé argued that like Captain Shotover's country house on the eve of the First

World War, South Africa in 1939 stood on the brink of chaos and war, and like the repellent characters in Shaw's play, white South Africans were oblivious to the impending disaster. Hoernlé reached for the Bible to reinforce his sense of imminent catastrophe, quoting the line, '"Watchman, what of the night?"' (Isaiah 21: 11): like the Israelites threatened by the Assyrian Empire, white South Africa is menaced by the African masses, and 'the watchman must report, not the breaking of the dawn, but the intensification of darkness'.[120] In terms that echo the words of Smuts quoted by Msimang, Hoernlé argues that the yearning for freedom of black South Africans will ultimately prove irresistible:

> Yet, it is as certain as anything can be in human life that the spirit of liberty is ineradicable and cannot in the end be denied. White South Africa may seek to entrench liberty as its own exclusive possession and withhold it from non-White South Africa. All the more will non-White South Africa continue to aspire after liberty and to demand liberty for itself. The very example of White liberty will act as a constant stimulus and irritant.[121]

Recognising that freedom in the past has not been a concession gifted by the powerful, but rather a result of the violent efforts of the powerless, Hoernlé concludes that if South Africa is to avoid violence and achieve change by peaceful means, 'then liberal-minded men and women must continue to bend all their strength to the task of spreading inter-racial good-will by example and precept'.[122]

To Msimang's alternative routes to freedom in South Africa of either two racially separated states or one racially assimilated state, Hoernlé adds a third alternative he terms 'Parallelism'. He defines the three options as follows: (1) Parallelism is a one-state solution in which the multi-racial society 'substitutes within it the *co-ordination* of racial groups for *domination* of the rest by one group, i. e. for the *subordination* of the rest to that one master-group'; (2) Assimilation is also a one-state solution, but 'abolishes race differences within it by the completest possible fusion, or amalgamation, of the races with each other'; and (3) Separation is a two-state (or multi-state) solution which 'organises the several racial components as mutually independent social units'.[123] The option of Parallelism is rejected because 'it cannot be regarded as a genuine alternative to, or an escape from, domination', and Assimilation because 'White South Africa, as a whole, is opposed to Total Assimilation with a fierce determination.'[124] Regarding the third alternative, Hoernlé's preliminary conclusion is that 'Total Separation is no more practicable than the preceding two alternatives [and offers] no ultimate hope for the liberal spirit.'[125] On further reflection, however, he argues that it represents the least bad option. Noting that Africans in the protectorates already enjoyed a version of 'total separation', Hoernlé concludes that 'separate areas of liberty for separate racial groups seem the only alternative to domination in a racial caste-society'.[126] Such a two-state solution, he believes, will create 'a favourable psychological atmosphere for co-operation [and] the growth of a vigorous and self-reliant national spirit among the Native peoples'.[127] The legal entrenchment of white racial prejudice in the Hertzog Bills provoked Msimang to abandon (temporarily) his liberal dreams of freedom and to contemplate the black South African masses emulating the Russian workers of 1917, and confirmed for Hoernlé the impossibility of a unified South Africa governed by liberal values promoting racial equality, prompting him to argue for a racially divided two-state solution.

THE ATLANTIC CHARTER AND THE WHITE MAN'S DUTY

The despondency following the enactment of the Hertzog Bills was partially lifted by the Atlantic Charter of 1941, which attracted the support of anti-colonial movements around the world, including the ANC. The ANC discussed the Charter at its annual conference on 16 December 1943, and published its response as *African Claims in South Africa*, which comprised two documents – 'The Atlantic Charter from the standpoint of Africans within the Union of South Africa' by ANC president A. B. Xuma (1893–1962), and the 'Bill of Rights', which was signed by twenty-eight leading members.[128] In his preface to the first document, Xuma calls upon all the nations which were signatories to the Charter, and in particular the white South African government, to acknowledge the ANC's interpretation of the Charter: '[A] just and permanent peace will be possible only if the claims of all classes, colours and races for sharing and for full participation in the educational, political and economic activities are granted and recognised.'[129] Noting that 'Roosevelt wanted the Atlantic Charter to apply to the whole world [whereas] Churchill understood it to be intended to be for the white people of the occupied countries of Europe,' Xuma insisted that in order for fascism to be 'uprooted from the face of the earth', the Atlantic Charter 'must apply to the whole British Empire, the United States of America and to all the nations of the world and their subject peoples'.[130] In reaching this conclusion, the ANC's 'Atlantic Charter Committee' addressed the ambiguities in the Charter that had produced the divergent interpretations of Roosevelt and Churchill: 'certain terms and expressions are somewhat loosely and vaguely used in the Atlantic Charter: "nations", "states", "peoples" and "men" . . . [T]he Committee decided these terms, words or expressions are understood by us to include Africans and other non-Europeans'.[131] In other words, the freedom promised by the Atlantic Charter to European nations under Nazi occupation would be extended to all subject peoples in the colonial world, including to African majorities under white settler rule.

For each of the eight points in the Atlantic Charter, the ANC Committee provided a short commentary, elaborating their application and relevance to South Africa. The Committee noted the Third Point as the most important one, identifying 'The Right to Choose the Form of Government' as an update of the right of small nations to self-determination as prescribed in Woodrow Wilson's post-First World War Fourteen Points. Applied to Africa, the Third Point of the Atlantic Charter means:

> Africans are still very conscious of the loss of their independence, freedom and the right of choosing the form of government under which they will live. It is

the inalienable right of all peoples to choose the form of government under which they will live and therefore Africans welcome the belated recognition of this right by the Allied Nations.[132]

In summary, '[T]he demands for full citizenship rights and direct participation in all the councils of state should be recognised. *This is most urgent in the Union of South Africa.*'[133] The Committee's commentary on the Atlantic Charter was reinforced by the Bill of Rights, which opens with the demand that Africans in South Africa acquire 'full citizenship rights such as are enjoyed by all Europeans in South Africa', and proceeds to set out in seven repetitious sections the conditions for an egalitarian society. The eleven-point opening section lists the most important rights and freedoms demanded by Africans, *inter alia* to vote for candidates and to stand in all law-making representative bodies; to equality before the law; to access to land occupancy and ownership; to unrestricted movement; and to work in all forms of employment. Sections Two to Six repeat and expand upon these demands, and for extra emphasis the final section lists the most important pieces of racist legislation which must be struck down in order for freedom to flourish. Compared to the ANC's 1923 Bill of Rights, the 1947 updated version is distinctive in its abandonment of any reference to Rhodes's citizenship test, and in its addition of certain rights and freedoms, notably the freedom of the press, and rights of access to education and the state's social services.

The hope of a better future expressed in the ANC's *African Claims* was not shared in the imagined history by the political historian Arthur Keppel-Jones, *When Smuts Goes: A History of South Africa from 1952 to 2010 first published in 2015* (1947). As the lengthy sub-title suggests, *When Smuts Goes* is written from the perspective of a historian looking back from 2015 at the tumultuous half-century following the death of Smuts. The key dates in this imagined history are: in 1952, the election of the Afrikaner Christian National Party; in 1957, the re-election of the National Party with an increased majority; in 1960, the passing of racist laws to restrict further the freedoms of Africans; in 1961, the mass emigration of white English-speaking South Africans (the first trek); in 1963, the replacement of the relatively liberal Jukskei as prime minister by the ultra-Nationalist Bult; in 1965, South Africa's departure from the British Commonwealth and the proclamation of an independent Afrikaner republic; in 1969–70, the devaluation of gold by the US and UK, precipitating a collapse of the South African economy, and the emigration of black South Africans to neighbouring states in search of work (the second trek); in 1972, an African uprising escalating to a civil war, and culminating in the secession of Zululand under British trusteeship; in 1977, an invasion of South Africa led by an international coalition defeating the white republican army, leading to a 12-year British-led occupation, and the mass migration of white Afrikaners to Argentina (the third trek); in 1989, the election of the first black government under the wise Mfundisi (Zulu for 'Teacher'); in 1996, a military coup led by the corrupt Funimali ('Want-money'); in 2002, the replacement of Funimali by the military despot Bulalazonke ('Kill-all'); in 2010, a mass plague killing large numbers of the population; and in 2011, the abolition of the racial classification of South Africa's citizenry.

Of greater interest than the specifics of Keppel-Jones's imagined history, however, are the competing conceptions of freedom set out in *When Smuts Goes*: Afrikaner freedom from British rule; British freedom protected by imperial rule; and African freedom from white settler rule. The first is couched in biblical terms: 'The Republican wing regarded the Chamber of Mines as the real power which had for so long kept the Volk out of the Promised Land';[134] after the 1962 elections confirming the increased support for the Republicans, 'From Pisgah the Promised Land could now clearly be seen';[135] and with the exit from the British Empire and declaration of the Republic in 1965, 'The Volk was represented by its Moses who had brought them from Pisgah and now, going one better than Moses, was leading them into Canaan.'[136] After 1965, the freedom of the Afrikaner republic was precarious, with the great powers still wanting to 'wreak vengeance on [the Afrikaners] because we wanted to be free'.[137] In the face of aggressive Afrikaner Nationalism post 1952, the second conception of freedom was on the retreat: 'People who still clung to the old liberal traditions were now convinced that their battle had been lost, and that in emigration lay the only escape from tyranny and persecution.'[138] The depleted United Party had attempted in vain 'to show the public the connection between the imperial tie and the principle of justice for all races', but there was at least the consolation that on the global stage liberal values enjoyed support:

> The representative of Columbia pointed out in the Assembly that one of the purposes of the United Nations, according to its Charter, was 'to reaffirm faith in fundamental human rights, in the dignity and value of the human person, in the equal rights of men and women and of nations large and small'. He pointed out that these words had been written by a great South African, and that the principle that they expressed was openly scorned by the present South African regime.[139]

For the white Republican leaders on the brink of war in 1977, the choice lay between Afrikaner freedom and 'a return to "British-Jewish imperialism", that is to say, giving rights and power to all the races'.[140] The destruction of the white Republic in the war represents both the short-term triumph for British liberal values, and the dawn of freedom for Africans.

This third conception of freedom, however, is compromised from the start. It was delivered not by the collective struggle of the African masses, but by the military intervention of the US–UK coalition, and was characterised by debauchery and ignorance: 'the liberated helots in district after district fulfilled the dream of years: they entered the abandoned houses of the White man, slept in his beds, ransacked his pantry and ate off his china, drank his wine';[141] and as the conquering army seized control, 'the Natives began to form a cheering crowd. A few words of English, such as "T'ank you, my baas!" and "African people not go'ng to wek now!" were distinguishable among sentences in Afrikaans and an incessant babble in the Native languages'.[142] These unpromising harbingers of African freedom were confirmed in the bleak post-independence scenario that unfolded after the British occupation ended in 1989: 'the characteristic trait of the South African . . . was unwillingness to make a greater effort than was absolutely necessary'; '[t]he pursuit and idolatry of wealth by the liberated black man was a part of his inheritance from his white mentors and predecessors'; 'South Africa was being exploited by a new class of capitalists, largely black but no better than the old for all that'; in sharp contrast to the neighbouring black-governed protectorates, South Africans of all races were known for 'the very low standard of work and achievement with which most of the people are content'; and by the dawn of the new millennium, the Republic had disintegrated into 'a primitive subsistence economy [tending] towards political chaos of the mediaeval type, with local chieftains exercising power and bandits preying upon strangers'.[143]

As in the case of the contrast between Flemming's cheerful 1922 article in *The Journal of the African Society* and his 1924 short story 'And So It Came To Pass', so too in the case of Keppel-Jones, fiction expressed his despairing nightmares of the future, whereas non-fiction provided the form for a more hopeful message. In contrast to the doom-laden images in the closing pages of *When Smuts Goes*, Keppel-Jones in his political history *Friends or Foes* (1949) optimistically predicts that segregation cannot survive because it contradicts 'the tendency of the democratic world . . . to extend the franchise to more and more groups of people till it is universal', and because '*freedom is indivisible* [italics in original]. You cannot for long preserve a system in which liberties are allowed to some people and not to others'.[144] His solution? A federal constitution, Keppel-Jones argues, will reconcile 'the realistic liberal and the sincere and idealistic advocate of apartheid'.[145] To continue enforcing segregation will lead 'to a revolution of the coloured races', and 'equality and assimilation [will be] frustrated by a revolution of the Europeans'; in order therefore to transcend the 'extremes' of segregation and assimilation 'let us take this [federal] road to freedom, justice and security'.[146] As a soothsayer, Keppel-Jones-the-fiction-writer fared better than Keppel-Jones-the-political-pundit: whereas his federal ideal for South Africa outlined in *Friends or Foes* failed to gain traction, some of his predictions in *When Smuts Goes* have proved uncannily accurate: the election of an Afrikaner Nationalist government (1952 v 1948); the transition from Union to Republic (1965 v 1961); and the election of a black majority government (1989 v 1994).

AFTER APARTHEID?

All hopeful prophecies were confounded by the election of the National Party in 1948: Lamont and Mqhayi's hopes of a benign British influence ameliorating racial oppression in South Africa were shattered; the 'liberal' element in Hoernlé's segregationist vision discredited; the ANC's request for a sympathetic adoption of the Atlantic Charter ignored; and Keppel-Jones's blueprint of a federal constitution rendered an irrelevance. Instead of edging steadily closer to the universal franchise, the National Party passed a series of laws that not merely halted, but reversed the journey of black South Africans to freedom: the Prohibition of Mixed Marriages Act of 1949; the Immorality Act of 1950; the Population Registration Act of 1950; the Group Areas Act of 1950; the Suppression of Communism Act of 1950; the Bantu

Authorities Act of 1951; the Abolition of Passes and Co-ordination of Documents Act of 1952; the Reservation of Separate Amenities Act of 1953; the Criminal Law Amendment Act of 1953; the Bantu Education Act of 1953; the Public Safety Act of 1953; the Natives Resettlement Act of 1954; and the Native Urban Areas Amendment Act of 1955; and the Riotous Assemblies Act of 1956.[147]

For white South Africans, the passage of apartheid legislation reinforced by the post-war economic boom produced a period of prosperity and stability. Anxieties about disenfranchised Africans seeking vengeance never disappeared, however, and as the Cold War intensified, these anxieties were supplemented by fears of nuclear destruction. Lewis Sowden's futuristic novel, *Tomorrow's Comet* (1951) captures the combination of white complacency and fear. Set in Johannesburg, the narrator John Lacey is a journalist who is the first to notice and report a comet flying towards the Earth. As the population grows increasingly frightened, the wealthy capitalist Kennaway Laver takes advantage of the panic to acquire immense wealth; the Africans leave Soweto *en masse* to protest in the city centre, waving banners with messages like 'JUDGMENT UPON THE WHITE MAN ... A COMET COMES TO JUDGEMENT ... A NEW WORLD COMES TO THE AFRICAN ... THROUGH THE FIRES TO FREEDOM' (capitals in original);[148] and the contending Cold War powers suspend their hostilities to seek ways of working together with their nuclear technologies to deflect the comet. The co-operation between the super-powers gives Lacey hope for a better future, as he exclaims to his fiancée, Philippa, '"We'll be so grateful to have dear old Mother Earth as our own again, to feel it belongs to us and we to her again, so we won't want to quarrel any more ... There'll be no more malice or mistrust, and ... it will be beautiful to live again and know there's a future."'[149] The attempt to deflect the comet fails, however, and the novel ends with Lacey waiting for the end, and appealing to God to spare someone somewhere so that 'life may revive again from chaos, and faith may flourish again under the heavens'.[150]

In contrast to the white South African characters in *Tomorrow's Comet* fearing the future, black South Africans faced a much more immediate constriction of their rights and freedoms. The new apartheid laws provoked a wave of popular protest, as leaders who had previously sought common cause with white liberals adopted increasingly independent positions. The shift is reflected in the trajectory of Z. K. Matthews (1901–1968). In 1940, Matthews had concluded that Hoernlé's '*South African Native Policy and the Liberal Spirit* 'richly deserves the serious consideration of all liberty-loving South Africans'.[151] In 1953, Matthews proposed convening a 'Congress of the People' in order to draw up a Freedom Charter. Matthews noted the artificial calm accompanying the imposition of apartheid laws, but warned (in terms that recall Winter's minor utopias in dark times) that it would soon be disturbed 'by the irrepressible urge for freedom for which all people yearn, irrespective of race or colour or creed'.[152] Rejecting the division of races under segregationist and apartheid laws, Matthews repeated the ANC's commitment to 'a united South African nation', and its 'vision of a South African State based upon justice, fair play, and equality of opportunity for all'.[153] To reinvigorate this vision, Matthews made his proposal:

> The main task of the Congress [of the People] will be to draw up a 'Freedom Charter' for all peoples and groups in South Africa. From such a Congress ought to come a Declaration which will inspire all the peoples of South Africa with fresh hope for the future, which will turn the minds of the people away from the sterile and negative struggles of the past and the present to a positive programme of freedom in our lifetime.[154]

Matthews was unable to attend the Congress of the People in Kliptown on 25–6 June 1955, but praised in the warmest terms the execution of his vision: the collective achievement of the Freedom Charter, he recalled in his autobiography, represented 'the people's finest hour'.[155] Turok, who drafted the final version of the Freedom Charter's economic clauses, concurred: 'the atmosphere was that of a celebration rather than a conference [and] we all knew that history was being made that week-end, and that it was a privilege to be there'.[156] But the euphoria of the Kliptown moment was exceptional, and Matthews noted that there was no prospect of meeting the aspirations in the Freedom Charter in the short term: '1955 seemed to be a particularly bad year [with] a sorry catalogue of assaults upon the rights of the people [making it] one of the blackest years in the history of the relations between the Union Government and the African people.'[157]

The Freedom Charter repeated all the elements of the vision for a free South Africa contained in earlier ANC documents like the 1923 Bill of Rights and the 1943 *African Claims in South Africa*: the right to vote ('Every man and woman shall have the right to vote for and stand as a candidate for all bodies which make laws');[158] the right to equality before the law ('All laws which discriminate on the grounds of race, colour or belief shall be repealed');[159] the right to own land ('Restriction of land ownership on a racial basis shall be ended');[160] the right to freedom of movement ('Pass laws, permits and all other laws restricting these freedom shall be abolished');[161] the right of access to all forms of employment ('Men and women of all races shall receive equal work for equal pay');[162] and the right to education ('The colour bar in cultural life, in sport and in education shall be abolished').[163] In addition, the Freedom Charter made demands which registered (much as Schreiner had done fifty years before) that economic inequalities would have to be overcome in order for freedom to be meaningful – that 'The People Shall Share in the Country's Wealth', and that 'There Shall be Houses, Security and Comfort'.[164] These additional clauses acknowledge that freedom might require more than the universal franchise; socio-economic rights protected by some form of welfare state are essential in order to give the political equalities material substance.

Matthews's sense of the distance between the bleak political terrain and the confident demands of the Freedom Charter was shared by Chief Albert Luthuli (1898–1967). In his autobiography, Luthuli captures the impact of apartheid legislation upon the black rural population. On white-owned farms, he observed that 'many of the people were depressed and oppressed to the point of hopelessness. Some of them perhaps had even acquired a sort of slave-mentality, a sense that their lot was incurable, and was best accepted'.[165] He encountered similar levels of demoralisation in the African rural areas, where black farmers had lost their land, leaving them with 'a couple of bony cows [and causing] many of the men to lapse into something near to apathy'.[166] Reinforcing 'this sort of depression', Luthuli notes further, was 'an unexpected and widespread misapplication of Christian trust. "Ah Chief," people say to me sadly, "God will give us freedom when he is ready" . . . Personal responsibility is abandoned [and] the product is a kind of resigned fatalism, a daydream about what God may do in the future'.[167] On Luthuli's diagnosis, rural black South Africans had lost their capacity to dream of freedom, lapsing instead into fatalistic daydreaming, with their faith in their own agency replaced by vague hopes of divine redemption.

Luthuli himself refused to succumb to defeatism. Addressing a meeting hosted by the Congress of Democrats in Johannesburg in 1958,[168] he set out in biblical cadences his 'gospel of democracy and freedom for South Africa'.[169] As an antidote to the desperate daydreaming he had witnessed among South Africa's rural poor, Luthuli proclaimed his 'vision of [South Africa] as a fully democratic country, [asking,] "Is this vision of a democratic society in South Africa a realisable vision? Or is it merely a mirage?" I say, it *is* a realisable vision'.[170] His confidence rested upon his conviction that the yearning for freedom is innate and inextinguishable: 'The germ of freedom is in every individual, in anyone who is a human being. In fact, the history of mankind is the history of man struggling and striving for freedom. Indeed, the very apex of human achievement is FREEDOM and *not* slavery. Every human being struggles to reach that apex.'[171] As contemporary examples of nations ascending successfully to the apex of freedom, Luthuli cites Ghana and Nigeria, and looking back in history, he commends the Afrikaners' efforts to win their freedom and 'full share in democracy'.[172] Luthuli exhorted his audience to resist pessimism, and to continue believing in the possibility of a humane and colour-blind South Africa: 'What is important, is that we can build a homogenous South Africa on the basis not of colour but of human values . . . [You] should do your best to work for the realisation of this POSSIBLE vision. It *is* possible, this vision of a multi-racial democracy in South Africa.'[173]

Three years later, in his acceptance speech for the Nobel Peace Prize, Luthuli repeated this message of hope, aligning his vision of a non-racial democratic South Africa with the United Nations Declaration of Human Rights, and quoting lines from the poem 'A Psalm of Life' by Henry Wadsworth Longfellow (1807–1882) in order to exhort Africans to take heart from the achievements of their ancestors: '"[Lives of great men all remind us/ We can make our lives sublime,/ And, departing, leave behind us]/ Footprints on the sands of time;/ Footprints, that perhaps another,/ Sailing o'er life's solemn main,/ A forlorn and shipwrecked brother,/ Seeing, shall take heart again."'[174] Like Longfellow's figure of the forlorn sailor uplifted by the records of great men of past generations, Africans can find hope and inspiration in the past, and can transcend the scars of racial oppression in the future, 'not in overthrowing white domination to replace it with a black caste, but in building a non-racial democracy that shall be a monumental brotherhood, a "brotherly community" with none discriminated against on grounds of race or colour'.[175]

Luthuli's Nobel acceptance speech had been written by Alan Paton (1903–1988), who shared Luthuli and Matthews's hopes of a non-racial future for South Africa.[176] Paton's best-selling novel, *Cry, the Beloved Country* (1948), sub-titled *A Story of*

Comfort in Desolation, ends with the elderly Reverend Stephen Kumalo returning from a desperately unhappy sojourn in Johannesburg to the Natal Midlands, where he detects a new spirit, telling a recently arrived agricultural adviser, '[T]here is a new life in this valley . . . There is hope here, such as I have never seen before.'[177] But Kumalo's hope is cautious, as he reflects that those seeking freedom and equality are so few in number, and recalls further his friend Msimangu's fear that 'when [the white people] turn to loving they will find [the black people] are turned to hating'.[178]

A decade later, Paton qualified his optimism in his column 'The Long View' in the magazine *Contact*, and in his political tract, *Hope for South Africa* (1958). In his first *Contact* column in February 1958, Paton declared that 'no one believes that the fortress [of white South Africa] will endure [and] our political problem . . . is to move from white supremacy to nonracial democracy as quickly, as soundly, as we can'.[179] In his final column a year later, however, he struck a more pessimistic note, first asking, 'Is there still a possibility of evolutionary adaptation away from a colour-bar society?', and then despairing at the feeble responses of the 'liberal' United Party and its leader, Sir De Villiers Graaf (1913–1999). Much like Matthews, Paton's attitude to Hoernlé's liberal 'separatism' hardened as apartheid was entrenched: in *Cry, the Beloved Country*, Hoernlé is described as 'a great and courageous fighter for justice',[180] but in *Hope for South Africa*, Paton dismisses Hoernlé's separatist model as a pipe-dream because 'there is no land for it, there is no money for it, there is no time for it, and there is no will for it'.[181] Instead, like Luthuli and Matthews, Paton favoured a 'liberal vision of a common society open to all',[182] and elaborated the essential elements of such a vision:

> All of us hope that whatever difficult times must be endured, South Africa will eventually become a democracy; and by that we mean a country with parliamentary institutions based on universal suffrage, with a written constitution and a bill of rights, and a distribution of power and authority, not only in respect of parliament, cabinet and judiciary, but also in respect of national, provincial and local bodies.[183]

Paton's vision was set out in greater detail in the Liberal Party's *Blueprint for South Africa*. Repeating substantially the same demands as the Freedom Charter, the *Blueprint* committed the Liberal Party to six goals: (1) One Man One Vote; (2) An End to Poverty; (3) Security for All; (4) Schools for All; (5) Land for All; and (6) Maximum Freedom.[184] In 1958, Paton was still confident that these goals were achievable, and that South Africa would ultimately arrive at the happy destination of a 'liberal society open to all'; what he was unsure about was whether it would reached via 'violence and revolution resulting in a black racial domination, or by an evolutionary process of a massive kind'.[185]

For all their differences, the dreams of the future produced in the 1950s are alike in their refusal to capitulate to despair (although Sowden's novel comes close): Matthews, Luthuli, the authors of the Freedom Charter, Paton and the Liberal Party all retain the hope that the goal of freedom in the form of a non-racial liberal-democratic nation can still be reached. As such, all of these texts could be added to

Winter's tradition of 'minor utopias' produced in moments of adversity. The intensification of apartheid in the 1960s, however, was to provide an even sterner test for those clinging to their dreams of freedom.

TO BLOOD RIVER OR THE PROMISED LAND?

Despite Matthews and Paton's loss of faith in Hoernlé's 'two/multi-state separation', a couple of novels of the early 1960s still attempted to imagine the future in his segregationist terms. Garry Allighan's *Verwoerd – The End: A Look-Back from the Future* (1961) is set in 1987, reflecting upon twenty-five years of happy progress during which Verwoerd's Bantustan policy has been taken to its logical conclusion by his successor, Dr Johannes Van Wyk, and two parallel states have been established. Whereas Verwoerd had conceded 'to the Bantu separate homelands with White supervision, [Van Wyk ceded] to them a large area as their own self-governed Bantu State', and since 31 May 1980 the independent Bantu State had flourished under 'the resolute and clear-visioned statesmanship of Ephraim Rametse'.[186]

Anthony Delius's *The Day Natal Took Off: A Satire* (1963) is set in the mid-1970s, with the feckless narrator John describing in gossipy detail the rapid fragmentation of South Africa into the Southern African Federation, made up of small independent states: the Good Hope Republic, the Free State, the South Sotho-Nguni Republic, Zululand-Swaziland, Bechuana-Ovambo, East Cape Republic, Outer Natal, Southern Rhodesia and Moçambique. As their names suggest, these new nations are extrapolations of the Bantustans created in 1959, with the addition of a couple of neighbouring protectorates and colonies. Admitting that 'covert apartheid ... seems to well up in us like gas in mineral water', John observes that the Free State is 'an Afrikaner homeland' or an 'Afrikaner Israel'.[187] The only complicating element is the Transvaal Republic, which has been colonised by the Soviet Union. However, its Afrikaner and Soviet citizens (according to the unreliable narrator) are happily united in their shared desire to nationalise the mines, to subordinate trade unions to the state, and to '[r]eject Western Liberal Humanism'.[188] The dark and jaunty humour of *The Day Natal Took Off* contrasts with the earnest confidence of *Verwoerd – The End*, but both novels nonetheless derive their visions of the future from the same template of 'separate development'.

In the decade following the Sharpeville massacre on 21 March 1960, the optimistic segregationist futures imagined by Nicholls, Mqhayi, Hoernlé, Allighan and Delius were discredited by the apartheid state's determined application of its version of separate development. Clamping down on opposition, and buoyed by an expanding economy, the state entrenched its hegemony. The period from Sharpeville to the Durban strikes of the early 1970s – the period of 'high apartheid'[189] – saw the state passing ever more draconian laws to suppress resistance to white rule: the Unlawful Organisations Act of 1960 (extending the 1950 Suppression of Communism Act in order to ban the ANC and PAC); the Indemnity Act of 1961 (to protect all state employees); the General Law Amendment Act of 1962 (extended in 1963, 1966, 1969 and 1970 to enable the police to exercise ever greater discretion in detaining political suspects without trial); the Publications and Entertainments Act of 1963 (allowing greater censorship); the Civil Defence Act of 1966 (reinforcing the 1953 Public Safety Act); the Terrorism Act of 1967; the Prohibition of Political Interference Act of 1968; and the Abolition of Juries Act of 1969.[190] The state backed these laws up by increasing expenditure on the police and military, and complemented their efforts to frustrate African opposition by the policy of 'separate development', which sought to reverse African urbanisation (and the collective resistance it enabled) by relocating urban Africans to rural 'homelands'/Bantustans. The Promotion of Bantu Self-Government Act of 1959 accordingly constituted eight homelands (later increased to ten), and by 1970, homeland citizenship had been imposed on all Africans in South Africa. In the process, 3.5 million people were forcibly moved under Group Areas and Separate Development legislation between 1960 and 1983; the populations of the Bantustans rose by 70 per cent; and during the same period the total populations of African townships in South Africa fell.[191]

Under high apartheid, dreams of a peacefully segregated Southern Africa all but disappeared, and were replaced by nightmare visions of a nation torn apart by violent racial conflict or ruled by police terror. The trajectory of Jordan K. Ngubane captures this shift. In the 1950s and early 1960s, he was the leading African member of South Africa's Liberal Party. Ngubane set out his dream of freedom in *An African Explains Apartheid* (1963), arguing that only when 'citizenship has a non-racial meaning [can the] African, the Afrikaner, the Asian, the colored, the British and the Jew . . . then march arm in arm to defend together those things they value most – their country, their freedom, and their independence'.[192] The rights of individual citizens must be paramount in a free South Africa, an emphasis Ngubane reiterated in several contexts: in his antipathy towards Communism, which paradoxically promises the individual 'the paradise of the classless society where no man exploits another, but [extracts] the price . . . that is the destruction of the individual';[193] and in his argument that 'the religion of the Sutu-nguni group (before the advent of the white man) revered the individual as the incarnation of a future ancestral spirit'.[194] However, Ngubane did recognise that the political freedoms of an equal citizenry could be undermined by economic inequalities. Accordingly, he looks forward to a future South Africa in which the laws 'must insure that the wealth is distributed and shared equitably, since the extremes of undiluted capitalism and Communism are not suitable for South African conditions. A welfare state would provide a practical system, half way between the two'.[195] He concedes that 'the advent of freedom will not transform [black South Africans] into a self-sufficient community', and that therefore in order to manage the transition to freedom, the fundamentals of South Africa's capitalist economy must continue to be supported. To curtail 'the inevitable pains of birth into freedom', African nationalists should accommodate 'the white man, who has the technical skills, the know-how, for maintaining the nation in a healthy condition, producing food for the millions, creating wealth, and distributing it'.[196] In addition, the principle of private property, modified by 'the repeal of all [racial] laws restricting the ownership of land',[197] should also persist unimpeded.

Very little of the optimism of *An African Explains Apartheid* survives in *Ushaba:*

The Hurtle to Blood River (1974). Written in exile in the United States, *Ushaba* attempts to forge a new genre beyond the English literary forms of the polemical essay and the novel.[198] In order to tell 'the tragic story behind the vicious power-struggle between the African and the Afrikaner in my country', Ngubane explains, he adapted the Zulu form of the *umlando*, the 'vehicle for developing the collective wisdom of the family, the clan, or the nation'.[199] Attuned to the history of ideas and the exploration of political themes, the *umlando* allows Ngubane to address his primary concern, namely 'the challenge of being human in the *ushaba* (the continuing provocation or proliferation of crises) which is steadily moving black and white in South Africa towards one of the ugliest bloodbaths in human history'.[200] The opening chapter establishes the centrality of the Battle of Blood River on 16 December 1838 in South African history, observing that on its annual anniversary, 'Zulus and Afrikaners emotionally dig up the bones of their dead and crack each other's political skulls with them', and further, that far from leading over time to reconciliation, 'in the last hundred years, the African and the Afrikaner have been moving inexorably to the moment of decision at Blood River'.[201] With frequent references to Afrikaner–Zulu hostilities of the past, the plot of *Ushaba* traces the escalation of the conflict between Afrikaner and African nationalisms after Sharpeville, with a vast cast of stereotypical characters populating the nation's inexorable march to a second Blood River. The most important African nationalist leader is Chief Bulube, who resembles the Inkatha leader Mangosuthu Buthelezi (1928–),[202] and who rejects definitions of 'freedom in terms of slogans borrowed from the white side', believing rather that 'the main ideological quarrels of the twenty-first century would be between the *Buntu* evaluation of the person and the one evolved by the Greeks, the Romans and the Hebrews'.[203] As the battle lines between Afrikaner and African nationalism harden, white English liberals (sympathetically discussed in *An African Explains Apartheid*) are exposed. The political activist Maggie Kuboni tells a black policeman, 'I once believed and told my own people that the white liberals were our friends ... I know now that they are not; they are the friends and allies of [Afrikaner premier] Willem Adriaan De Haas!'[204] Even the word 'freedom' is treacherous: Zandile Makaye, another Zulu woman character, explains that freedom defined as 'the right to determine our lives ... is the white man's definition', and she argues *contra*, 'I want to know how to feed, clothe, house, educate and cure every person. Freedom won't enable me to do that. In your great democracies, people are free to starve'.[205] Stripped of the illusory promises of liberal freedom, *Ushaba* closes with the clash of contending nationalisms. The troubled African policeman Bashise Basengi warns his boss Paul Kritzinger:

> You are the prisoner of your power and I am the prisoner of my anger. That is true of your people, Sir; it is true of mine, too. We are caught in a trap set by history. A cruel force drives us relentlessly to destruction; it moves events slowly, inevitably, to a catastrophe we cannot escape. Your people and my people hold each other in a grip of death ... This cruel force I have just spoken about – we call it *ushaba* in my language – will not stop before it has destroyed everything beautiful in this land (and ugly too, he thought).[206]

Bashise's words are prophetic, as *Ushaba* culminates in violent racial conflict and the death of the Afrikaner nationalist premier De Haas.

Written at the same time as *Ushaba*, but set further in the future, *Na die Geliefde Land (The Promised Land)* (1972) by Karel Schoeman (1939–2017) imagines a rural Afrikaner community under a black government. *Promised Land* gestures to earlier South African fiction – in its setting to Schreiner's *The Story of an African Farm* (1883), and in its title to Paton's *Cry, the Beloved Country* (the Afrikaans title 'Na die Geliefde Land' translates literally as 'To the Beloved Land').[207] It also echoes the earlier dystopias of Flemming and Keppel-Jones in its depiction of cowering Afrikaner characters menaced by a black police state. However, whereas the dystopias of Flemming and Keppel-Jones alternate between satire and paranoia, Schoeman's novel is elegiac, with the central characters trapped by their anachronistic dreams of freedom. The protagonist George Neethling, a publisher living in Geneva, returns to visit his old family farm in post-apartheid South Africa, but discovers it had been used to hide fugitives and munitions, and as a consequence had been destroyed by the new regime's military. He registers the emptiness of his long-held dream of returning to the land of his fathers:

> And yet there must be an answer, he thought, somewhat taken aback and uncomprehending; it was indeed time for summing up and decision, now that all dreams had been realised and what had so long been desired had become actuality. This was, after all, the promised land, possessed by birth and inheritance, the land about which so much had been spoken and dreamed, the object of such endless longing, for which so much had been endured – even exile and death.[208]

George recognises that his futile longing for the family farm was shared by all exiled Afrikaners: 'The dream endured, its lustre untarnished, and their existence was a perpetual attempt to deny the pressure of the reality surrounding them, while they remembered and longed and waited for the hour when it would all be over and they would return to the beloved land.'[209] For the Afrikaner men who remained in South Africa, freedom is no less elusive. Fanie Raubenheimer, the teacher-poet, tells George, '"It's only in the outposts that a person can still be free, and we keep the campfires burning, or try to anyway!"'[210] To keep the flame of freedom burning, Fanie explains, he writes poetry, because '"it's also a weapon in our struggle, it's something with which to rouse our people and inspire them!"'[211] But the hollowness of Fanie's words are exposed at the party on George's final night. In a rare satirical passage, Fanie reads one of his nationalist poems, which includes the lines, '*Our leaders in their deep despair accosted . . ./ And whatever the battle we started to fight/ Before we're halfway we've lost it.*'[212] Such poetic words, however, prove to be ineffectual, as the police arrive, humiliate Fanie, and arrest three of the men involved in the resistance.

A third response to the eclipse of Afrikaner rule is provided by the daughter of George's hosts, Carla Hattingh, who resembles Olive Schreiner in her independence of spirit and intelligence.[213] Visiting George's destroyed farm, Carla tells him,

'"You people with your dreams... It wasn't proof against reality. The first gust blew it apart... I'm tired of all the dreams and memories; I don't want to live in the past, I don't want to come and grieve over an old overgrown garden. There's work to do, life must go on."'[214] Carla extends her disdain for George's dreams of returning to the Promised Land to the dreams of her Afrikaner nationalist teachers: '"They wasted years of our lives... with their patriotic songs and speeches and sacred covenants. There wasn't any sense in it... They should rather have taught us how to keep quiet, how to forget, how to be humble and patient, how to stick it out and cling to life whatever happens."'[215] In her farewell conversation with George, Carla repeats her sense of exasperation with the decaying culture of Afrikaner nationalism represented by Fanie and her brothers, and asserts her own acceptance of an irreversibly changed society:

> 'My own brothers dashed off with a mouthful of threadbare slogans, they set off to regain a world they themselves hadn't even known... When something becomes irrevocable, you have to recognise the fact and accept it... The old world has disappeared, and it will never, in all eternity, come back, even if we give our lives to try to regain it. We must learn to live in the new world.'[216]

If any dream of freedom can be extracted from *Promised Land*, it resides not at the collective level of the post-apartheid society described in the novel, but rather at the individual level in the character of Carla, whose capacity to adapt to the authoritarian social dystopia and inhabit a *locus* of existential freedom, represents a version of Arendt's journey of 'inner migration', a personal solution to a terrifying future.

CONCLUSION

For all their differences, the dreams of freedom surveyed in this chapter share two assumptions about how South Africa's future will unfold: first, that the nation will continue as the primary form of political community; and secondly, that capitalism (however modified) will continue as the dominant form of economic system.

The dreams of freedom shaped by these two fundamentals can be grouped into three loose groups. The first two are characterised by a spirit of hope – the Mandela and the Hoernlé traditions. The Mandela–Daniels dream of freedom is of a sovereign and unitary nation-state made up of an equal citizenry enjoying universal franchise and the protection of the rule of law, and includes the dreams of Schreiner, Smith, the 1923 ANC Bill of Rights, Lamont (with qualifications), Msimang, *African Claims*, Luthuli, the Freedom Charter, Matthews and Paton. The Hoernlé group of dreamers share the dominant group's hope that all races will one day enjoy the liberal freedoms, but believes such freedoms can only be secured within the framework of (at least two) independent racially segregated states. The dreams of Nicholls, Mqhayi, Allighan and Delius fall into this category, but this tradition dies out with the consolidation of high apartheid in the early 1960s. The third group is the 'lineage of despair', the tradition that abandons all dreams of a free South Africa governed by liberal values, and foresees instead their betrayal, abandonment or perversion – the dystopian futures imagined by Flemming, Keppel-Jones, Sowden, Ngubane and Schoeman. Part warning, part paranoid racial fantasy, these dystopian visions (particularly those of the period of high apartheid) cast some doubt on Winter's faith in the resilience of utopian thought. In contexts of enduring oppression, which are not uncommon in colonial and postcolonial history, the imagination can as easily abandon hope, and either lapse into silence (as in the 1960s), or extrapolate from the grim present to ever more pessimistic visions of the future.

In the closing lines of his 1976 Robben Island essay, Mandela made a plea for unity among the different resistance movements, naming as possible allies of the ANC *inter alia* Yusuf Dadoo of the SACP, I. B. Tabata of the NEUM, and Potlako Leballo of the PAC.[217] None of these figures, nor the parties they represented, shared the ANC-Liberal Party's hopes for a future framed by liberal nationalism and capitalism. How each of them (and the ICU before them) dreamed their different and distinctive dreams of freedom is the focus of the chapters to follow.

2 The Industrial and Commercial Workers Union (ICU) and the Language of Freedom

INTRODUCTION

The ICU grew from modest beginnings in Cape Town in 1919 to a membership of over 100,000 across Southern Africa by the mid-1920s. In 1926, at the zenith of its power, the ICU adopted a Manifesto, which criticised racist legislation (the Pass Laws and the Sedition Bill); made specific demands (a minimum wage, an eight-hour day, and the extension of the franchise to African men and 'European' women); and set out its dream of freedom. The ICU's dream had both a national and an international dimension. It promised firstly that freedom in South Africa would be achieved 'by according full political, economical, civic and social rights to all citizens who make up the South African nation, irrespective of colour, race or creed'. Beyond national liberation lay a further dream:

> [The ICU] stands for the industrial organisation of the African workers, who must be organised 100% strong, so that in due course these oppressed peoples of Africa should take their rightful place in the Labour movement of the world for the complete overthrow of capitalism and the establishment of a Socialistic Commonwealth of all nations and races.[1]

These heady words are followed by practicalities, as the Manifesto closes with a request to its members to pay for the union's ongoing legal battles: 'our members as a whole can contribute towards a fund designated for battling for their freedom. THE HOUR FOR FREEDOM HAS STRUCK [capitals in original]! Will the African workers throughout South Africa rally to the great call?'[2]

In looking at the first of the unfulfilled dreams of freedom, I consider how the many contending factions within the ICU developed a critique of the status quo, and dreamed of a future society that exceeded the liberal-nationalist dreams of the ANC and its supporters.[3] I argue that Kadalie and his ICU comrades did much more than borrow from or 'write back' to the axioms of European liberal nationalism; rather, they expressed their own distinctive dream of freedom, drawing upon

Christian discourse, the political ideologies of Garveyism and Communism, a wide range of literary resources, and their own vernacular language of freedom.[4]

CHRISTIANITY: I WILL NOT PRAY AGAIN UNTIL WE ARE A FREE PEOPLE

The ICU leaders frequently cast their dreams of freedom in biblical idiom, both their critiques of settler power and their utopian longings for a society more humane than 1920s South Africa. In his autobiography, Kadalie describes his education at Livingstonia Missionary Institute in Nyasaland between 1906 and 1912, emphasising that he 'passed through the hands of only Scottish teachers'.[5] He refers only twice further to the content of his education. In the first reference, he recognises that Christianity taught compassion and empathy, qualities that became the basis of his politics: 'I went through a theological course, which I think has helped me since to understand the sufferings of my fellow-men.'[6] And in the second reference, he embraces as his own the Christian ideal of equality: observing the brutal exploitation of African mine-workers in Southern Rhodesia in 1915, he recalls, 'I nearly forgot the good missionaries in Nyasaland, at my college in particular, who taught me the Christian faith that all men are equal and that their lives were valuable.'[7]

In their attacks on white power, ICU leaders drew extensively upon the Bible, frequently comparing black South Africans to the Israelites in Egypt/Kadalie to Moses/white South Africa's rulers to the Egyptian pharaohs. At a well-attended rally in Pietermaritzburg in 1926, Kadalie dismissed the dangers of white hostility, declaring, 'Naturally, I ignored the threat of being shot at, for I had a holy mission to speak to the modern Pharaohs.'[8] On his return from Europe in 1927, Kadalie explained, 'To me it now appeared I was in the role of the Biblical Moses, who had gone to Mount Sinai, returning with the new commandments to the children of Israel below. To Africa I must now return with new ideas to further the cause of the new trade unionism.'[9] In a speech in East London in January 1930, the ICU leader P. S. Sijadu declared, 'God sent Moses to Pharaoh to release Israelites, but the King of Egypt refused to do so. Kadalie has been sent by God to teach the native people as to how to live a happy life.'[10] And at another meeting the same month, Sijadu's message was amplified by Alex Maduna: '[W]e have been praying for 400 years, yet we have not been replied to, now we are going to do as Moses did and take our freedom.'[11]

Complementing the identification of Kadalie with Moses were a number of references to Kadalie as Jesus. In a speech in 1928, Kadalie identified his mission with that of Jesus, casting his adversaries as modern-day Judases:

> Some intellectuals do not want to join the I. C. U. for they say it is for the illiterate natives. When Christ came into the world he did not go to the Pharisees but to the raw Jews. I am proud of being leader of raw natives. The intellectuals do not matter, they spent their people's monies through lawyers, those people are traitors like Judas.[12]

A year later, Kadalie's ally, Keable 'Mote, endorsed his leader's message, telling his audience, 'You have been told by [Theo] Lujiza and [John] Mzaza [Kadalie's critics] that Kadalie has stolen I. C. U. money, I am not afraid to say they are damn liars, they helped to betray Kadalie, like Judas did Jesus Christ.'[13] Following his release from prison in May 1930, Kadalie told a large crowd, 'We were not afraid, we have all come back from gaol a free race. Jesus Christ died and came back to Earth again. I have come back from gaol to fight for a new Africa.'[14] Kadalie repeated the same message a few months later, adding the apostles as exemplary freedom-fighters: 'Look at Christ and the 11 Apostles when they [were] persecuted by the gentiles through preaching the gospel of God and they organised and fought for their right even the Bible tells you so.'[15]

In several speeches, Kadalie drew Old and New Testament antecedents together. At a meeting in King William's Town in 1930, he stressed the continuity of oppression, telling his audience, 'The oppression you are now suffering started in the days of Pharaoh, when the children of Israel were in Egypt until delivered. Herod also acted likewise on hearing that a child was born: all male children were slaughtered.'[16] Speaking in East London at the same time, he emphasised the continuity of resistance, arguing, 'Jesus Christ and Moses were Agitators because they wanted people to do God's will. I am then an Agitator because I want the freedom of our people.'[17] By strategically appropriating the stories of Moses v Pharaoh and Jesus v Herod to serve the cause of union recruitment, Kadalie transformed these Old and New Testament tales into inspirational political allegories.

In conjunction with these affirmative biblical appropriations were attacks upon the failure of white South Africa to live up to the ideals of equality prescribed by Christian doctrine. For example, a newspaper report on a speech by Kadalie in Bloemfontein in 1926 recorded:

> [Kadalie] hoped, he said, that the heavens would also watch o'er him. They should not be misled by the Bishop of Bloemfontein addressing them as 'my dear brothers'. He did not mean it. The British bishops of today were all hypocrites, so were all ministers of religion, or they would have raised their voices against the colour bar legislation of the Government . . . Kadalie reminded his hearers that he had been brought up under the Christian church, but he had since lost all faith in white Christianity. 'I am in revolt,' he exclaimed, and proceeded to inveigh against all authorities in heaven and in earth. He had no more time for religion or the church. All white ministers of religion, he said, would go to hell. They were all hypocrites.[18]

Kadalie was not the only ICU leader to attack white Christianity and its ministers: at a meeting in East London in 1930, first Alex Fifani told the audience, '[W]e must pray to God but we have not found the right one yet as the one we got is the one the white people showed us so we can't pray for him';[19] and then John Mciza, reinforcing the point, argued, 'I believe that the word of God given to us by white people is wrong. Look how simply our farms were taken away from us by these white people.'[20] For Dorrington Mqayi, speaking a year later, the solution lay in the existence of a

God who treated all races equally: 'The white people tell lies that God is a white man. God is not a white man at all. God is not after those who default to pay poll-tax or to carry passes. The true God is sympathetic with all the people of all various nations.'[21]

In explaining his own disillusionment with Christianity, Kadalie emphasised the historical dimension of white Christian betrayals. At the 1927 annual congress of the ICU, he linked his personal loss of faith to the duplicity of the missionaries, declaring, 'I am not a religious fanatic, as I ceased to pray in 1910 and will not pray again until we are a free people by fair means or by foul means. The missionaries who brought the Bible here did it as an instrument of capitalistic hypocrisy.'[22] A year later at the General Missionary Conference, he accused the first missionaries of being 'thoroughly reactionary and drifting from Christ's teaching [by siding] with the rich against the poor, opposing every effort toward social and economic freedom for the masses.'[23] White hypocrisy is the unbroken thread in South African history linking the first missionaries to Prime Minister Hertzog in the 1920s. In the speech transcribed and presented as evidence in Kadalie's trial in May 1928 for his promoting 'hostility between Natives and Europeans' under the 1927 Native Administration Act, he elaborated:

> This country belongs to the Lord and the fullness thereof. This land was robbed by the forefathers 500 years ago. They came here only with the Bible. They stole this country . . . We are going to tell them that they came here as Christians, as civilised people, and they are blessed hypocrites because our rulers today know nothing . . . I am just wondering when 500 years ago the Missionary came here whether my forefathers asked him for his pass. He had the Bible. What happened when they got this country? This country became a land in which the Pass Law was introduced.[24]

Kadalie's compressed history recounts how land was stolen 500 years ago by Bible-bearing white colonisers, who spurned the hospitality of the indigenes and established laws (pre-eminently the pass laws) to deny black South Africans access to the land. Kadalie links the long history of white Christian hypocrisy to present injustices under the Pass Laws by asking the court to '[i]magine the Angel Gabriel coming down from Heaven into Colonel Beer's bedroom with his sweetheart and asking the Chief of Police where his Pass is'.[25] Kadalie continued repeating such arguments well after the heyday of the ICU. At a meeting to protest Hertzog's Native Bills in 1936, he declared, 'White people had given them the Bible which taught equality, charity and brotherhood, but ungrateful General Hertzog and his gang did not believe the Biblical doctrine which they preached to the Natives but did not practise themselves.'[26]

For all that he believed that Christianity was complicit in effecting the dispossession of Africans, Kadalie did not abandon its teachings. The Christian values of 'equality, charity and brotherhood' retained their utopian force, and more than once, Kadalie argued that the ICU shared the same values as Christianity. In a speech in Middelburg in 1927, for example, he used biblical tropes in exhorting his

audience 'to look forward to the star which is guiding you from the house of bondage
... That star is the ICU which is organising all the non-European workers. Hear the
ICU – it is something like a religion'.[27] A year later, in a speech in Ermelo, Kadalie
again located the ICU's Christian roots, proclaiming, 'We are brothers, we must live
together, we are brothers in the Lord.'[28] The Bible also has the capacity to lift the
spirits of the exhausted and demoralised worker. In a speech in East London in 1932,
Kadalie used the story of the Israelites fleeing slavery in Egypt in order to uplift his
audience:

> Some of you may be tired and fed up with the I. C. U. but you don't realise you
> have got to go through hardships and troubles before you reach the promised
> land. Many times I get disgusted with you and when I feel like going home to
> my mother, I hear a small voice of God say, carry on, you have not finished
> your work. Let's not get disheartened and fed up, let's carry on, that is the way
> to success.[29]

Another rhetorical ploy was to weave together biblical and historical tales of heroic
freedom struggles. Kadalie told a large East London crowd in 1930:

> There is not a single nation that was not under slavery. The English and
> Germans were slaves under the Romans. They struggled for their freedom and
> at last they got it. We in our days are slaves under the Europeans and we have
> to fight hard for our freedom before we get it. The native and European enemies
> do not see, but I myself see descending from heaven a new Jerusalem. They
> think to get freedom is an easy matter and forget that it takes some years before
> it comes. The way to liberty passes through Gaol, thorns, aeroplanes, big flying
> machines and Great Government authorities.[30]

Kadalie thus positions his audience as the inheritors of a tradition of resistance that
starts with the English and Germans fighting the Roman Empire and culminating in
a religious vision of freedom identified with a New Jerusalem. There are echoes too
of *Pilgrim's Progress*, as 'the way to liberty' is strewn with multiple obstacles virtuous travellers must overcome in order to reach their destination of freedom. In yet
another variation of the same story, Kadalie told workers in Port Elizabeth in March
1927 that they have every right to expect a better life:

> We have made the blind eye to see, which is the greatest accomplishment
> going. Today ... you are not contented with the wages paid you by your
> employer because you have the eyes to see that it is insufficient, and that you
> cannot live a decent life, and bring up your children decently. Today, you do
> not want to live in hovels, locations and in the slums. The ICU is responsible
> for all those things that you now rightly detest as unsuitable for a civilised
> nation. The main object of the ICU ... is like the children of Israel to deliver
> you from bondage ... Like the Israelites, you will eventually be emancipated
> from bondage.[31]

Old and New Testament images are mobilised, as Kadalie's reference to the once-blind exploited workers now able to see as a result of ICU echoes the tale of Jesus healing the man born blind, and his promise of deliverance from bondage for the enslaved Israelites repeats the archetypal Old Testament journey to emancipation. What the workers can 'see' for the first time is a 'decent' world beyond the markers of their current poverty – the 'insufficient wages', the 'hovels' and the 'slums'. The ICU, Kadalie claims, has activated a vision of freedom 'suitable for a civilised nation'.

The ICU's invocations of the Scriptures thus serve the dual but related functions of utopian literature. First, the critique of white South Africa is expressed in biblical idioms of despotic Pharaohs and greedy Pharisees, and the gulf between Christian ideals and (white Christian) practice repeatedly highlighted. Secondly, Bible stories are inspirational, with the ICU cast as the successor to the Israelites fleeing bondage in Egypt for the Promised Land. Finally, the imagining of a better future is realised by reactivating the goals of 'the Christian faith that all men are equal and that all lives are valuable'; of 'equality, charity and brotherhood'; of a New Jerusalem; and of 'the promised land'.

The contrast between the ICU and the ANC's use of Christianity is instructive: the ANC's Sol Plaatje combined his bitter criticism of white land grabs with an unwavering conviction that '[t]he Christian voice has been our only shield against legislative excesses of the kind now in full swing in the Union'.[32] For the ICU leaders, Christianity was much more than a defence; it provided an invaluable resource in criticising settler power and in dreaming of a future beyond their present suffering.

GARVEYISM: THE BLACK MAN'S DESTINY FREE AND UNTRAMMELLED IN AFRICA

The ICU's insurrectionary Christianity was complemented by the ideology of Marcus Garvey's (1887–1940) supporters in the ICU, who relayed their leader's assertions of black pride, psychological liberation, self-reliance and racial separatism to receptive Southern African audiences.[33] In a letter written in 1920 to Samuel Michael ('S. M.') Bennett Ncwana (1890–c. 1948), Kadalie confessed that his 'essential object is to be the great African Marcus Gorvey [Garvey]'.[34] It was an object he pursued in the ICU's early years, as the union entertained close links with South African Garveyites like Ncwana and James Saul Mokete Thaele (1888–1948).[35] Several Garveyites from the Caribbean served as officials in the early ICU: A. James King was elected the first ICU president, and James Gumbs and Emmanuel Johnson both served terms as vice-president. Garvey's ideas were disseminated via Ncwana's *The Black Man* (1920), the first newspaper of the ICU; the many articles Thaele wrote for *The Workers' Herald* in 1922–4; and Thaele's *The African World* (1925), the ANC paper for the Western Cape. Garveyism's impact in Southern Africa was acknowledged by the Xhosa historian W. D. Cingo, who in 1927 criticised the Garveyites for peddling false dreams to 'large numbers of uneducated Africans', but nonetheless conceded that 'the mad dreams and literature of Marcus Garvey' had revived '[h]opes for political and economical emancipation [and] today the word America (*iMelika*) is a household word symbolic of nothing else but Bantu National Freedom and Liberty'.[36]

Both Ncwana and Thaele emphasised the primacy of Christianity to the Garveyite political mission. In *The Black Man*, Ncwana argued that black South Africans yearned in the first instance for unimpeded access to 'the benefits of Christianity', and that 'not until the whole population of the Black race have been Christianised'[37] would they be in a position to contemplate the next stages in their journey to freedom – economic and political liberation. In a similar spirit, Thaele argued that 'the white man has failed morally here in Africa to govern the subject race in the light of Christianity', and that the imperative therefore was for 'the negroid elements from the Occident to the Orient to create a quasi-spiritual regeneration among the already suspicious aboriginals'.[38] To this end, 'The policy of non-co-operation with us here in Africa must begin in the field of religion; that is, the time has arrived when the white church must be for the white man, and the black church for the black man.'[39] Only once black South Africans have achieved religious independence can they proceed to economic self-sufficiency, and then ultimately to political freedom. The catalyst for liberation was to be a black Messiah (invariably from beyond Southern Africa), who would lead the African masses to spiritual and political salvation. Garvey himself was adept at inhabiting just such a redemptive identity, and his Southern African surrogates attempted to mobilise black South African supporters by couching their appeals in similar terms. For example, one of the South African Garveyite Wellington Buthelezi's close associates, Ernest Wallace, addressed a crowd in the Transkei in December 1925, declaring that he had come to promote 'a general confraternity among the scattered negro race [and] to ask Africa to trim her land and await the time when the Son of Man shall come on His chariot of fire to redeem his people'.[40] For Buthelezi and Wallace's Xhosa-speaking audiences, the conflation of the political and the religious was reinforced by the translating of the English words 'freedom' and 'redemption' into a single word – *inkululeko* – in the Xhosa Bible.[41]

In the same way that Christianity transcended national boundaries, Garveyism imagined a trans-national community embracing all black people. Thaele spoke on behalf of all Southern African Garveyites when he declared:

> Africans here at home should seek co-operation with the Africans abroad. The Universal Negro Improvement Association and African Communities League is the biggest thing today in Negro modern organizations. Its programme must be scrutinised, imbibed and assimilated by us . . . [Garvey's] *The Negro World* . . . must be a Bible to us in order to realise and bring to immediate fruition the inevitable practicability of the African Empire.[42]

Thaele's tribute to Garvey was reinforced by invocations of other anticolonial leaders like Gandhi and Da Valera, as he argued that his Southern African comrades should 'foster that spirit of independence and the uplifting of our brothers and sisters, and as the Brown man is working out his own destiny in Japan, the Yellow man in China, so must the Black man work out his destiny free and untrammelled in Africa'.[43] Thaele's exhortation was met by the rapid spread through Southern Africa of Garveyite organisations, notably in the Transkei, Southern Rhodesia and South-West Africa. As the ICU established branches in South-West Africa in 1920, in Southern Rhodesia in 1927 and in Northern Rhodesia in 1931, it established close working relationships with these Garveyite organisations outside South Africa, frequently sharing the same platforms.[44] In its internationalism, the Garveyite thread in the ICU ideological fabric therefore exceeded the liberal-nationalist dream of freedom. Stretching from Africa to the Americas, and in solidarity with anti-colonial struggles in India and Ireland, Garvey's variety of freedom could never be corralled within national boundaries.

Fundamental to the South African Garveyites' campaign against settler racism was the assumption that while white domination might initially have been achieved by military conquest, its ongoing hegemony was secured by imprisoning the minds of Africans in the chains of white supremacist myths. The elevation of European history and culture at the expense of African achievements was central to the process, as an anonymous poem published in *The Black Man* made clear: 'You'd think [the white men] had built the Pyramids/ Because with guns they fight./ They are the sun, and more than that,/ The black man's only night.'[45] The first step towards challenging such cultural imperialism and initiating the journey to freedom was to attain psychological liberation; racist-colonial lies of African inferiority must be reversed, and the right of all Africans to full independence proclaimed. Thaele set out his version of the strategy for psychological liberation thus:

> The salvation of the African race lies in its uncompromising organisations – organisations that will uncompromisingly *undo* the spurious teaching of the whiteman of fifty years! We must point out, it is our belief, the destructive teaching and propaganda of these fellows from Europe to the young of the race ... The laws of psychology are laws that have more or less to do with the human mind. It is from this point of view that we should organise the young Africans – from a psychological point of view. The serpentine cunningness and subtlety of the whiteman, his method of exploitation, his teaching of the bible – which amounts to nothing more than *do as I tell you, but don't do as I do* must be analysed, exposed and opposed.[46]

The mental enslavement of Africans, however, is not due exclusively to the 'cunningness and subtlety of the whiteman'; he has been aided by the indispensable contributions of African sell-outs, described by Thaele as '"the notorious good boys", the singers at the shrine of white autocracy, the "yes-sir-hat-in-hand-type-of-me-too-Boss-Native"'.[47] But Thaele was confident that the lies of 'the whiteman' and his compliant 'good boys' would be exposed and defeated, and that the '300 years the African race has meandered in the prairies of Caucasian subtle hypocrisy'[48] were soon to end.

The South African Garveyites' ideological struggle to liberate the minds of

Africans was rejoined in *The Workers' Herald*. One strategy was the republishing of Pan-Africanist poems like the 1920 poem by Kadalie, which declared, 'Oh Africa! Greater Continent,/ yet exploited/ For Goodness' Sake Arise!'.[49] Another strategy was to publish advertisements for Garvey's many publications. One full-page advertisement for Garvey's *Africa for the Africans* described it as 'a book that will set you thinking right. A second *Uncle Tom's Cabin* with the appeal of Bunyan's *Pilgrim's Progress* . . . Like John Bunyan in prison, [Garvey] sends a message to the World that Time shall not efface!'[50] The precarious financial state of the *Herald*, however, compelled its editors to sell advertising space for products at odds with Garvey's message of black pride and self-reliance, notably hair-straightening and skin-lightening products. In the same issue as the advertisement for *Africa for the Africans* was an advertisement for Percine Hair Straightener:

> Percine Hair Straightener and Beautifier as sold in America. Has it ever occurred to you? In these up-to-date times the vital necessity of a commanding and dignified appearance. Do you want to improve your position? Every man and woman has this desire, but perhaps there is a slight suspicion of colour, accentuated by frizzy hair, and you are barred. Percine removes that suspicion, and opens up avenues in the employments field at wages that were previously unthought of. Percine straightens the most obstinate frizzy hair, and has become a daily toilet preparation for those with advanced ideas who desire a commanding and distinguished appearance.[51]

Whether the *Herald*'s readers spent their wages on *Africa for Africans* or Percine Hair Straightener is hard to ascertain. But the two advertisements reveal at the very least the contradictory escape routes out of poverty South African workers had to negotiate.

Another key component of Thaele's understanding of freedom was his embrace of free market capitalism. Captivated by the achievements of the United States, Thaele used the pages of *The Workers' Herald* and *The African World* to praise American freedom and decry Communist servitude. On one occasion, he declared:

> [We do not believe in the destruction of] the government of the United States; we believe that white and black labour can secure justice and fair play in our industrial system, and it has gained much in the last half century by peaceful agitation and legislation; nor do we believe it any more necessary to substitute the Soviet or any system of government for that of the United States, because we believe it the best system ever devised through which men can work out themselves their social, civil and economic values, or can be devised. The people are the rulers in this country. They govern themselves. They make and enforce their own laws. There is no appeal from themselves except to themselves.[52]

What was particularly attractive about the United States – 'the best system ever devised' – was its dynamic capitalist economy. Garvey had argued that 'capitalism is necessary to the progress of the world, and those who unreasonably and wantonly oppose or fight against it are the enemies of human advancement', and further, had asked, 'Why should not Africa give the world its black Rockefeller, Rothschild and Henry Ford?'[53] Garvey's conviction that US capitalism provided sufficient space for black-owned commercial enterprises to emerge and thrive in parallel with white-owned businesses was shared by Thaele, who exhorted black South Africans to copy the economic model developed by Garvey and the UNIA:

> Our brothers in America have shewn us how it can be done and by following their example in opening up industry, teaching, and commercial businesses of every description under *our own control*, so can we ... Is it not looking too far into the future to expect to see large businesses owned by blacks? But why not if these things have been done in America, surely we can do the same in the Homeland – Africa.[54]

Thaele's determination to constitute a separate and independent black economy led him – as it had with Garvey – to seek ways of accommodating the policies of white segregationists.[55] Thaele's endorsement of Hertzog's 1924 pro-segregation election campaign represents a Southern African parallel to Garvey's negotiations with the Ku Klux Klan in the United States in 1922.[56]

The corollary of Ncwana and Thaele's enthusiasm for the US variety of freedom was their conviction that Communism was the very antithesis of freedom. Ncwana claimed that 'the doctrines of Bolshevism do not in the least attract the attention of the true aboriginal [and further] we want no communistic government as taught by the Bolshevist propagandists'.[57] Thaele looked to North American Garveyites for ammunition in his fight against Communists in South Africa, quoting with approval the labour leader William Green's warning that 'Communism in America is comparable to the boll-weevil in the cotton fields. Both are importations and both are equally injurious ... Negro members of trade unions are being led into a trap [by the Communists] that'll eventually be their undoing.'[58] Convinced that 'we do not believe in the Soviet theory of government nor in the destruction of the industrial system',[59] Thaele translated his anti-Communism into concerted efforts to expunge all Bolshevik influence from first the ICU and then the ANC.

The CPSA retaliated with interest.[60] The June 1930 issue of *Umsebenzi* declared that 'many [ANC] members were at a loss to understand [Thaele's] dislike of non-European Communists, like Comrade [John] Gomas', and in order to clinch its argument that Thaele's anti-Communism effectively served the interests of Pirow and the white regime by coining one of its most unpronounceable neologisms – 'Thaelopirowism'.[61] For the CPSA, Thaele's anti-Communism therefore located him not on the side of those fighting for freedom, but rather in the service of those enforcing oppression. In relation to liberal nationalism, Thaele (and by extension South African Garveyism) therefore occupied a contradictory position: on the one hand, his internationalism exceeded nation-bound definitions of political freedom; on the other, his enthusiasm for capitalism failed even to contemplate alternative economic dispensations.

COMMUNISM: EMANCIPATION FROM THE BITTER GALLING CHAINS OF CAPITALISTIC OPPRESSION

The ICU and the Communist Party of South Africa (CPSA) initially viewed each other with suspicion.[62] The ambivalences of their relationship are captured in the 18 May 1923 issue of *The Workers' Herald*, which included one article attacking the Third International and another praising the workers' soviets in Russia. However, the fading influence of Garveysim in the ICU coincided with members of the CPSA and Young Communist League (YCL) assuming important roles within the union: by the end of 1925, Thomas Mbeki was the Transvaal secretary of the ICU, John Gomas Cape provincial secretary, James La Guma general secretary and Eddie Khaile financial secretary. *The Workers' Herald* reflected their influence, as its political and economic analyses increasingly adopted Marxist terminology:

> We must prevent the exploitation of our people on the mines and on the farms, and obtain increased wages from them. We shall not rest there. We will open the gates of the Houses of Legislation, now under the control of the white oligarchy, and from this step we shall claim equality of purpose with the white workers of the world to overthrow the capitalist system of Government and usher in a co-operative Commonwealth one, a system which is not foreign to the aboriginal of Africa.[63]

The Garveyite binary opposing the 'white oligarchy' to 'the aboriginal in Africa' is thus supplemented, but also superseded, by the Communist opposition between exploited (black and white) workers and 'the capitalist system of Government'. The ICU's sympathetic incorporation of Communist critique into the pages of *The Workers' Herald* was reciprocated in the CPSA's newspaper *The International*, which noted a couple of months later that 'Lenin insisted that an essential condition of revolution was that it stirred the masses, including the most backward sections of the population. That is what the ICU is doing.'[64]

Marxist language percolated not only the ICU's reportage and opinion pieces; it also began to appear in occasional poems published in *The Workers' Herald*. The best example is the three-stanza poem 'Awake! Africa!' by James La Guma (under the pseudonym JALAG), which appeared in June 1925. The opening stanza invokes the Garveyite image of 'Ethiopia', whose hand has been 'Blistered and scarred by toil,/ That others may gorge their fill of/ The Wealth,/ Wrested by you from your own/ Mother soil', and the second stanza switches to the Marxist *telos* that anticipates workers struggling towards '[t]he day of emancipation,/ From the bitter galling chains,/ Of capitalistic oppression/ That sucks the life blood from your veins'.[65] The racial oppression emphasised by Garveyites (stanza one) and economic exploitation emphasised by Communists (stanza two) are transcended in the final stanza, as workers are summoned to 'Come rally to the banner,/ Determined to be free,/ That the blessings of a fuller life/ May be your gifts to posterity'.[66]

The synchrony between Garveyism and Communism imagined in La Guma's poem was short-lived, however, as the CPSA's period of direct influence on the

ICU ended when dual membership of the two organisations was prohibited by the ICU executive in December 1926, and all CPSA members consequently expelled. The fractious exit of Communists from the ICU did not, however, result in the disappearance of Marxist-inflected critique in the pages of *The Workers' Herald*. For example, an article in May 1928 explained the wording of the revised ICU constitution with reference to a quotation from Marx insisting upon the interconnectedness of the economic and the political:

> The new constitution . . . establishes the I. C. U. as a trade union, albeit one of the native workers whose rights of organisation are only now earning recognition. In these circumstances it has become necessary for the organisation to have a clearly defined economic programme, corresponding to the interests of the organisation at large. At the same time it must be clearly understood that we have no intention of copying the stupid and futile 'non-political' attitude of our white contemporaries. As Karl Marx said, every economic question is, in the last analysis, a political question also, and we must recognise that in neglecting to concern ourselves with current politics, in leaving the political machines to the unchallenged control of our class enemies, we are rendering a disservice to those tens of thousands of our members who are groaning under oppressive laws and are looking to the I. C. U. for a lead. [Lists the tactics to be pursued by the ICU.] Only in this way can the organisation grow and become an effective agency for liberating the African workers from the thraldom of slavery.[67]

Registering that as a trade union, the ICU's principal activities must be of an economic nature, the constitution nonetheless notes the dangers for trade unions of ignoring politics, and proposes – *contra* the approach pursued by the white unions – to challenge the political strategies used by the 'our class enemies' in order to advance the cause of its members. By thus waging both an economic and a political struggle, the ICU hopes to lead African workers to freedom.

Written long after the event, the final chapter of Kadalie's autobiography provides his stock-taking of the influence on the ICU of both Garveyism and Communism:

> When the Marcus Garvey movement was at its height, these Negroes in South Africa tried their best to use the ICU as an auxiliary of the Universal Negro Improvement Association, but, just as was the case with the Communist Party of South Africa, I became the stumbling block against their machinations, since I abhor serving two masters at the same time in my political make-up . . . I believed, as I believe now, that the salvation of the Africans in this country will be brought about by their own sweat and labour.[68]

For Kadalie, his primary allegiance to the African workers of Southern Africa was threatened by these two northern hemisphere ideologies that had substantially shaped the first seven years of the ICU. The final sentence implies that both Garveyism and Communism undermine the faith of African workers in their own agency, as the two ideologies obfuscate the fundamental principle that only through 'their own sweat and labour' can African workers win their freedom.

LITERATURE (1): I AM THE CAPTAIN OF MY FATE

It was not only the Bible, the lectures of Garvey and Communist doctrine that the ICU leaders drew upon to justify their politics; literary works too were recruited to articulate their dreams of freedom. One frequent strategy was to rewrite northern hemisphere poems to fit the South African political landscape. An early example was Kadalie's adaptation of John McCrae's First World War poem 'In Flanders Fields'. Writing in the socialist African American magazine *The Messenger*, Kadalie used the famous elegy to describe the killing of twenty workers by the South African police in Port Elizabeth on 23 October 1920. Instead of addressing the reader in the voice of the First World War's dead soldiers as per McCrae's poem, Kadalie's adaptation assumes the voice of Port Elizabeth's murdered black workers: '"We are the dead, short days ago/ We lived, felt dawn, saw sunset glow,/ Loved and were loved, and now we lie,/ In the trenched graveyard" [not "In Flanders fields"]'.[69] By substituting white British soldiers in the First World War trenches with black South African workers in 1920, Kadalie insists upon the equivalence of white and black deaths, and proclaims the humanity of the black victims of police violence.

A comparable but more private act of appropriation was Kadalie's interpretation of Swinburne's poetry. Edward Roux recalls his first meeting with Kadalie early in 1925, when Kadalie took Roux's copy of Swinburne's *Songs before Sunrise* (1871),[70] and read aloud a couple of stanzas of the poem 'Messidor'. For Roux, the lines of the poem – 'The dumb, dread people that sat,/ All night without screen for the day,/ They shall not give their harvest away,/ They shall eat of its fruit and wax fat'[71] – resonated for both men: exploited Italian peasants and black South African farmworkers alike should enjoy the fruit of their labours. Roux concludes, 'Kadalie, the tough politician, the leader, the orator who swayed the multitude, was essentially a poet ... As he read Swinburne that night he glowed and was kindled.'[72] Roux's projection of Kadalie-as-poet might have had something to do with Roux's own great enthusiasm for Swinburne,[73] but it is at least plausible that for Kadalie, poems evoking the sufferings of Italian peasants – like poems about the deaths of English soldiers in the trenches – could be adapted to express the sufferings and deaths of black South African workers. By such appropriations, Kadalie used the poems to enhance his critique of white political and economic power in South Africa.

In addition to McCrae and Swinburne, Kadalie cited two further literary works as important influences on his political career: William Ernest Henley's poem 'Invictus' (1888), and Nicholls's *Bayete!*. As in his rereadings of the Bible, so too in his interpretations of these two literary works, Kadalie disrupts coloniser-settler readings. Henley's short poem was written in 1875, but only appeared (without a title) in his first volume *Book of Verses* (1888). Subsequently anthologised and given the title 'Invictus' in Arthur Quiller-Couch's *The Oxford Book of English Verse, 1250–1900* (1901), the poem has had a prolific afterlife, not least in South Africa, where it acquired a fresh readership when it was revealed to be Mandela's favourite poem.[74] Both Kadalie and Mandela were mission-educated, and it is likely that they first encountered the poem at school, where the prevailing pedagogy would have demanded they memorise its lines for recitation. In four stanzas, the lyric 'I' of the poem simultaneously evokes formidable obstacles and dangers, and declares a determination to struggle against them. The final stanza encapsulates the message: 'It matters not how strait the gate,/ How charged with punishments the scroll,/ I am the master of my fate:/ I am the captain of my soul.'[75]

There are three records of Kadalie quoting the poem. In a report in *The Workers' Herald*, Kadalie uses military analogies to describe how much the government ban on his freedom of movement damaged the ICU: 'I sent out each month words of encouragement to our soldiers on the battle front which was on the retreat. With all our inspiring writings, the results were not promising: the soldiery desired to see someone from the War Office who could verbally arouse them.'[76] On the brink of despair, Kadalie remembers the words of 'Invictus', quotes three of the four stanzas (he leaves out stanza three), and returns revitalised to the struggle: 'I had now received a new baptism and was more determined to save the Organisation from collapse.'[77] Kadalie's mention of 'baptism' combines the religious and literary: like the Bible, literary works can strengthen the black workers' resolve in the daunting battle against racial capitalism.

The blurring of the line between the religious and the secular-literary is also evident on a second occasion Kadalie quoted 'Invictus'. At a meeting of the Independent ICU at the East Bank Location, East London, attended by 4,000 people on 24 January 1930, Detective Sergeant S. D. Mandy, the police informer transcribing Kadalie's speech, recorded his pleas to the crowd to answer the call to strike:

> If you start picketing the police will start shooting. Are you prepared? Again a few shouted out yes. Are you prepared to die? A few shouted yes. If you are prepared to die sing Onward Christian Soldiers. On Monday we must aim my people to stop the whole town, there must not be a single man or woman go to work. If you agree, we are going to stop the cowards from going to work. I want you now to make a solemn resolution. He then quoted a biblical expression saying I am the master of my soul, I am the captain of my fate.[78]

Detective Sergeant Mandy's failure to recognise the Henley poem, or to transcribe its lines accurately, are honest mistakes; the final couplet does indeed have biblical echoes, and it also complements Kadalie's appeal to sing 'Onward Christian Soldiers'. In this charged context, the poem itself assumes a more insurrectionary meaning. No longer functioning as consolation and encouragement amidst times of defeat, 'Invictus' becomes the clinching element in Kadalie's defiant summons to collective action.

The associations of 'Invictus' with collective struggle in Kadalie's 1930 speech are absent, however, a decade later in his quoting of the opening stanza of the poem towards the end of his autobiography. Immediately preceding the quotation from 'Invictus', he describes buying a house in 1936 at No. 8 Hope Street in East London, where 'I now live happily with my family', as he looks back with a sense of relief at having endured the trials of his earlier life: 'Who could have imagined that I could have survived all the storms which beset me and my family in the early 1930s?'[79] Kadalie's ambitions have changed, from dreaming in the 1920s of a mass workers' movement that could liberate the sub-continent to taking solace in the 1940s in his capacity to provide a materially secure existence for himself and his family. As in 1927 and in 1930, so again in the 1940s, 'Invictus' provides a vocabulary for summing up his thoughts and feelings. In this final case, Kadalie uses Henley's words – '"I thank whatever Gods may be/ For my unconquerable soul"'[80] – to explain that the combination of fate and his own agency had seen him through two turbulent decades of economic and political conflict, but that he was now ready to withdraw from the public struggle for freedom.

Although Kadalie's use of 'Invictus' changed in different contexts, his various interpretations do not deviate too far from the poem's central message. His reading of Nicholls's novel *Bayete!*, however, diametrically opposed the author's declared intention to warn complacent white readers about the imminent danger of a revolutionary black uprising. Quite how radically the meaning of the novel can change when consumed by readers outside its immediate target audience is demonstrated by Kadalie's interpretation of *Bayete!*. Responding in 1928 to pressure for regional autonomy from the Natal branch of the ICU, Kadalie invoked *Bayete!* as a lesson in the need for African unity:

> But what is the real truth of talking about the federation of the I.C.U.? The real motive underlying this is to divide African Workers into tribal groups. The interests of the Natives are quite identical throughout South Africa. No achievements can be made in Natal without the support of other Provinces and vice versa. All of us as a race are labouring under economic and political oppression. By Mass Organisation, we have achieved many things. Perhaps the leaders of the Federal Movement have not read the book 'Bayete' written by the honourable member for Zululand, Mr Nicholls. In that book, Mr Nicholls puts it clearly how the natives of South Africa supported by the Coloured people would gain their economic and political freedom by Mass Industrial Organisation. I commend this book to the leaders of that Movement.[81]

Kadalie does not interpret Nelson's death and the defeat of the rebellion in the closing chapters of *Bayete!* as any kind of deterrent to building the ICU and struggling for 'economic and political freedom'; rather he ignores the ending, and instead reads the novel as an appeal to overcome tribal differences and build worker unity in order to fight white domination. Kadalie's interpretation thus enacts Nicholls's worst fears. The rhetorical context of Kadalie's reading is also significant: in wrestling with the problem of threatened defections from the ICU, the antidote he reaches for is a literary work – *Bayete!*. Were more black trade unionists to read the novel, they too would appreciate its lesson of black unity, and act accordingly.

A second interpretation of Kadalie's reading of *Bayete!* is provided by William Ballinger (1892–1974). Brought out to South Africa in 1927 by English liberals as an adviser to the ICU, Ballinger's initially cordial relationship with Kadalie deteriorated swiftly into one of enmity, and within eighteen months, he engineered Kadalie's expulsion from the ICU. In an unpublished essay on 'Winifred Holtby and Africa' written in 1937, Ballinger recalled the impact of *Bayete!* on Kadalie:

> Kadalie was also inspired to think that he was the black man from the North whom it was ordained should save the black people from the South from their harsh white oppressors. The inspiration was strengthened at a later date by his reading of a somewhat fifth-rate novel entitled 'Bayete' written by Heaton Nicholls, M. P. for a Durban constituency, and now one of the three members of the Native Affairs Commission, a body that advises the government on all matters connected with Native affairs. The novel tells the story of how Nelson a black man from the North comes to the South, marries a white woman and eventually releases the black race of the South from the bondage of their white oppressors. It is interesting to note that in trying to live up to Heaton Nicholls' 'Nelson' Kadalie got as near as conditions would allow to marrying a white woman by actually marrying a Cape Coloured woman. The novel has certainly greatly influenced Kadalie's whole life.[82]

Like Kadalie, Ballinger reveals a partial and imperfect knowledge of the novel's plot. First, Nelson does not marry a white woman, although Ballinger's perception that he does so might reveal his own anxieties about miscegenation, and secondly, (to repeat) Nelson does not 'release the black race of the South from bondage', but rather dies violently in attempting to do so. Whereas Kadalie himself reads the novel as a powerful imprimatur to black readers to strive for unity in their struggle against exploitation, Ballinger sees the novel's influence as fuelling both Kadalie's political hubris and his sexual desire for white women. For Kadalie, *Bayete!* inspires the fight for freedom, but for Ballinger, the novel, with its model of politics centred on a charismatic leader and its racially permissive sexual morality, was much more likely to derail the journey to liberation.

LITERATURE (2): KEEP ON WITH YOUR WEARY BATTLE

Kadalie's most substantial comrade and rival within the ICU, A. W. G. Champion, also used poems (both his own and those of others) to fortify his critique of the many adversaries he faced in the world of trade union politics. In three pamphlets in Zulu and English published at the end of the 1920s,[83] Champion adopted the same rhetorical structure, setting out in detail his economic and political arguments, spliced through with biblical allusions, and concluding with a short poem distilling his position. In *The Truth About the I. C. U.* (1927), Champion describes the aims of the ICU as akin to those of Christianity: the preamble of the ICU's constitution 'is an attempt to put into modern language the teachings of Christ, namely, "Love thy neighbour as thyself." '[84] The ICU's goal is to help its members 'advance like any other citizen(s) under the British flag', and accordingly, the ICU regards 'the Colour

Bar Act as a piece of slavery and a disgrace to any British Statute Book'.[85] The remedy sought by the ICU is 'to give the Native full freedom and liberty to develop every faculty and quality with which Nature has endowed him'.[86] Elaborating the impact of racist laws on workers' livelihoods, Champion commits the ICU to unite workers into 'a broad, non-racial African Trade Union Organisation ... fighting for ... economic emancipation, justice and industrial peace'.[87] To clinch his arguments, Champion first invokes (in prose) the example of Christ, and then in the closing eight-line stanza of his poem, he appeals to the collective fortitude of workers. According to Champion, 'Christ was born with a glory in His bosom which transfigured the employer and employed [and] as he died to make men Holy let us die to make men free.'[88] The transition from prose to poetry presages a shift in focus from Christ to the workers, as labouring men and women 'crushed by the power of gold' are implored to 'Keep on with your weary battle/ Against triumphant might./ No question is ever settled/ Until it is settled right.'[89]

In *Mehlomadala: My Experiences in the I. C. U.* (1929), Champion recounts his experience of the internecine rivalries within the ICU, attacking erstwhile allies Kadalie and Ballinger. The former is accused of losing all judgement during his trip to Europe: '[H]e came back from overseas with a sudden revolutionised mind. He wanted a European private secretary, white girls as shorthand typists,'[90] and Ballinger is charged (incorrectly) with taking money from 'Moscow which is looking for new fields for the furtherance of Soviet government', and more broadly, for exceeding his brief – he was brought in 'not to control the affairs of the I. C. U. but merely to advise us'.[91] Champion's acute sense of grievance is expressed in his two poems on the final pages of the pamphlet. In the first, his anger is directed at 'the rulers of this Land,/ Who make laws to suit their own/ Purposes in life'.[92] But in the second, longer poem, entitled 'Believe It Or Not', his target switches to treacherous comrades in the ICU. The first two stanzas liken the sufferings of Africans to those of the Israelites in the Old Testament, but in the third, the biblical parallels are adapted to cast Champion's adversaries in the ICU (like Kadalie) as Eve tempted by the serpent: 'The snake that tempted Eve of old,/ Whispered low to Champion's pals;/ "Call him a thief and down he sinks,/ While up ye go."'[93] Invective follows, as Champion dismisses his gullible ex-comrades as 'fools' and 'hypocrites'.[94]

Champion's third pamphlet, *Blood and Tears* (1930), is more measured, as he sets out the history of the Durban beer hall riots, criticising the government for trying to 'prevent him from addressing his people and publishing resolutions passed by the Natives [in pursuit of] full civic rights'.[95] For Champion, the state's attempts to curtail his freedom of speech threaten to 'precipitate a racial struggle the possibilities of which are too dreadful to contemplate especially in their impact on European civilisation in this country'.[96] The poem Champion quotes in support of his argument – John Greenleaf Whittier's abolitionist plea 'Stanzas for the Times' (1835) – is particularly apposite, as it too was written in defence of freedom of speech, specifically the freedom of abolitionists to criticise Boston's pro-slavery elite. The fifth stanza of Whittier's poem is the one quoted by Champion, and comprises a series of rhetorical questions: '"Shall tongues be mute, when deeds are wrought/ Which well might shame extremest hell?/ Shall freemen lock the indignant thought?/ Shall

Pity's bosom cease to swell?/ Shall Honor bleed? – shall Truth succumb?/ Shall pen, and press, and soul be dumb?."[97] Like the North American abolitionists praised in Whittier's poem, the ICU leaders refused to 'lock the indignant thought', and instead argued and wrote in opposition to the racist restrictions inhibiting the freedoms of black workers in 1920s South Africa. The pamphlet closes with Champion's own poem, 'Blood and Tears'. Whereas 'Stanzas for the Times' encourages a secular comparison between North American plantation slaves and black South African workers, Champion's poem reverts to biblical tropes. Addressed to 'Jehovah, who is mighty', the final two stanzas conclude with the lines: 'Says the I. C. U. – feed thy people/ With food and give them health./ All offenders will disappear like the mist/ Before the sun./ Speak with your Mighty Spirit/ To all the Ministers of Christian Religion/ And let them see your Everlasting Truth.'[98] Material sustenance for its members is the ICU's ambition, and Jehovah is entreated to help in achieving it.

LITERATURE (3): BE PATIENT! WAIT!

Literature was not only recruited by ICU intellectuals to pursue the class struggle; literary works were also disseminated via ICU publications in order to contain revolutionary impulses. *The Workers' Herald* regularly published poems, but unlike Kadalie's promotion of *Bayete!* because he believed it taught Africans how to 'gain their economic and political freedom by Mass Industrial Organisation', and Champion's exhortation to workers to battle against 'triumphant Might . . . Until [the battle] is settled right', many of these poems expressed messages of reconciliation, acceptance and deference. The poems in *The Workers' Herald* were chosen by Ethelreda Lewis (1875–1946), South African novelist, proponent of segregation and unwavering opponent of Communism.[99] Lewis enjoyed the confidence of Kadalie, and oversaw the literary contributions to *The Workers' Herald* via her regular column 'The Book Shelf'. Her work included publishing (or not) occasional original poems submitted to the paper. For example, she approved the inclusion of a couple of short poems by James La Guma (like 'Awake! Africa!'), but a third of his poems were rejected because although 'it was something better than doggerel . . . it also dwelt on propaganda subjects, [and] it cannot be included in this column or accepted for competition. This is a literary not a political Book shelf'.[100]

Lewis's own favourite poet was William Blake. A couplet from Blake – 'The wild deer, wandering here and there,/ Keeps the human heart from care' – provided the title and epigraph of her novel *Wild Deer* (1933). Blake's 'The Little Black Boy' from *The Songs of Innocence* (1789) was retitled 'Pathos' by Lewis, and appeared on the front page of *The Workers' Herald* of 15 October 1927. The title 'Pathos' directs attention away from the voice of 'the little black boy' seeking equality before God with the 'little English boy' in the final two stanzas, and the poem's deceptive complexity is inflected in Lewis's edited version towards a singular evocation of noble suffering.[101]

Lewis also liked black US poetry and culture, publicising it in the pages of *The Workers' Herald*. But in the same spirit as her suppression of La Guma's political verse and her conservative appropriation of Blake, Lewis's selections for *The Workers' Herald* eschewed the many expressions of black America's culture of resistance in favour of conciliatory alternatives. For example, Lewis summarised faithfully an article 'Singing soldiers' from *Scribner's Magazine* on the spirituals sung by black American soldiers in the trenches of the First World War. According to the article (endorsed by Lewis), the songs born of enduring plantation slavery in North America travelled successfully to the killing fields of Europe, and consoled black and white Allied soldiers alike. As a consequence, 'Negro music had some part in the success gained by American arms in the past war.'[102] A month later, Lewis published an extract from 'Dialogue' by the Harlem Renaissance poet, Countee Cullen (1903–1946), describing it as a 'conversation between the brave Soul and cowardly Body'.[103] In Cullen's poem, Soul claims that, 'There is no stronger thing than song,' but Body disagrees – 'Song is not drink, song is not meat.' Lewis's extract gives Soul the last word, thus tilting the dialogue in favour of 'the brave Soul'. But Cullen's own final stanza is in the voice of Body, who asks, 'But will Song buy a wooden box/ The length of me from toe to crown,/ To keep me safe from carrion flocks, / When singing's down and lyre laid down?'[104] The dialectical tension in Cullen's original, as well as the claims of material survival, are thus sacrificed in Lewis's elevation of Soul's love of 'Song'.

Lewis returns to the function of 'song' in the next issue, as she pairs extracts from Paul Laurence Dunbar's famous 'I Know Why the Caged Bird Sings' (1899) and Ethyl Lewis's 'The Optimist' (1920). While the former registers that the bird's song 'is not a carol of joy or glee', but rather 'a plea that upward to Heaven he flings', Lewis's poem addresses America's black oppressed and counsels, 'be patient awhile,/ And carry your load with a nod and a smile', before repeating in conclusion, 'Be patient! Wait! See what may yet befall.'[105] The need for black South Africans to exercise such patience when confronted with fresh suffering is repeated in the edition of *The Workers' Herald* immediately following a major railway accident at Mapleton in which twenty-nine were killed. Lewis dedicates her column to 'our brothers who were killed in the Mapleton disaster', and as solace for her readers, reproduces 'verses and songs by American negroes in times of loss and grief'; each of the lyrics, Lewis continues, 'carries that note of hope in despair which is going to raise the black man to his feet among nations'.[106] Extracts from 'Somebody's Buried in the Graveyard', 'Swing Low, Sweet Chariot', 'Burial at Night', and 'Watching by the Dead' are then reproduced.

Lewis's enthusiasm for black American culture extended to the singer, Paul Robeson (1898–1976), and from 1929 to 1935 she tried with the help of other ICU sympathisers like Winifred Holtby, Mabel Palmer (1876–1958) and William and Margaret Ballinger (1894–1980) to bring Robeson out to South Africa. These efforts came to nought, but in her novel *Wild Deer*, Lewis compensated by imagining a Robeson-figure (the protagonist De la Harpe) visiting South Africa and being converted to her segregationist 'solution' to the country's racial problems. The character of Colenbrander (based on Ballinger, although deviating from his political beliefs) expresses Lewis's views, as he persuades De la Harpe that Africa's only hope of freedom lies with the few autonomous African communities continuing to evade

European industry and culture. An honorary chief of the fictional 'Maca' tribe, Colenbrander exhorts De la Harpe to listen to their singing, which has '"a quality in it you don't hear north of the Zambesi. A vigour and freedom"'.[107] Having fled in order to escape slave traders, the Maca had settled in the south east (presumably in the region of Mozambique), and according to Colenbrander, '"they've become the finest, care-free race in Africa . . . They are negroes . . . who made a great bid for freedom – *and found it!*"'.[108] Attributing the Macas's state of freedom to their proximity to Nature, and lauding the wisdom of Thoreau and Blake, Colenbrander concludes, '"There's only one way to do it and that is to save the native from contact with the civilised."'[109]

LITERATURE (4): EPHEMERAL BUT REMUNERATIVE FICTION

Winifred Holtby endorsed many of Lewis's commitments: they both supported the ICU in its fight on behalf of South Africa's black workers, and they both wrote novels, sharing a faith in the power of literature.[110] But they also differed in important respects, as Fanny Klenerman's recollections of the two women highlight. Klenerman met the two of them while teaching at the ICU night school, and recalled Lewis to be 'an extremely narrow, conservative woman; she was very religious, and wanted Christianity in the night school . . . She was bourgeois and not able to understand working people'; Holtby, by contrast, 'had such a good, open heart . . . I remember that she was extremely interested in things, the conditions of people, the kinds of lives'.[111] Their different personal qualities aside, Holtby never shared Lewis's uncompromising anti-Communism, and she also expressed doubts about the segregationist solutions Lewis promoted for South Africa.

In both her fiction and her journalism, Holtby questioned the limits of British definitions of freedom. In *Mandoa, Mandoa* (1933), Holtby's novel set in a fictional East African nation, the different varieties of British freedom are satirised. To the Tory MP Maurice Durrant, the British constitution is 'a sign of political genius', parliament is 'holy ground', and the frescoes in Westminster represent 'decisive incidents in a story of freedom slowly broadening down from precedent to precedent'.[112] To the ineffectual radical Arthur Rollett, Liberty must be defended, and he 'spent his time tracking down its enemies. Any assault against free thought, free speech, free voting, free motherhood, free trade or free love stirred him to fiery protest'.[113] Neither Durrant nor Rollett's versions of freedom prove to have any purchase in Africa, but neither does the nostalgia for pre-colonial Africa promoted in Lewis's *Wild Deer*. The sympathetic Mandoan leader Talal explains as much to his English guests: 'To be primitive means to sleep in dirty huts, to ride on donkeys, to do the same things day after day . . . Would you like to have no books, no photographs, no motor cars? If these were such evils, why did your nations make them? Why did you stop being a primitive people if it was so nice?'[114] The closest the novel comes to an affirmative commitment is when the protagonist Jean Stanbury copies out her favourite quotation from Olive Schreiner, a passage declaring that *'man as man is a great and important thing, that the right to himself and his existence is the incontestable property of all men*' (italics in original).¹¹⁵ But even embracing Schreiner's humanist faith fails to console Jean, as the novel closes with her brooding on the principled Rollett's lonely death in Africa, and her friend Bill Durrant contemplating Mandoa's unpromising future: 'He saw it as a place of poverty and squalor, without arts, or learning, or dignity, or discipline, or science, a place ruled by a corrupt and irresponsible aristocracy, a place where human effort was subject to a million accidents of nature, of chance, of man's unmerciful caprice.'¹¹⁶

In her journalism, Holtby pointed out repeatedly that black South Africans were excluded from the democratic freedoms enjoyed by white citizens, but she also went further, identifying how such patterns of exclusion had long been embedded in Western political thought and practice:

> The vision of freedom, of 'the greatest light which has yet dawned on our human horizon', has not yet gleamed upon South Africa. Why? Because of a very simple reason. Because, for General Smuts and his contemporaries, the human horizon does not yet extend to coloured races, as, for Fox and his eighteenth-century contemporaries, it did not extend to English women ... These abrupt failures of the imagination are among the most fruitful sources of injustice in the world. They are more common than deliberate sadism, more insidious than fear. Indeed, they breed fear ... The Jews to Nazi Germany, the Catholics to the Ku Klux Klan, Negroes to a southern states lynching party, women to eighteenth-century liberals – they are not human; they need not be accorded human privileges.¹¹⁷

Holtby's insight into such failures of empathy and imagination imply that the best that black South Africans can hope for is to be included in Holtby's Western-democratic 'vision of freedom'; they nonetheless stop short of allowing the possibility that South Africa's 'coloured races' might generate their own independent ideas of freedom.

Holtby also differed from Lewis in her views on the potential of both artists and writers to accelerate the journey of black South Africans to freedom. Once it became clear that Robeson was not coming to South Africa, Holtby confided in a letter to Margaret Ballinger:

> I wish you had not built so highly on Robeson so that you are not so disappointed. I, who spend so much of my time with musicians and artists, was surprised to find him willing to go so far as he does. I knew Polish pianists who would never reach out a hand to the Poles (not [Ignacy] Paderewski. He's almost the only musician who is a politician). I know Jews who care nothing for Zionism or refugees. Their work is their art. They make beauty. The world must take it or leave it. Robeson is not indifferent. He will do things for American Negroes and for coloured people in London. I don't really know why we should <u>expect</u> him to do things for African Negroes. My racial ancestors are Danes, I suppose, but I'm damned if I'd buy Danish bacon for that reason.¹¹⁸

Ultimately sceptical about recruiting artists and writers to the cause of African emancipation, Holtby tried to advance the cause of black workers by collecting books for the ICU's library. In a letter to the *New Statesman*, reprinted on the front page of *The Workers' Herald*, Holtby lists the kinds of books required for black South African readers, with utility prioritised above aesthetics: 'standard works on economics and sociology . . . good histories and books dealing with racial problems, simpler books for the beginners, and works of general literature'.[119] Although such works are of a different order from Lewis's selection of black American poetry, Holtby believed that they too would have the effect of moderating the influence of the revolutionary elements within the ICU. She observes that the unions display 'an admirable moderation and statesmanship in face of all appeals to raise animosity',[120] but concludes that such moderation should be consolidated by giving the workers access to a library with the right books.

Within a few years, Holtby's faith in the ameliorating effects of educative reading was superseded by a more pragmatic conception of how literature might serve black trade union politics. In a letter to the Ballingers written a year before her death, Holtby contemplates in playful and generous spirit the competing claims on her royalties of politics (African trade unionism) and friendship (the Ballingers). Disillusioned by the collapse of the ICU, she chooses the route of inner migration, and opts for the latter:

> Ten days ago I received from America an entirely unexpected cheque for 375 pounds. It is the result of continued sales of *Mandoa Mandoa!* Far beyond my expectations. 75 will go for taxation and American transfers and agent's fees. 100 I want to put by against emergencies. But the 200 is a completely unexpected gift from Heaven, as it were. I was going to send it to the Friends of Africa Fund . . . Then it struck me, why shouldn't you have it instead as a wedding present to buy a motor car? It would buy one, wouldn't it? Are they much dearer in S. Africa than here? Anyway, unless you would <u>prefer</u> me to hand it to the Fund, I very much want to write the cheque to you personally, as a token of my admiration and wishes to your adventure together. And whether you prefer to use it for car or furniture or something else, is your concern. I don't care a button.[121]

In a letter written at the same time to her confidant, Vera Brittain (1893–1970), Holtby concedes that writing popular fiction itself might be an elaborate detour, and that writing non-literary appeals directly on behalf of her political causes might be more effective. In the context of her South African commitments at least, Holtby resolved the tension between her identities as artist and social reformer in favour of the latter:

> I have written literally millions of words about Ballinger since 1927. Perhaps they are the only words I have ever written which will deserve immortality [but] better to be a willing scribe of one permanent movement for releasing the human spirit, than produce nothing but ephemeral if remunerative fiction.[122]

For her writing to serve an emancipatory function, Holtby sees two options: write popular literary fiction and give the royalties to trade union leaders to pursue the struggle for economic and political freedom; or write non-literary journalism/pamphlets/petitions/letters that support the trade unionists directly.

VERNACULAR FREEDOMS: FREEDOM AND BREAD AND BUTTER

Certain versions of the ICU dream of freedom amounted to the bare alleviation of white domination. For example, Kadalie, James La Guma and James Gumba concluded their statement to the government's Economic and Wage Commission in 1925 with the declaration, 'Non-European workers do not ask for equality in any way with the whites in all things social, but will insist at all times on the proper distribution of equal opportunities in all spheres of labour.'[123] Such incremental demands for freedom rooted in familiar white institutions were echoed in a speech by William Ballinger during his brief honeymoon with Kadalie and the ICU. According to Ballinger, white South Africa must learn that 'the native was not merely a wage slave but a man', and that ultimately '[t]here would come a time when natives would sit side by side with white people in Parliament and help in the forming of laws to govern all communities'.[124] Looking back many years later, ICU sympathiser Mmereki Molohlanyi recalls Kadalie promising no more than 'to influence the government to be more lenient on us, so that the whites mustn't be so free in their treatment of blacks'.[125]

However, such cautious and pragmatic expressions of the ICU's political aims alternated with more ambitious declarations, as Kadalie in particular encouraged workers to dream more boldly. In a speech in Bloemfontein at the beginning of 1925, for example, he told his audience, '"You must be free men and free women in the land of your fathers" (Loud cheers) [He told them] that vision they must ever keep before them and visualise it in their dreams.'[126] He claimed that the ICU had changed its members' horizons of expectation by enabling them to dream of hopeful alternatives to the tough world they inhabited. The optimistic futures 'visualised in their dreams' had at least four qualities that distinguished the ICU discourse of freedom from liberal-nationalist visions of freedom.

First, there are several speeches that appeal to the pre-colonial past and to African prophets, whose prophecies supersede all other religious/literary/historical authorities. Sijadu at Cambridge Location in East London in 1930 told his audience:

> I advise you all to join the I. C. U. Do not listen to the Ministers of churches who do not like the I. C. U. They only collect money from you and send it to England to make aeroplanes for you to be killed. Do not pray for King George, pray for this organisation, your time of freedom has come which was told by Ntsikana the prophet some time ago.[127]

A year later, Mqayi appealed to another prophet:

A Bible which says there is nothing which can stand before the white people is telling a falsehood. I must tell you that something serious is coming, but I won't say what it is. The late prophet Umlangeni prophesied about our Union, but no record was written about him ... Church natives are liars, where will they get by worshipping God? They are every day under oppression and are not like the Israelites, who did their worshipping after they were delivered from Egypt. This is now the last time in which the natives are hanging between Hell and freedom.[128]

Both Sijadu and Mqayi criticise Christianity, with the former attacking the Church's ministers for taking black South Africans' money and handing it over to their white oppressors, and Mqayi declaring the Bible's support for white domination to be lies, and the 'Church natives' who acquiesce in such beliefs to be liars. The Xhosa prophets Ntsikana and Umlangeni predict the coming of the ICU and the consequent freedom of black South Africans. Kadalie by contrast did not refer to pre-colonial African prophets by name, but on numerous occasions proclaimed the superiority of African societies before 'the white man ... came to this continent with Bible in his hand to Christianize the African native'.[129] For Kadalie, 'Whatever may have been our primitive way of government in those days gone by, we look to the past with pride in the knowledge that our forefathers lived a communal life and shared everything in common.'[130] Much more than writing back to imperial discourse, Sijadu, Mqayi and Kadalie reactivate memories of pre-colonial prophets and communities whose examples inspire resistance to contemporary suffering.

A second distinctive quality of ICU discourse was its foregrounding of the economic hardship suffered by its members. Overlapping with the Communist discourse of capitalism exploiting the proletariat, the ICU's critique of South Africa's rulers emphasised the primacy of the economic over the political. For example, the ICU Manifesto of 1926 argued:

[T]he I. C. U. is of the opinion that the Segregation policy of General Hertzog is designed to perpetuate a caste of white labour aristocracy which should defend the present system of exploitation and keep the African worker in perpetual slavery; besides this, the terrible injustice of political disenfranchisement sinks into insignificance.[131]

For the ICU, the significance of Hertzog's laws therefore lay less in their threat to (already much-diminished) political freedoms; rather it lay in their power to intensify economic exploitation. If the economic was to the fore in the ICU's language of critique, it was equally prominent in its visions of a happier future. Kadalie grasped that the ICU was a product of straitened economic conditions, and that its success lay in its promise to deliver black South Africans from poverty:

The ICU could never have flourished easily in this country if economic hardships of the non-Europeans had been satisfactorily redressed by the powers that be. Notwithstanding the high cost of living, there was no corresponding adjustment of the wages of the African workers. The feeling of frustration was soon evident. In the northern provinces passes were forcibly loaded on the African people. Nowhere was there a silver lining to show the masses the way to human freedom. In this hopeless frustration the advent of the ICU was like a beacon of light on the horizon. There was a great desire to find the way towards emancipation, and the advent of the ICU promised the only way.[132]

Diagnosing the economic conditions that produced support for the ICU – high living costs, low wages and pass laws restricting access to employment – the argument continues that by promising relief from such hardships and by showing 'the way to human freedom', 'the way to emancipation', the ICU functioned as a 'beacon of light'. In its constant emphasis on the economic, the ICU differed fundamentally from the ANC, as the Natal ICU supporter, Charles Khumalo noted: 'The ICU fought for freedom. Those of Congress also fought for freedom but didn't talk about money. The ICU was concerned with wages . . . [and helping the evicted] back onto the farms . . . and claimed that in freedom people would be liberated and not stopped for passes.'[133] Even historians broadly sympathetic to the ANC confirm Khumalo's judgement on the two organisations, and concede that at this stage the ANC prioritised campaigning for citizenship rights for the black elite; such tactics meant that 'the mid-1920s saw little apparent open ANC support for, or from, workers'.[134] Kadalie expressed the same sentiment in 1930, when he first asked rhetorically 'Why are the natives gathered here in all weathers?', and then answered, 'They want freedom and bread and butter, and . . . there is not going to be any law or Government to stop the people from asking for their freedom now that they have made up their minds.'[135]

A third distinguishing characteristic of how the term 'freedom' was deployed in ICU discourse was the yoking of 'freedom' and quotidian demands for specific changes in the treatment of black South Africans. There are many examples, but perhaps the most resonant one was the ICU's campaign for black South Africans to enjoy the freedom to walk on pavements. The formation of the ICU was triggered when Kadalie was pushed off a pavement in Darling Street, Cape Town by a white constable in December 1918,[136] and the subsequent campaign played a role in transforming the consciousness of ICU members. As the campaign gathered momentum, ICU member Rose Sibanyoni of Mhluzi Township in Middelburg recalled, 'They began to be free. They were given little red cards. So they began to be free. They began to be free to move on pavements, away from the streets of the cars. They were made to walk on pavements, walking side by side with the whites and rubbing shoulders with them.'[137] Crucially, such quotidian protests were linked to larger demands. Freedom of movement – not only to walk on pavements, but to enjoy unrestricted access to land – was identified as central to the ICU's concerns. Champion, for example, looked back to an earlier age, when '[p]eople were free and not waked up at night to be asked for permits . . . Places like Cato Manor, Lennoxtown, Newcastle, Kingsley were demolished when people were free and not troubled by anything'.[138] But by the 1920s, this (doubtful) golden age had passed, as the state's new racist legislation restricted the movement of black workers.

Kadalie spelt out the connections between these political restrictions, the economic rationale they served, and the need to mobilise against them in order to win freedom. Reporting on the 1925 ICU conference resolutions, he summarised, 'all passes, no matter in what shape or form, are nothing more or less than an institution of the present capitalistic system of government . . . to reduce the African worker to a state of abject servility so as to facilitate their utmost exploitation'.[139] A year later, he reinforced his opposition to the pass laws in characteristically personal terms, but again connected the campaign against them to the struggle for a more comprehensive freedom:

> If there was a grievance that warranted a revolution, it was the pass laws. These obsolete pass laws were anti-British, un-Christian and opposed to civilised government. The progress of the black man in South Africa depended on the overthrow of this bad law . . . I say that the pass laws interfere with a man's liberty, and that if any man interferes with Kadalie's liberty he will meet opposition, because I am not a slave. But for goodness sake, let us convince the white man and everybody else that we are not out for disruption and disturbance, but that we are out for freedom, and will exhaust all constitutional means to attain that end.[140]

The passage suggests at least two interpretations. One reading might emphasise how Kadalie's language of freedom is contained within the dominant discourse of Western liberal freedoms. In its appeal to the 'British', the 'Christian', the 'constitutional', Kadalie's words appear to parrot the hegemonic vocabulary of South Africa's rulers. But a second reading is possible, namely that Kadalie's words enact a rhetorical tactic identified by James C. Scott as a '[strategic appeal] to the hegemonic values'.[141] Scott describes as 'public transcripts . . . performances of deference, respect, reverence, admiration, esteem',[142] and Kadalie's words published here in *The Workers' Herald* could be read as an instance of a subversive 'public transcript'. Anterior to the public transcript lies a conception of freedom that welcomes the prospect of escalating protests against the pass laws to revolution.

Finally, the ICU's message of trade union fellowship imagined a community that broke down both racial and national barriers.[143] Within the imagined national community of South Africa, Kadalie attacked white workers because he argued that '[t]rade unionism can only succeed when it realizes that if one member of the family suffers, be it white, black or yellow, the whole family will suffer'.[144] For Kadalie, the 'family' of workers fighting against capitalism and its racist proxies transcended national boundaries. At a meeting 'of large proportions' in Johannesburg on 31 January 1926, he told his cheering audience, 'I am looking forward to the day when both black and white workers of South Africa – the proletariat – will stand united under one banner'; and, he continued, if Hertzog insisted on pursuing segregationist policies, 'the black man of this land is going to be supported by the niggers of America, the people of India, and all the coloured races of the East generally'.[145] In Figure 2.1 by the ICU cartoonist J. Scott and published in *The Workers' Herald* of 18 March 1927, two white South African workers are represented, one as an obstacle to trade union fellowship, and one as a comrade in an egalitarian community.

Figure 2.1 Cartoon by J. Scott, 'The African workers receive international recognition through the affiliation of the ICU to the International Federation of Trade Unions. The South African white worker is annoyed at the victory of the blacks', *The Workers' Herald*, 18 March 1927.

Beginning within the political boundaries of the South African state, the ICU vision of freedom expanded to embrace the ideal of international solidarity. In one of his articles in *The Messenger*, Kadalie sets out a *telos* for political and economic emancipation: start by improving the economic conditions of South African mine- and farm-workers; continue by asserting equal political rights for black South Africans within the nation state; and conclude the journey by defeating capitalism and ushering in an international commonwealth synchronous with communal African forms of government:

> We must prevent the exploitation of our people on the mines and on the farms, and obtain increased wages for the workers. We shall not rest there. We will

open the gates of the Houses of the Legislature, now under the control of white oligarchy, and from this step we shall claim equality of purpose with the white workers the world over – throw the capitalist system of government and usher in a co-operative commonwealth one, a system of government which is not foreign to the aboriginals of Africa.[146]

Kadalie expressed a similar hope in an article published in the British *Labour Monthly* of 1927, invoking a pre-colonial African brotherhood consistent with the trans-national workers' collective in the making: '[W]e are not going to follow the narrow path of nationalism. We shall be guided by the spirit that permeated old Africa, of accepting every man as his brother. We are utterly opposed to nationalism. Our goal is international Socialism.'[147] Such a utopian fellowship is depicted in a second cartoon by J. Scott in *The Workers' Herald* (Figure 2.2), in which racial and national antipathies are forgotten as workers of the world unite.

CONCLUSION

Helen Bradford concedes that the ideology of the ICU was so flexible 'that it was often a higgledy-piggledy jumble of "inherent" and "derived" ideas', but she nonetheless insists that 'it contained some valuable political insights, and certainly converted tens of thousands of rural Africans to visions of radically altered lives in a transfigured social order'.[148] The ICU-inspired visions of a transformed future, in whatever fragmentary and contradictory forms, disrupted the axioms of settler-colonial and liberal-nationalist discourses, most notably by providing a critique of capitalism and by dreaming of international worker solidarity.

For many ICU members, the union's credibility was shattered by the gulf between its words of freedom and its failure to improve the workers' material circumstances.[149] Many of the interviews conducted between 1979 and 1985 with former ICU members emphasise how their hopes were betrayed. Ramakgelo Dinkebogile of Phokeng, Rustenburg describes Kadalie as 'a great cheat [who] ate our money pretending to be our spokesman . . . He took away a lot of money from people. Mh! Many people lost their things because of him'.[150] L. H. Mathebula of Vryheid recalls Champion with some affection, but dismisses Kadalie as a charlatan: 'Kadalie was with the ICU Heh heh heh that was a snake . . . Very clever and very educated . . . He used to talk a lot, talking lies. He wasn't good at all. Kadalie was not a good man at all, he was very bad.'[151] Ephraim Zondi of Greytown recalls the ICU's failure to keep its promises: 'ICU came here and claimed it would put the land question in order. We popped out our money and gave it to them. We hoped that they would help us, only to find that we were the losers.'[152] What several interviewees stress is the ICU's failure to leave any enduring legacy. Elijah Ngcobo of Bulwer, for example, complains, 'It just vanished into thin air . . . They were beaten. They did nothing. It all ended up in talking.'[153] And Lucas Nqandela, a farm-worker in the Orange Free State, contrasts the ICU's bold promises and ultimate disappearance from the political landscape. He recalls the excitement accompanying Kadalie's

Figure 2.2 Cartoon by J. Scott, 'Coming events. Socialism can only be brought about by unity of all workers, irrespective of colour or creed', *The Workers' Herald*, 14 October 1926.

arrival in the region when he gave speeches 'insulting the whites and promising us liberation from oppression'. But optimism turned to despondency, as the combination of Kadalie's failure to deliver and the white farmers' suppression of the ICU destroyed the movement, with the result that Kadalie 'just vanished like water vanishing under the ground'.[154]

Contradicting such bleak conclusions, however, are the memories of other ICU members, who were encouraged by the union's modest if short-lived victories. Thabiso Bogopane of Phokeng, Rustenberg, remembers messages of defiance – 'Kadalie spoke for every black man . . . He wanted every black man should be paid. He must also be free'[155] – as well as specific improvements achieved by the ICU: 'During Kadalie's time we got increases. They paid [messengers] one pound seven and eight pence. Drivers were paid three pounds ten'; and 'This man [Kadalie] helped us, even ordinary shop workers, bicycle riders.'[156] Rose Sibanyoni recalls how Kadalie succeeded in convincing white farmers to give some black tenants time off to cultivate their own land; as a consequence, 'we too tasted freedom'.[157] And Kas Maine of Ledig, Rustenburg, also drew strength from Kadalie's message of freedom, but interpreted it as a long-term aspiration, inspiring at the time of its enunciation, but demanding patience: 'He was also talking of us being freed. He said that the whites were treating us badly, the law would free us . . . He was talking figuratively, saying that the time will come gradually it cannot be today [1980] but a year or fifty years or ten, twenty years but we will be freed.'[158]

3 Soviet Freedom in South Africa

INTRODUCTION

In the decade following Union, a third group of dreams of freedom took root in South Africa. Inspired by Marxism and the Russian revolution, freedom in this dream was pursued via a synthesis of northern hemisphere ideas about class conflict and the material struggles of Southern Africa's working class. This synthesis was pursued by the Soviet-inspired radicals associated with the International Socialist League (ISL) and the Communist Party of South Africa (CPSA) in the 1920s and 1930s.

Marx and his successors were critical of rigid blueprints for future societies.[1] In 1873, Marx rejected prescribing what form any future free society under socialism should take, pledging to confine himself to 'the critical analysis of actual facts, instead of writing recipes ... for the cook-shops of the future'.[2] In 1880, Engels criticised the ahistorical idealism of the utopian socialists Fourier, Saint-Simon and Owen, arguing that 'the more completely [their utopias] were worked out in detail, the more they could not avoid drifting off into pure phantasies'; what was required instead, he argued, was a dialectical-materialist approach in which 'Socialism was no longer an accidental discovery of this or that ingenious brain, but the necessary outcome of the struggle between two historically developed classes – the proletariat and the bourgeoisie.'[3] In 1902, Lenin refuted the 'stern questions' asking Marxists to confine themselves to short-term tasks, and quoted *contra* a passage from the novel *What Is To Be Done?* (1863) by Nikolay Chernyshevsky (1828–1889) on the importance of dreaming of freedom:

> [I]f man were completely deprived of the ability to dream in this way, if he could not from time to time run ahead and mentally conceive, in an entire and completed picture, the product to which his hands are only beginning to lend shape, then I cannot at all imagine what stimulus there would be to induce man to undertake and complete extensive and strenuous work in the sphere of art, science, and practical endeavour ... The rift between dreams and reality

cause no harm if only the person dreaming believes seriously in his dream, if he attentively observes life, compares his observations with his castles in the air, and if, generally speaking, he works conscientiously for the achievement of his fantasies.[4]

The fate of this tradition in South Africa – its reception, its mutations and its betrayals – is the focus of this chapter.

FREEDOM AFTER WAR AND REVOLUTION

The two most interesting socialist-inflected dreams of freedom in South Africa after 1910 took their co-ordinates from the First World War and the Russian Revolution. The first was contained in an obscure utopian novella, *1960 (A Retrospect)* (1919) by James and Margaret Scott Marshall, and the second was expressed in the letters and journalism of Olive Schreiner. Completed in 1916, but only published in Los Angeles three years later, *1960 (A Retrospect)* is set on the veranda of a Natal farmhouse in December 1960, and is in the form of an extended conversation between 79-year-old George Brierley and young Harry Simpson. Prompted by questions from Harry, old George recounts the history of the world and in particular of South Africa from the First World War to the present (i.e. 1960). Paraphrasing the 'Master Mind', a charismatic seer, George explains, 'all strife and struggle and contention in the individual, the family and the community, leading ultimately to war between nation and nation, are part of the evolutionary processes acting under divine laws'.[5] For evolution (capitalised as Evolution) to run its true course, individual self-sufficiency must be demonstrated: 'it is only by one's own individual efforts that righteousness and purity of life can be attained, this being the method of true Evolution, the true evolvement from lower to higher states'.[6] Such self-sufficiency is in accord with the dictates of Reason: 'man ... must climb the spiritual heights by his own efforts [and] Reason is man's only true guide, and the pivot upon which he evolves'.[7] The penultimate chapter sets out a seven-stage journey from the dinosaurs to advanced civilisation. Starting from the first era 90 million years ago, George dwells at greatest length on the fifth era, which encompassed the First World War and the destruction of European civilisation, and the sixth era, which was dawning in 1960 and was destined to be centred in Africa, 'the greatest and the most illustrious of all the continents of the coming races'.[8] After the devastation of the fifth age, George on his veranda is confident that 'the Car of Progress is once again on a good hard road'.[9]

The differences between the pre-Union projections and the Marshalls' utopia are striking. For one, in contrast to the acceptance of a version of capitalism in Smith and Schreiner's writings (and the enthusiasm for capitalism in Rhodes's case), the Marshalls' *1960 (A Retrospect)* blames capitalism (termed 'Commercialism') for the suffering of the fifth era. Looking back, George recalls, 'Commercialism ... was a monstrous, soul-killing, inhuman machine of vast ungainly proportions, and it was one of the chief reasons why the brotherhood of man was well-nigh killed in those days.'[10] A 'mighty octopus that strangled the higher faculties in men and women',[11] Commercialism was itself destroyed during the War in a necessary process of purification that cleared the way for the next evolutionary era. A second contrast concerns the management of race relations. Whereas Rhodes, Smith and Schreiner were prepared to countenance a racially mixed polity, the Marshalls were determined segregationists. In South Africa, the effects of introducing black workers into the white cities and factories had been disastrous, with 'the natives . . . becoming extremely impudent, very lazy [and] picking up and absorbing all the vices of the white man . . . [C]ontact of the white races with the black invariably demoralized the latter'.[12] With great success, George explains, the urbanisation and corruption of the African race had been reversed in the decades after the First World War by re-separating the races, and returning Africans to their ancestral lands: 'It was a blessed day for this country when the natives were thrust out from the towns and farms altogether, and segregated in portions of the land, all of which had at one time belonged to them, and which had been wrested from them by the cupidity of the white people.'[13] At the happy dawn of the sixth era, miscegenation is accordingly dismissed as being 'as reasonable as trying to mix water with oil',[14] and eugenics is promoted in its stead as the key to reinvigorating the race: 'man is not sufficiently developed to be trusted with entire freedom in the propagation of the species, [so] defective ones are consequently weeded out, [resulting in] a great improvement in the health and soundness of the community'.[15] The third and most important difference lay in the Marshalls' supreme confidence that capitalism's demise was inevitable, and that a socialist future lay ahead. For all its lurid scenes of mayhem, *1960 (A Retrospect)* is optimistic that by the end of the sixth era, 'we are now on the highway which will ultimately lead us into the true Brotherhood of Man, the true Divine Socialism: the realization of that mighty truth that by helping others we are in very deed helping ourselves'.[16] This 'Divine Socialism' to be realised in a future South Africa will ensure that all industry is nationalised; equality between men and women accepted; private property abolished; the death penalty a distant memory; and vegetarianism the norm.

Like the Marshalls' novella, Schreiner's thoughts in the decade after Union were dominated by events in Russia and the First World War. Schreiner's letters reveal a fascination with Russia going back to the 1880s. In a letter to Karl Pearson in 1885, she confessed, 'I do feel intense interest in "the Russian". For a time it was almost an absorbing interest. I believe the next great blow for human freedom that will be felt all round the world, will be struck there.'[17] During the Russia–Japan war of 1905, Schreiner confided in her friend Betty Molteno, 'I am so glad over the victory of the Japs. It may not be a good thing for them but it may be the saving of Russia & will teach all fair skinned folk to leave off talking of the darker as "inferior races",'[18] and in a similar vein, wrote to Edward Carpenter, 'My heart is very much in Russia now; I sometimes seem almost living more in Russia than [in South Africa].'[19] Her most impassioned expression of solidarity with Russia's oppressed was contained in a public letter to the Social Democratic Federation in Cape Town, expressing her support for the uprising in progress:

I shall yet be ... with those who in far-off Russia are today carrying on that age-long war of humanity towards a larger freedom and a higher justice, a war which has been waged through the ages, now by this people, and now by that; now a small nation against one that would subjugate it; then by a class; then by a race; now, for religious freedom, then for the right of free thought and free speech; but which, when looked at from the highest standpoint, has always been essentially one battle, fought with one end, now with success, and then with seeming failure, but always bringing nearer by minute and imperceptible degrees that time, in the future, when for a free and united humanity, a truly human life shall be possible on earth. To-day the flag is passing into the hands of the great Russian people ... One very beautiful fact is brought home to us by this struggle of our fellows in Russia. Divided and half-developed as our human race yet is, a certain dim consciousness of human solidarity is beginning to dawn. From the drought-smitten, barren plains of South Africa, from the hearts of the great cities all over the world thoughts of sympathy and fellowship are stretching themselves out to our brothers in Russia, so that whether they are lying in Russian fortresses or perishing in the streets of Poland, they are not really dying or suffering alone. We are all with them.[20]

After the defeat of the 1905 Revolution, Schreiner's interest in Russia was undiminished, as two years later she confessed to John X. Merriman that Russia had replaced South Africa at the centre of her interests: 'I feel far more interested in European (Russian, Irish & other) affairs just now than in South African. The world's centre of interest has passed away from us.'[21]

At the beginning of the First World War, Schreiner's pro-Russian sympathies were aroused afresh, as she wrote to several of her friends abominating Britain's alliance with Czarist Russia, complaining to Havelock Ellis, 'To me this is the most sordid war in which England has ever engaged. She is backing Russia, not because she loves Russia but because millions of her money are invested there, and millions more in France, whose money system will break if the Russian autocracy falls';[22] and to Mrs Georgiana Solomon, 'As to the war, I feel it is more wrong, much than [sic] the Boer war – that England's league with Russia, has been the greatest crime in our history.'[23] However, when Britain's self-interested scheming in Russia unravelled, and the revolution of 1917 transformed the political landscape, Schreiner was exultant. In a letter to Ellis in 1919, she declared, 'The world is full of great men of genius and ability now. A greater genius than Lenin has not appeared in these last hundred years – unless it was Karl Marx',[24] and in her finals days, Schreiner told Molteno, 'Things seem going well with Russia, for which I am so grateful.'[25] Three months before her death, she wrote to Smuts, warning that if South Africa's rulers continued oppressing the populace, revolution in Russia would assuredly be succeeded by revolution in South Africa: 'The next few years are going to determine the whole future of South Africa in 30 or 40 years' time. As we sow we shall reap. We may crush the mass of our fellows in South Africa today, as Russia did for generations, but today the serf is in the Palace & where is the Czar?'[26] Reinforcing her warning, she ended with a portentous post-script: 'The day of princes and Bosses is gone forever: one must meet the incoming tide & rise on it, or be swept away forever.'[27]

Whereas the Russian Revolution gave Schreiner hope, the First World War had the opposite effect. In a letter to Carpenter at the start of the War, Schreiner looked forward to decades of unremitting slaughter:

> I wish I could feel with you that this war is going to bring the kingdom of heaven. I feel it is the beginning of half a century of the most awful wars the world has seen. First this – then another war of probably England & Germany against Russia, then as the years pass with India, Japan & China & the native races of Africa. While the desire to dominate, & rule & possess empire is in the hearts of men there will always be war.[28]

A couple of years later, as the horrors of the War became ever more apparent, Schreiner developed this theme further in a letter to her brother William, remarking upon the fact that so many Germans had fought with Wellington at Waterloo, that '[y]esterday it was German English & Belgians against France: today Germans against English French & Belgians; tomorrow, perhaps ... it will be English, Germans, & other Western peoples against Russia backed by Japan', and concluding, 'A curious nightmare life when you study it historically! Never the less the dawn of civilization will break on Earth one day – though the day may yet be far off.'[29] In her uncompleted essay, 'The dawn of civilisation', written in 1915–16, Schreiner repeated these gloomy reflections in abstract form, asking, 'Why did the strong always crush the weak? Why did we hate and kill and torture?', but recalled a consoling vision from her childhood of a world that transcended such cruelties: 'I seemed to *see* a world in which creatures no more hated and crushed, in which the strong helped the weak, and men understood each other, and forgave each other, and did not try to crush others, but to help.'[30] Reverting to the allegorical idiom of her *Dreams*, Schreiner eschews the kind of detailed predictions provided by the Marshalls, detailing instead her symbolic vision of a socialist fellowship in the distant future.

A NEW JERUSALEM

Like the leaders of the ICU, most of the first-generation members of the ISL and CPSA were schooled in Christianity.[31] For example, David Ivon Jones (1883–1924) was a Methodist who converted to Unitarianism; W. H. Andrews (1870–1950) served as a Methodist Sunday-school teacher and choir-boy; and Sidney Bunting (1873–1936) was descended from generations of distinguished Wesleyan churchmen. R. K. Cope's observation on Andrews's early Christian influences stands as a fair assessment of the trajectory followed by his comrades: 'Protestantism and Dissent were the first steps on a road that leads logically to atheism. The first use of reason in the break with the established church is a vigorous blow for emancipation.'[32] Christianity played if anything an even more prominent role in the early lives of the first black members of the CPSA, all of whom received mission school educations: William Thibedi (1888–1960), James La Guma (1894–1961), Gana Makabeni (1897–1955), Edwin Mofutsanyana (1899–1995), John Gomas (1901–1979), Josephine Mpama (1903–1979), J. B. Marks (1903–1972) Albert Nzula (1905–1934) and Moses Kotane (1905–1978). Different catalysts prompted the shift from Christianity to Communism. Nzula, for example, credited his reading of Montgomery Brown's *Communism and Christianism: Analysed and Contrasted from the View-point of Darwinism* (1920) for clinching his conversion to Marxism.[33]

The abandonment of the Church for the Party did not, however, result in an immediate disappearance of religious language, as biblical allusions abounded in the early issues of the ISL and CPSA newspaper, *The International*.[34] An editorial in 1917, for example, expressed the conviction that the Russian proletariat were on the brink of freedom: 'The Russian workmen are simply wonderful ... They are going to reclaim the lost sheep of the Socialist International ... Hail the coming revolution, now within sight.'[35] In a letter Jones wrote in December 1917 to his friend in Wales, George Eyre Evans, he explained how Russia's 'lost sheep' had won a new form of freedom quite different from the compromised freedoms of the bourgeois revolutions of the eighteenth and nineteenth centuries. Again, he adopts the language of the Bible, with echoes of Marx, in order to amplify the distinction:

> The extension of the liberation movement from Russia in the East to the countries of the West is inevitable ... In the alchemy of progress the old names of democracy and justice and freedom of small nationalities become the repositories of the new tyrannies. And the new liberty comes in gusts, unknown to the prophets of liberty who preached to the old world. And the people walked in great darkness, saw a great light. But the light is pictured as a great terror by the paid charlatans of the press and the pulpit. And it shall come to pass again as of yore that the message of liberty shall go forth, not from the scribes and Pharisees of the capitalist temple who repeat the words of democracy, justice and equality, but from the unknown fishermen and unpaid working people. Look out for the new dawn. Its crucifiers will be Asquith, Lloyd George, and other scribes and Pharisees.[36]

The ambition expressed in *The Manifesto of the Communist Party* (1848) to abolish 'bourgeois individuality, bourgeois independence and bourgeois freedom'[37] is reiterated in Jones's conviction that the old appeals to democracy, justice and freedom have become the repositories of the 'new tyrannies', and in his hope that that 'the gusts' of Communist freedom will blow away bourgeois forms of freedom. Biblical references dominate Jones's prose: in his casting of the fall of the Czar and triumph of the revolution as a journey from darkness into light; in his association of the capitalist press with the scribes and Pharisees expelled from the temple by Jesus; in his conviction that 'the unknown fishermen' – a gesture to Christ's promise to make his disciples fishers of men – will herald the new freedom; and in his identification of Asquith and Lloyd George with Christ's 'crucifiers'. In another arresting comparison, Jones likened the veteran French socialist Marcel Cachin's conversion to communism to 'a Moses on Mount Pisgah having perceived the promised land, a Galahad having found the Grail'.[38]

Direct experience of the Soviet Union increased Jones's enthusiasm for the revolution. Having arrived in Moscow in 1921 for a short visit as the South African delegate to attend the Third Congress of the Comintern, he ended up spending the remaining three years of his life in the Soviet Union. They were difficult years. In 1922, Emma Goldman (1869–1940) looked back on her fifteen months in the Soviet Union, expressing deep disillusionment: 'I did find the revolutionary faith of the people broken, the spirit of solidarity crushed, the meaning of comradeship and mutual helpfulness distorted. One must have lived in Russia . . . to appreciate fully the disintegrating effect of the Bolshevik principle and methods.'[39] In his memoir, Victor Serge (1890–1947) remembered that by 1921, 'With the political monopoly, the Cheka and the Red Army, all that now existed of the "Commune-State" of our dreams was a theoretical myth.'[40] But such demythologising judgements were rare, and for the many non-Russians who like Jones had come to the Soviet Union seeking a promised land, Serge believed, 'the majesty of the Russian Revolution disarmed its supporters of all critical sense; they seemed to think that approval of it entailed the abdication of the right to think'.[41]

Jones was not entirely blind to the difficulties facing the Soviet Union, but he never doubted the integrity and vitality of the revolution, continuing to describe its achievements in biblical idiom. There are many examples. In his address to the Third Congress of the Comintern, Jones declared, 'The Negro has been the Ishmael of the human race'; the challenge facing all socialists is to ensure that '[h]e must become the Benjamin of the Communist International'.[42] In a letter to Evans, he described the suffering Russian people as martyrs: they had endured 'the privations of seven years of war and civil war, and the blockade, and now the drought and the failure of crops', but he remained convinced that '[t]hey have done wonderfully, performed epics of martyrdom. And will do it again'.[43] A couple of years later, the ritual of baptism is invoked to herald the inspirational achievements of the workers of the Donetz Basin in the Ukraine: 'Anyone who wishes to be re-baptized in the revolutionary faith, let him go to the Donetz Basin.'[44] In a front-page article in *The International* attacking the capitalist class, his apocalyptic imagery recalls *The Book of Revelations*:

> In the name of the great God Kapital [sic] they have commanded all to fall down and worship their putrid institutions and rotten glories . . . The past is written in letters of blood and fire and cannot be wiped out . . . And the sun of the rising day throws its first early beams across the sky. It is a new dawn.[45]

And in his final article in *The International*, written in a sanatorium in Yalta shortly before his death, Jones compares the Soviet Union to a garden: 'If my letter seems, as usual, inordinately optimistic, that is not because I wish to convey that everything in the garden is lovely. No! But what is unlovely is not significant of the trend of things – an indisputably disappearing factor which the revolution is sweeping away.'[46] Old and New Testament language thus percolates Jones's prose, as he utilises the rhetorical power of religious discourse to express both his critique of the capitalist West and his anticipation of the (Soviet) socialist future.

A few years later, Josiah Gumede (1867–1946) echoed Jones's biblical rhetoric in his enthusiastic response to the Soviet Union. Gumede's effusive words carry the authority of a convert, as up until his sixtieth birthday, he had been deeply suspicious of Communism. Indeed, he had gone so far as to declare that the African's position under Communism would be akin to slavery.[47] For most of his life, his dreams of freedom were framed by his faith in the capacity of the British Empire to protect the rights and freedoms of black South Africans. Along with Sol Plaatje, Gumede had been a member of the 1919 South African National Congress delegation to the British government to protest against the Union's racist laws. In response to a request from Leo Amery (1873–1955) to write a report summarising the plight of Africans in Natal, Gumede produced the pamphlet 'A cry for freedom, justice, liberty and fair play', which concludes:

> The good work that was done by great Englishmen, whose names we honourably mention, such as Bishops Colenso, Callaway, Merriman, Sir Theophilus Shepstone, Sir Bartle Frere, Messrs Grant, Saul Solomon, Molteno, and Missionaries Moffat, Dr. D. Livingstone, Harry Escombe Esq., Sir John Robinson, Revs. John Ayliff, James Allison, Dr Adams, Rev. Mr. Wilder, Wilberforce, Buxton, President Lincoln, and others who stood for the great Heavenly principles of Freedom, Liberty, Justice and Fairplay [sic], is a living monument that, had they lived still, we should never for one moment be placed in the hands of such incompetent law givers as are forming the majority in the Union of South Africa. No laws would be made on our Colour – no one would attempt to deny us Freedom, Liberty, Justice and Fairplay because we are merely black or coloured.[48]

Appealing to a Victorian golden age when the British Empire ruled without racial prejudice, when 'great Englishmen' from Bishop Colenso to President Lincoln dictated imperial policy, and when the 'Heavenly principles of Freedom, Liberty, Justice and Fairplay' held sway, Gumede berates 'incompetent law givers' for failing to protect the freedom of black South Africans. The many missionaries in the list of great Englishmen attests to Gumede's faith in the congruence of God's Empire and the British Empire.

However, Britain's failure to protect the 'Heavenly' principle of freedom on behalf of the Union's increasingly impoverished black population provoked Gumede's conversion to Communism. In February 1927, Gumede attended the inaugural conference of the League Against Imperialism (LAI) in Brussels, where he renounced the British Empire:

> When Great Britain occupied South Africa the Union Jack was pointed out as meaning justice, liberty, freedom and fair play. We find it means just the opposite . . . I am glad to say that in South Africa there are Communists. I am not a Communist, but we find that the Communist Party are the only people

who are with us in spirit ... There are two forces working today, imperialism and a workers' republic in Russia. We hear little of it. We hear much against it. I would point out that I wish to learn more and more of it. We shall have to put these two on a scale and see which would be the best to ally with.[49]

On his return to South Africa, Gumede addressed the first non-European conference in Kimberley on 23 June 1927, and reiterated Britain's betrayals: 'We are British subjects and were promised freedom, justice, liberty and fair play. With these four principles it was heaven, without them we are hopeless ... We simply want the four principles.'[50] In Moscow at the Tenth Anniversary Celebrations of the Russian Revolution, his new-found political faith was reinforced, as he explained to an audience in Johannesburg soon after his return:

> South Africa is hell for the black man now, we mean to make it a heaven. I am one of the blessed sons of your mothers for I have seen the new world to come, where it has actually begun. I have been to the new Jerusalem ... All the states of Russia are presided over by a peasant – a Jacob – a sheep herd, and I found that all are equal there, men and women, black and white ... I have brought back a key with me if you will accept it; we need your help and support to turn that key and unlock the door to freedom.[51]

For Gumede, the Soviet Union is like heaven in contrast to the hell of South Africa; it is a new Jerusalem; and its supreme leader (Stalin) is like the Old Testament shepherd Jacob tending all of his flock. The model of socialism he discovered in the Soviet Union is likened to a key that can unlock the door to freedom in South Africa. Further, Gumede argues that the pre-colonial communalism of Africans predisposed them to the new Jerusalem of Soviet Communism: 'The Bantu has been a Communist from time immemorial. We are disorganised, that's all! ... I believe the land belongs to the people and not to individuals. We Bantu don't eat alone, we share our food with each other.'[52]

After the reports on Gumede's speeches, biblical references diminished in number, but still appeared occasionally in the pages of *The International* and successor CPSA newspapers, *The South African Worker* (1926–30) and *Umsebenzi* (1930–7).[53] In a cartoon in May 1930 (Figure 3.1), the figure of a black Christ on a crucifix is flanked by soldiers representing Boer imperialism and British imperialism. Prompted by the police killing of six farm-workers in Worcester in May 1930, Roux's cartoon identified the victims with Christ and the police and farm-owners with His persecutors.

Four years later, the same image of Christ flanked by soldiers representing Boer and British imperialism was recycled in *Umsebenzi* (Figure 3.2), headed 'South Africa's new constitution', with a quotation by Patrick Duncan (1870–1943 – the Minister of Mines at the time) added beneath it: '"The British Commonwealth of Nations can be held together only by complete freedom and mutual agreement."'[54] The pretext on this occasion was different, but the symbolism of the cartoon communicated in broad terms that the victims were still the same, as were the colluding factions of the white ruling class.

Figure 3.1 Cartoon by Edward Roux, 'After Worcester – what?', *The South African Worker*, 16 May 1930.

Figure 3.2 Cartoon by Edward Roux, 'South Africa's new constitution', *Umsebenzi*, 7 April 1934.

In a third example (Figure 3.3), a cartoon of an African hiker emblazoned with the word 'Umsebenzi' is entering a dark valley titled 'Pirovian Dictatorship', with the caption quoting from the 23rd Psalm, followed by its translation into Xhosa, and a paragraph explaining the reference:

Figure 3.3 Cartoon by Edward Roux, '"Yea, though I walk through the valley of the shadow of death"', *The South African Worker*, 30 May 1930.

Yea though I walk through the Valley of the Shadow of Death'. Yo! Nokuba sendilhamba etunzini lokufa. With the gazetting of the Riotous Assemblies Amendment Act we enter upon a period of open dictatorship by the slave drivers' government. With the support of the masses, however, we shall continue to publish our paper, to drive back the vile beasts of oppression from our path, and passed through the Valley of Darkness, emerge on the other side in the sunshine of the African Republic.[55]

The disappearance of biblical language was hardly surprising given the CPSA's official hostility towards religion, which was economically summarised in a fourth cartoon (Figure 3.4) of a white soldier named Pirow brandishing a bayonet over a cowering black worker, and a white priest holding aloft a cross and a book titled 'Bible Dope'. The caption on three separate lines and in three different fonts reads:

'Religion is the Opium of the People' – Marx.
Pirow: Pray, you damn nigger, PRAY!.
Government has prohibited all meetings, except exclusively religious ones, in the country districts of the Western Cape.

Figure 3.4 Cartoon by Edward Roux, '"Religion is the opium of the people"' – Marx', *Umsebenzi*, 20 June 1930.

Biblical imagery thus functions in Roux's cartoons alternately as an expression of outrage at the sufferings of black South Africans (as in the identification of Christ on the cross with black workers), as a spur to the working class to show fortitude in the struggle for freedom (as in the adaptation of the 23rd Psalm), and as a weapon deployed by the ruling class to subdue the people's resistance (as in the Pirow figure brandishing the 'Bible Dope').

Marx's hostility towards religion was premised upon the conviction, '*Man makes religion*, religion does not make man,' and that accordingly, 'The criticism of religion disillusions man, so that he will think, act and fashion his reality like a man who has discarded his illusions and regained his senses, so that he will move around himself as his own true sun.'[56] In subjecting religion to criticism, 'man' regains his senses, and in the process becomes the agent of his own history. In more specific terms, the proletariat takes responsibility for its own emancipation, and no longer looks to religion for either comfort or salvation. An essential element in Marx's conception of proletarian self-emancipation was the eschewal of messiahs. Messiahs were a lingering presence in the writings of the utopian socialists, and for Marx, 'it was beyond comprehension that messianic utopianism continued to thrive [in the 1850s] when the proletariat was able to emancipate itself without the aid of messiahs'.[57]

In considering how Marx's critique of religion might illuminate the biblical imagery in Jones, Gumede and Roux, South Africa's early Communists in most respects observe his strictures: Jones fused biblical and Marxist vocabulary to critique bourgeois freedoms; Gumede drew on the Bible to expose the hypocrisy of the British Empire; and Roux used the Old and New Testaments to attack the racist state and provide hopeful images of a socialist future. But in one important respect, in their elevation of Lenin and Stalin to messiah status, they fail to heed Marx's warnings, and they repeat the mistake of the utopian socialists. Seeing Lenin as a saviour, or Stalin as 'a Jacob', limits the agency and imagination of the South African proletariat in its struggle for freedom.

JOHN BALL'S DREAM IN AFRICA

Complementing the articles with biblical allusions in the ISL/CPSA newspapers were a large number of borrowed, adapted and original poems, reviews of literary works and articles on left-leaning literati. For many first-generation white socialists in South Africa, literature provided a more than adequate substitute for the Bible, and they never hesitated to clinch political arguments with quotations from their favourite poets or authors. From a slightly earlier generation, J. T. Bain venerated William Morris; Jones's favourite was Shelley; Bunting was inspired by Browning; and Roux quoted Swinburne at every opportunity.[58] Novels too could contribute to the socialist cause, as in the case of Henry Glazer (1874–c. 1935), whose son Joseph recalled how his father had borrowed Upton Sinclair's *The Jungle* (1906) from the Johannesburg Public Library, and how the novel 'transformed my father's views about the world and about the conditions of the working class. In such a manner he became a communist [and] was one of the first to organise the working class in South Africa'.[59] More significant than these individual enthusiasms, however, was the collective left literary culture in the pages of *The International* and its successors.

The majority of the poems reproduced (nearly always in abbreviated form) provided inspirational words exhorting readers to intensify their collective struggle against capitalism, socialist versions of 'Onward Christian Soldiers'. All such poems had the same three-part structure: an opening evocation of the suffering of the poor; a transitional moment of awakening, when the poor understand their common oppression and their revolutionary potential; and a concluding vision of freedom. This structure resembles conversion narratives, as it reproduces a collective version of the individual convert's three-stage journey: from sinfulness and suffering; to crisis and conversion; to redemption in Christ's mercy. And indeed, several of the poems retain a residue of Christian imagery. For example, the third stanza of the anonymous 'The Forges of the Nations' asks, 'They have sealed man's eyes with darkness, have they blinded him for good?', and answers, 'They have rent his garments from him, they have spat upon his face,/ Given him a reed for sceptre, till the cross was in its place.'[60] As the genre requires, exploitation is overcome by the collective agency of the workers, and freedom is ultimately won: 'Then rise, rise, rise, all ye men who live to labour!/ Up, up, up, go tell it to your neighbour!/ Though you're burdened with the load, though you're bloodied by the goad,/ Oh, prepare, prepare to follow, for FREEDOM'S on the road.'[61]

Other poems eschewed Christian imagery, and simply exhorted workers to have confidence in their own agency. Francis Perkins Gilman's poem 'To Labour', for example, is addressed to workers, and ends with the rousing words, 'And show as was never shown before,/ The power that is in you! Stand all as one!/ See justice done!/ Believe, and Dare and Do'.[62] And (untypically for *The International*), Gilman's short poem 'Woman' anticipates women's liberation in its portentous closing lines, 'Slow advancing, halting, creeping/ Comes the Woman to the hour!/ She walketh veiled and sleeping/ For she knoweth not her power.'[63] Several of the workers' anthems were preceded by a line telling readers which tune should accompany the words. An anonymous marching song opening with the lines 'Long have we laboured in darkness and sorrow' is to be sung 'to the tune of the Warshavyanka'.[64] Another anonymous poem titled 'Emancipation' is be sung to the tune of '"Tramp, Tramp, Tramp, the Boys"', and the lyrics of the original were adapted to fit South Africa's political landscape: 'From the broad Zambesi's roar, / To Agulhas' rocky shore, / Fling the message far and wide throughout the land,/ Yes "all one people we"/ But that people must be free,/ From the cunning, cruel, greedy, grafting Band.'[65] The words of 'The Red Flag' were published in several issues, as were those of 'The International', with the latter also translated into Afrikaans and Zulu.[66]

In addition to providing rousing words for exploited workers, literature fulfilled a second function, to criticise the powerful. The poems appeared unaccompanied by any introductions, and many of them satirised the hypocrisies of ruling-class ideology. Most were from the works of famous poets, with the Romantics prominent. An early issue of *The International* introduces a selection of seven quotations from Byron's *Don Juan* (1819–24) with the assertion that 'the beauty of Byron's words' are particularly apposite to the 'large hypocrisy of the bourgeois jingo [and] the ingenious trapdoors in the capitalist conscience'.[67] Following the quotations from *Don Juan* mocking Britain's rulers, the column concludes by contrasting Byron's courage in speaking truth to power and the timidity of 'every writer of today [who] pot-boils the taste of his capitalist masters'.[68] In another extract reproduced in *The International*, a stanza from 'Lara' (1814), Byron describes how words like 'freedom' are misappropriated by the powerful, and thus implicated in the suffering of 'mankind': 'Religion – freedom – vengeance – what you will,/ A word's enough to raise mankind to kill;/ Some factious phrase by cunning caught and spread,/ That guilt may reign, and wolves and worms be fed!'[69]

To help readers of *The International* make connections between the words of English and American poets and South African society, many of the adaptations made their relevance explicit. William Covington Hall's poem 'Might is Right' (1915), reworked and published in *The International* twelve years after its first publication, is one such example.[70] The title is attributed to Nietzsche, and its logic ridiculed in a sequence of examples, starting with those in Hall's original, and culminating in South African additions. The poem's argument is established in the ironic opening two couplets – 'Might was right when Christ was hanged/ Beside the Jordan's foam;/ Might was right when Gracchus bled,/ Upon the stones of Rome'[71] – and is adapted in subsequent stanzas to fit South African politics. The logic repeated is that the might of the South African state was 'right' to exploit and kill its workers, and to protect the material interests of its capitalists: 'Might was right when Stassen died, when/ Long and Smith followed him,/ When Smith and Dowse's lives were beaten/ out by Smuts' murderous band,' and 'Might was Right when Jagger builds, A hell/ round every hearth;/ Might is Right when Solly Joel, his peons/ off the earth doth starve.'[72] Examples of might prevailing, of the powerful crushing the weak, accumulate, with the final line of every stanza concluding, "Tis the logic of the Ancient World, and the/ Gospel of to-day.' In the final stanza, however, the despairing conclusion to the mantra is reversed: 'And so, O Hearts of Toil, Awaken, O working men Unite;/ Unite! Unite! For Might is Right, 'tis/ freedom's only way.'[73] By uniting, working men acquire the power to vanquish the hitherto mighty capitalist.

Adaptations like those of 'Emancipation' and 'Might is Right' out-numbered original South African poems by some distance. One of the few anonymous poems, 'Tot System in the North', responds to Cabinet Minister Oswald Pirow's decision to address the depression in the Cape wine industry by introducing the 'tot' system[74] for black farm-workers in the Transvaal. The poem's opening stanza speculates, 'In the future it seems we shall have one right,/ When all other freedom is taken away,/ The right to get drunk on a Saturday night,/ And lie drunk in the gutter till break of day,' and concludes ironically, 'It will thrill dear old Liberty, doubtless, to know/ We're allowed to get drunk on South African wines!'[75] Realism replaces irony in a second anonymous poem, 'Ndabeni', which accumulates images of poverty and squalor – 'sand and fleas', corrugated-iron shacks, 'filthy lavatories', 'stinking urinals' and 'dustbins piled with refuse'.[76] The church is the target of criticism, as a minister tells the black township's congregation, '"You must be good, obey the laws,/ And keep yourselves within your proper stations."'[77] A third original poem, James La Guma's 'Awake! Africa!', first published in *The Workers' Herald* in 1925, was republished in *The South African Worker* in 1928.[78]

On occasions, poetry in the service of critique was more directly instrumental, as quotations from poems were woven into articles on economic and political issues. A typical example is provided in an unsigned front-page article in *The International* of January 1918. The article opens with the generalisation, 'Petty nationalism is the most reactionary apparition of our times,' and proceeds to argue along Marxist lines that universal appeals to 'freedom' cloak the sectional interests of the ruling class, in this case, South Africa's Afrikaner nationalists:

> A body of men who are continually whining about freedom, and justice and language rights . . . and bandying the words 'Vrede' and 'Vryheid' in long-faced calvin countenances, – as soon as they are up against it betray the odious fact that what they mean is only freedom for their little clique to exploit the labour of the native worker . . . Opportunist in everything else, the Nationalist farmer is only sure of one thing, that he wants freedom to sjambok the native in his own sweet way as in the days of long ago.[79]

How is the Afrikaner farmer's freedom to exploit the agricultural labourer guaranteed? By keeping the farm worker in a state of ignorance – the answer provided by an extract from Edwin Markham's poem 'The Man with the Hoe' (1898), written after seeing Millet's painting of the same title:

> Bowed by the weight of centuries he leans
> Upon his hoe and gazes on the ground,
> The emptiness of ages in his face,
> And on his back the burden of the world.
> Who made him dead to rapture and despair,
> A thing that grieves not and never hopes,
> Stolid and stunned, a brother to the ox?[80]

This poetic image of the crushed farm worker thus established, the argument continues, 'that is what Nationalism wants to preserve in the labourer'.[81] However, a Marxist grasp of history promises that such interminable exploitation will end: 'Capitalism however can only increase its efficiency by raising the forces that are going to bring about its downfall,' which in South Africa will be 'the native workers as soon as they escape clean from the sjambok rule of the peasant farmer'.[82] Markham's image of the worker under capitalism as 'a brother to the ox' is transcended by Marx's image of the worker as 'the gravedigger of capitalism'.[83]

Markham's depiction of the down-trodden worker, however, contrasted with the many poems providing messages of hope for workers. This was the third function of the literary contributions in the ISL and CPSA newspapers – to provide a language, however inchoate, for imagining utopian possibilities beyond present sufferings. As with the poems attacking the powerful, so too in the poems looking to a hopeful future, the Romantics provided inspiration. Extracts from several of Shelley's poems written in optimistic spirit were published, notably the final stanza of *Prometheus Unbound* (1820), with its lines dedicated '[T]o suffer woes which Hope thinks infinite;/ To forgive wrongs darker than death or night;/ To defy Power, which seems omnipotent;/ . . . to hope till Hope creates/ From its own wreck the thing it contemplates.'[84] A long extract from the Chorus of the enslaved Greek women in his play *Hellas* (1822), expressing a similar message of despair defeated, appeared a year later: 'The world's great age begins anew,/ The golden years return,/ The earth doth like a snake renew/ Her winter weeds outworn:/ Heaven smiles, and faiths and empires gleam/ Like wrecks of a dissolving dream.'[85] The hardships endured by workers in their struggle for freedom is registered in these extracts, but in the closing stanzas, disappointments are reversed and utopian futures anticipated.

CPSA intellectuals also found resources of hope in the Victorian poets, notably Swinburne and Morris. Roux's love of Swinburne was evident in the publication in *The South African Worker* of a stanza from 'Messidor' (1871), accompanied by a three-quarter page image of a black farm-worker scything down a field entitled 'Harvest of African Liberation', with three snakes named 'Labour Party', 'Nationalists' and 'SAP' and a rat named 'Pirow' fleeing his sickle (Figure 3.5). In contrast to the unending exploitation suffered by the workers in 'The Man with the Hoe', the final stanza of Swinburne quoted by Roux promises freedom:

> The dumb dread people that sat
> All night without screen for the night,
> All day without food for the day,
> They shall give not their harvest away,
> They shall eat of its fruit and wax fat:
> They shall see the desire of their sight,
> Though the ways of the seasons be steep,
> They shall climb with face to the light,
> Put in the sickles and reap.[86]

Swinburne's own outraged sensibility, railing against injustice in nineteenth-century Europe, is thus transposed to South Africa. His hopes of defeating tyranny and exploitation, inspired by the triumph of Mazzini in Italy, function as a model for black South Africans' struggles in the twentieth century.

Morris was prominent in CPSA publications, with an extract from his 'The March of the Workers' (1885) on the front page of *The International* in April 1918.

Figure 3.5 Cartoon by Edward Roux, '"Put in the sickles and reap!"', *The South African Worker*, 22 May 1930.

From the collection *Chants for Socialists*, the poem opens with the question 'What is this, the sound and rumour?'[87] and the succeeding stanzas provide the answer: the sound and rumour are of workers gathering together and marching against the bosses. For many a hundred year, workers 'have laboured deaf and blind', but now 'the cry comes down the wind', and 'rich men hear and tremble'.[38] The final two lines quoted proclaim the workers' irresistible momentum: 'On we march then, we the workers, and the rumours that ye hear/ Is the blended sound of battle and deliverance drawing near.'[89] Conceived to be sung to the tune of 'John Brown', the poem itself communicates 'the sound and rumour' of working-class insurrection. According to E. P. Thompson, for Morris 'the Socialist movement stood for "life", and if his poems helped to feed this life, they found their immortality in the spirit of the movement which they helped to shape'.[90] In Britain in the 1880s, Thompson claimed further, poems like 'The March of the Workers' 'caught fire in the hearts of the comrades whose feelings were already high within them';[91] for the anonymous author writing for the readers of *The International*, the aspiration was for the message of socialism to catch fire in the hearts of South African workers. Picking up on the theme of the poem, the article opens with the claim that change is imminent, 'not in political boundaries, but in the whole form and Spirit of Society'.[92] The 'sound and rumours' of the Russian Revolution have reached South Africa, and 'the oppressed races and classes of this country . . . are silently groping and reaching towards an emancipation the nature of which they scarcely yet realise'.[93] Such an absence of a prescriptive post-emancipation script for South African workers coincides with Morris's utopianism, which Thompson describes as a 'leap out of the kingdom of necessity into an imagined kingdom of freedom in which desire may actually indicate choices or impose itself as need'.[94] Notwithstanding the many obstacles, *The International* article continues, 'hope predominates and spreads like fire'.[95] Morris's faith in workers educating themselves and marching together to freedom is adapted and applied to South Africa's racially divided working class:

> 'Ah, but you mustn't cause native unrest,' they say. Who causes unrest among natives today but their oppressors and exploiters? . . . 'Ah, but they are not educated up to freedom.' Who bolts the compound doors against all enlightening influences? Who has turned the old free agricultural native into a cringing wage slave? This whole domination over, and denial of civilisation to, natives is an utterly untenable position, and the more thoroughly the domineering whites appreciate that the native workers are destined to free themselves from it just as their white fellow workers have struggled all these years to free themselves from what is essentially the same thing, the smoother will be their transition to emancipation.[96]

Like the British workers in Morris's poem who 'laboured deaf and blind', South Africa's 'agricultural native' has been denied 'enlightening influences' and 'civilisation'. Whereas colonial discourse conventionally scripts a journey from African darkness to European light, the journey here is from an exploited and racially divided working class to a common struggle against (and triumph over) 'domineering whites'. In the same way that Morris's poem brings a message of deliverance, so too does *The International*, as the article concludes with the confident promise that the united struggle of black and white workers will vanquish the opportunistic alliance of 'white capitalists and white artisans': 'It will be another fight of Might v Right; and . . . we know Right must win.'[97]

Morris's popularity amongst South African radicals in the early twentieth century was also evident at a lecture on him by Bain for the Workers Educational Association at the Johannesburg Public Library in July 1916.[98] *The International*'s unnamed reporter picked up on comments by one audience member, who argued for a rejection of Marx in favour of Morris, and a return to the ethical side of socialism. Incensed at the idea of opposing Morris to Marx, *The International*'s reporter insisted upon their compatibility:

> If anyone has a notion that William Morris aimed at superseding Marx, he is very much mistaken . . . The poetic genius of William Morris was informed by the constructive genius of Marx . . . As for Morris, who that has read his 'Dream of John Ball' can ever imagine that he was prey to that fantastic notion that you can divide the ethics of socialism from its economics.[99]

The dangers of separating the ethics from the economics of socialism are again foregrounded in J. M. Gibson's critique of the ideas of Morris's disciple, A. R. Orage (1873–1934), editor of *The New Age* and author of *National Guilds* (1914). Characterised as 'one of those ill-digested schemes put forward by middle-class intellectuals with an eye to the main chance of conserving to their section of the community the loaves and fishes of office as statesmen', Gibson derides Orage's proposed model of national guilds based upon consumer (as opposed to producer) interests as one offering no more than the 'amelioration and reform'[100] of capitalism. What is required is 'organising at the bottom on a class conscious basis', and the single-minded pursuit of strategies 'controlled and guided by the clear cut issue of eliminating the capitalist state, not amending it'.[101]

Finally, novelists like Upton Sinclair and Jack London were reviewed with an eye to how they might promote socialism. Marx and Engels had argued in *The German Ideology* that the early nineteenth-century systems of the utopian socialists like Saint-Simon, Fourier and Owen 'appeared in the early days of the communist movement and had at that time propaganda value as popular novels'.[102] Jones in his caustic review of London's *The Iron Heel* (1908) in *The International* applied the same criterion to literature, and measured the novel in terms of its propaganda value. For Jones, capitalism 'survives only by the artificial oxygen of militarism', and 'the Co-operative Commonwealth is therefore the only conception of society today . . . that can preserve the productive forces'.[103] However, London's vision in *The Iron Heel* is 'a travesty of the Socialist idea, casting a lurid and uncanny gloom over the whole conception'; by contrast, Jones concludes, 'there is more humanity, beauty and truth, in fine, more Socialism, in Jack London's unsophisticated *White Fang* than in all his conscious propaganda efforts'.[104] Marx and Engels are attuned to the literary qualities of the political writings of the utopian socialists – 'Cabet calls his *Icarie* a "roman philosophique" [and in] Fourier's system there is a vein of true poetry'[105] – whereas Jones demonstrates a sensitivity to the political qualities of London's literary fiction.

BEYOND CAPITALIST FREEDOM

The pages of the ISL and CPSA newspapers also included a number of theoretical articles on the meaning of freedom. Most of these were initialled by J. M. Gibson,[106] and they both outlined the false freedoms under capitalism, and also looked forward to true freedom under socialism. The fundamental criticism repeated in all the articles is that without economic security for all, the political freedoms promised under capitalism are of little value. Contrasting the chattel slave and the modern 'wage slave', Gibson argues that 'the [latter] possesses certain political rights which his predecessor the chattel slave did not possess. But these rights have not sufficed to free him from the thraldom of economic slavery'.[107] As a consequence, 'workers are notwithstanding this boasted freedom nothing but slaves under the heel of the capitalist class'.[108]

This nexus of political freedom and economic enslavement under capitalism is focused in several columns on Britain, and in particular on the role of British nationalism in obfuscating the true meaning of freedom. The antipathy towards nationalism is captured in the opening line of the Chartist Charles MacKay's poem 'British Freedom', which was published in an early issue of *The International*: 'We want no flag, no flaunting rag, for liberty to fight.'[109] Elaborating the critical attitude towards nationalism, one of the unsigned articles paraphrases Marx's critique of British apologists for free trade, and argues that Britain's hostility to 'Prussian tyranny' is based upon British shopkeepers resenting 'the interference of German shopkeepers with their elbow room to buy and sell . . . By freedom, under the present bourgeois condition of production, is meant free trade, free buying and selling'.[110] The duplicitous yoking of 'freedom' and 'Britain' is not confined to the trading interests of British shopkeepers; it also extends to labour relations, where the terms are combined in order to disguise the exploitation of workers: '"Free born Briton" is a shibboleth that when analysed is found to be one of those meaningless phrases that is used to dupe the workers into submission to the capitalist class.'[111] In an essay on citizenship, Gibson argues further, 'The fallacy of citizenship like other shibboleths such as "patriotism", "your country", "liberty", "justice", is but a red herring to divert the workers from the real issue at stake.'[112] The appeals to citizenship/patriotism/nationalism/liberty/justice are controlled by 'press, pulpit, platform and cinema', with the result that workers 'embrace the shadow of citizenship to the neglect of the substance of economic liberty'.[113]

The critique of how 'freedom' is opportunistically identified with official nationalisms and imperialisms is also applied to the United States, India and South Africa. One of several articles on the United States is titled ironically 'The land of the free',[114] and a second unsigned contribution describes the US government's clampdown on workers' rights, concluding, 'Socialists on the side of peace are lynched or imprisoned . . . Freedom for the workers is withheld, in speech and in print.'[115] With respect to India, an article by Blanche Watson republished in *The International* in July 1923 points out the hypocrisy in the British Colonial Office phrase 'freedom within the Empire', as she argues that 'profit is at the bottom of the British connection [with India, and that] India free cannot tolerate that profit.'[116] In relation to the official nationalisms in South Africa, an unsigned article headed 'Nationalism: freedom's foe' reports on a meeting of the South African Native National Congress (SANNC) in December 1918, complaining of the meeting, 'i[I]t is felt to be sacrilegious to assert the common interest of all involved in the class struggle as paramount above national peculiarities.'[117] Describing further the 'capitalist speakers [telling] the natives to be thrifty and docile, and not to waste their money in riotous living', the report concludes that nationally or racially defined organisations like the SANNC should be replaced by 'organisations of the wage workers, irrespective of race, colour or creed'.[118]

The critiques of bourgeois freedom in *The International* were supplemented with optimistic projections arguing that true freedom under socialism was imminent. Gibson believes that 'the modern form of social production clearly and distinctly points to ending this enslaving form of society, and giving that freedom, that economic liberty that should be the right of every human being'.[119] He is careful at the same time to differentiate his own 'scientific' confidence in the rise of true freedom in a socialist future from the varieties of utopianism derided by Engels:

> The cry for 'Absolute Liberty' is reactionary, based upon the Utopian ideology of an exploded philosophy of emotionalism and the mistaken idea that natural laws are the foundations upon which society should rest. It overlooks the fundamental economic basis upon which all phases of society since the advent of civilisation, including the present one, have been raised, and neglects to take into account the co-operative nature of the economy of the future society.[120]

Scientific (as opposed to utopian) socialism provides Gibson with a confident understanding of society's 'fundamental economic basis'; hence his conviction that a 'Co-operative Commonwealth [will be] the immediate heir of the capitalist system'.[121] Under such a socialist co-operative economy, 'Liberty will be such as will free the individual from the enslaving restrictions of class-made laws and regulations necessary to safeguard the interests of the possessing class in their economic power.'[122]

Such theoretical reflections on freedom only occasionally referred to South Africa's colonial past or the racial politics of its present, but implicit in CPSA ideology was the assumption that 'progress' from feudalism to capitalism, from barbarism to civilisation, had ill-served Europe's workers, and that such 'progress' would benefit black workers in South Africa even less. A cartoon on the front page of a 1923 issue of *The International* headed 'And this is capitalist civilisation' featured an image of a white worker on a bench with the caption:

> If I was an African savage I would have a kraal to sleep in. I would be able to maintain food by hunting and fishing. But I am a civilised white man, and I have

no shelter, no food or possibility of obtaining any. If I creep into some hole to sleep, the forces of 'law and order' rout me out. If I take food, the forces of 'law and order' throw me into prison. All the forces of 'civilisation' are combined to reduce me to utter misery and starvation. Some 'civilisation', isn't it?'[123]

Like Morris, who always used the terms 'civilisation' and 'barbarism' with ironic inversion,[124] the caption suggests that the 'barbarous' pre-colonial African is much better off than the 'civilised' European. Rather than arriving at the destination of freedom, the 'progress' of the journey to capitalism has led to greater suffering. The challenge for South African socialists of this generation was to persuade black workers that socialism was their best option for a happy future, one pithily described by the CPSA leader Douglas Wolton as: 'Yesterday a tribesman; to-day an industrial worker; tomorrow freedom.'[125] As black workers and peasant farmers suffered ever greater poverty after the First World War, both the Christian conversion narrative and the progressive narrative of capitalism lost authority, and the alternative socialist dream of freedom found a ready audience.

'DEEPENING ECONOMIC CRISIS'

Biblical and literary language in South African socialist publications of the early 1920s was embedded within a political discourse comprising humanist and modernising elements. These two elements are captured in a letter from Sidney Bunting to Edward Roux from Moscow in 1922 while he was attending the Fourth Congress of the Comintern. Proclaiming Moscow as 'the Mecca of the working class movement', Bunting described a mass rally on Red Square:

> One hundred thousand were there in serried ranks with scores of bands and countless banners, expressing confidence in the revolution and vowing death to world capitalism ... Here, after all, is the secret of Soviet Power. And what humane and intelligent faces! Yes, the soldiers and police too; not those brutalised dogs we know too well, but decent kindly fellows ... To us, for our part, this first Marxian step of proletarian political control, as the prerequisite of workers' control of industry, seems more important, more valuable, more far-reaching and wonderful than ever.[126]

For Bunting, the abstract dream of 'the dictatorship of the proletariat' was becoming a concrete reality on the streets of Moscow, where the 'first Marxian step of proletarian political control' was being taken. His impressions were not, however, entirely positive, as he shared Serge's critical views on the foreign delegates attending Comintern congresses. Contrasted with the Comintern leadership, they 'seemed of quite mediocre calibre ... making it easy to understand why the Communist Parties of the world are not merely content but well advised to "take orders from Moscow"'.[127] He was especially caustic about the CPSA, with its factions and splits, arguing that it should subordinate its wishes to the commands of the Comintern:

> Today the Comintern is an engine, a conquering force . . . It is a power determined to win the world in our day. It should be our privilege, not to stand on a Cape Town dunghill and crow that we know better, but to march in solidarity with it to win the world victory we all desiderate.[128]

Bunting's military-industrial images of the Russian Revolution – 'serried ranks', 'engine', 'conquering force' – convey a progressive impulse dedicated to accelerating the Soviet Union from Czarist backwardness to modernity as quickly as possible.

Six years later, Bunting's wife Rebecca reiterated his enthusiasm in describing to South African readers their experience of the Sixth Comintern Congress, opening with a paean to Lenin's beneficent presence, casting him as a messiah figure:

> Among our many wonderful experiences at the VIth Comintern Congress at Moscow, one of the most striking was the emblem of the spirit of Lenin brooding over the Congress. At the right hand of the platform, encircled by beautiful flowers, with a red light shining over it, stood a bronze bust of the great leader, as if he were watching like a soldier over proceedings and guiding them. And, indeed the Congress felt his presence all the time: it was the Leninist policy that all strive to follow up.[129]

Lenin's inspirational example, which continued to capture the Russian people's imagination long after his death, ensured the flourishing of the revolution: 'A new morale, a new outlook on life, unknown anywhere else in the world, is growing up in Russia . . . So long as the USSR is left in peace from outside . . . everyone will enjoy the free and glorious life.'[130] But belying Rebecca's public praise for the Soviet Union were her private doubts about the new regime. Accompanying her and Sidney in Moscow in 1928 was Roux, whose recollections of their visit – and of Rebecca's impressions – were quite different:

> Mrs Bunting found the social atmosphere at the Sixth Congress very different from that of the Fourth Congress in 1922. Then there had been a spirit of comradeship; comrades had exchanged news about conditions in their different countries. They had all been friends together, members of one big revolutionary movement. But now there were numerous factions and cliques, each trying to curry favour with the powers at top, each with its own axe to grind. Comrades were afraid to discuss things openly for fear of being accused of political deviations.[131]

The uneasy atmosphere at the Sixth Congress portended a seismic transition in the fortunes of the CPSA. Up until that moment, the Comintern had left the South African party to proceed with relatively little interference from Moscow; but with the adoption of the Native Republic thesis at the Congress, that was to change.[132] Drafted by Bukharin and James La Guma in 1927, the Native Republic thesis was passed in Moscow in October 1928, despite initial opposition from Bunting and others, and endorsed as the CPSA's official policy in Johannesburg in late December of the same year. The Native Republic slogan proclaimed '"an independent Native Republic, as a stage towards a workers' and peasants' government"', which was interpreted as '[black] majority rule as a stage towards socialism'.[133] Hotly debated in South Africa, with La Guma, Douglas and Molly Wolton and Mofutsanyana in favour of the thesis, and Bunting, Thibedi and Makabeni opposed to it, the Native Republic thesis was ultimately adopted, with the authority of the Comintern decisive in determining the result.

The repercussions of the Native Republic thesis were still reverberating in South Africa, when a second Comintern imprimatur designated 'the New Line' was promulgated in 1930. Repudiating the cross-class African coalition demanded by the Native Republic thesis, the New Line required instead the uncompromising struggle of the African working class against social democracy and its capitalist sponsors.[134] The results were disastrous, with endless splits, expulsions and defections. Martin Legassick points out the ironies: 'expelled from the CPSA were both the leading proponent of the black republic, Jimmy La Guma (the first time in June 1929 and the second in October 1931), and the leading opponent, S. P. Bunting (in September 1931)'.[135] The consequences of Comintern interventions in this period are summarised by Allison Drew:

> The Native Republic thesis and the New Line were the first two experiences of direct Comintern intervention in the CPSA's affairs. Both indicated the pitfalls of applying policies derived overseas to South Africa. The Native Republic thesis reoriented the CPSA away from a primarily class-based approach towards a mechanical view of the relationship between national liberation and socialism. The New Line depleted the Party's membership and set the black trade union movement back several years. From a claimed peak of almost 3,000 [mostly black] members in early 1929, by April 1931 the Party's membership had plummeted to 100 [mostly white members] . . . The Comintern's role in the CPSA led to the stifling of discussion and debate, which was replaced by the correct interpretation of dogma, by the use of personal abuse against dissenting voices and by the expulsion of dissidents.[136]

The casualties of the Comintern's policies were not limited to those (like Bunting and La Guma) who were expelled; those enforcing the Comintern diktats were themselves ultimately held responsible for the devastation they wrought, and were punished. The pre-eminent example was the Latvian communist Lazar Bach (1906–1941), who together with the Woltons engineered many of the expulsions. Bach was summoned to Moscow to explain the falling numbers of CPSA members, and died in a gulag. The New Line itself was superseded in 1935 by the Popular Front strategy, which required the CPSA (and all Communist parties affiliated to the Comintern) to seek once again alliances with nationalist political organisations.

As the CPSA mutated in the late 1920s under Comintern influence, so too did the language of its publications. The humanist appeals of Jones and Bunting diminished; biblical and literary allusions all but disappeared; and a new language fusing progressive modernising rhetoric and what Roux called 'Imprecor language, the formal phraseology of the doctrinaire Communist'[137] became hegemonic. Whereas the biblical language of Gumede and Jones scripted the journey of black South Africans from the racist hell of settler-colonial rule to a socialist heaven, and the literary language of Bunting and Roux anticipated workers 'deaf and blind' being enlightened by the 'sound and rumour' of socialism, Imprecor language encoded a secular Marxist-Leninist *telos* from exploitation under feudalism and then capitalism to the dictatorship of the proletariat.

Under the editorial leadership of Douglas and Molly Wolton and Bach, *Umsebenzi* transmitted in content and register the Comintern's messages of imminent socialist victory. For example, one front-page article was headed 'Theses of the twelfth plenum'; subtitled 'The development of the revolutionary upsurge and the preparation for the struggle for the dictatorship of the proletariat'; and opened with the sentence, 'To the extent that the economic policy of monopolist capital is adapted to the special conditions and difficulties of the economic crisis, social democracy adapts ideology to the requirements of the crisis policy of the financial oligarchy.'[138] Such language repelled readers, and sales of *Umsebenzi* plunged. According to Roux, Wolton's facility with Comintern clichés led the African members of the CPSA to call him 'Deepening Economic Crisis' (behind his back), and according to Kotane, Bach 'spoke a language none of us understood, nor were some of his actions and political theses understood by anyone in South Africa, not even by himself!'.[139] For the veteran anarchist/socialist, Wilfrid Harrison (1871–1947), it was not only the inaccessible Imprecor language that drove away black members from the party; the abstract blueprints of a socialist future seemed remote from workers' everyday concerns. In the idiom of his generation of white socialists, Harrison observed:

> Native psychology is not capable of visualising Utopian schemes that may in the dim future mean emancipation. The pass laws, the poll tax and the compound system were still some of his many grievances, and naturally he thought that if the Communists could do so much in the future why not relieve him of such burdens now.[140]

Harrison's views on the limited capacity of 'native psychology' to understand 'Utopian schemes' bear the imprint of colonial ideology, but he himself had little patience with such schemes, as he complained bitterly about Russia 'sending us slogans and delegating to us leaders who knew very little'.[141] Although from a different generation and aligned to a different faction within the CPSA, Kotane agreed with Harrison's criticisms: the party's senior members, he argued, 'subordinate South Africa in the interests of Europe', and its black constituency are alienated by over-theoretical projections –'Socialism and proletarian revolution to our rural population (the majority) is but a vague expression which sounds more as a dream than a reality.'[142] At odds in other respects, Harrison and Kotane were united in the view that the Comintern programmes failed to appeal to black South Africans.

In contrast to the Woltons' and Bach's faithful regurgitation of Comintern discourse, Roux chafed against 'the heavy Imprecor-style explanations in *Umsebenzi*',[143] and attempted to develop creative ways of translating Marxist vocabulary into

African languages. The challenge was provoked in the first instance by the discovery that African-language translators at CPSA meeting were rendering 'capitalist' as 'ma-Juda', as Africans thought of 'capitalism in terms of his experience with a local Jewish shopkeeper'.[144] With the help of Josiah Ngedlane, Roux addressed this specific problem by translating capitalist into the Xhosa 'word *ungxowankulu* which meant literally "the man with the big bag"'.[145] In a series of short didactic pieces in *Umsebenzi*, Roux and Ngedlane introduced Marxist terms in Xhosa, Zulu and Sotho, and their efforts were subsequently summarised in an academic article by I. L. Sneguireff in the Moscow-based journal *Africana*. Adopting an appropriately materialist method of analysis, Sneguireff argues that before the influx of Europeans, Southern African 'tribes' were 'at the stage of a fully developed clan society, with a vocabulary reflecting the concepts of this particular historic stage of social development'.[146] With the transformation of pre-colonial African society under colonialism, new words were coined to reflect 'the new social relations of capitalism and capitalist oppression [and] terms reflecting the struggle against capitalist slavery led by the heroic class, the proletariat'.[147] Despite the aspiration to forge a vocabulary of resistance, or even more ambitiously, to provide a language giving expression to the socialist vision of a post-capitalist world, the overwhelming number of translated terms listed by Roux and Ngedlane in *Umsebenzi* are concerned with the everyday here-and-now of black workers' experiences: *imali yamakanda* (Zulu for 'tax'), *ukubala* (Xhosa for 'to write'), *ibandhla* (Zulu for 'political party'), and so on.[148] Roux conceded that his efforts at translating Marxism into African languages remained embryonic, admitting 'as with so many things in my life I did not carry it through',[149] and Sneguireff concluded in a similarly downbeat fashion that 'things are not well at the present day regarding new economic and social terminology'.[150]

Roux and Ngedlane's efforts to translate Marxist terms into the African languages of South Africa were exceptional, however, as the combination of Imprecor prose and Comintern policy in the CPSA's newspaper was repeated in academic studies too, most notably in the Moscow-published *Forced Labour in Colonial Africa* (1933). Co-authored by Albert Nzula, Ivan Potekhin, Aleksander Zusmanovich, *Forced Labour* surveys the history of imperialism in Africa, analysing the political economies of individual African nations. Robin Cohen, the editor of the English translation, argues persuasively that in the division of labour between the three young writers, Nzula wrote the chapters on South Africa. The influence of Soviet thought is ubiquitous, as it is assumed that Czarist Russia and twentieth-century South Africa are alike in most essentials. First, both nations have agricultural economies reliant on cheap labour. That abundant cheap labour slows the introduction of machinery is established by juxtaposing a white South African farmer's comments on the relatively few tractors on South African farms and a quotation from Lenin confirming that '"low wages are one of the main obstacles to the introduction of machinery"'.[151] Secondly, both nations are structured in the interests of exploitative landlords. The creation of forced black labour by South Africa's Native Servant Contract Act is likened to the modes of exploitation in Czarist Russia: 'What, one may ask, is the difference between this draconian law and the "good old days" of the Russian landowner Saltychikha?'[152] Thirdly, both nations are made up of many different races, nations and tribes, and the ruling elites manipulate their differences in order to exploit all workers. The point echoes an argument repeated over and over in the pages of *Umsebenzi*:

> The bosses of this country set race against race; for they know that while workers are disunited capitalists will always be able to make money out of them. The old Russia of the Czars also had its different races, of different colours and religions, of different degrees of culture and civilisation. And in old Russia these different peoples were continually fighting and quarrelling with each other. It suited the Czar and the big landlords and rich men to keep the people divided so that they could be more easily exploited. And so Russia was a land of racial strife and hatred like our present day South Africa.[153]

How to defeat such regimes and win the struggle for freedom? The answers provided by Nzula follow closely the Comintern script, as he gives uncritical support to the Native Republic thesis throughout *Forced Labour*. He notes examples of white working-class racism, and embraces the need to prioritise the Native Republic: 'Clearly, one cannot involve black and white miners in a united front and joint struggle against the capitalists with prejudices of this nature.'[154] Dismissing the strategy of building a community of black and white workers in favour of a cross-class alliance of black South Africans, he argues, 'Such a mistaken view contradicts the line of the Comintern and the Profintern on this question. The need for systematic work within reformist and national-reformist [black] organizations must be explained to all politically conscious workers.'[155] Similar support is evident in Nzula's concluding assessment of the Dingaan's Day protests in 1929 and 1930, where he argues that the result of police killings has been African workers 'realizing that the only way out of imperialist bondage and economic misery is the revolutionary way out – a South African Black Republic as a stage towards a Workers' and Peasants' Republic'.[156]

ENEMIES OF FREEDOM

An important element in the Soviet-inspired critique of South African state capitalism was the identification of the many enemies of the workers' struggle. The racist state, frequently represented by the Nazi-sympathising Minister of Justice Oswald Pirow, and British and English South African capital, symbolised by the figure of 'Hoggenheimer', were constant targets for vituperation. An *Umsebenzi* cartoon of 1934 (Figure 3.6) lampoons both factions simultaneously, with an article by Roux sub-titled 'Clear Hoggenheimer out!' and a cartoon with the caption 'Tata amapasi ako asiwafuni' [Hurry along; we don't want your support], and an image of a black warrior carrying a shield engraved with the word 'Umsebenzi' and a spear with the initials C. P. pursuing a fat white figure in a suit with the words 'Pirow' and 'Pass Laws' on his jacket. Roux's article concludes by insisting upon the shared interests of white English capital and white Afrikaner republicanism, and upon the common interests of black and white workers in opposing them: 'Let us clear Hoggenheimer

Figure 3.6 Cartoon by Edward Roux, 'Tata amapasi ako asiwafuni', *Umsebenzi*, 15 December 1934.

out. And when we clear them out we shall also clear out the sjambok and pass law, colour bar and curfew regulations. We shall do away with poor-blackism as well as poor-whiteism. We shall build a Soviet South Africa, a workers and peasants republic.'[157]

A second group singled out for insult were black leaders accused of colluding with white rule. The standard term of derision was 'good boys', and the insult was embellished and hurled with great frequency. Nzula quotes and derides Professor D. D. T. Jabavu's words '"The natives love their British masters (and curse the Boers), and they are happy to live under the Union Jack,"' and proceeds to describe him and other such black reformist leaders as 'black lackeys' and 'native lickspittles'.[158] Kotane singles out H. Selby Msimang, 'an employee of the Chamber of Mines, one of the lackeys of the capitalist class, who has the audacity to put into his propaganda circulars, "Beware the Communist danger – its danger to the race is more than Pirow's fiendish laws"'.[159] And an unsigned front-page article in *Umsebenzi* quoted the ANC leader Pixley K. Seme praising Hertzog as '"a statesman who laid the foundation of a great temple of justice, peace and goodwill for all peoples of our country irrespective of race or colour"', and then asked, 'How can a person who licks the boots of this bloody imperialist robber so shamelessly be a leader of an oppressed people against imperialism?'[160] Such vituperation had to be silently forgotten (rather than explicitly retracted) when the Comintern switched from the New Line of 1930 to the Popular Front Line of 1935, as the latter demanded a cross-class alliance of all Africans.

The third group of enemies of socialism were those accused of deviating from the Comintern line. Nzula refers on several occasions to those expelled from the CPSA after 1928, describing his former comrades as 'the right, opportunistic leadership in the Communist Party', and he attributes the failure of the CPSA to influence the black trade union movement in the 1920s to 'the then opportunistic, chauvinistic character of its leadership in the person of Bunting and others, now expelled from the Party'.[161] The pages of *The South African Worker/Umsebenzi* were even more vituperative, publishing a steady barrage of articles attacking the alleged traitors to the cause. When Manuel Lopes criticised the Native Republic thesis, suggesting it resembled Marcus Garvey's 'Back to Africa' slogan, John Gomas accused him of failing 'to make himself conversant with Lenin's views on the national question', and of succumbing to the false doctrine of Trotskyism, which 'is like a dustbin full of all sorts of political rubbish right and "left" wing thrown out from the Communist parties'.[162] The most vicious attacks were directed at Bunting, who had initially queried the Native Republic thesis but soon after acquiesced with the Comintern line.[163] He stood accused of 'revealing a complete lack of understanding of this line'; of demonstrating 'a fundamental lack of faith in the Native masses [and a] liberal, muddled-headed, petty-bourgeois outlook'; of exhibiting the attitudes of 'a bourgeois liberal or social democrat . . . still to acquire a Leninist outlook'; and of attempting 'to cover up his white chauvinism by revolutionary phrases'.[164] Bunting's expulsion from the party was announced on 4 September 1931, along with 'Comrade W. H. Andrews', 'Comrade C. Tyler', 'Comrade E. S. Sachs', 'Comrade F. Glass' and 'Comrade B. Weinbren'. Their offences are listed as: 'passivity, opportunism and a complete inability to correctly estimate the changing situation which confronts the toiling masses'; 'the complete neglect and sabotage of red trade unions'; and 'hostile and counter-revolutionary acts aligning with Social Fascist forces against the revolutionary movement'.[165] The attacks on Bunting culminated in accusations that he had aligned himself with Trotsky:

> Trotsky and his fellow renegades launch ever more vicious attacks against the Soviet Union and clamour for world imperialism to speed up its military preparations to attack the U. S. S. R. – the Fatherland of the working class and its toilers. Likewise Bunting and his handful of disciples in their impotent way join in slandering the Unions of Socialist Soviet Republics, and call for the blood of the heroic workers and peasants, the Socialist builders of the First Workers' Republic.[166]

CPSA rhetoric thus established an opposition between a virtuous party of the workers set against a coalition made up of the white Afrikaner state, white English capital, black reformist leaders, ex-comrades out of step with the party line and Trotskyists.

THE DICTATORSHIP OF THE PROLETARIAT

Whereas South African Communists borrowing from the Bible promised a new Jerusalem, Heaven or the Holy Grail, and those quoting the poets promised 'the golden years return' or a world where workers 'shall eat of the harvest and wax fat', those using the language of the Comintern promised either the abstract utopia of the dictatorship of the proletariat or the concrete template of the USSR. Like Marx, certain early South African socialists were opposed to laying down a fixed route to the socialist future. Harrison, for example, mocked the stock image of workers overcoming 'street barricades and civil turmoil in the final struggle, with the final march to the Guildhall with the red flag unfurled and the chief heroic revolutionary proclaiming the Social Revolution'.[167] But attitudes like Harrison's became increasingly heterodox, as the CPSA adopted increasingly rigid visions of the future. At their seventh annual conference in January 1929, for example, the programme identified the ultimate destination as:

> the final abolition and domination of class by class, of man by man, the final stage of the Social Revolution for the establishment of Socialism under which all men shall be socially, economically and politically free to share alike in the fruits of their joint labour, with equal opportunity and equal access to all the comforts of life.[168]

Adapting this general prognosis of a socialist future to South Africa, with its class conflicts reinforced by racial divides, the programme argues that 'race emancipation and class emancipation tend to coincide. Hence the conception and realisation of native rule merges into that of the Workers' and Peasants' Republic, non-imperialist, non-capitalist, non-racialist, classless and in effect Socialist'.[169] Rather than an image of the workers' triumphant march and the red flag unfurled in victory, the CPSA provides the image of a destination featuring a combination of positive (social/economic/political) freedoms and equalities (of access to opportunity and the comforts of life), and negative freedoms – from all existing class and racial oppressions (freedom from imperialism, capitalism, racism and class oppression). With the same vigour that the now-spurned Bunting had acclaimed the Red Square parades in 1922, the CPSA's new leaders at the end of the decade looked forward to a Soviet-inflected 'dictatorship of the proletariat'.[170]

Expositions of the abstract rights and freedoms guaranteed by the dictatorship of the proletariat were rare, however, with breathless descriptions of the Soviet Union, the model of Communist progress, far more frequent. Variations on the paragraph below from *Forced Labour* were repeated endlessly in the ISL/CPSA newspapers:

> The history of Russia since the epochal event has been one triumphant march. Formerly oppressed nationalities are enjoying complete freedom and are recording with every day the new achievements in the spheres of economic, cultural and social progress. Racial discrimination and oppression

have been completely wiped out, and isolated manifestations of chauvinism by counter-revolutionaries are dealt with in a merciless and ruthless manner by the Workers State. The gigantic achievements of socialist construction in the Soviet Union are in striking contrast to the decay and disintegration in the capitalist and colonial world, arousing the fury and hatred of the capitalist class. Therefore the Negro workers and toiling peasants who find inspiration in the achievements of the Russian workers and peasants must put forward in the front rank the slogan: 'Defend the Soviet Union, the fatherland of all toilers.'[171]

The absence of racial discrimination in the USSR is given particular prominence. Specific contrasts were enumerated, with one article describing first how in South Africa a court acquitted 'a European farmer who had shot and killed a Native for the "crime" of picking wild date leaves on a farm', and then how a European engineer who had hit a Negro worker in Stalingrad had been sentenced to ten years in prison, concluding 'The Soviet power will not, and does not, tolerate any form of national or social prejudice or chauvinism such as sjambokking or murder of natives'.[172] The egalitarian treatment of non-Russian races in the USSR is praised – 'Backward people (Eskimo, Kirghiz, etc.) are not kept ignorant, colour-barred, exploited, enslaved, as the Bantu in South Africa' – and this functions as inspiration for South Africa's oppressed races: 'our bosses do not want us to know what has happened in Russia [but] when we know the truth nothing will stop us from doing what the Russian workers have done and making a Soviet Africa'.[173]

CONCLUSION

The November 1930 issue of *Umsebenzi* republished an extract from an article by Stalin entitled 'Former "backward races" marching to socialism'. Stalin concludes with the confident prescription that 'only under the conditions of the development of national cultures will it be possible really to initiate the backward nationalities into socialist construction'.[174] Six months later, a lead article echoed Stalin's message, reassuring readers that their liberation was on schedule. The crises besetting the capitalist West are diagnosed: 'The rapidly deepening economic crisis throughout the world is primarily an agrarian crisis, sweeping millions and millions of Farmers and Peasants into a vortex of poverty, starvation and misery.'[175] But whereas in the past, South Africa's poor had lacked the resources to resist such destructive economic forces, the CPSA was now on hand to guide them:

> [The CPSA] declares that the land hunger of the masses of the farming people, Black, White and Coloured, calls for joint action for the confiscation of the land of the rich farmers and its redistribution amongst the mass of the people. It calls for the setting up of a republic, independent of British Imperialism in which the democratic rights of full equality shall be established for all people without regard to race or colour, under the slogan of 'a South African Native Republic as a stage towards a Workers and Peasants Republic with full and

equal rights for all National Minorities'. The Communist Party of South Africa will lead the fight of the workers, employed and unemployed, organised and unorganised, of Poor Farmers and Peasants, irrespective of race or colour, in struggle against the Imperialist system of exploitation and for the freedom and liberation of all peoples.[176]

Stalin's plan 'to initiate the backward nationalities into socialist construction', faithfully applied by the CPSA to South Africa, contrasts sharply with Marx's determination not to 'write recipes for the cook-books of the future', with Engels's conviction that socialism must always be more than 'an accidental discovery of this or that ingenious brain', and indeed with David Ivon Jones's conviction that 'the message of liberty shall go forth . . . from the unknown fishermen and unpaid working people'. Within fifteen years of the Russian Revolution, Marxist dreams of freedom for Southern Africa had been translated into the language of Imprecor, and had turned into an African version of the Soviet narrative of 'backward nationalities' led by the Communist Party towards 'the dictatorship of the proletariat'.

In the dark times of 1920s South Africa, the Communist dream of freedom challenged the liberal-democratic dream expressed in the ANC's 1923 Bill of Rights, Lamont's *South Africa in Mars* and Mqhayi's *U-Don Jadu*. It rejected an economy based upon a reformed version of capitalism in favour of one based upon the redistribution of land and wealth, and working-class ownership of the means of production. In political terms, however, the CPSA's position was more equivocal, as it paid lip service to the slogans of international solidarity, while simultaneously endorsing the exclusive nationalism required by Stalin's policy of 'socialism in one country' and its South African derivative, the Native Republic thesis. The many defeats and reverses suffered by the CPSA in the 1920s – both self-inflicted and inflicted by the state and the employers – left deep scars. By the end of the decade, Communist dreams of freedom had mutated into something quite different. The optimism inspired by 1917 failed to survive 'the rapidly deepening economic crisis', the racist laws from Pretoria and the inflexible left imperialism from Moscow, with the result that by 1930 the Soviet dream of freedom was fatally compromised by the nightmare shadow of the gulag.

4 Anti-Stalinist Dreams of Freedom

INTRODUCTION

The early 1930s were haunted by defeat, although those committed to the ICU and the CPSA still clung to their dreams of freedom. Glossing over the ICU's fragmentation and collapse, Kadalie in 1936 declared, '"Nothing could check the forward march of the Natives,"'[1] and a decade later, was still arguing that 'the advent of the ICU was like a beacon of light on the horizon'.[2] Those loyal to the CPSA also continued expressing optimism. In 1932, a report in *Umsebenzi* concluded that '[t]he CP aims at . . . the abolition of all exploitation of man by man and the building of a socialist society in South Africa',[3] and in 1936, John Gomas re-emphasised the CPSA's confidence in the triumphant outcome of 'the struggle for national liberation'.[4] Notwithstanding these brave words, police arrests and sectarian dissensions took their toll, as the CPSA ceased publishing its magazine in 1938, its Johannesburg branch collapsed, and only thirty members remained in Cape Town.[5]

Beyond the shrinking core of ICU and CPSA members, others looked elsewhere to nourish their dreams of liberating South Africa's masses. William Thibedi, an expelled member of the CPSA and experienced trade unionist, wrote to Leon Trotsky in August 1932 to ask for help in the search for an alternative socialist vision of freedom. He asked Trotsky for 'more literature of the left opposition because the Stalinist bureaucrats have for some years been hiding such literature to be known by the African Negro workers'.[6] From the 1930s onwards, Thibedi was joined by other South African activist-intellectuals who sought guidance from Trotsky directly and from his writings in an effort both to develop political strategies effective in their struggles against the state and capital, and in order to avoid the pitfalls of the ICU's populism and the CPSA's Stalinism. The reception, circulation and mutation of Trotsky's thought in South Africa from the 1930s to 1950s is the focus of this chapter – the critiques of liberalism, nationalism and private poverty, and the conception of literature as critique and utopia.

TROTSKYISM IN SOUTH AFRICA

No substantial Trotskyist party ever survived in South Africa; rather, Trotskyist ideas were expressed in the publications of several short-lived radical organisations and in the writings of the individuals connected with them. His ideas were first introduced in Johannesburg in 1930 by the ex-CPSA member Frank Glass, who owned a left-wing bookshop. When Glass left the country for China, he handed over the bookshop to his wife, Fanny Klenerman, who reopened it as Vanguard Books in July 1931. Looking back, Klenerman recalled the impact of reading Trotsky in Johannesburg:

> In the early stages of my bookselling career I managed to read about a publication ... called *The Militant* [and] began to import this newspaper [and] sell it to a small coterie of people. As a result, I became interested in a book published by Trotsky called *The Real Situation in Russia* ... I read it with great concern and great interest, and I began to think that not only was the USSR not practising Socialism or Communism, but that it was an increasingly backward country with a bureaucracy swelling up with power. It seemed to me a coterie of officials enjoyed new privileges, not in any way experienced by the ordinary workers of the country. The more I read about Russia, the more worried I became about what was happening there, and I realised that this was no revolution, it was a counter revolution ... I could not find a single aspect of the state concerned with improvement of workers' wages or conditions. It was yet another bureaucratic machine created only as an oppressive force against workers and dissident intellectuals.[7]

Inspired by Trotsky's critique of the Soviet Union, Klenerman and her Johannesburg comrades hoped 'to organise workers to accept change in society, and to resist the Communist alternative. We did get some worker members ... But this movement did not thrive. We did not attract large crowds to join us'.[8] At the same time, Thibedi formed the Communist League of Africa, which had (he claimed) fifty African members in the Transvaal, and published one issue of its magazine, *Maraphanga*. The Communist League of Africa was succeeded two years later by the Bolshevist Leninist League, with Thibedi prominent. In 1935, the Rand-based Bolshevist Leninist League merged with the Cape-based CLSA/Lenin Club to form the Workers' Party. Unsuccessful in building a mass-based party, the Johannesburg Trotskyists made greater inroads via Thibedi and Max Gordon's trade union efforts with African workers. The African Mine Workers Union was resuscitated; Gordon organised the Laundry Workers Union; a newspaper *Umlilo Mollo* (*Flame*) appeared for a few issues; and Gordon established the Joint Committee of African Trade Unions, a federation with affiliates from several industries.[9]

The first explicitly anti-Stalinist socialist organisation in Cape Town was the International Socialist Club, which came together in 1931. The US Trotskyist magazine *The Militant* was circulated; individual members pursued propaganda work; and a reading group called the Marxist International League was established.

Superseding the International Socialist Club was the Lenin Club, which amalgamated the International Socialist Club and the Marxist International League, organising a socialist Sunday school, rallies and public lectures. In early 1935, the Lenin Club expanded further to form the Communist League of South Africa (CLSA), but soon after, a faction split off to form the Workers' Party of South Africa (WPSA). The remaining members of the CLSA/Lenin Club continued running lectures and discussions, and published their own magazine *Workers Voice* (1935–6). The new WPSA established the Spartacus Club as a rival to the Lenin Club, and published *The Spark* (1935–9) under the editorship of Clare Goodlatte (1866–1942). Both Cape-based Trotskyist groups prioritised propaganda efforts, with the CLSA (renamed first the Workers' Party, and then the Fourth International of South Africa – FIOSA) organising events through the Lenin Club and *Workers Voice*, and the WPSA doing likewise through the Spartacus Club and *Spark*. Even the CPSA historian Roux praised the efforts of the two groups, noting that 'lectures and debates at the Lenin Club drew large audiences', that the *Spark* 'published a number of interesting articles and contributed a searching analysis of South African conditions in terms of Bolshevik theory', and that the Spartacists produced propagandistic plays which 'merited wider audiences, never achieved publicity, being performed only before small and rather select audiences'.[10] Roux distinguished between the audiences of the two groups: 'most of the "intellectuals", university people and so on, went to the Spartacist Club, while the others who wanted to hold street corner meetings stayed with the Lenin Club'.[11]

With the decision of the Workers' Party to disband and go underground in 1939, its members and other activist-intellectuals of the left opposition pursued their political commitments within the larger broad-front organisations that emerged in the years immediately before the Second World War. Despite not being a founder member of the National Liberation League (NLL) in December 1935, Goolam Gool (1904–1962) exerted a significant influence through its magazine the *Liberator*, contesting the CPSA-inclined leadership of Cissie Gool (1897–1963), John Gomas and James La Guma. I. B. Tabata was one of the guiding spirits of the All African Convention (AAC), which assembled for the first time on 15–18 December 1935 with 400 delegates from across the country, and briefly promised an effective coalition of black organisations united against the segregationist state. Goolam Gool was again to the fore in establishing in 1937 the New Era Fellowship (NEF), which provided a forum for political and cultural debate in District Six.[12] And despite conceding the leadership of the Non-European United Front (NEUF) to CPSA 'Popular Frontists' in 1938, Gool also remained prominent in NEUF politicking, which in March 1939 culminated in 20,000 supporters marching to parliament to protest against residential segregation. By the onset of the Second World War, however, these black united-front organisations – the NLL, the AAC and the NEUF – had lost impetus, as they focused increasingly on electoral politics, and passed radical resolutions unsupported by mass political or trade union action.

The war years provided fresh opportunities for left opposition figures to intervene in political developments. Ben Kies played a leading role in the coloured Teachers' League of South Africa (TLSA), the NEF and the Anti-CAD Movement, which represented an alliance of coloured organisations formed to oppose the state's latest instrument for enforcing segregation, the Coloured Affairs Council/Department (CAC/CAD). Together with Tabata, Dora Taylor, Leo Sihlali (1915–1989), Goolam Gool, A. C. Jordan (1908–1968) and other anti-ANC and anti-CPSA activists, Kies found a new political home in the Non-European Unity Movement (NEUM), which was formed in 1943 in the wake of the AAC's fragmentation. The NEUM was conceived as a federal structure linking the numerous sectional organisations. The two biggest affiliates at its outset were the AAC (representing black organisations) and the Anti-CAD (representing coloured organisations), and they were joined by *inter alia* the TLSA, the NEF, the African People's Organisation (APO), Society of Young Africa (SOYA) and the Transvaal African Teachers Association (TATA).[13] These political organisations, informal reading groups, newspapers and magazines, and public lectures together constituted a 'counterpublic sphere',[14] a political-intellectual milieu that enabled the propagation of radical ideas. The independent magazine *Trek* provided Taylor with a forum for her literary and political journalism,[15] and Kies reached popular audiences both through his polemics for the Anti-CAD's news-sheet *The Bulletin*, and in his regular column under the pseudonym 'Fandum' for the mainstream Cape newspaper *The Sun*.

In the 1950s, the NEUM continued to provide a congenial space for anti-Stalinist intellectual-activists, with a younger generation, including Livingstone Mqotsi (1921–2009), Baruch Hirson (1921–19199), Hosea Jaffe (1921–2014) and Neville Alexander (1936–2012), reinforcing but also contesting the efforts of their older comrades.[16] Under the broad auspices of the NEUM, three influential books were published, namely *The Awakening of a People* (1950) by I. B. Tabata, *The Role of the Missionaries in Conquest* (1952) by Taylor (under the pseudonym of Nosipho Majeke) and *Three Hundred Years* (1952) by Hosea Jaffe (under the pseudonym Mnguni). At least as significant were the many more ephemeral publications – the feature articles in sympathetic newspapers and magazines like *The Torch* (1946–63), *Ikhwesi Lomso* (*The Morning Star*) (1958–60), the TLSA's *Educational Journal* (1929–71) and *The Citizen* (1956–8); the lectures at the non-aligned Forum Club, which were published in its journal *Discussion* (1951–2); and occasional pamphlets, like *The Boycott as a Weapon of Struggle* (1952) by Tabata, *Jan van Riebeeck: His Place in South African History* (1952) by Kenneth Jordaan (1924–1988) and *The Contribution of Non-European Peoples to World Civilisation* (1953) by Kies.[17] Many of these publications first appeared anonymously or under pseudonyms, a convention motivated not only by the need to protect individual writers from the attentions of the police, but also by a commitment to the collective ownership of the ideas they expressed. In 1958, the NEUM split, with the two main factions – the one broadly associated with the AAC and the other with the Anti-CAD – parting ways in order to form two new organisations.

BEYOND LIBERAL FREEDOMS

Trotsky's early writings express dreams of a socialist freedom that would exceed the bourgeois liberties achieved by the Jacobins in the French Revolution. In *Our Political Tasks* (1904), he argued that Russia's revolutionaries could gain the freedom denied to France's revolutionaries if the Jacobins' blind spots were apprehended: 'The Jacobins were utopians ... They wanted an egalitarian republic based on private property; a republic of reason and virtue in the framework of the exploitation of one class by another. They straddled a gigantic contradiction and called the blade of the guillotine to their aid.'[18] Close in spirit to Marx's writings of the 1840s, Trotsky spells out the contradictions that entrapped the Jacobins – egalitarian republicanism against private property; the utopian dream of rule by reason against the economic exploitation of the masses; and the securing of freedom by state violence – arguing that Russia's revolutionaries would supersede the Jacobins by embracing the agency of the proletariat. He claims that 'what separates us from the Jacobins [is] *our attitude towards the elemental social forces, and therefore towards the future, [which] is one of revolutionary confidence* [italics in original]', and he concludes with the stark choice: 'Either, you end up making your theoretical "bridge" between bourgeois-revolutionary democracy (Jacobinism) and proletarian democracy ... or you give up the practice which leads you into such a theoretical attack. Either Jacobinism, or proletarian socialism!'[19] In an essay written just before the October revolution, Trotsky once again drew an impenetrable line between the liberal bourgeoisie and the socialist proletariat: 'Whoever thinks about the experiences of 1905 ... must see how utterly lifeless and pitiful are the hopes ... for revolutionary co-operation between the proletariat and the liberal bourgeoisie.'[20] To hold out any such hopes, Trotsky concludes, is to ignore the lessons of 1905, which demonstrated dreams of 'co-operation between capital and labour [to be] a miserable Utopia'.[21]

In adopting Trotsky's critique of bourgeois freedom, South Africa's left opposition intellectuals directed their criticisms at South African and international targets alike. Their writings in all cases were animated by a drive to expose the tensions between bourgeois liberty (politics) and capitalist exploitation (economics), and to bridge the gulf between liberal/bourgeois ('Jacobin') freedom and proletarian democracy. Trotsky's analysis of liberalism as the ideology legitimising bourgeois class interest in the Soviet Union was modified in order to explain South African liberalism. Kies applied Trotsky's critique to South Africa, identifying liberal ideology with the interests of South Africa's ruling class, arguing that reformist African leaders had been duped by the promise of liberal freedoms:

> Our reformist leaders were always deeply attached to the Liberal ... [We] are finding them all out, these liberals, past and present, whom our reformist leaders used to trust so pathetically! We have also seen through the United Party puppet, the 'Liberal' Press ... which helped to dupe the Africans in 1935–36 ... These are the agents and lackeys of the ruling class who blindfolded our reformist leadership for fifty years and more.[22]

Such attacks on African leaders seduced by liberalism were repeated in the NEUM's newspaper *The Torch*. For example, after a 1948 report by the Institute of Race Relations (IRR) bemoaning the fall-off in its African membership, a lead article declared that 'political helotry, economic enslavement, injustice, and inequality cannot be glossed over by the sugar-coating ... of the liberals'.[23] Whereas the decline in African membership of the IRR 'fills us with hope that the Non-Europeans ... have broken with their leader-goats and that we are at the dawn of liberation, the liberals are filled with fear'.[24]

Following a meeting with the IRR in Cape Town, Tabata reflected bitterly upon what he perceived as the duplicity of its leading members. His reflections begin with an extended metaphor comparing liberalism to a poison contaminating the pristine African landscape:

The liberals are a poison, an insidious poison that soaks through the surface of the earth and poisons the very roots of young plants. Imagine a field of young green mealies growing out of rich black soil in a valley surrounded by mountains whose stones are barely visible through the vegetation that covers the mountain sides; with springs only known because of its music that is made by the water running over the falls, and its crickets singing near it at night. Think of the young mealies bursting out of this virgin soil, green and beautiful with the freshness of young life; think of this all suddenly strangled with vitriolic poison that scorches its very roots, making it shrivel up even as it is being born. When you have imagined all this, you will have understood the effects of liberalism on the great majority of S. A. society – the Blacks. Liberalism is the most deadly of all poisons on the race that is struggling to be born.[25]

Switching from liberalism as an ideology to its proponents, Tabata describes the IRR's members as 'viragos, bandits and savages with a veneer of civilisation', and concludes by singling out Hoernlé and J. D. Rheinnalt-Jones (1884–1953) for particular censure: 'They never say a harsh word against the Non-Europeans. They are like a poison that can enter your body without the slightest pain and make for your heart to stop.'[26] Tabata's metaphor of liberalism as a poison destroying African life indigenises the Marxist critique of liberal ideology, while at the same time suggesting that the serum of socialist critique is essential to inoculate the African race 'struggling to be born'.

Other left opposition intellectuals foregrounded the specific historical circumstances of South African liberalism. Goolam Gool turned to the nineteenth century to explain the origins of liberalism in South Africa, identifying the passing of Ordinance 50 in 1829 as the key event. By extending the protection of British law to '"all Hottentots and other free persons of colour residing in the Colony"',[27] Ordinance 50 appeared to exemplify a humane instance of liberal freedom in action. But for Gool, 'the important thing is to see the economic reason for this law, and to strip it of all its liberal, humanitarian and hypocritical meanings. We ... must see the basic economic needs of the law and not be misled and deceived by the sanctimonious phraseology'.[28] Gool employs Marxist categories to look beyond the legal words to the economics determining the law: '[I]t is not the Herrenvolk human consciousness and ingenuity that determines the economics, but the economics that determines Herrenvolk human consciousness and ingenuity.'[29] Like Tabata, Gool was preoccupied with the capacity of liberalism and its agents to deceive those opposing oppression and exploitation: '[O]ne of the primary functions of the liberals, most of whom have had a legal training ... is to hide the *real aims* of the Herrenvolk and to clothe the law in such language for the purpose of deceiving the oppressed leadership.'[30] The deception by the law-makers is reinforced by liberal historians, who assiduously occlude the fact that 'the change-over from the chattel slavery practised by the Trek-Boer republics to modern capitalism was a murderous process'.[31]

A more nuanced historical account of South African liberalism was provided by Arthur Davids, who distinguished between the liberalism that justified the primitive accumulation of the Chamber of Mines from the 1870s onwards, and the liberalism that legitimised the profiteering of the manufacturing industries from the early twentieth century. According to Davids, 'the two wings of "Liberalism" are merely the reflection in politics of the dichotomy in the two main spheres of imperialist exploitation – gold mining and industry'.[32] Despite apparent divergences, both varieties of liberalism agree that 'the struggle for democracy is something apart from the class struggle – the lie of supra-class politics'.[33] For the labour movement, the convergence of liberalism and capitalism dictated a non-collaborationist strategy of resistance: workers are 'entitled to take advantage of the progressive element in liberalism [but] cannot be permitted to mix the banners or make programmatic concessions'.[34] In a critique of Tabata's conception of liberalism, Davids argued further that it amounted to 'intellectual laziness' to anatomise liberalism as by definition toxic; liberalism – and opposition to liberalism – should always be historicised: 'When the unenlightened old Coloured and African leaders turned to liberalism, they were not utter and complete idiots. Seeing no possibility of a militant road, after a series of unrelieved defeats, it was not so asinine after all for them to prefer a liberal to a reactionary regime.'[35]

The left opposition's critique of liberalism extended well beyond its South African manifestations. Kies in particular railed against what he perceived as liberal hypocrisies on the world stage, returning repeatedly in his polemics in *The Bulletin* to attack the Atlantic Charter.[36] Arguing that the strategic liberalism of Smuts during the Second World War paralleled Roosevelt and Churchill's bogus liberalism embodied in the Atlantic Charter, Kies attacked the abuse of the word 'freedom':

> No doubt this veteran-son of Imperialism and servant of Finance-Capital [Smuts] has made invaluable contributions to the biggest fraud of our time: the Atlantic Charter ... What are these 4 Freedoms [promised by the Atlantic Charter]? The Freedom of Capitalism to exploit Labour. The Freedom to restrict production and create scarcity, wherever it is profitable for Capitalism. The Freedom to create monopolies, trusts, cartels, to corner markets and divide the world into spheres of influence. The Freedom to plunder the Colonies, to oppress and exploit the Colonial peoples in order to obtain raw materials for

their industries. These are the Four Freedoms which the Atlantic Charter seeks to preserve.[37]

In contrast to the ANC's positive attitude to the Atlantic Charter. Kies was hostile to those he thought had failed to realise that the Charter was a false dream peddled by the Allied leaders, those who 'still clung pathetically to the illusion that the Churchill–Roosevelt Atlantic Charter . . . would usher in the Four Freedoms for the oppressed'; rather, he observed, they ought to have discovered that 'while they may dream, the ruling class does not dream. The ruling class sells dreams'.[38]

Once the war ended, however, the capacity of cynically disseminated dreams of freedom like the Atlantic Charter to be turned against their progenitors became apparent to Kies. No longer describing the Charter simply as 'the biggest fraud of our time', he acknowledged that it had in certain contexts become a strategic resource the oppressed could mobilise to support anti-colonial resistance. Kies noted that 'the Chinese people took the Atlantic Charter seriously and started a Civil War', and further, that Smuts never anticipated that 'anyone in his own country would be so disloyal, if not treacherous, as to take his preamble to the Charter seriously', but that he had returned from the war to discover 'talk going on about war-promises and houses and jobs and African trade unions and fundamental human rights for all'.[39] The short-term strategic potential of the Atlantic Charter notwithstanding, Kies insisted upon a fundamental distinction between political leaders exploiting the Charter's words in their efforts to extract concessions from their rulers, on the one hand, and the collective struggle of the oppressed, on the other:

> Now we have never concealed from the people the fact that both the Atlantic Charter and the preamble to the World Charter are just plain frauds. But we must also make it quite clear that there is a fundamental distinction between those honest, working people who may not know anything about politics but who are turning the ideas contained in those documents into weapons for use in their direct fight for liberation, and on the other hand, those so-called political leaders who hope to obtain freedom by reminding the rulers of the words of the Charter.[40]

Kies concludes that the oppressed will never win their freedom 'by holding up the Atlantic Charter or chanting snatches of the preamble'; they will only prevail if 'they stand up and fight'.[41]

That liberal freedoms could function both as ruling class chimera and as anti-colonial resource was a contradiction Gool and other left opposition activist-intellectuals confronted both in developing their critique of racial capitalism and in scripting a political programme envisioning a socialist future. Although consistently critical of the ANC's *African Claims* and the CPSA's two-stage strategy of pursuing national liberation as a first step towards socialism, the left opposition generated their own foundational document demanding liberal freedoms as interim essentials in the journey to socialism – the NEUM's Ten-Point Programme of 1943. A version of Trotsky's 'theoretical bridge' between Jacobinism and proletarian democracy, the

NEUM's Programme expressed ten minimum demands for a democratic society: (1) the franchise; (2) *habeas corpus*; (3) equal access to education; (4) freedom of association; (5) freedom of movement; (6) abolition of racist statutes; (7) revision of land legislation; (8) reform of the criminal code; (9) redistribution through tax reform; and (10) reform of labour laws. The rationale for making the franchise the first demand, Gool explained, was because any state's refusal of political rights and freedoms directly served economic exploitation: 'the lower the oppressed are forced from the point of view of citizenship rights, the more they are exploited'.[42] Shifting from this abstract point to the specifics of South Africa, Gool argued, 'It is precisely because of the lack of the franchise that we are a landless, rightless people, deprived of the main source of our livelihood, cattle and sheep.'[43] To campaign effectively for the franchise, the pre-eminent liberal freedom, would therefore ultimately lead to the fundamental economic redistribution promised by proletarian democracy.

THE LIMITS OF ANTI-COLONIAL NATIONALISM

Not only was the struggle for the enfranchisement of black South Africans contingent upon political struggles being tied to economic liberation; political struggles in individual nation states also had to be understood as part of the global struggle against feudalism and capitalism. In a letter to Wycliffe Tsotsi in 1942, Tabata explained the limits of an exclusively national analytic:

> It is my conviction that it is impossible for a man to understand fully the problems in this country . . . without first understanding the World problem . . . Our problems here are fundamentally the same as those to be found in all backward colonial and semi-colonial countries elsewhere. The differences are small and superficial. For instance, the fact that the Russian peasants were white and our peasants are black does not remove the fact that our peasants here have the same tasks as the Russians prior to 1917. In fact the Russian Revolution was successful because there had been a French Revolution and a Paris Commune (1871) before it. The leaders of the Russian Revolution were for many years avowed students of the French Revolution, which they used as a model, but striving, successfully, to avoid the mistakes which the French Revolutionists made. Again, the fact that the Indian people have different customs and different religions does not remove the fact that they have identical tasks to perform in order to achieve liberation.[44]

At a conceptual level, South African history is thus connected to revolutions of the past in France and Russia, and to the contemporary anti-colonial struggles in India. The assumption is that because capitalism is an international system, opposition to it must be conceptualised on a global scale. The history of segregation in South Africa on this perspective is therefore but one specific version of imperial and colonial history. Kies, for example, argued that 'the world has been segregated into East and West, and both East and West have been segregated into nations and states . . .

in the interests of despotism'.⁴⁵ Enumerating German Nazism, Italian fascism, and American and Japanese imperialism, he added the South African ideology of 'white trustees and non-white child races'⁴⁶ as yet another instance of the global system of divide-and-rule that prevents the workers of the world from grasping their common interests. For Kies, the limits imposed by national consciousness made no sense in an international economic system: 'Through the development of the world market, production everywhere has taken on a cosmopolitan character; national self-sufficiency is a thing of the past and national seclusion, whether in material or intellectual production, is as difficult for South Africa as it is for the Llamas of Tibet.'⁴⁷

The end of the Second World War provided an opportunity to challenge the division of the world into contending races and nations. Capturing the optimism of the moment, the Non-European Unity Committee issued the pamphlet 'A Declaration to the Nations of the World' (1945), which stated, 'ten years of war and bloodshed have taught us that ... there can be no real peace when tyranny is eliminated in one continent but left undisturbed in another ... Hitlerite tyranny must be uprooted not only in Europe but also in South Africa and every corner of the globe'.⁴⁸ Not only 'Hitlerite tyranny', but also its accomplice global capitalism was identified as a target for international resistance, with *The Bulletin* warning that 'as long as the factories, and forests, lands and mines remain in the hands of the few, the world will always be at the mercy of the Finance Sharks and will continue to be plunged into economic depressions and mass unemployment and bloody slaughter every few years'.⁴⁹ Appeals for trans-national opposition to fascism and capitalism were accordingly frequent, with both European and colonial workers included as essential elements in an international anti-fascist, anti-capitalist alliance. During the War, *The Bulletin* had embraced European workers surviving under Nazi occupation, declaring 'our full moral support and our solidarity go out to Greek and Belgian people', and warning, 'Let us not make the blunder of thinking ... we are not directly affected by the battles in Greece and Belgium. They are OUR battles. A victory for the people in Europe will undermine the walls of Jericho in this country and make it easier to storm them.'⁵⁰ At the end of the war, *The Bulletin* argued that French and South African workers share a common enemy, likening the Non-European Unity Committee's 'Declaration' to 'Emile Zola's "I Accuse" in which he made an indictment not only against the military clique which had conspired against Dreyfuss, but against the whole corrupt and rotten ruling class of France'.⁵¹ Like Zola's famous letter, the 'Declaration' addressed both short- and long-term ends – to expose the lies about 'trusteeship' in the first instance, and ultimately 'to unfurl the banner of the S. A. oppressed alongside the banners of all the oppressed throughout the world'.⁵²

Expressions of solidarity with colonial workers and peasants were even more frequent. A war-time issue of *The Bulletin* argued, '[T]he struggle of the common people for freedom is the same in South Africa as it is in India, in Malaya, as in South America: it is the struggle for liberation from the yoke of colonial exploitation, whereby we are exploited twice – once as wage slaves and doubly for our dark skins.'⁵³ At the end of the war, *The Bulletin* singled out the anti-colonial activists of Java and China as examples for black South Africans to emulate: 'although thousands of miles may separate him or her [in South Africa] from the scenes of these life and death struggles, [they share] the triumphant knowledge that... nothing can now extinguish the fire of liberty which now to-day influences and inspires the colonial peoples in Asia and the Pacific'.[54] Conceding that South Africa's struggle for freedom lags behind the national movements in China, Indonesia and India, *The Bulletin* concludes with the optimistic claim that the NEUM with its Ten-Point Programme represents a fundamental advance on the ANC, the APO and the ICU because it transcends narrowly national interests: 'it views the question of the liberation of the oppressed from the NATIONAL angle and through the eyes of ALL the oppressed'.[55]

In the 1950s, international solidarity with colonial workers continued to occupy a prominent place in left opposition thinking, with Tabata explaining the relationship between the specifics of the South African struggle and the global anti-colonial struggle in the following terms:

> When, for instance, we think of the trade union problem, the peasant problem, the relation between the workers and the peasants, and finally, the national problem, these objective conditions invest the situation with what may be called a unique quality. It is in this sense, and in this sense only, that there is a uniqueness in the problems of the Non-Europeans in South Africa. Nevertheless, the struggles in South Africa are basically the same as those of all the oppressed throughout the history of mankind. It is a struggle at this very moment [1952] convulsing Asia, Europe, the Middle East, North, Central, East and West Africa – everywhere where people are striving to throw off the yoke of oppression.[56]

For some left opposition critics, Tabata's anti-nationalist emphasis could have been clearer, with Baruch Hirson in his commentary on *The Awakening of a People* (1950) cautioning against blurring the line between nationalism and socialism. He charges Tabata with oscillating between statements 'sometimes appearing to propound the ideas of socialism and sometimes appearing to espouse the ideas of nationalism, no different from the politics of the petty-bourgeois nationalists who have captured control of the nationalist movements in south-east Asia and in Africa'.[57]

Hirson's attention to the theoretical distinctions between socialist internationalism and anti-colonial nationalism highlights a fault-line in Trotsky's own positions on South Africa. In 1934, Trotsky had advised the left opposition to forge strategic alliances with the ANC, whenever it came under attack from 'the white oppressors and their chauvinistic agents', and whenever the progressive tendencies in its programme might be supported, but he insisted that any such alliances be negotiated within 'the framework of strictly defined practical tasks'.[58] In his willingness to recognise the right of oppressed nations to self-determination, Trotsky repeated V. I. Lenin's position on anti-colonialism as set out at the Second Congress of the Comintern in 1920. Trotsky makes no concession in his analysis of South Africa to M. N. Roy's critique of Lenin, which identified the dangers posed by the nationalist bourgeoisie in the colonies to the cause of socialist internationalism.[59] Far from parroting Trotsky's line on South Africa in the 1930s, critics of anti-colonial nationalism like Kies and Hirson were therefore much closer in spirit and content to Roy's denunciations of India's anti-colonial bourgeois nationalists than they were to the Lenin–Trotsky pronouncements on the need for strategic alliances with nationalists in the colonial struggles of the 1920s and 1930s.[60]

Complementing Hirson's critique of nationalism was the closely related attack on anti-colonial leaders. Left opposition intellectuals drew a clear distinction between the exploited masses in the colonies and their leaders: for the former, unequivocal solidarity, for the latter, critical scrutiny. The distinction derived in part from their reading of twentieth-century South African resistance politics as fatally undermined by pusillanimous leaders – labelled 'policemen-chiefs' and policemen-intellectuals'[61] by Tabata – betraying the mass of African workers and peasants. The same tension between the masses and their leaders beyond South Africa was observed in the anti-colonial struggles of other African and Asian countries. Reinforcing the critique of the conflict of interests dividing nationalist leaders from their constituencies was the application of the Marxist vocabulary of class analysis. An editorial in the Forum Club's publication, *Discussion*, for example, insisted upon the need to appreciate the class differences within all nationalist movements:

> Thus each class reads into the term 'national movement' its own meaning according to its own class position and interest ... Each class will finally attempt to identify the interests of the national movement with its own peculiar class aims, and dress its class political policy in the guise of a national ballroom dress. Thus it will not only attempt to speak in the name of the entire nation, but in order to ensure the success of its class policy, it must gain the backing of the other classes as well.[62]

With the nationalist leaders representing 'the native bourgeoisie', the editorial concludes, it is inevitable that they will broker a deal serving their narrow constituency, while at the same time wearing 'the national ballroom dress' to disguise their true interests: 'constitutional independence is merely a screen for continued economic exploitation ... This arrangement [has been] made possible by an agreement between the Imperialists and the native bourgeoisie, an agreement made behind the backs of the peasant and proletarian millions'.[63]

As successive colonies achieved independence and then failed to fulfil their dreams of freedom, South Africa's left opposition intellectuals sharpened their critique of postcolonial betrayals and comprador elites. The contradictory achievements of Indonesian independence in 1945 were analysed in both *The Bulletin* and *The Torch*. In 1947, *The Bulletin* warned:

> Woe to the people of Indonesia if they follow the advice of their collaborator [Sutan] Sjahrir [the first prime minister of Indonesia], if they rely on the UNO and allow themselves to be disarmed by paper resolutions and foul compromises. In that case their heroic fight for freedom will have been in vain, they will end again in slavery. The road to liberty is a hard road. It requires courage

and sacrifice and the people are prepared to give – it is the leaders who have to be watched.[64]

Three years later, *The Torch* argued along the same lines that although the national struggle against Dutch colonial rule represented progress, it was but the first phase of a longer struggle for political *and* economic self-sufficiency. The anti-colonial nationalists, 'the twin doctors, Hatta and Soekarno', had indeed driven out the 'Dutch master', enabling 'the Indonesian today [to] walk upright in his own country as an Indonesian', but by shooting down 'the most democratic section of the anti-imperialist armies, the working men under the leadership of Tan Malakka',[65] the leaders had betrayed the people. However, *The Torch* continued, 'we shall yet see the end of Hatta and Soekarno, who dared to replace the Dutch exploiter with the Indonesian exploiter, who like the Nehrus and Jinnahs just exchanged masters, on the strength of a battle won by the working man'.[66] In subsequent issues of *The Torch*, further anti-colonial leaders were added to the list of the duplicitous nationalist elite: 'too closely dependent upon the imperialists ... we see that Chiang Kai Shek, Nehru, Nkrumah, Soekarno and others were quite incapable of driving the imperialists out, of unifying their countries, and of achieving national independence on anything like their own terms'.[67]

After Indian independence in 1947, *The Bulletin* commented at length on developments in India. Indeed, the only issue of *The Bulletin* to break with the convention of a single double-sided A4 page of typed commentary followed Gandhi's assassination, which was discussed for four pages.[68] There were two main elements to the left opposition's critique of India's Congress leaders. The first echoed their criticisms of both the APO and ANC leaders in South Africa and of anti-colonial nationalist leaders across the decolonising world. The attack on Nehru is typical:

> The workers were led to believe that Nehru was the friend of the worker, a Socialist himself, almost a Communist. And now those who worshipped Nehru see that it is not Sirdar Valabhai Patel, but Nehru himself who is personally conducting the campaign to split the Trade Unions, to smash strikes, to gaol Trade Union leaders and militant leaders with whom but yesterday he was sitting as a prisoner of British Imperialism. And they cannot understand it! Similarly the peasants whom Congress promised land, relief from tax collectors and moneylenders, now feel the hand of the Congress Government descending more heavily on them than even the British Raj did. They now stand aghast to see their Congress siding openly with the landowners and moneylenders. And they don't understand it![69]

Congress's post-independence *volte-face* is explained in the final paragraph: Nehru is the servant of India's capitalist class, and accordingly is 'now liquidating the old Congress and transforming it into a tool of counter-revolution'.[70] The second element in *The Bulletin*'s critique of Indian anti-colonial nationalism is its objection to Congress's cult of individual leaders like Nehru and Gandhi at the expense of the politics of collective struggle practised (so they claimed) by the Anti-CAD and

NEUM: '[W]e have built on the principle that the liberation of the people is everything and the individual leader is only a small and subordinate part of the movement ... We would like to see the death-blow to the cult of leader-worship which began with Gandhi and Kadalie.'[71]

After Ghana's independence in 1957, its leader Kwame Nkrumah too came in for frequent criticism. Hirson attacked Nkrumah for fetishising political freedoms, with the 'economic struggle against exploitation ... relegated to the distant future', arguing that he ultimately had 'the aspirant bourgeoisie behind his party and he was protecting his own class interests'.[72] What makes such leaders hard to read is their facility with the radical language of anti-imperialism, but '[e]ven where men like Nehru and Nkrumah mouthed socialist slogans we declared that they did so to pay lip service to the workers' aspirations in order to utilise these workers for their own class ends'.[73] As the disappointments of Ghanaian independence became increasingly apparent, the NEUM critique hardened. A 1959 NEUM statement emphasised the sharp divergence between the interests of the African masses and the newly installed elites:

> This is the matter and spirit of Ghana's message to Africa. To the African masses: hot air and drums: but to the African middle class and intelligentsia a new Timbuctoo and a new Mecca of 'hope and glory', of careers as 'leaders' or, more correctly, as leader-goats, of jobs carrying with them a cut of the profits derived from the exploitation of the masses. The layer of the comprador class whom Nkrumah-Nasser-Nehru represent do not want to see real liberation of the masses, because the privileged positions they and their kind occupy, their power, their profits, may be swept away (as in China) in the process, together with the foreign exploiters with whom their interests are inter-locked.[74]

The state-generated national culture, with 'hot air and drums' for the masses, and myths of a 'new Timbuctoo' for the elite, is dedicated to protecting the material interests of the postcolonial 'comprador class' and its sponsors, 'the foreign exploiters'. Such uncompromising pronouncements on Nkrumah's postcolonial betrayals were however moderated when certain of the left opposition activists confronted the *realpolitik* of African exile politics. Tabata, for example, wrote to Nkrumah after meeting him in 1964, describing their encounter effusively: '[I]t was like meeting a kindred spirit. Meeting a keen intellect is always a treat, particularly if the person is knowledgeable and devoted to the cause of liberation of man from the toils of man.'[75] The theoretical stand against the neo-colonial comprador elites produced by Kies in the 1940s and by Hirson in the 1950s in South Africa was thus strategically moderated by Tabata in African exile in the 1960s.

LAND AND LIBERTY!

From the earliest days of Trotsky's reception in South Africa, land ownership was a major point of contention. In 1934, soon after Thibedi's first letter to Trotsky, two 'theses' (position papers) by opposed factions of the South African left opposition were sent to Trotsky for adjudication.[76] The majority thesis insisted that 'the far greater part of the Native Question is the Agrarian Problem'; that 'the so-called national liberation movements of the African National Congress here ... can lead to nothing except the betrayal of the workers'; and that the class struggle must precede national liberation because 'a man needs first of all bread, then liberty'.[77] The minority thesis rejected the emphasis on the agrarian problem, arguing *contra* that 'the Native problem is not the Agrarian problem at all, but the problem of Imperialism and Capitalism', and that accordingly, 'we have to support the National Bourgeois in so far as they struggle and are forced to fight against Imperialism', or, we need to 'march separately and strike together ... as Lenin patiently and unceasingly hammered in the heads of the communist parties in relation to the colonial and semi-colonial countries'.[78]

In his reply, Trotsky conceded his ignorance of the specifics of South African society, but declared that he had '*no differences in principles* with the authors of these theses'.[79] Accordingly, he endorsed in general terms the South African left opposition's commitment to overthrow British imperialism; its ambition to awaken 'the Native masses' and to support the struggle of black South Africans for 'self-determination, *with methods of proletarian class struggle*'; and its aspiration to proceed always 'with the spirit of revolutionary internationalism'.[80] In his concluding summary, Trotsky remained true to Lenin, following the Bolshevik itinerary for the journey to freedom in South Africa. The revolutionary resolution of both the agrarian and the national questions, Trotsky argued, 'leads inevitably to the Dictatorship of the Proletariat which guides the Native peasant masses [which in turn] will open an era of a Soviet regime and Socialist construction'.[81] This optimistic *telos* was distinguished from contemporaneous Stalinist projections by the commitment to permanent revolution, the antidote to Stalin's 'socialism in one country'. Several subsequent commentators, however, have pointed out that both the minority position and Trotsky's adjudication bear traces of the Comintern/CPSA Native Republic template of national-bourgeois liberation preceding socialist freedom. Hirson noted that 'the black republic slogan ... might have been an obvious corollary to their programme',[82] and Drew that 'in striking respects, [the South African Trotskyists'] arguments replicated the Communist debates of the previous decade'.[83]

A decade on from these exchanges with Trotsky, Tabata's polemic, *The Rehabilitation Scheme: A New Fraud* (1945), refuted the Secretary for Native Affairs, D. L. Smit's scheme purporting to make the best use of the land available and combat soil erosion by culling the livestock of African peasants. Exposing the gulf between the scheme's ostensible intentions and its actual effects in impoverishing African peasant farmers, Tabata reiterated the centrality of the 'agrarian problem' to South Africa's liberation struggle, declaring that 'no amount of juggling with words will alter the plain fact that the problem is LAND HUNGER'.[84] In an extended metaphor likening Africans to water channelled along canals to irrigate white-owned farms and mines, Tabata argued that the state's complementary laws governing peasants and workers produced a comprehensive system of control:

The rulers have indeed laid their plans on a nation-wide scale. In the towns they propose creating bottlenecks at the labour-depôts; in the Reserves the bottle-necks are to be the so-called village settlements. Here we have a picture of the whole population forced through bottle-necks and damned up in labour reservoirs. From these reservoirs channels are created, leading to the white farms and the mines. This will result from their Rehabilitation Scheme in the Reserves. This will result from their Housing Scheme and their Pass Regulations in the town.[85]

In subsequent speeches like 'Land and liberty' (1951) and 'The agrarian problem' (1954), Tabata expanded upon his analysis, observing that the 'Rehabilitation Scheme is able to operate because we have lost our human rights, our independence, our manhood'. Linking the land problem to the national problem, he argued further that 'landlessness is an instrument for economic exploitation and national oppression'.[86] In order to resist the state's legislative attempts to regulate and exploit the African peasantry, Tabata counsels a strategy that attends both to the national (political) and agrarian (economic) problems: '[W]e must unreservedly throw in our lot with [the landless peasantry] in their struggle for their right to the land. At the same time we must teach them that the national, i. e. political question is the key to the solution of their problems.'[87]

Several literary works also stressed the bond between the South African peasant and the land. Taylor's short story, 'The Return', depicts how the Rehabilitation Scheme destroyed the livelihoods of rural Africans. Set in the Transkei in the 1940s, the protagonist Takane returns with his three cattle to his wife Noswe and rural homestead after five years working for a white farmer. Arrested immediately upon his return under the new laws regulating the Scheme, Takane is obliged to sell his cattle below their market value to a white butcher in order to pay his fine. Impoverished once again, Takane has to leave the Transkei for a second time, this time to work on the mines. The fragility of Takane's dreams of freedom are signalled in the couplet from the Yeats poem 'The Cloths of Heaven' which introduces the story – 'I have spread my dreams under your feet;/ Tread softly because you tread on my dreams.'[88] Takane's bucolic vision of life with a wife, land and cattle is destroyed, as the law compels him to return to the white-owned economy as a wage-labourer on the mines.

Taylor's pessimism about the prospects for land redistribution in 'The return' contrasts with the more defiant message of Livingstone Mqotsi's novel, *House of Bondage* (1990). Written in the 1970s, but only published in 1990, *House of Bondage* is set in the Transkei in the years between the imposition of the Rehabilitation Scheme and the introduction of the Bantu Authorities Act (1951) and Bantu Education Act (1953). The plot centres on the struggle for land and liberty in the Transkei village of Devilworth, with the popular leaders Vusumzi, Nkwitshi and Shushu set against the collaborator Ngcothoza, who is helping the Native Commissioner Smith to enforce the new apartheid laws. Shushu explains to Smith the centrality of land to all political struggles in the Transkei, past and present:

'[The land] is yours by usurpation. You have taken it by force and trickery. We do not own it, that is, the nation does not own it. Whatever little patch is allocated to us, we do not own; we merely occupy it, and this without security of tenure. You and your Government ought to know that every chief must have land which he holds in trust for those under his jurisdiction. If, as you say, you are going to restore generously, the power of the chiefs, which your people took away from them after conquest, then you must also return the land of our forebears to us. If you do not do this, then there can be no question of self-rule and self-determination by us. This whole plan must then be a fraud. Is our land by right of birth going to be restored to us by those who robbed us of it?'[89]

Shushu's address cuts through the segregationist/apartheid discourses of 'separate development', pointing out that without the redistribution of land, promises of 'self-rule' or 'self-determination' for African leaders are meaningless. He refers to pre-colonial African modes of land ownership, when the chief held land 'in trust for those under his jurisdiction'. In a subsequent speech Vusumzi reiterates the difference between Western modes of land ownership anchored in private property and Xhosa modes of collective land ownership: 'Even when we held the land in trust for our people before we lost it, its distribution was a matter for public discussion and decision. I do not decide anything for my people. They discuss things and arrive at decisions by consensus.'[90]

The emphasis on the collective in the past is sustained in the novel's vision of the future. Exiled to Bethal, Vusumzi meets other political dissidents, and upon hearing their difficult plight, 'assured them that they were not alone in the struggle for land and liberty and that the stories they told could be repeated in all essential details throughout the length and breadth of the country'.[91] Such shared suffering, Vusumzi tells his fellow exile-prisoners, means, '"If we believe in ourselves, we shall win. We cannot depend on others. We welcome whatever help they can give, but we are our own liberators. I personally believe in the genius of the struggling masses of our people at war with a system that is historically doomed."'[92] Vusumzi dies on the prison-farm in Bethal, but his message survives. His funeral in the Transkei is followed by heavy rain, which transforms the countryside, so that it 'began to smile as the grass and the trees turned greener'. The transformation of the land is interpreted as 'a vision or waking dream' that inspires the peasants to heed Nkwitshi's 'summons to arms, to take up the call in the name of liberty'.[93]

Takane and Vusumzi's dreams of land ownership were enshrined as an aspiration in Point Seven of the NEUM's Ten-Point Programme, which provided:

Revision of the land question in accordance [with the Ten-Point Programme] ... The relations of serfdom at present existing on the land must go, together with the Land Acts, together with the restrictions upon acquiring land. A new division of the land in conformity with the existing rural population, living on the land and working the land, is the first task of a democratic State and Parliament.[94]

But the precise meaning of Point Seven proved contentious. The assumption initially had been that all land lost under the racist land acts would be reappropriated, held collectively after liberation, and redivided among the black peasantry. From 1957, however, the AAC element of the NEUM led by Tabata reinterpreted Point Seven, arguing that the clause prescribed the unrestricted right of black South Africans to buy and sell private property. The Anti-CAD element led by Kies and Jaffe rejected any such concession to capitalist property relations, arguing that 'without the solution of the land question on a democratic basis – according to the new relationships in the emancipated society – no country in the world has yet achieved freedom from imperialism, nor the abolition of poverty and caste'.[95] The fall-out over Point Seven led to the end of the NEUM, with Tabata's faction leaving to form the African People's Democratic Union of Southern Africa (APDUSA) in 1961, and in 1964 re-naming the exile NEUM the Unity Movement of South Africa (UMSA).[96]

As to why the AAC and Anti-CAD dreams of land were incompatible, ex-FIOSA member Kenneth Jordaan asked, 'is the term "acquiring land" the same as "buying land" from private holders or is land to be acquired only from the democratic state as the sole owner?'[97] Or, in slightly different terms, '[S]hould the NEUM hitch its destiny to the star of private property as a plenary power or should it seek to abolish private ownership in land?'[98] For Tabata, the answer was the former; for Kies the latter. For the individual African peasants like Takane or Vusumzi, Jordaan suggests, realising the dream of buying land might indeed free individual peasants from the poverty produced by the combination of hyper-exploitation by white capitalist farmers, landlessness and unemployment (Tabata's perspective). But such freedom for individuals to buy land and cattle might in fact amount to no more than freedom for a small minority of black farmers, as it amounts to little more than 'a reactionary dream to universalise small-scale farming . . . and endow everyone with economic equality under capitalism'.[99]

LITERATURE AS CRITIQUE

As the stories of Taylor and Mqotsi exemplify, original poems, short stories, plays and novels, as well as innumerable literary allusions and quotations, percolated the published and unpublished writings of South Africa's left opposition. Literature is understood dialectically – on the one hand in materialist terms as a form and expression of consciousness 'determined' by economic/political/historical conditions, and on the other hand, as having the capacity to exceed its determinants and to serve a variety of political ends: to express social critique; to inspire the collective struggle against capitalism; and to imagine future societies free from oppression.

These dual assumptions are integral to Trotsky's reflections on the Russian literary culture of his own epoch. Acknowledging in *Literature and Revolution* (1923) the centrality of military and economic considerations, Trotsky at the same time insists upon a privileged place for literature. He argues that without the military victory of the Red Army, 'we would not be thinking now about economic problems, much less about intellectual and cultural ones', but he nonetheless asserts that 'the development of art is the highest test of the vitality and significance of each epoch'.[100] Consistent in applying historical-materialist method, Trotsky asks rhetorically, '[W]hat are the social conditions of these thoughts and feelings [expressed in Soviet literature and art of the 1920s]?'[101] Declaring that 'it is silly ... to pretend that art will remain indifferent to the convulsions of our epoch', he argues, 'the art of this epoch will be entirely under the influence of revolution', and accordingly, it is 'incompatible with pessimism, with scepticism ... It is realistic, active, vitally collectivist, and filled with a limitless creative faith in the Future'.[102] In turning to the subject-matter of post-revolutionary Soviet art, Trotsky shifts focus to consider literature's capacity to serve a social/revolutionary function. With this question in mind, he rejects the prescriptions of Proletkult:

> It is not true that we regard only that art as new and revolutionary which speaks of the worker, and it is nonsense to say that we demand that the poets should describe inevitably a factory chimney, or the uprising against capital! Of course the new art cannot but place the proletariat at the centre of attention. But the plough of the new art is not limited to numbered strips. On the contrary, it must plough the entire field in all directions. Personal lyrics of the very smallest scope have an absolute right to exist within the new art.[103]

To his endorsement of new 'personal lyrics' under socialism, Trotsky adds his optimistic hopes for new varieties of tragedy, new forms of comedy and a revitalisation of the novel. Trotsky's antipathy towards Proletkult orthodoxy hardened in his years of exile. In 1930, he recalled that 'the struggle for "proletarian culture" ... had at the beginning of the October Revolution the character of utopian idealism ... In recent years it has become simply a system of bureaucratic command over art and a way of impoverishing it'.[104] Trotsky's polemic against Proletkult art and literature thus paralleled his opposition to the Stalinist bureaucratisation of the Communist Party, but it did not extinguish his faith in the capacity of writers and artists to support his socialist vision. In a 1938 manifesto co-signed by Diego Rivera (1886–1957) and Andre Breton (1896–1966), for example, he declared: 'The opposition of writers and artists is one of the forces which can usefully contribute to the discrediting and overthrow of regimes which are destroying, with the right of the proletarian to aspire to a better world, every sentiment of nobility and even of human dignity.'[105]

Trotsky's literary-critical legacy influenced South Africa's left opposition. In terms of critical method, Taylor reprised Trotsky's dual insistence that 'a work of art should, in the first place, be judged by its own law, that is the law of art', and secondly that '[art/literature] is not a disembodied element feeding on itself, but a function of social man indissolubly tied to his life and environment'.[106] Taylor reformulated these two methodological commitments as follows:

> The development of literary (artistic) movements is not a simple thing to be traced mechanically in each country in parallel lines according to the development and decline of capitalist society in each. While the economic base is an

invaluable and essential guide in tracing the rise of certain ideological concepts, literature at the same time has its own laws of growth, change, assimilation, imitation and revolt . . . The laws of uneven development would seem to hold in literature as well as economics.[107]

Conceding a degree of autonomy to art and literature did not, however, extend to endorsing the Romantic elevation of the poet. Rather, Taylor recognised that 'revolutions cannot be made by literary or cultural movements; the deep social discontent of the masses must supply the urge to action'.[108] Taylor also shared Trotsky's abhorrence of Stalin's centralised autocracy and its strangling of Soviet economic and cultural life alike: in creating 'weapons of defence not only in iron and steel, but in every medium of art as well, Art became state-controlled like any other form of labour'; as a consequence, the Proletkult contradicted 'Lenin's whole purpose in liberating the proletariat'.[109]

Both in her own original literary works and in her many literary reviews, Taylor strove to mobilise literature in the service of critique. Her memory of her first encounters with the Cape Town left in the 1930s foregrounds her literary priorities:

> It was [Frederick] Bodmer who introduced me to the [Spartacus] Club several years later – 1935. I was totally ignorant politically, as Jim was. But there was one big difference between us (i. e. Jim and me), at first totally unconscious and unforeseen. I had already written my poem 'Red', which showed in a groping way that I was aware of the profound oppression in S. A. society – long before the [National Party] came to power. And being always serious-minded, I began to be drawn into the Club, not just an ignorant onlooker.[110]

Composed in an accordingly critical spirit, Taylor's poem 'Red' (1935) does indeed display an awareness of 'the profound oppression in S. A.', as it evokes in five stanzas a work-gang of black convicts. The poet-observer yearns for an act of defiance from the gang: 'If only the flag of anger had stood out on their temples,/ . . . /To turn the axe from the living wood/ And feel the joy of the blade/ Deep in the corrupt body of the oppressors!'[111] But instead of an image of resistance, the poem closes with the poet-observer registering the convicts' submission to power: 'I met only the sullen lip,/ And the burnt embers of dark eyes,/ Unquestioning, vacant, dead.'[112]

As a literary critic, Taylor's aesthetic was orientated by her Marxist political compass. Her reviews of two familiar South African writers exemplify her weaving together of literary and political critique. In her 1942 review of Nicholls's *Bayete!*, she begins by lamenting the novel's literary flaws: '[t]he style is artificial, the characterisation is inconsistent and in the frequent melodramatic incidents one hears the machinery creaking'.[113] Following a plot-and-character summary, Taylor asks whether the warning the novel issues to its white readers carries any conviction. The answer, she argues, must be sought by applying the materialist critical method – 'by relating the novel to the social and political life which was its background'.[114] By relating text to context, Taylor finds that *Bayete!* appeared to have had the effect that Nicholls desired: since its publication in 1923, racial oppression had increased, legislation restricting African workers had been passed, and white complacency had diminished. In short, she concludes, 'It almost looked as if the warnings had not fallen on deaf ears.'[115]

For Taylor, Nicholls's literary limitations, failures of imagination, and racist politics contrasted with Olive Schreiner's imaginative capacity to make the leap from her own individual experience of oppression to write sympathetically on behalf of other oppressed groups: 'Her first battles had been personal ones, but in the course of that fight she learned things which she was to fight for to the end of her days on a larger impersonal scale.'[116] During her nine years in England, Schreiner discovered much about 'the evils of capitalism and the oppression of workers', but succumbed – Taylor chides gently – to 'the common bogey that the socialist state means death to individual freedom'.[117] Taylor praised Schreiner's courage in denouncing 'imperialist aggression ... the terrible corruption of racial prejudice and passion ... [and in standing up] for individual freedom, irrespective of race, colour, sex or creed',[118] but she then proceeded to locate Schreiner's protests in their mutating ideological context(s). In the late nineteenth century, Taylor argues, 'it was then possible to entertain enthusiastic hopes of what the liberal spirit might do', and as a consequence, Schreiner 'believed in democracy, in the principle of individual freedom, not realising fully that with its class basis, bourgeois democracy was a travesty of true democracy'.[119] The South African War and First World War, however, exposed the limitations of liberal ideology, as well as the modest impact of artists' appeals against injustice. Schreiner responded to the changed context by correcting her misplaced faith in liberalism and her unrealistic belief in the power of art/literature to influence society. She concludes by quoting with warm approval Schreiner's letter to Havelock Ellis in which she declared, '"A greater genius than Lenin has not appeared in the last hundred years ... Art and fine writing are in this age secondary."'[120]

Taylor-the-critic's commitment to historical materialism seldom wavered, but Taylor-the-creative-writer's willingness to subordinate her own literary ambitions – anchored to Trotsky's principle that literature can serve revolution – did come under pressure. Like Schreiner, who had conceded in 1917 that 'art and fine writing' are secondary to politics, Taylor in 1946 turned from literary pursuits to the writing of polemical histories. Aside from her own efforts in fiction, poetry and drama, Taylor had by 1946 written thirty-four book reviews and opinion pieces on literary topics for *Trek*, as well as longer articles for *The Critic* and *Forum*.[121] Taking stock in November 1948, Taylor reflected, 'I had the gift, the eye, I had the time. I had the feeling for words – poured out in many letters. But only 2 or 3 stories; 2 imperfect novels; 2 poor plays; oh, and good literary criticism in *Trek*.'[122] From the mid-1940s, her labours increasingly were directed to collaborating (without public acknowledgement) with Tabata on *The Awakening of a People* (1950), and to writing (under a pseudonym) *The Role of the Missionaries in Conquest* (1952).[123] By 1949, however, Taylor regarded with some regret her uninterrupted dedication to Tabata's political and historical writings, and her own enforced withdrawal from literary work: 'By this time, I was not writing literary criticism for *Trek*, a mistake, this deliberate decision to stop contributing ... I thought I had to be loyal to the "group" – idiot.'[124] Obedient to the hierarchy that elevated writing about politics and history above the writing of literary works or literary criticism, Taylor thus subordinated her own interests to those of her comrades. Literature might have some social utility, but in dark times, Taylor observed the consensus that the fight for freedom is more effectively served in the discourses of politics and history.[125]

Taylor's hesitations about abandoning literature entirely for history and politics are also evident in a waspish aside in her diary about Tabata's reading: 'It is strange how much he had imbibed our reading of Shakespeare. Yet his reading (when he had time) was first and foremost Lenin, Marx, Trotsky. And he was a slow reader, having had imperfect training at Lovedale.'[126] While Tabata might indeed have favoured Lenin over Shakespeare, he too was alive to the potential political utility of literature. For example, in a lecture 'The future of industry in South Africa' (1942), he opened with a quotation by the character of the arch-capitalist Undershaft in George Bernard Shaw's *Major Barbara* (1905):

> I am the government of your country. Do you suppose that you and a half-dozen amateurs like you, sitting in a row in that foolish gabble shop, can govern Undershaft? No, my friend, you will do what pays us. You will make war when it suits us, and keep peace when it doesn't . . . When I want anything to keep my dividends up, you will discover that my want is a national need. When other people want something to keep my dividends down, you will call out the police and the military. And in return you shall have the support and applause of my newspapers, and the delight of imagining that you are a great statesman.[127]

According to Tabata, '[T]he fact that [this speech] occurs in a play and is spoken with a cynical frankness, does not invalidate its accuracy as a description of the true state of affairs.'[128] Nor were Tabata's uses of literature for politics limited to quoting other writers; he himself produced stories for political ends. During his tours to the Transkei in the 1940s and 1950s, he included animal stories in his speeches to African peasants in order to teach political lessons.[129] For example, 'The Dog Story' illustrates the danger of Africans internalising a slave mentality. Dog, once 'a proud animal roving in the forests' is captured by Man, who wipes out all Dog's memory of his past existence, 'until the poor thing began to think that he could not exist without his master',[130] and spends all his days labouring in the service of Man in return for scraps of offal from Man's table. In the closing paragraphs, Tabata spells out the analogy between Dog and his peasant audience in a succession of rhetorical questions, asking first, 'Who has built up the civilisation of this country? It is our black hands'; then, 'And what do we get for all our labour? They throw us only offal to eat and hovels to live in'; and finally, 'What has happened to us? Just as man breeds certain dogs to catch other animals, so has the white ruler turned some of us into his dogs, the chiefs and the quisling intellectuals, to keep the rest of us as chattel slaves.'[131]

Tabata's animal stories contrast with those of another leading NEUM intellectual of the 1950s, A. C. Jordan. An intimate of Tabata, Jordan was also on occasions a source of frustration.[132] In a letter to Tsotsi in 1944, Tabata suggested that Jordan was prone to 'chauvinism' and 'conservatism', qualities he regarded as 'dangerous', 'especially since he has the gift of a writer, thus placing him in a position of being able to disseminate his poisonous ideas under the cloak of art'.[133] Their respective animal stories reveal their political differences. Jordan pioneered the study of Xhosa literature in a series of articles in the magazine *Africa South* from the late 1950s (subsequently republished in *Towards an African Literature: The Emergence of Literary Form in Xhosa* (1973)), and in a collection of animal stories he selected from African oral sources, *Tales from Southern Africa* (1973). Less interested in Marxist (or Trotskyist) theories of literature than Taylor, Jordan was nonetheless committed to materialist modes of reading African literature. The Introduction to *Towards an African Literature* by Lindi Nelani Jordan insists that the distinctive quality of Jordan's literary method was that 'the writers and their works are placed in their proper historical perspective'.[134] Such an approach requires that the literary critic 'has to know the historical forces that shaped that society'; in summary, '[t]he dialectical approach also gives the reader a context in which to analyse both the literature and academic works on the literature'.[135] Shared literary-critical methodological commitments did not, however, produce the same kinds of literary works. Whereas Tabata's political priorities framed his animal stories, Jordan's intentions were less didactic, as he sought to rescue disappearing African oral story-telling traditions. In introducing African traditional literature, he distinguishes between riddles, 'which present a mental problem' and are associated with younger people, and proverbs, which are a 'criticism of life [with] a more serious and didactic intent',[136] and are associated with older people and especially men. He provides the following example of a proverb:

> 'The rock-rabbit has no tail because he trusted to others (to bring him one).'
> After the creation, when all the animals were invited to come and receive their tails, the Rock-rabbit, preferring to sit and bask in the sun, requested the Monkey to bring him a tail. But on being supplied with the extra tail, the Monkey decided to add it on to his own. Hence the 'knot' on the Monkey's tail. This proverb exhorts people to do things themselves and not to trust to others to do things for them.[137]

Jordan's animal story and its associated proverb could conceivably be adapted to teach political lessons, but for the most part, his proverbs derive moral lessons with no explicit political message.

Another left opposition intellectual to absorb and reanimate the legacy of Trotsky-the-literary-critic was Ben Kies. In his weekly column in *The Sun* newspaper, Kies ranged widely in topic, but Marxist-inflected literary allusions were a staple. In an aside in an article attacking the coloured teaching establishment, Kies provides his own accessible version of the argument for reading literature in its historical context:

> [E]very age, every historical epoch, creates its own ... characteristic atmosphere. This applies as much to the machine, food, clothing of that epoch, as it does to the philosophy and literature. That is why, if you know your stuff,

you could pick out any number of anonymous passages of literature, prose or poetry, of any historical epoch, and you could say, this must have been written during such and such a period and that during such and such a time. The ideas, but also the vocabulary, the lengths of sentences, the balance, prose or poetic rhythms – all these will help you assign the passages to their period. Why? Because, as we said earlier, the style is the man. And the man is the product of his time.[138]

Kies's confidence in applying historical materialist methods to literature is matched by his embrace of Trotsky's second assumption, namely that literature functions in a dialectical relationship with the material world. In an article mocking the dogma of 'art for art's sake', Kies in Orwellian terms argues, 'I believe that all art is propaganda'; that the aspiration to be unbiased can only produce works that are 'colourless and shallow and unworthy of consideration'; and that therefore the writer's 'work must be an interpretation of the world about him, a criticism, i.e. a critical and therefore selective evaluation of the object'.[139]

There are many examples in his columns of Kies adopting literary works in order to bolster his political arguments. An attack on a coloured educational leader guilty (in Kies's view) of opportunistically seeking favour with his masters is likened to the briar in Edmund Spenser's 'The Shepheardes Calendar', who entangled and ultimately killed the oak tree, with fatal results for itself: ' "Now stands the Briar like a Lord alone,/ Puffed up with pride and vain pleassaunce:/ But all this glee had no continuance./ . . ./ Such was th' end of this ambitious briar." '[140] The political lesson is clear: any coloured leader (the briar) tempted to collaborate with the segregationist state (the oak) is ultimately destined to die when the state itself succumbs. (The extended metaphor does not map precisely on to Kies's broader political ideology: the logic of Spenser's poem suggests that the briar/collaborator will kill the oak/white state and thence die itself, whereas for Kies, the oak/white state will be vanquished by the black proletariat, and the briar/collaborator will then die along with its doomed master. The agency of the briar/collaborator is greater in Spenser's poem than in Kies's politics.)

Finally, Trotsky's pre-eminence as the guide to literary-critical practice for South Africa's left opposition was challenged in the 1950s by the discovery of Bertolt Brecht. Encountering Brecht in Germany as a student in 1958, Neville Alexander wrote several letters to Dora Taylor extolling Brecht's qualities. His first letter attacked the attempts by literary critics to de-politicise Brecht, insisting on the importance of appreciating Brecht's plays in context, as well as his sense of their didactic social function:

The professor could go so far as to say, 'Of course ideology is not to be ignored, but it is so secondary as to be negligible. We are interested in Brecht's stage craft, in the iambic pentameter and the obscurantism which is really exposure, as it were,' etc. Thus when you [Taylor] say that the formalists would like to forget that Brecht is a revolutionary, you hit the nail resoundingly on the head. Because that is the fundamental thing . . . I have studied carefully all Brecht says about his art, and he makes no bones about it, his opinions are clear as crystal. Firstly, the theatre has a social function in all societies. The theatre he envisages is one in which moral teaching, i. e. education must be accomplished in an enjoyable manner.[141]

Trotsky's axioms are thus given fresh life in Brecht's plays and prescriptions for the theatre. Alexander's parody of the 1950s formalist critic provides the necessary contrast to the historical materialism he and Taylor embrace. For Alexander, an important element in his encounter with Brecht in Germany is the potential to import his ideas and practice to South Africa:

> The good thing about Brecht is that he is fresh, with his soul and heart in the centre of modern life, its problems and its controversies. We must not only find the time to bring some of this to our chaps, but also establish the dynamic link between literary criticism, the theatre, and the social movement, <u>which is precisely what Brecht and his ensemble did</u> (underline in original). Can you imagine the effects of an 'Arturo Ui' on an audience which had to swallow Hitler only yesterday? . . . Can you imagine what is possible at home, if only we find the people who are willing to work hard all the time? I am not very pessimistic.[142]

Whereas Taylor had looked to Trotsky as her ally in forging her historical-materialist literary criticism and her use of literature for critique, Alexander found in Brecht an equivalent ally.

LITERATURE AS UTOPIA

Alexander and Taylor were not the only members of South Africa's left opposition to be inspired by Brecht. In the same year, there had been a production of a Brecht play in Cape Town – *The Good Woman of Setzuan* at the University of Cape Town's Little Theatre. An anonymous review of the production in *The Citizen* was broadly approving, noting that 'it is impossible to sit through a Brecht play and feel detached intellectually: he engages on provocatively with his remarkable characterisation and profound statements'; the only flaw is that the play's ending reveals the playwright's 'indecision – with what is to be done'.[143] A month later, Albert Thomas responded to the initial review and the production, rejecting the complaint about Brecht's 'indecision', and arguing *contra* that Brecht's strength is his capacity to convey through the theatre life's complexity. For Thomas, Brecht is unique in his ability to fuse 'his economic interpretation of human existence, his materialism [and] his more finely humane, ironic, salty appreciation of human nature'.[144] Of the production, Thomas condemns both its location at UCT's Little Theatre as a betrayal of Brecht's aesthetic, as well as the extensive cuts to the original play-text. Referencing the recent passage of the Suppression of Communism Act, Thomas quotes a passage cut from the play that emphasises the importance of solidarity and community:

'"Unhappy men!/ Your brother is assaulted and shut his eyes!/ He is hit and cries aloud and you are silent!/ . . . /When injustice is done there should be a revolt in the city./ And if there is no revolt, it were better that the city should perish in fire before night falls!"'.[145] Thomas therefore shares Alexander's reading of Brecht as especially relevant to 1950s South Africa, but in addition finds in Brecht an image of collective resistance able to inspire the South African struggle for freedom.

From the earliest stages of Taylor's encounters with Marxism, she had attempted in her creative writing to imagine a community of resistance that was in closer conformity to Trotsky's prescription for literary works to be 'realistic, active, vitally collectivist'. In contrast to her short story 'The Return' and her poem 'Red', Taylor's plays for the Spartacus Club dramatised black South Africans fighting back collectively. In 'The Spark' (1937), for example, the young farm workers Lukosi and Anna combine with their cousin the teacher, Ntombela, and the white trade unionist, Bill Martin, to lead a mass strike of dock-workers. After Lukosi's arrest for his role in the strike, Anna leads a protest march of 3,000, but is shot and killed by the police. Anna's death is not the final event of the play, however, as the surviving workers sing first a lament to her and then 'The Internationale'.[146] The defiant sentiments closing 'The Spark' are echoed in another unpublished poem, 'For the Future – A Prophecy' (1940). In the opening stanza an erotic embrace is evoked between a white woman ('her milk-white loveliness gleamed soft as a flower') and a black man ('the ebony sheen/ of rippling muscles'),[147] while the second stanza shifts from the intimate world of the lovers to the hostile South African landscape beyond. Several lines contrasting 'savage white faces' and 'toiling black bodies' are followed by the hopeful conclusion that 'the love' of the white woman and black man will function for the black masses as 'a symbol, a challenge and a prophecy/ Of the day to come'.[148]

Taylor's ideas of freedom echoed Trotsky's dream of a proletarian revolution that superseded Jacobinism. In a letter to Tabata, Taylor contrasted the (limited) individual freedoms accompanying the bourgeois revolutions of the seventeenth and eighteenth centuries with the (authentic) individual freedoms promised by the socialist revolutions of the twentieth century: 'But [the bourgeois individualism of the past] is nothing compared with that individualism which will blossom when the forces of socialism are planting the deserts with corn and conquering nature to man's needs.'[149] As to whether literature could express socialist dreams of freedom, Taylor found most literary works wanting. Taylor praised Ignazio Silone's *Fontamara* (1933), picking out the protagonist Berardo Viola's self-sacrificing speech in which he decided not to betray his companions in prison: ' "If I die, I shall be the first peasant to die not for himself but others . . . For the unity of peasants. That is – strength. That is – solidarity. That is – liberty. That is – land." '[150] But *Bread and Wine* (1936), with its focus on the priest Don Benedetto, is assessed more critically: although it shows the life of an individual man 'who strives to be free, loyal, just, sincere, disinterested . . . more than that is wanted to solve the problems of a people'.[151] John Steinbeck's *Grapes of Wrath* (1939) is praised for its evocation of the collective; Taylor argues that 'the people show an indomitable spirit and above all they are able to learn from their destitution that strength lies in their unity.'[152] The collective voice of the workers in *The Grapes of Wrath* replicates in novel form the community of resistance Taylor attempted to dramatise in the closing scene of her play 'The Spark'. Erskine Caldwell's *Tobacco Road* (1932), in contrast to Steinbeck's novel, describes with documentary realism the poverty, isolation and despair of poor white farmers in Georgia, with the only glimmer of hope a retrospective one: instead of toiling as individual farmers, the protagonist Jeeter Lester realises too late, '"Co-operative farming would have saved them all."'[153] The same criteria are applied in Taylor's assessment of André Malraux's novels *Storm of Shanghai* (*Man's Fate*, 1933) and *Days of Contempt* (*Days of Wrath*, 1935), as Malraux is charged with being 'more interested in the individual and his ceaseless quest to find a meaning and a significance in life'.[154] Only one passage in *Days of Contempt* meets Taylor's requirement of capturing 'both elements, emotion and action, the individual and the mass, [and fusing] into a magnificent whole', namely the description of the climactic sacrifice of the Russian Katow and his Chinese comrades, which Malraux characterises as a triumph of collective resistance that will inspire future generations.

Taylor's diaries describe evenings spent with Tabata and Goolam Gool in the late 1940s when they enjoyed listening to Dvorak, and reading anti-colonial testimonies, Cicero's speeches and poems by writers ranging from Shakespeare to Taylor herself.[155] As for Tabata, so too for Gool, his appreciation of literature was more than a private affair; literature was a resource to be used to enhance the impact of political arguments. In his presidential address to the AAC on 17 December 1951, for example, Gool declares that ruling-class repression will never deter 'us from pursuing the path which we have pledged ourselves to follow, the path of liberation. And let us leave this place armed with the will to fight with undaunted courage for land and liberty',[156] and then quotes two stanzas for A. H. Clough's 'Say Not the Struggle Nought Availeth'.[157] The final line of the first stanza quoted ends with the line, '"As things have been they remain,"' but the second stanza quoted expresses hope: '"For while the tired waves, vainly breaking,/ Seem here no painful inch to gain,/ Far back through creeks and inlets making/ Comes, silent, flooding in, the main!"'[158] In his gloss on the meaning of Clough's poem, Gool exhorts his audience, 'Yes! If we persist in our course the main will indeed come flooding in.'[159] In other words, for Gool the struggle ultimately 'doth avail', and 'we' – the collective represented by the AAC – will return like the tide to wash away the enemy. Gool's technique of concluding his political speeches with a rousing literary quotation was copied by other NEUM leaders, with Leo Sihlali, for example, quoting Claude McKay's poem 'If We Must Die' at the end of his presidential address to the Cape African Teachers Association in June 1953. More incendiary than Clough's muted appeal to maintain the faith, McKay's final couplet quoted by Sihlali exhorts his audience: '"Like men we'll face the murderous, cowardly pack,/ Pressed to the wall, dying, but fighting back!"'[160]

Complementing Kies's use of literature to embellish his radical critique (or to sharpen the edge of his invective) were his efforts to employ it to imagine brighter futures. In a column on the role of intellectuals in political struggles, Kies argues that the majority 'never plan, socially or politically, because they are comfortable cowards, who have no confidence in each other or in the masses'.[161] Turning his focus to his favourite target, conservative coloured teachers, he finds them especially culpable, invoking an unlikely literary authority in order to make his point: 'I think it was Kipling who said, "Where there is no vision, the people perish." The Coloured teacher is going to prove him correct.'[162] In order to provide his readers with a vision to cherish, Kies refers them first to Ernest Hemingway's Spanish Civil War novel *For Whom the Bell Tolls*, and then quotes ten lines from the John Donne poem that gives the novel its title – 'No man is an island, entire of itself'. The immediate context provoking Kies to quote the poem was the collapse of a conference on black education led by the TLSA. Accusing his readers of indifference – 'you might assert that it is not your funeral'[163] – Kies uses the lines from Donne to try and shame his readers into caring about the failed conference, and by extension, about black education, and ultimately about the struggle against the racist state. By means of the poem, Kies badgers his readers to think of themselves not as isolated individuals, but as members of a collective, as active participants within a community of resistance.

CONCLUSION

For three decades, South Africa's anti-Stalinist left fought for freedom from capitalist exploitation and liberal-nationalist compromise. Why didn't their dreams of freedom come to fruition? The most obvious reason was the strength of their adversary: the segregationist-apartheid state backed by South African and international capital. From the 1930s onwards, the state deployed increasingly brutal measures to crush the organisations and individuals associated with the left opposition: police surveillance, banishment and banning orders, and imprisonment. As a consequence, many activists went into exile, withdrew from politics, or (more rarely) joined other political organisations.[164] For their critics, the efforts of the state were aided by the tactical inflexibility of the NEUM. Alexander, one of the most gifted of the anti-Stalinist intellectuals, argued in retrospect that 'The policy of non-collaboration was often transformed from being one of the most creative ideas of the South African struggle into a pharisaic cliché which was used to assassinate the political characters of any who did not agree with the NEUM leadership.'[165] To this objection, many more were added: that the NEUM failed to build meaningful connections with working-class organisations like trade unions; that it never sustained political alliances beyond the Western Cape; that its theoretical sophistication was never matched by effective praxis; and that its organisational culture shifted from a collective ethos to one built upon the authority of individual leaders like Tabata.[166]

An example of how the left opposition's dreams of freedom faded under harsh conditions is illustrated in the trajectory of Tabata and Mqotsi's relationship. The two comrades forged a close bond in South Africa in the 1950s, but first Tabata and then Mqotsi were forced to flee into exile in Zambia. Tabata recalled Mqotsi's arrival in Lusaka in 1961:

> I cannot forget your face that first day you caught sight of me [in Lusaka]. The overwhelming shock was written all over it. It was a day of great pleasure for

me, too. It is no small matter for a man coming out of confinement to see his fellow fighters face to face . . . You can imagine my joy at seeing your children none the worse for the period of penury and Nizimazana looking like the queen of her domain. The sight of her and you convinced me that the herrenvolk can no longer break our spirit, no matter what they do.[167]

Tabata's confidence in 'our' unbreakable spirit, in the collective resilience of the left opposition, came under pressure as the 1960s unfolded. Despite initial successes in forging links with other African leaders (like Nkrumah) and in developing an infrastructure for his party in exile, Tabata and his comrades were out-manoeuvred by the ANC and SACP. The succession of defeats, both those inflicted by the state and by rival anti-apartheid organisations, intensified internecine conflict. The clash between Tabata and Mqotsi was one of many, and culminated in a special hearing on Mqotsi's conduct presided over by Tabata on 21 April 1966. Mqotsi's opening statement starts by refuting the specific charges against him, and then proceeds to turn the spotlight on his former comrades:

These frightened little men and women [his adversaries within APDUSA, including Tabata] have degenerated into a bureaucracy that does not brook criticism, including self-criticism of any kind. Their politics have been reduced into lies, gossip-mongering, smears, slander and vilification . . . [I]n fact, it is these drawing room intriguers, masquerading as revolutionaries and not Mqotsi who should be put in the dock. It is they who . . . have deviated from the basic tenets of the Unity Movement, particularly the concept and practice of collective leadership.[168]

No trace of the 'unbreakable spirit' of a radical community resisting the 'herrenvolk' proclaimed by Tabata in 1961 remains; nor, indeed, is there evidence in the record of these hearings of the optimism expressed by Mqotsi in his novel *House of Bondage*. Instead, Mqotsi alleges, bureaucratic authoritarianism, duplicity in inter-personal politics, and a retreat from the 'concept and practice of collective leadership', have destroyed (at least in the short term) the dreams of freedom held dear by South Africa's anti-Stalinist intellectual-activists.

5 Pan-Africanism: Freedom for Africa

INTRODUCTION

In June 1958, the popular South African magazine *Drum* carried an article on the All-African People's Congress in Accra, Ghana. Accompanied by photographs of the heads of state and their entourages, the article describes the discussions on future cultural and economic co-operation between African nations, concluding on an optimistic note: 'After the last speech had been spun, and the last goodbye said . . . there was a feeling of satisfaction in Accra, a feeling that the words had perhaps not been in vain. The road to a new vision of Africa had been shown.'[1] Inspired by the Accra conference, Robert Mangaliso Sobukwe, the head of South Africa's newly formed PAC, extended the Accra Congress's message of hope to South Africa:

> Nobody disputes our contention that Africa will be free from foreign rule. What *is* disputed by many, particularly the white ruling minority, is that she will be free either 'within our lifetime' or by 1963, or even 1973 or 1984. However, the African nationalist movements which met at the All-African People's Conference in 1958 put down 1963 as the target date for African freedom. If, however, by this date there are still parts of Africa that are under foreign rule, then certainly, they said, by 1973, every part of Africa must be free. Even though I live in South Africa, I have no doubt that this prophecy will be fulfilled.[2]

By 1963, the apartheid regime remained more entrenched than ever: the PAC had been banned on 8 April 1960; its leadership was in exile or prison, with Sobukwe himself on Robben Island; and its armed wing Poqo had suffered mass arrests from April to June 1963. The prophecy of African freedom for black South Africans was no nearer fulfilment in 1973: the National Party continued governing with increased white support; the PAC-in-exile had been weakened by internecine conflict and out-manoeuvred by the ANC; and Sobukwe was isolated by a banning order confining him to Kimberley.

This chapter examines Pan-Africanist dreams of freedom, tracing their evolution through two phases. The first phase includes the political, literary and philosophical reflections of Africanists of the 1940s like Lembede and Solomzi Ashby Peter ('A. P.') Mda (1916–1993), and the second the writings of PAC members in the 1950s and 1960s – the speeches and letters of Sobukwe, the polemics of P. K. Leballo (1924–1986), the journalism in publications like *The Africanist*, and the novels of Lauretta Ngcobo (1931–2015) and Bessie Head (1937–1986).

NATIONAL FREEDOM FOR AFRICAN PEOPLE

The Pan-Africanism in South Africa after the Second World War was anticipated by the Southern African Garveyites of the 1920s, but by the Second World War, the moment of South African Garveyism had passed. Its demise was the consequence of several factors: the intensification of state repression; its failure either to penetrate or align with organisations like the ANC or ICU; and the inability of its leaders like Thaele to deliver on promises of imminent salvation. Although the Garveyite dream of freedom may have receded from the South African political landscape, the disillusionment produced by the non-appearance of African-American saviours was the catalyst for the emergence of a new conception of political agency. No longer did dispossessed black South Africans look to be liberated by saviours from abroad; rather they began declaring a new-found confidence in their own collective capacity to propel them to freedom. This transformed conception was captured by S. E. K. Mqhayi, who rejected any reliance on 'gentlemen overseas', and insisted that Africans in South Africa would liberate themselves: 'Our nation is alive, and on top of that, perfectly healthy; we must work amongst our own people in our own nation. That's where our salvation and that of our nation lies.'[3]

In the 1940s, the new generation of South African activists drew a line between Garveyism and its own philosophy of Africanism.[4] Based largely at the University of Fort Hare, and coalescing in April 1944 in the ANC Youth League (ANCYL), this generation included figures like Lembede (the first president and leading theorist of the ANCYL), Mda (Lembede's closest interlocutor), Sobukwe, Walter Sisulu (1912–2003), Oliver Tambo (1917–1993), and Nelson Mandela.[5] After Lembede's death in 1947, one obituary described him as 'a protagonist of a new philosophy of Africanism, in contradistinction to that of Marcus Garvey'.[6] The contrast was amplified a year later in the second Manifesto of the ANCYL, which was drafted by Mda, and included a sub-section headed 'Two streams of African nationalism':

> One [stream of African nationalism] centres round Marcus Garvey's slogan – 'Africa for the Africans'. It is based on the 'Quit Africa' slogan and on the cry of 'Hurl the Whiteman to the sea'. This brand of African Nationalism is extreme and ultra revolutionary. There is another stream of African Nationalism (Africanism) which is moderate, and which the Congress Youth League professes. We of the Youth League take account of the concrete situation in South Africa, and realise that the different racial groups have come to stay. But we

insist that a condition for inter-racial peace and progress is the abandonment of white domination, and such a change in the structure of South African Society that those relations which breed exploitation and misery will disappear. Therefore our goal is the winning of National freedom for African people, and the inauguration of a people's free society where racial oppression and persecution will be outlawed.[7]

Viewed in retrospect, far from being more 'moderate' than Garveyism, the second 'stream of African Nationalism' was in at least two respects more radical – in its faith in collective agency, and in its gestures towards socialism. Reiterating Mqhayi's insistence upon the mass character of political struggle, the Manifesto defined the ANCYL's approach in opposition to the fetishising of individual leaders:

But despite the Christian tradition [in the ANC], which gives people the idea of a messiah, most people didn't accept this notion, not that we didn't sometimes try it. But we didn't want any 'cult of personality'. This is what we had seen with Xuma and his 'heavy hand'. We didn't want anyone pretending he was better than the rest. The people hated any such attempt by anyone.[8]

In addition to replacing the messianic leader with the collective, the ANCYL's reconceptualisation of Africanism also eschewed the Garveyite accommodation with US capitalism, favouring instead a broadly defined version of socialism. Although the ANCYL adopted a hostile stance towards both the white members of the CPSA in the ANC and the Trostkyists in the NEUM, Mda conceded that Marxism had certain analytical strengths, and Lembede discerned continuities from pre-colonial African communalism to modern forms of socialism. Mda acknowledged that 'Marxist ideas can have a power and impact on oppressed people. [Marxism] appeals to a person and tells him why he is oppressed. But . . . it is also a prescription for action, a *modus operandi* for change.'[9] Lembede drew a distinction between Marxism and Communism, on the one hand, and socialism, on the other, with the former rejected as a foreign import, whereas 'the fundamental structure of Bantu society is socialistic. There was no individual ownership of land in ancient Bantu society . . . Socialism is . . . our valuable legacy from our ancestors. Our task is to develop this socialism by the infusion of new and modern socialistic ideas.'[10] Socialism remained, however, secondary to Africanism, as Lembede scripted an African nationalist version of the Comintern/CPSA's two-stage theory:

After national freedom, then, socialism. Africans are naturally socialistic as illustrated in their social practices and customs. The achievement of national liberation will therefore herald or usher in a new era of African socialism. Our immediate task however is not socialism but national liberation.[11]

The ANCYL's Africanism thus assimilated the anti-individualistic elements of socialism, as well as the liberal freedoms of Western democracies.

The Africanists' desire to attain liberal freedoms was intensified by the Allied war against fascism, and especially (as we have seen) by the Atlantic Charter. Mda characterised the 1940s as 'the golden age of schemers and planners',[12] singling out the NEUM's Ten-Point Programme as the more influential model for the ANCYL members than the less familiar anti-colonial initiatives from abroad.[13] The 1944 Manifesto of the ANCYL proclaimed national liberation as the primary aim: '[The African] demands the right to be a free citizen in the South African democracy; the right to an unhampered pursuit of his national destiny and the freedom to make his legitimate contribution to human advancement.'[14] Lembede repeated this message in his journalism: in 1946, he declared pessimistically that '[u]nless Africans achieve national freedom as early as possible they will be confronted with the impending doom and imminent catastrophe of extermination', and in 1947, more hopefully, he looked forward to 'the overthrow of oppression and the free participation of Africans in the government of the land. When Africans achieve their national freedom and are able to . . . make laws for themselves all these ills and anomalies will vanish into thin air like a morning mist'.[15] Like Kadalie, Kies and Xuma, Lembede began to connect the liberation struggle of black South Africans both to contemporary anti-colonial struggles and to past struggles for freedom in European history. Noting on one occasion that 'Non-European races all over the world are clamouring for freedom – India, Indonesia, Egypt, Madagascar,' Lembede included Africans as participants 'in a colossal struggle for human freedom'; and on another, he located the freedom struggle of black South Africans in the tradition 'of the French Revolution, of England after 1215, of South Africa after 1833, of Russia after 1917, of India, Egypt and Indonesia today'.[16]

Although the ANCYL's nationalist struggle was committed to achieving the same political freedoms as those won in France, England and Russia, 'foreign' ideological imports as a general rule were treated with caution: 'Africans cannot be mere doers and imitators of other nations and their ideologies . . . [T]hey must at all costs retain and determinedly preserve their own essential character and identity.'[17] However, this determination to forge an independent African-nationalist ideology was expressed inconsistently, with the ANCYL's uncompromising hostility towards foreign/white/European Marxism contrasting with its initial sympathy towards foreign/white/European ultra-nationalism and fascism. In Lembede's discussion of Marxism in his MA thesis on the conception of God in the writings of philosophers from Descartes to the present (1945), for example, he characterises the Marxist attitude towards religion – and its limitations – as follows:

> According to this theory, God is merely a complex of ideas engendered by the ignorance of mankind and by its subjection firstly beneath the forces of nature, and secondly by class oppression. By spreading and disseminating scientific knowledge among the masses and by abolishing social classes, religion and the belief in the gods will automatically disappear.[18]

The authorities Lembede invokes to demolish the foreign ideas of the white atheist Marx are the Afrikaner nationalist philosopher-politician Nicolaas Diederichs (1903–1978) and the Flemish Catholic priest and poet Guido Gezelle (1830–1899).

In *Die Kommunisme: Sy Teorie en Taktiek* (1938), Diederichs condemns Marxism for its 'superficiality' and 'childish optimism'; its elevation of Marx and other Communist leaders 'to the status of prophets who have brought the message of salvation'; and for 'locating its worldview not in God, but in man as social being, the proletariat'.[19] For Lembede, Diederichs's key insight into the Marxist conception of religion is its failure to appreciate that only through Christ can adversity be overcome: Marxism 'deplorably overlooks... the problem of human suffering which cannot be removed, abolished or done away with, even in a classless society'.[20] To support his argument, Lembede quotes Diederichs's sarcastic question asking whether 'in communist civilisation sickness and death cease to exist', and his claim that 'aside from the path of suffering, there is the path that leads to God, namely the path of joy and gratitude'.[21] Lembede concludes by expressing his own Christian feelings via a quotation (in the Flemish original) from a Gezelle poem, which expresses the human soul's sense of awe as it looks up to heaven.[22]

Diederichs was not the only Afrikaner intellectual/politician Lembede cited in his efforts to theorise a robust Africanism that could withstand all the contending '-isms' of his day. He quoted approvingly Paul Kruger's insistence on the need to learn from history,[23] and ended an article on African nationalism in *Ilanga lase Natal* by exhorting his readers to take inspiration from the words of the Afrikaans poet, A. G. Visser (1878–1929), quoting the final stanza of his poem 'The Awakening' (1927): 'The time for begging has passed,/ And sweet-talk is no longer the plan;/ A place in the sun for me – / The right of a free man'.[24] According to Mda, Lembede studied Smuts's *Holism and Evolution* (1927), but found an even more useful resource in the journalism of H. F. Verwoerd (1901–1966). In Verwoerd's regular column in *Die Transvaler*, Lembede discerned parallels between Afrikaner and African nationalism, and according to Mda, 'read avidly and discussed [Verwoerd's column] with [Jordan] Ngubane'.[25] Lembede did not restrict his reading to South African theorists of ultra-nationalism; Mda describes his fascination with European fascism:

> At the time [1939–45], Lembede was much taken with Mussolini's ideas, 'corporatism'. We discussed this, and fascism and Nazism, to try and formulate our ideas about these philosophies ... Lembede had also read *Mein Kampf*, and Hitler's propositions on the nature of leadership had a direct impact on Lembede's thinking.[26]

Lembede's sympathetic references to European fascists provoked angry responses at the time, with Edwin Mofutsanyana reporting in the CPSA newspaper *Inkululeko* in 1944 that 'Hitler is rapidly losing all his supporters in Europe but he has found a new recruit [in Lembede] in South Africa [and] if one were to close one's eyes when [Lembede] was speaking, one would certainly think one was listening to Hitler broadcasting from Berlin.'[27] Lembede's reply to the article peremptorily denied the charge, focusing instead at greater length on the priority of liberating black South Africans psychologically, and on the need to find common ground between African nationalism and Communism. Lembede proclaimed, 'I stand for the revolt against the enslavement of my people. I strive for the eradication of this "Ja-baas" mentality, which for centuries has been systematically and subtly implanted into the minds of Africans,' and he pleaded with the editors of *Inkululeko* not to widen the gulf between 'Communism and African Nationalism in this country [because] it must be remembered that practically every African is a nationalist at heart'.[28] Despite Lembede's demurral, the association of the Youth League's nationalism with Nazism lingered, as four years later, Mda in a letter to Godfrey Pitje still felt the need to spell out that the nationalism of the ANCYL 'has nothing to do with Fascism and Nationalism Socialism (Hitleric version) nor with the imperialistic and neo-Fascist Nationalism of the Afrikaners (the Malan type). Ours is the pure Nationalism of an oppressed people, seeking freedom from foreign oppression'.[29] Several decades later, Mda claimed the credit for Lembede abandoning his enthusiasm for fascism: 'I clashed with Lembede and argued with him until he ceased to seem to be taking this fascist/Nazi line.'[30]

Lembede's eclectic reading extended from Diederichs and Hitler to Europe's philosophical and literary tradition. His MA thesis includes summaries and discussions of the religious ideas of Plato, Descartes, Spinoza, Leibniz, Berkeley, Hume, Kant, Hegel, Darwin, Marx, William James, Bergson and Samuel Alexander (1859–1938, the author of *Space, Time, Deity* [1920]). As a young teacher, Lembede had told his students – echoing, perhaps unconsciously, Stefan Trofimovitch in Dostoevsky's *The Possessed* (1872) – that 'a pair of boots is more important to an African than all the works of Shakespeare'.[31] But by the time he wrote his MA, he had modified his views, signalling a more generous estimation of literature by concluding three of the chapters with quotations from poems: the chapter on Spinoza with the opening lines of Wordsworth's 'Tintern Abbey' (1798); the chapter on Berkeley with the final stanza of Gezelle's poem 'God is Daar' (1859) in the Flemish original; and the chapter on Kant with the opening lines of 'In a Strange Land' (1893) by Francis Thompson (1859–1907). All three philosophers extend or challenge conventional Christian doctrine, and Lembede turns to poetry both to answer their challenges, and to express his own deeply felt religious faith.

Following a sympathetic paraphrase of Spinoza's teaching that God is immanent in Nature, Lembede identifies Wordsworth as his literary successor, quoting lines from 'Tintern Abbey' to clinch his argument: 'hearing oftentimes [in Nature]/ The still, sad music of humanity'/ . . . / I have felt a presence that disturbs me with the joy/ Of elevated thoughts'.[32] In the same spirit, Lembede interprets Berkeley's philosophy as a refutation of materialism in favour of 'the proposition that ultimate reality is fundamentally spiritual', closing the chapter with Gezelle's lines expressing a pantheistic faith: 'The leaves on the trees/ . . . / The wavelets of the stream/ . . . / The sighing winds and clouds,/ Though far away from God's Holy Throne/ Tell of and interpret/ The sweet mysteries of His Hidden Word.'[33] Unlike Spinoza and Berkeley, Kant proved difficult for Lembede to assimilate to Christianity, so his summary of Kant's agnosticism is followed by his conceding the domain of Reason to Kant, while insisting that Christianity rules the universe beyond Reason. His argument concludes with parallel quotations from the cleric John Thomson and the poet Francis Thompson. From the former's *An Examination of Various Aspects of the New and Old Theology* (1908), he quotes the assertion that 'the doctrines of

Christianity and the great facts upon which they rest, are supernatural and as such, outside of [Reason's] domain', and from the latter's poem 'In a Strange Land', the lines, 'O world invisible, we view thee/ O world intangible, we touch thee/ O world unknowable, we know thee/ Inapprehensible we clutch thee.'[34] The poetry extracts at the ends of the chapters serve a rhetorical function akin to the choruses of hymns, repeating in compressed form the Christian message contained in the content of the verses. In the Epilogue of his thesis, Lembede likens religion to art, music and literature, arguing that they all 'attempt to create harmony between man and the world'.[35]

In his journalism, Lembede enlisted literature in the service of nationalism. Specifically, he proposed an African-nationalist equivalent of the Afrikaans 'Akademie vir Wetenskap en Kuns', laying down the role for all art and artists:

> Our Art (including literature) can also receive a great impetus and fillip from a cultural society or academy of art . . . Art is indispensable to a nation in the process of being born. We need artists to interpret to us and to the world our glorious past, our misery, suffering and tribulation of the present time, our hopes, aspirations and our divine destiny and our great future; to inspire us with the message that there is hope for our race and that we ought therefore to draw plans and lay foundations for a longer future than we can imagine by struggling for national freedom so as to save our race from imminent extinction or extermination. In short we need African artists to interpret the spirit of Africa.[36]

For historical novels, Lembede adds to this exacting aesthetic the criterion that they should 'give an insight into, or knowledge of, the social practices and conditions of the times', citing Thackeray's *Vanity Fair* (1848) and the Afrikaans novel *Vreemdeling* (1944) by Mikro (1903–1968) as exemplars. Applying these criteria to B. W. Vilikazi's novel *Nje-Nempela* (1944), Lembede finds the work wanting: in formal terms, 'the story was pieced together too quickly',[37] but more substantially, it fails to serve the cause of African nationalism by depicting the Zulu nation and its heroes in less than laudatory terms. In judgments that echo Stalinist aesthetics, Lembede lambasts Vilikazi on several counts: for installing as his novel's hero a traitor from Zulu history – 'it is highly undesirable to give [such traitors] publicity or emphasis [because] this may sew [sic] the seed of a defeatist mentality or an inferiority complex in the minds of our children'; for narrating the defeat of the Zulu nation by white people as a humiliation, instead of emphasising that in the face of impossible odds, 'we were compelled to lay down arms – but our National Spirit is invincible, unconquerable'; and for failing to censure the treachery of Chief Bambatha's wife, whose behaviour was 'deplorable', in sharp contrast to 'our African women [who are] of a noble and heroic mould, and that is what should be stressed'.[38] Literature thus serves a didactic function, correcting settler-racist histories, generating narratives of anti-colonial heroics, and forging an African nationalist mythography. In the ANCYL's 1948 Manifesto, Lembede's uncompromising aesthetic was supplemented with a utopian requirement: 'African works of Art can and should reflect not only the present phase of the National liberatory struggle but also the world of beauty that lies beyond the conflict and turmoil of struggle.'[39] In conjunction therefore with the demand for realism was the need for visions of a better world beyond the present struggles for liberation.

A UNITED STATES OF AFRICA STRETCHING FROM CAPE TO CAIRO, MADAGASCAR TO MOROCCO

In its founding Manifesto, the ANCYL described itself as 'the brains-trust and power-station of the spirit of African nationalism',[40] but throughout the 1940s subordinated itself to the ANC, which Lembede described as 'the Mother Body'.[41] The Youth League's influence was especially prominent in what was to become a defining document in the histories of both the ANC and PAC – the 1949 'Programme of Action'. In addition to signalling the tactical transition from petitions and appeals made by reasonable leaders to manifestos and boycotts initiated by collective action, the statement accompanying the Programme of Action drew a distinction between the white ruling minority and the black disenfranchised majority. In its second sentence, the Programme explained:

> By National freedom we mean freedom from white domination and the attainment of political independence. This implies the rejection of the conception of segregation, apartheid, trusteeship, or White leadership, which are all in one way or another motivated by the idea of White domination or by the domination of the White over the Blacks. Like all other people the African people claim the right of self-determination.[42]

For Youth League members like Sobukwe, this conceptual distinction between white domination and black oppression was fundamental. For others like Sisulu, Tambo and Mandela, however, it was superseded six years later by the ANC's Freedom Charter, which declared that 'South Africa belongs to all who live in it, black and white, and that no government can justly claim authority unless it is based on the will of all the people'.[43] PAC leaders subsequently attributed their organisation's genesis to the betrayal by erstwhile Africanist comrades of the Programme of Action. For Leballo, the PAC were the true heirs of the Africanism expressed in the Programme, whereas 'Mandela, Sisulu, Tambo and others had turned against their promise of 1949 [because] they were completely in the clutches of the Communist Party ... and some liberals in Johannesburg [and] were able to say this programme was racialistic and chauvinistic'.[44] Sobukwe was similarly dismissive, describing the ANC leaders as 'a very mediocre lot [who had] abandoned the Program of 1949 altogether. Our aim was always to bring the ANC back to the Program of Action'.[45] For Mda, who sympathised with but never actually joined the PAC, the split between the two factions was caused by their irreconcilable visions of freedom. His pronouns disclose an identification with the PAC's Africanist vision of freedom, and an alienation from the ANC's hope that dialogue with the white government might lead to black liberation: 'We had our "utopia" and the ANC had its "utopia". Their utopia was that someday we could magically "sit down to tea with Verwoerd". It was our utopia versus theirs. But we were ... more pragmatic than they were ... We want freedom, and we want it at all costs.'⁴⁶

The defining element of the PAC's 'utopia' was the extension of its constituency from the nation to the continent, from South Africa to Africa. The forging of a Pan-Africanist collective identity was a response in the first instance to the divide-and-rule logic of European nationalism. In the opening issue of the short lived magazine *Mafube* (*The Dawn of Freedom*), the roots of Europe's antipathy towards insurgent nationalisms were traced back to the Congress of Vienna, which favoured the great nations 'by annexing or dislodging parts of European land, without the slightest consideration being given to the wishes of the small nations living in such lands'.⁴⁷ The damage inflicted upon Europe's smaller nations in 1815 was extended to Africa with the Berlin Conference of 1884, when the European powers imposed artificial boundaries in creating colonies 'without the least consideration being given to the wishes of the people of Africa'.⁴⁸ The 'historic duty [of the PAC] is to right that wrong, and to erase European-imposed boundaries from the face of Africa'.⁴⁹ The specifically Southern African history of Europe's divide-and-rule was elaborated by Sobukwe in a 1957 speech to the Basotho Congress Party (BCP), in which he first listed examples from the colonial period when the English had set African chiefs or tribes in conflict with each other – Ngqika against Ndlambe; Mpande against Dingaan; the Sekukuni against the Swazi; then described how Europeans had generated further divisions by 'setting up the so-called "Christian" Africans against the so-called "heathens", the educated against the uneducated'; and concluded by warning his audience to distinguish between the 'Mosotho' and 'the black European', characterising the latter as 'one of the "good boys", the "moderate respectable and responsible leaders"',⁵⁰ who foments division by serving the white man instead of the African masses. PAC ideologues acknowledged that the founding fathers of the ANC (the SANNC in its original incarnation) had in 1912 laid the foundations for overcoming tribal divisions by inscribing their supporters as South Africans, rather than as Xhosa, Tswana or Zulu, or so on. But Sobukwe in the address to the BCP went further, extending his 'imagined community' by speaking on behalf of all Africans and thus constituting a collective exceeding the nation: 'We cannot forget that we are part of the vast continent of Africa, which is today demanding the right of self-determination.'⁵¹

The rhetorical construction of a Pan-Africanist community transcending the nation concealed class tensions dividing the new party's membership. From its inception, the educated urban minority epitomised by Sobukwe was outnumbered by the much larger body of less formally educated and predominantly rural supporters, whose spokesman was Josias Madzunya. The bookish Sobukwe condescended to Madzunya, suggesting he 'was not an educated man. He probably didn't grasp the full import of our philosophy. His thinking was rather "primitive"'.⁵² Madzunya in turn regarded Sobukwe and his faction as incapable of effective political action, accusing them of failing to 'organise Orlando West, because they say they are intellectuals and they only drink tea in their houses'.⁵³ In 1959, the year the PAC was formally established, Sobukwe's faction prevailed, denying Madzunya a post on the party's executive.

A flurry of publications communicating an optimistic vision of a united Pan-Africanism ensued. In an article in the January 1959 edition of *The Africanist*, Sobukwe claimed that African nationalism 'is the only liberatory outlook that can bind the masses by providing them with a loyalty higher than that of the tribe'.[54] Four months later at the inaugural convention of the PAC, he invoked inspirational Pan-Africanist figures like Nkrumah, Padmore and Du Bois, concluding that 'it is the sacred duty of every African state to strive ceaselessly and energetically for the creation of a United States of Africa, stretching from Cape to Cairo, Morocco to Madagascar'.[55] The Manifesto adopted by the PAC at the convention proclaimed Africanism 'the third social force in the world', contending as an equal with capitalism and Communism, and serving 'the material, intellectual and spiritual interests of Africa'.[56] Confident that Africanism 'operates to liberate Africa and to create a socialist social order, original in conception, Africanist in orientation, and creative in content', the Manifesto concluded in Hegelian terms: 'In its dialectical march towards the final synthesis of Africanism, African nationalism is destined to create the conditions favourable for the development of the African personality.'[57] For another leading PAC intellectual, Peter Raboroko (1917–2000), integral to Africanism were the concepts of 'Nationalism', 'Socialism' and 'Democracy', and taken together, they ensured the defeat of white rule and guaranteed freedom for Africa:

> The crucial issue today is whether the interests of the five million Europeans throughout Africa must continue to dominate over those of the two hundred and eighty million Africans, or whether the reverse should obtain ... Nationalism demands that the interests of indigenous peoples should dominate over those of aliens, because the country belongs to the indigenous peoples. Socialism demands that the interests of the workers should dominate over those of their employers, because their contribution to the creation of wealth is more significant than that of their bosses. Democracy demands that those of the majority should dominate over those of the minority, because they are a majority. In Africa in general, and in South Africa particular, the African people are indigenous to the soil, are the real workers and are the majority. Their right to the effective control of their interests is, therefore, unchallengeable.[58]

In addition to PAC's 'continentalism', its 'positive neutralism' and its loosely defined socialism, the journalist Peter Rodda in his report on the 1959 inauguration added two further commitments that defined the new party: its 'emotional and sometimes eccentric and exclusive Christianity',[59] and its anti-Communism. In the popular imagination, the PAC appeared as a defiant alternative to the ANC. An article in *Drum* in early 1960 described the PAC leadership as a 'tough-talking group of angry young men', and recounted Raboroko telling the reporter, '"I'm pleased the whites are so proud of the houses they have built us in Meadowlands ... It's a good job BECAUSE THE WHITES ARE GOING TO BE LIVING IN THEM, AND WE'LL BE LIVING IN LOWER HOUGHTON, MAN" [capitals in original].''.[60]

OUR OWN ESSENTIAL AFRICAN GENIUS

For several members of the Africanist intelligentsia writing in the 1950s, culture and literature had an important role to play in promoting African nationalism. For Sobukwe, the first task of the writer is to explain the complexities of society. In his 1949 address on behalf of his graduating class at Fort Hare, he had deferred to the exceptional insight of poets and novelists, telling his audience, 'This is a difficult period to analyse. It is a confused period, as only a Mqhayi [the Sotho poet Theko], Bering or Dickens could describe.'[61] Mda in the pamphlet 'Comment on the 1949 programme of African nationalism' (1954) repeated Sobukwe's requirement that artists and writers should describe reality, adding the further expectation that they should provide images of hope: 'our artists could very easily advance the liberatory struggles by reflecting in their works the concrete reality of the sufferings of the oppressed millions, as well as the triumph, peace, beauty, and glory of freedom'.[62] For Leballo, writing in *The Africanist* three years later, literature was particularly useful in describing oppression, and to illustrate, he notes how 'ably' Harry Bloom (1913–1981) in his novel *Episode* (1956) captures the impact of the pass system on black women.[63]

The most extended reflection on how art and literature might serve Africanism was Mda's essay 'Some targets to be aimed at in art and literature' (1956). Although Mda opens with the Keats quotation, 'Beauty is truth, truth beauty/ That is all ye know on earth/ And all ye need to know', and closes with a quotation from H. I. E. Dhlomo's long poem 'Valley of a Thousand Hills', 'God who created sights so fair/ Create again, but leave out pain,/ A world of love and beauty,/ Divinity fair',[64] the core of the essay takes an instrumental view of art and literature at a variance to Keats and Dhlomo's elevation of 'beauty'. Insisting that 'the Programme of African Nation-Building should include a cultural aspect, whose aim should be to encourage the development of African enterprising genius',[65] Mda proceeds to lay down guidelines for the different genres. For painting and sculpture, 'we should use the "European" media and forms to express our own essential African genius'.[66] For music, we should both 'sing of our past heroes and the long road of struggle', and 'cultivate in [the masses] the habit of faith in victory and in the final triumph of the forces of freedom'.[67] For literary fiction, we need novels 'which deal with the people as they are in the actual South African society, [which] grasp the underlying forces in the general struggle for National Liberation and for Africanist democracy [and] give an impetus to, and map out the direction of the liberation struggle'.[68] And for drama, we should learn from the techniques of Shakespeare and Bernard Shaw, but then deploy them in forging a 'new renaissance of African drama' dedicated to accelerating the 'march [of the masses] to their destiny as a free people'.[69] Expressed in disconnected fragments, Sobukwe, Leballo and Mda's occasional comments on literature and aesthetics therefore accommodated the appropriation of elements of European culture (Dickens, Keats, Shakespeare, Shaw), but prescribed that literature should combine critical realism and inspirational utopianism in serving the 'Programme of African Nation-Building'.

As Lembede and Mda had done, so too Sobukwe continued to recruit literary works from Europe and North America to promote African nationalism. In his speech to the BCP in 1957, for example, he quoted from the poem 'Horatio' in *The Lays of Ancient Rome* (1842) by Thomas Babington Macaulay (1800–1859) and from the novel *My Glorious Brothers* (1948) by Howard Fast (1914–2003). Both quotations proclaim heroic sacrifice in the course of resisting a terrible enemy. In Macaulay's much-anthologised poem,[70] the Roman soldier Horatio stands with his two companions on the Sublician Bridge and confronts the mighty Etruscan army of Lars Porsena. Sobukwe identifies Horatio's defence of Rome as a precursor to anti-colonial resistance in Lesotho: '[W]e are looking forward to the dawn of the day when the young herdboys will listen to the call of [the BCP] and say with Macaulay's soldier, "And how can man die better/ Than facing fearful odds,/ For the ashes of his fathers,/ And the temples of his Gods."'[71] In Fast's novel, the Jewish-Maccabee rebels in second-century BCE Palestine face the ruthless occupying forces of the Greek-Seleucid Empire. Rather than attempt to negotiate peace with their oppressors, their spokesman Simon declares, '"[S]o long as two men walk free on Judaean soil, the fight goes on . . . it goes on until all the world knows that in Judaea there is a people who will not bend their knee to man or god! We were slaves in Egypt, and we shall not be slaves again."'[72] Sobukwe seizes on Simon's defiant words, exhorting his Basotho listeners to direct them at those in Lesotho seeking limited concessions instead of unqualified freedom: 'Tell the "good boys" that! . . . Tell the Christian Democratic Party that! . . . Tell British Imperialism that!'[73] For Sobukwe, Macaulay's and Fast's words function as a riposte to those seeking to negotiate or compromise with the oppressor.

My Glorious Brothers was cited repeatedly, both in PAC publications and by Sobukwe in his personal correspondence. The front cover of the January 1959 edition of *The Africanist* contains two lines: 'THE CAUSE OF AFRICA MUST TRIUMPH' (capitals in original), and a quotation from *My Glorious Brothers*, '"Resistance to tyranny is the first obedience to God."'[74] In a letter from Robben Island to Benjamin Pogrund in April 1966, Sobukwe confided, 'I do not believe that [Fast's novel] *Spartacus* can compare with *My Glorious Brothers*, describing the struggle of the Maccabees. My wife and I read it together, page by page from beginning to end, and we wept as we read.'[75] Six weeks later, Sobukwe explained in another letter to Pogrund why the novel meant so much to him:

> In your reading of *My Glorious Brothers*, you have by now presumably reached what to me is the whole message of the book: 'Tell Ragesh that the Maccabee is in Judaea, the Maccabee and his brother Simon, etc. etc.' A similar configuration appears in *Spartacus*, 'Tell the Senate, etc.' And what a message! And yet I have always felt that the message in *Spartacus* was a political testament. The message to Ragesh [in *My Glorious Brothers*] was in the genre of the great utterances of the prophets – a timeless message for all oppressed. And when Ragesh, the High Priest, received it, he wept. It reminded him of what he was. I can never forget that passage.[76]

Sobukwe's intense identification with the struggle of the Maccabees, and in particular with the message of no compromise in the struggle for freedom sent to the rabbi Ragesh, elevates *My Glorious Brothers* above *Spartacus* (1951), as he favours 'the prophetic' above 'the political'. Sobukwe's interest in Jewish-Israeli history and literature is expressed throughout his correspondence with Pogrund, but it had its limits, as one of his last letters from Robben Island indicates: 'Without sounding like Oliver Twist, may I ask you for more books by Jewish authors – particularly Malamud, Golden and others. Only don't send me anything by Leon Uris. I have become allergic to him.'[77]

Notwithstanding Sobukwe's preference for *My Glorious Brothers*, it was *Spartacus* that enjoyed the wider readership in PAC circles. Prompted by interviewer Gail Gerhart, Z. B. Molete recalled that in the 1950s and 1960s, the novel 'was popularised by the Africanists themselves. Because every time the *Bulletin* came out, it carried a quotation from *Spartacus*. And then [readers] got interested because the Africanists used to have that practice of quoting from various revolutionary books'.[78] In *The Africanist* of May/June 1959, a page-long extract from *Spartacus* was published. Like the passage Sobukwe quoted from *My Glorious Brothers* in 1957, the extract from *Spartacus* expresses uncompromising defiance and a yearning for freedom. The extract is Spartacus's message to the Roman Senate following first major victory of the slave rebels over the Roman army in Capua:

> Tell [the Senate] that they sent their cohorts against us, and that we destroyed their cohorts. Tell them that we are slaves – what they call the *instrumentum vocale*. The tool with a voice. Tell them what our voice says. We say that the world is tired of them, tired of your rotten Senate and your rotten Rome ... The world is tired of the song of the whip. It is the only song the noble Romans know. But we don't want to hear that song any more. In the beginning all men were alike and they lived in peace and they shared among them what they had. But now there are two kinds of men, the master and the slave. But there are more of us than there are of you, many more. And we are stronger than you, better than you. All that is good in mankind belongs to us ... You have made a mockery of all men dream of, of the work of a man's hands and the sweat of a man's brow ... And you have built your grandeur by being a thief to the whole world. Well, it is finished. Tell your Senate that it is all finished. That is the voice of the tool ... The whole world will hear the voice of the tool – and to the slaves of the world, we will cry out, Rise up and cast off your chains![79]

The identification of black South Africans under apartheid with Fast's fictionalised second-century BCE Maccabees under Greek-Seleucid tyranny is thus extended to Fast's fictionalised first-century BCE slaves under Roman domination. For Sobukwe and his comrades, the same elements are present in all three contexts: an exploited and oppressed majority fighting for freedom; a vicious and hypocritical ruling elite clinging to power; and the ultimate certainty of freedom for the oppressed, even if it is short-lived in Fast's novels, and lies in the future for the PAC.

The PAC practice identified by Molete of 'quoting from various revolutionary books' in order to draw in more readers was also on display in the magazine *Mafube (The Dawn of Freedom)*. Under the heading 'Freedom for its own sake?', the magazine quoted the following passage from Amanke Okafor, the Nigerian Marxist and author of *Nigeria: Why We Fight for Freedom* (1949):

> We fight for freedom not for its own sake nor in order to create opportunities for careerists to become politicians. We fight because of the chance freedom will give us to organise the resources of our country and use them to establish healthy and decent conditions of life for our people; to wipe out the miseries and degradations which have been the lot of the Africans hitherto. **And to enable the black man wherever he may be to get back his self-respect and raise his head as an equal among men.** (Bold in original.)[80]

The emboldening of the final sentence in the quotation from Okafor declaring that freedom enables the recovery of black self-respect (rather than the earlier sentence arguing that freedom enables the establishment of 'healthy and decent conditions of life') reveals PAC priorities, which complicate (at least) the sequence of Okafor's Marxist argument that has improved material conditions preceding the restoration of black self-respect.

If the PAC appropriation of Okafor involved some shift of emphasis, *Mafube*'s recruitment of Walter Scott in the service of Pan-Africanism required even more ingenuity. In an essay arguing that the European theft of African land is condoned by the Freedom Charter's declaration that '"South Africa belongs to all who live in it,"' Scott's poem 'Lay of the Last Minstrel, Canto VI' (1805) is quoted to affirm the intimate bond between autochthonous identity and land. Black South Africans have not only been 'physically emasculated through alienation of land'; they have been subjected to 'a corrosion of the spiritual attachment to it, cutting them adrift in the wide world – a rootless, vagabond people'.[81] Scott's words – '"Breathes there a man with soul so dead/ That to himself hath never said/ This is mine own, my native land"' – capture the power of the attachment to land, and only by restoring black South Africans to their stolen land can 'this national soil erosion'[82] be arrested. The words from 'Lay of the Last Minstrel' quoted in *Mafube* open a stanza that had frequently been anthologised as a stand-alone poem with the title 'Patriotism', and in this decontextualised form, its (conservative) Romantic message celebrating the sanctity of 'native land' resonated for (radical) Pan-Africanists seeking land restitution.

That the PAC at the moment of its inception aspired to go beyond invoking or quoting inspirational literary works of the past – whether African (Mqhayi, Bering, Dhlomo or Okafor), British (Dickens, Keats, Shaw, Shakespeare, Macaulay or Scott), or American (Fast) – and to produce its own literary tradition, is revealed in an urgent notice published in *The Africanist* of February 1960:

> Extremely valuable manuscripts. ABOUT 25 POEMS, AVERAGING 100 LINES EACH, AND 15 'SHORT – STORIES' OF UNUSUAL BEAUTY HAVE BEEN LOST. THEY WERE BEING TYPED AT 52 KING'S CHAMBERS, 49 COMMISSIONER STREET WHEN THEY MYSTERIOUSLY DISAPPEARED UNDER VERY SUSPICIOUS CIRCUMSTANCES. THE MSS. BELONG TO MR. KANG ALSO R.

SOBUKWE. BOTH THE POEMS AND THE STORIES HAVE BEEN PRAISED TO THE SKIES BY BOTH LITERARY CRITICS AND RANK-AND- FILERS AS OUTSTANDING, UNUSUAL, REALISTIC AND VERY BEAUTIFUL. (Capitals in original.)[83]

There is no record of the twenty-five poems and fifteen short stories ever having been recovered, and they have never turned up in any of the PAC archives. What the notice does disclose, however, is a sense of what kind of literature the PAC intelligentsia valued. To qualify for praise, poems or short stories had to be 'UNUSUAL', 'REALISTIC' and 'VERY BEAUTIFUL', and in addition, they had to appeal both to 'LITERARY CRITICS' and to 'RANK-AND-FILERS'. Whatever the explanation for the disappearance of these particular forty poems and short stories, they were never replaced; the hostile political environment ensured that literary works enjoying PAC patronage and satisfying these criteria never saw the light of day. Instead, the first literary representations of the PAC were produced by writers hostile to the party and its ideology.

DISGRACE TO THE BLACK NATION

Following its inauguration in April 1959, the PAC launched campaigns aimed at liberating the enslaved minds of the African masses: a 'status campaign' encouraged the boycott of white-owned shops that racially denigrated black customers, and an anti-pass campaign proposed in September 1959 and launched shortly afterwards, aimed to challenge the central pivot of the apartheid economy, and to act as the trigger for further (ultimately revolutionary) acts of civil disobedience. State repression was swift and violent: the crowds of Africans led by PAC cadres attempting to hand over their passes at police stations were met with arrest and gunfire, most notoriously at Sharpeville on 21 March 1960, where sixty-seven were killed and 186 wounded. The outraged response to Sharpeville both in South Africa and internationally prompted the state to suspend pass law arrests on 26 March, and the extended stay-away observed by black workers (particularly in Cape Town) in the same week provoked short-term capital flight and panic on the Johannesburg stock market. A state of emergency was declared on 30 March, the same day 30,000 peaceful marchers led by Philip Kgosana (1936–2017) entered central Cape Town. Intensified repression followed, with the PAC and ANC banned under the Unlawful Organisations Act on 8 April, the pass laws reintroduced, and the police taking full advantage of the emergency legislation to clamp down on further resistance. In the vacuum left by the imprisonment and exile of the PAC leadership, an armed insurrection was initiated by the PAC's military wing Poqo made up of fifty-eight semi-autonomous cells of militants. Targeting white civilians and black agents of the apartheid state, Poqo 'task forces' killed twenty-four people in fifteen different attacks between March 1962 and February 1963.[84] Aided by infiltrations, betrayals and internecine conflict within the PAC, the state arrested 3,246 Poqo members and convicted 1,162 on a range of common law and statutory charges, with 124 found guilty of murder, and forty-two executed at Pretoria Central Prison between 1963 and 1968.[85] Under such wide-ranging political pressures, PAC members unsurprisingly directed little attention to literature and culture, and as a consequence, most of the literary representations of the PAC and its struggle against the apartheid state in the 1960s were by writers loyal to competing political traditions – Melikhaya Mbutumu and Peter Abrahams to the ANC;[86] Richard Rive to the NEUM;[87] and Alex La Guma to the SACP and ANC.[88]

Between September 1959 and March 1963, Mbutumu, the *imbongi* (praise poet/bard) to the Themba paramount chief Sabata Dalinyebo (1928–1986), produced a number of *izimbongo* (oral/praise poems) commenting on the apartheid state and its conflict with the PAC in the Transkei. Transcribed by Archie Mafeje, Mbutumu's poems attacked the racist state and its puppet-leaders like Kaiser Matanzima (1915–2003). Mbutumu addresses Matanzima directly to criticise his greed, ambition and in particular his opportunism in seizing upon the false 'freedom' offered to the Transkei by the white regime: 'But opportunists have grabbed [independence for the Transkei] with both hands./ . . ./ The way this "freedom" is being offered is puzzling./ Perhaps, they see it as the last straw in their dying days.'[89] If Matanzima's opportunism was one false road to 'freedom', Poqo's strategy of targeting white civilians was another. In a March 1963 poem, Mbutumu censured a specific Poqo attack, the killing of the five white civilians at the Mbashe Bridge in Thembuland on 4 February 1963:[90]

> For what has happened in Thembuland is a disgrace and a scandal.
> It has not been done by Thembu but by invaders and foreigners.
> A Thembu, a Coloured and a white is one and the same thing.
> We all share a common bond of belonging to a single nation.
> Grobelaar's death is an obvious sign of political degeneracy.
> Why kill an innocent poor white? The curses of the Almighty be upon
>   you murderers of children? Where were those who stand in your way to
>   liberty?[91]

Mbutumu extends his disapproval of this singular instance of violence to a blanket condemnation of Poqo's tactics, declaring, 'You Poqo members, you are excluded,/ For you have acted stupidly and irresponsibly./ You have disgraced the black nation.'[92] With both Matanzima's comprador route and Poqo's millenarian violence rejected, the only road to true freedom, 'the only remedy' for curing the diseased racist state, Mbutumu argues, is for 'the black multitudes . . . to unite under one leader'.[93] Dalinyebo is just such a leader, 'the only weapon that can cut Matanzima down to size'.[94]

Written in 1961 and 1962, Rive's *Emergency* (1964) is set in Cape Town in the weeks after Sharpeville, and follows the protagonist Andrew Dreyer as he confronts the rapidly changing political landscape. Dreyer wrestles with the alternatives provided by his two friends, the NEUM intellectual Abe Hanslo and the ANC supporter Justin Bailey. In an argument between the two shortly after the Sharpeville massacre, Abe sets out the NEUM critique of the PAC:

> The PAC started this campaign in a spirit of bravado and political opportunism ... All this was somehow intended to bring freedom to the so-called African people by 1963 ... I don't for a moment think that the people responded to the PAC call as such. I don't think that they were aware of its policy then or that they are aware of it now. They were simply prepared to attend any meeting critical of the Government ... Quite apart from [the PAC's] Africanist orientation which is as bad as white racialism, they haven't even begun to consider fundamental problems such as the kind of society they envisage. They don't take into account, or even understand, the kind of oppression they are fighting against.[95]

In responding to Abe's critique, Justin does not defend the PAC, but rather defends the activist tradition of *both* Congress parties and attacks the intellectualism of the NEUM:

> Do we sit on our backsides discussing the finer points of political theories? ... All you do is talk, talk, talk! You never *do* anything. Your whole outlook on life is negative. You oppose everything ... You talk of principles while people are starving, gaoled and banished. You talk about humanity in high-faluting academic terms while the dead of Sharpeville are crying for revenge.[96]

At this stage of the novel, Dreyer does not choose between his friends' contending positions, nor does he attempt to formulate any kind of synthesis or third way. In other passages, the conflict between the NEUM and the Congress parties is presented as one between rationality and sentiment.[97] But at the end of the novel, having just marched with the 30,000 into Cape Town on 30 March, Dreyer reaches a temporary resolution by expressing his commitment to an Africanist community as a corrective to Abe's unrelenting criticisms: '"I felt part of it all. That was me. I was the crowd milling outside the Police Station. I felt for the first time in my life that I was Africa. They might gaol our bodies, but they can never break our spirits."'[98]

Unlike the critical but nuanced representation of the PAC post-Sharpeville in Rive's novel, Abrahams's *A Night of Their Own* (1965) and La Guma's *In the Fog of the Season's End* (1972) give minimal credit to the contribution of the PAC to anti-apartheid resistance. Abrahams's novel is dedicated to 'my friends Walter Sisulu and Nelson Mandela and all the others, the captured and the still free, who are at war against the evils of this night of their own'. *A Night of Their Own* narrates the clandestine arrival in South Africa of Richard Nkosi/Dube; his passionate affair with the Indian woman Dee Nunkhoo; and his escape once again into exile. In the only substantial mention of the PAC in the novel, Sammy Naidoo, the leader of the Indian underground opposition in Natal, explains to Nkosi the threat posed by Poqo to the Congress tradition:

> 'Poqo challenged the old Congress leadership and asserted the methods of the counter-terror ... Poqo and the Africanists reacted by repudiating and denouncing all co-operation between black and white. They went further.

They insisted that nobody could help the Africans win their salvation and that they therefore did not need anybody's help. This shocked everybody, the African moderates included. The liberal and progressive types in all the minority groups – the coloureds, the whites, the Indians – had assumed that all they had to do was declare themselves on the side of the Africans and they would be welcomed with open arms and invited to lead the poor blacks. So, when the poor blacks said we don't need you and we don't want you, it was a nasty shock. But more shocking was the apparent warmth with which the African masses welcomed the stand of the new leadership.'[99]

Naidoo explains to Nkosi that in such a racially polarised context he and his Indian comrades 'have to beg for an opportunity to prove the commitment of the Indians; we have to beg for a chance to make such a contribution',[100] and the unfolding plot of the novel refutes the exclusive Africanism of the PAC – Nkosi's escape is enabled by a wealthy Indian businessman and a white sea-captain. After Naidoo's brief analysis of Poqo, the novel makes no further mention of the PAC, Sharpeville or the march of the 30,000 into Cape Town; rather, the ANC's non-racial humanism as expressed by the saintly Nkosi in the final chapter provides the defining message of the novel: '[T]he great South African adventure . . . can only begin when the land is rid of this racial ugliness . . . [A] good society provides for and protects its minorities . . . Democracy is the rule of the majority, but the full flowering of the human spirit needs more.'[101] The challenge to the ANC posed by Poqo and summarised by Naidoo at the beginning of the novel is thus contained by a restatement of the Freedom Charter's racially inclusive humanism at the novel's conclusion.

Whereas Mbutumu, Rive and Abrahams acknowledge the PAC, providing at least partial snapshots of its ideology, La Guma's *In the Fog of the Season's End* (1972) writes the PAC out of history. Chapter 9 of the novel narrates the Sharpeville massacre in allegorical mode, transmuting Van der Byl Park into 'Steel Town', Sharpeville into 'the Township', the police into 'the Sergeant', and the black victims of the massacre into individual archetypes – 'the Child', 'the Washerwoman', 'the Bicycle Messenger' and 'the Outlaw'. As for the PAC, who initiated the campaign to hand in passes at police stations, it is never mentioned by name, and its very existence doubted: 'Who were calling on the people [to hand in their passes]? A rival organisation, *agents-provocateur*, the real leaders?'[102] Even La Guma's sympathetic biographer struggles to justify taking such liberties with history, suggesting that the novel succumbs to 'the worst traditions of authoritarian historiography'.[103]

SOBUKWE'S BOOKS

Sobukwe's love of literature was by no means restricted to Western literary works like Fast's novels and Macaulay's poems; during his period of employment at the University of the Witwatersrand, he took a professional interest in African-language literature, publishing five book reviews between 1957 and 1959 in the university's journal *African Studies*.[104] The first review of Guybon B. Sinxo's didactic short stories is neutral, providing plot summaries and pointing out typographical errors, but in the subsequent reviews, Sobukwe passes increasingly confident judgments. Noting the dramatist Witness K. Tamsanqa's plea for indulgence because 'drama is still a comparatively unexplored field in Xhosa literature', Sobukwe adds drily, 'indeed such a plea is necessary',[105] as he proceeds to point out the many flaws in Tamsanqa's melodrama *Buzani kubawo*. In the last review he wrote, Sobukwe found E. S. M. Dlova's novel *Umvuzo wesoono* lacking in nuance and complexity. At the level of character, Sobukwe complains, 'the hero is thoroughly noble . . . while the villain is thoroughly bad . . . The theme of good versus evil, with good reserved for the christianized and evil for the heathen, besides being hackneyed, is not realistic. It savours too much of propaganda'.[106] The flaws in characterisation were compounded by the polarised representations of the different Southern African tribes, with 'sweeping condemnations of both the Hlubi and the so-called Fingoes [whereas] the Xhosa are not once censured. It is again the same picture of all-black versus all-white, except that now the canvass is larger, accommodating tribes, instead of individuals'.[107] Sobukwe's literary criticisms of the crude character-and-tribe binaries in the novel coincide with his political criticisms of the racial binaries legislated by the apartheid state.

Like Tabata and Jordan, Sobukwe turned African oral literature to political ends. In an interview in *Drum*, for example, he told the story of two wolves, one lean and hungry, the other fat and contented. The fat wolf explains to the thin wolf that his master gives him food and a room, and invites the thin wolf to come and live with him. The thin wolf agrees to join him, but then notices the fat wolf wearing a collar, and discovers that his master ties him up at night. Changing his mind, the thin wolf says, '"I won't go with you. I'd rather be free, even if I must stay hungry,"' and Sobukwe ends by spelling out the meaning of the story: 'The Africanists are like the thin wolf.'[108]

After leaving his job at the university and entering full-time politics, Sobukwe's opportunities to read literature disappeared: he was arrested in March 1960 in the wake of the pass campaign, and convicted under the Criminal Law Amendment Act of 1952 to three years in prison. On 23 April 1963, he was transferred from Pretoria Central Prison to Robben Island, where he was detained under a clause in the Suppression of Communism Act of 1950 (as amended by the General Laws Amendment Act of 1963) that empowered the Minister of Justice to extend the prison sentence of anyone convicted under security legislation if he considered the prisoner likely to further the ends of Communism (as defined by the state). Known as 'the Sobukwe clause', the legislation was used to detain Sobukwe in solitary confinement on Robben Island from April 1963 until his release in May 1969.

During his imprisonment, Sobukwe established regular correspondences with Benjamin Pogrund (1933–), journalist and friend, and Nell Marquard (d. 1981), lecturer in English at Stellenbosch University and the wife of the liberal intellectual Leo Marquard (1897–1974). In both correspondences, substantial attention was dedicated to literature, with Sobukwe asking for books, and then discussing them with Pogrund and Marquard.[109] As he revealed in his crushing review of Dlova's novel in *African Studies*, Sobukwe was swift to dismiss literary works he disliked.

We have noted his aversion to Leon Uris's novels, but in addition, he scorned the popular fiction of Ian Fleming,[110] the contemporary South African poetry of Guy Butler,[111] the modernism of Faulkner[112] and the liberal fiction of Alan Paton.[113]

Sobukwe's most extended expression of literary animus, however, was directed against Shakespeare's *Hamlet*, which he elaborated in several letters to Marquard between April 1965 and July 1968. In his first mention of the play, Sobukwe concedes that he has never seen Shakespeare performed on stage, but that nonetheless, 'I cannot share the enthusiasm of most students of English for *Hamlet*. I have never liked *Hamlet* and find it impossible to read any criticism that is favourable to the play.'[114] To challenge Sobukwe's hostility, Marquard asked him to reread the play as well as an article she had written on *Hamlet*, in which she followed John Dover Wilson and G. Wilson Knight in providing a redemptive interpretation of the play. According to Marquard, 'it is difficult to reconcile Shakespeare's Hamlet, so essentially civilised, intelligent and imaginative, with the idea of vengeance',[115] and accordingly, she argues that Hamlet's killing of Claudius in Act V is quite distinct from revenge; it is an act of public justice that restores social harmony. The ultimate meaning of *Hamlet*, for Marquard, lies in its reassurance that justice and virtue prevail over evil:

> It is not only justice that is vindicated by the action of the play – revenge would have been a rough justice – but that heightened awareness, that fullness of life, that can see and rejoice in man's godlike qualities, and see and repudiate the most specious evil . . . Virtue in *Hamlet* is not charactering of precepts and rules of conduct, but the awareness that is life in its fullness. When Hamlet has come out of the grave and his perceptions and feelings are harmonised with his will and judgment, virtue prevails and justice is established.[116]

In his response to Marquard's challenge, Sobukwe first explains his general objection to her sanguine reading, and then identifies specific flaws in her interpretation. In tentative terms, Sobukwe rejects Marquard's disavowal of vengeance, as well as her argument that Hamlet ultimately embodies public justice and social equilibrium: 'No, I do not think vengeance poses any difficulty for us [modern readers]'; and with respect to the final Act, 'you say that Hamlet [kills Claudius] as a judge, that he is fully integrated. I have my doubts'.[117] More specifically, Sobukwe questions the characterisation of Gertrude – 'what baffles [Hamlet] is how his mother could possibly fall for another man'[118] – and where Marquard hears an assured tone in Hamlet's words in the final Act, Sobukwe hears cadences of continuing self-doubt.[119] Two years later, Sobukwe was still wrestling with *Hamlet*, and conceded that his antipathy to the play could be attributable to his own resistance to its sacrosanct status:

> I dislike *Hamlet*, I believe, because from the first I was told that it was Shakespeare's greatest tragedy. My teachers waxed poetic when they described the play. I read *Julius Caesar*, *King Lear* and enjoyed them. I read *Hamlet* and, I am afraid, didn't feel that it was greater than the others, either in language or in characterisation . . . With respect to *Hamlet*, then, I believe my dislike stems

from sheer perverseness. Because all the others think highly of him, to show my indifference of mind I have to class the play as indifferent. I'll try and find the reason through ruthless self-analysis![120]

Sobukwe's reluctance to venerate *Hamlet* contrasts with the respectful annotations by other prisoners on Robben Island of Sonny Venkatrathnam's 'Shakespeare Bible': Saths Cooper selected Hamlet's speech in Act 1 scene 4 ('This heavy-headed revel east and west'); Strini Moodley Hamlet's soliloquy in Act 2 scene 2 ('What a piece of work is a man!'); and Michael Dingake Polonius's advice to Laertes in Act 1 scene 3 ('The wind sits on the shoulder of your sail').[121]

Sobukwe's refusal to worship at the altar of *Hamlet* was complemented by a confidence in his own eclectic literary enthusiasms, as he praised the comic novels of Wodehouse;[122] the middlebrow fiction of C. P. Snow;[123] and the tragedies of Sophocles.[124] He returned most frequently to Snow's novels, with *The Masters* a particular favourite. Snow's characters, Sobukwe declares, 'leave me limp with pain. They seem to suffer simply and purely because they are themselves. Their suffering is written into the code of their personality'.[125] He recalls his brother as a boy killing a snake with a sharp knife, and compares the snake's death throes to the suffering described in Snow's novels: 'The blade would cut into [the snake's] soft belly and as it felt the pain it would push forward more firmly, hoping to escape the pain, but merely succeeding in disembowelling itself. That is how I feel Snow's tragic characters behave.'[126] Wrestling with why he finds Snow's characters so affecting, Sobukwe speculates that he is so moved because 'we find the suffering of a good man insupportable'.[127]

In letters to Pogrund, Sobukwe confessed to feeling guilty about his susceptibility to literature, berating himself for preferring novels to books on economics and politics. On one occasion, he recalled working on a 'stolid volume' of political theory when a box of novels arrived for him: 'it has demanded tremendous self-discipline to continue with it in the face of the blatant coquetry of Shaw, Somerset Maugham, Oscar Wilde, George Orwell and other luscious characters'.[128]

If the masculine world of politics succumbed to the feminine world of literature in Sobukwe's personal reading preferences, the hierarchy was reversed when he prescribed the political responsibilities of writers and artists. In a letter to Marquard, he wrote approvingly of Soyinka's interventions in postcolonial Nigerian politics, asking, '[H]ave you read that Soyinka went and took over the broadcasting station in Western Nigeria and called Chief Akintola a thief and a robber? ... Africa compels her intellectuals to be involved – no neutralism.'[129] In a letter to Pogrund, he recounted an anecdote about Mqhayi, which exemplified how literature – in this case the performative oral literature of the *imbongi* – should criticise political authority:

> The late S. E. K. Mqhayi, the African 'Poet Laureate' who, during the last War attended the opening of the Ciskei Bunga clad in his regalia. When Van der Byl, then Minister of Native Affairs, got out of his black cabinet car, Mqhayi met him with the words: '*Yehla, yehla, yehla, ingwe emithini*' (Down comes the

leopard from the trees). Van der Byl and his retinue were flattered, even when the words were correctly interpreted to them. But the tribesmen were warned: When a leopard leaves the tree, while people are around, its purpose is to destroy![130]

In a third example, he praised Mayakovsky extravagantly, copying out 'these stupendous lines' from 'A Cloud in Trousers', and exclaiming to Pogrund, 'How these boys can write!'[131] Sobukwe does not draw explicit conclusions from these examples, but unlike the 'coquetry' of Shaw/Somerset Maugham/Wilde/Orwell, which seduces the reader away from politics, he implies that Soyinka/Mqhayi/Mayakovsky by contrast inspire the reader to move from the personal/feminine space of literature into public/masculine space of politics.

LITERATURE AS INTERNAL CRITIQUE AND UTOPIA

Whereas Sobukwe used literary quotations and commentaries to express his political criticisms and ideals, other PAC members wrote poems and novels to similar ends. J. D. Nyaose (1920–), one of Sobukwe's closest allies, wrote the poem 'The Party Dictator' while in exile in Ethiopia in 1966 in order to express his internal critique of the PAC in the 1960s. Nyaose was the head of the Federation of Free African Trade Unions of South Africa (FOFATUSA), formed in 1959 with seventeen unions, and affiliated to the PAC. A member of the PAC's national executive, Nyaose remembered Sobukwe in April 1959 telling the executive, 'I am no demi-God and I don't wish to be one ... Let us be a Collective Leadership – that means we are equals in the NEC.'[132] In the difficult years immediately after Sharpeville, however, Sobukwe's ideal of collective leadership collapsed. With Sobukwe in prison, the general secretary Leballo took control, and fell out with many of his comrades, including Nyaose. In an interview in 1969, Nyaose accused Leballo of dishonesty, stealing party funds, carelessness, vetoing a plan in 1964 to rescue Sobukwe from Robben Island, being a police spy and ultimately of fulfilling the government's ambition 'to smash [the PAC] into fragments'.[133] In eight stanzas of concentrated vituperation, Nyaose's poem 'The Party Dictator' lists Leballo's flaws and misdemeanours, condemning his 'avidity for craven power and praise'; describing him as 'neither a Scholar nor Patriot [but] an ignoramus swindler'; accusing him of 'bundling husbands [of women he seduced] into jail; and of 'thriving in corruption, deft murders [and] gossipy tiffs'.[134] In the penultimate stanza, Nyaose himself appears as 'Jaidee', a victim of Leballo's machinations, 'banished', and together with his few loyal comrades traduced by 'the party dictator' as 'dissidents, party subversive elements'.[135] That 'The Party Dictator' is the only surviving poem by Nyaose suggests that prose was unequal to the task of expressing the intensity of his antipathy towards Leballo; only in the form of a poem could his feelings be conveyed.

For Lauretta Ngcobo, the wife of another member of the PAC executive, A. B. Ngcobo (1931–1997), Leballo's failures as a leader were symptoms of the organisation's patriarchal culture. Looking back at her experiences of the period, she recalled realising that 'mine was a cheering role, in support of the men. I had no voice. I could only concur and never contradict nor offer alternatives. In short, men had (and still have) the exclusive right to initiate ideas ... All decision-making positions are still in the hands of men'.[136] In her first novel, *Cross of Gold* (begun in 1969, but published in 1981), Ngcobo corrects the marginalising of the PAC in the novels of Abrahams and La Guma. Foregrounding the PAC's role in the anti-pass campaign, she acknowledges the historical influence of Sobukwe, and identifies her characters as PAC members. In the opening chapter, we learn that the husband of Sindisiwe Zikode was arrested with Sobukwe on 21 March 1960,[137] and in the closing chapter, the police convict the protagonist Mandla Zikode for being 'involved in Poqo work, spreading dangerous ideas against white people'.[138] More compelling than the sympathetic identification of the main characters with the PAC are the several passages in the novel expressing a Pan-Africanist critique of the apartheid state and dreams of a post-apartheid future. In an early passage, Mandla registers the racist basis of the oppression he and all black South Africans confront: 'he felt a new spiritual affinity with all those on his side of the colour line ... He was enduring everything in the name of all Black people ... if he was Black, [he] had to suffer one or all the pains that go with being Black in South Africa'.[139] The PAC insistence on psychological liberation as the first step in combating such oppression is emphasised by Mandla's more experienced activist-friend Marumo, who tells him, '"We must tell [black people] that they are as human as any man on earth ... We mean to change our people's way of thinking ... They will no longer plead, they will demand what is theirs by birthright ... We shall teach them that they are men and worthy of that honour."'[140]

The novel's vision of freedom, again voiced by Marumo, combines the Pan-Africanist insistence upon vibrancy of pre-colonial African societies with confidence in Africa's capacity to forge a new order based on equality and freedom:

'Before [the Europeans] came we had no crime. We lived in well ordered societies politically, socially and economically ... They destroyed a great system of government where we ruled ourselves by consensus and they replaced it with this instrument of death ... We have a vision of a new order – the order of equality where men have the right to live in liberty and happiness, a society that will remake us.'[141]

After Mandla's execution in the final chapter, the Epilogue of *Cross of Gold* provides an image of hope in synchrony with Sobukwe's oft-repeated humanist mantra that 'there is only one race to which we all belong, and that is the human race'.[142] Mandla's son Manqoba spares the white Afrikaner Piet Swanepoel because he senses for the first time a common humanity transcending race: '[H]e's human, I saw it, I saw *ubuntu* there, he loves, he longs for peace, he bleeds, he dies, he's human, they're human.'[143]

Like Ngcobo, Bessie Head combined support for the ideals of Pan-Africanism (and for principled PAC leaders, pre-eminently Sobukwe) with criticisms of how routinely the ideals are betrayed by PAC followers. In a letter to Sobukwe in 1972,

Head admitted, 'I was not, in the final analysis attracted to the P. A. C. as much as I was attracted to your personality. I met too many types of voracious people in that political party and disliked them.'[144] In her novel, *When Rain Clouds Gather* (1969), Head combines critique of Pan-Africanist apparatchiks with an optimistic image of Pan-Africanist ideals enacted in postcolonial Africa. Crucially, Head's novel is set not in South Africa, but in neighbouring Botswana, and Head's pessimism about the prospects for freedom for South Africa contrasts with her confidence in the possibilities for freedom in post-independence Botswana. Insofar as South Africa registers in *When Rain Clouds Gather*, it is a prison the South African protagonist Makhaya has escaped. On his arrival in Botswana, he declares, '"I just want to step on free ground ... I want to feel what it is like to live in a free country."'[145] Makhaya's physical journey from the prison state of South Africa to the free state of Botswana enables his personal journey: he 'saw this suffering mass of mankind of which he was part, but he also saw himself as a separate particle', and in embracing his life in Botswana, he reflects, 'if you can find a society that leaves the individual to develop freely you ought to choose that society as your home'.[146] A few months later, he confirms that Botswana has allowed 'a putting together of the scattered fragments of his life into a coherent and disciplined whole'.[147] In addition to describing Makhaya's individual freedom, the novel contrasts two collective forms of freedom – the false freedom expressed in the Pan-Africanist slogans of the opportunist Joas Tsepe and the communitarian utopian freedom of Makhaya and the English agricultural adviser Gilbert. The Pan-Africanists in Botswana are dismissed: 'To many, Pan-Africanism is an almost sacred dream, but like all dreams it also has its nightmare side, and the little men like Joas Tsepe are the nightmare. If they have any power at all it is the power to plunge the African continent into an era of chaos and bloody murder.'[148]

Much more sympathetic than the trans-continental rhetoric of Pan-Africanism is the village-based appeal of communitarianism. In their first conversation, Gilbert tells Makhaya that '"[the village of Golema Mmidi] is Utopia, Mack. I have the greatest dreams about it"',[149] and in the course of the novel, Makhaya comes to share this view. As the collective agricultural initiatives introduced by Gilbert gradually bear fruit, Makhaya observes that they 'blended with his own dreams of Africa ... [C]ommunal systems of development which imposed co-operation and sharing of wealth were much better than the dog-eat-dog policies, take-over bids, and grab-what-you-can of big finance'.[150] Towards the end of the novel, Makhaya and Gilbert discover a youth from Golema Mmidi starved to death at a distant outpost, and the loss leads Makhaya to accept the importance of community:

> Therefore, he, Makhaya, could run so far in search of peace, but it was contact with other living beings that a man needed most. Maybe Utopias were just trees. Maybe. Maybe he walked around in hopeless circles, but at least he was attempting to reach up to a life beyond the morass in which all black men lived. Most men were waiting for the politicians to sort out their private agonies.[151]

Makhaya and Gilbert's dreams of African freedom lay well beyond inherited tribal fealties. In his dispute with the people of Golema Mmidi, the despotic local chief

Matenge was doomed to defeat because '[t]here were too many independent-minded people there, and tragedies of life had liberated them from the environmental control of the tribe'.[152] And even the days of the benevolent Chief Sekoto were numbered, because there was 'a quiet and desperate revolution going on throughout the whole wide world [in which] [p]eople were being drawn closer and closer to each other as brothers, and once you looked at the other man as your brother, you could not bear that he should want for anything or live in darkness'.[153]

CONCLUSION

Notwithstanding the depleted state of the PAC within three years of its formation, the historian Gerhart draws some consolation from its record. In terms that echo Bradford's belief that the ICU had in the 1920s given black South Africans 'a taste of freedom', Gerhart argues that as a result of the Pan-Africanist-inspired resistance of the early 1960s, 'African action had forced a brief suspension of the pass laws and had threatened for a short time to paralyze the nation's industries. Many Africans had at least glimpsed the potential power of civil disobedience and economic disruption.'[154] Gerhart's judgment is confirmed in Lembede and Sobukwe's influence on the Black Consciousness generation of the 1970s. For post-apartheid South Africa, however, Pan-Africanist dreams contend with the xenophobia that has blighted the nation since the 1990s.

Conclusion

FUTURES OF THE PAST

In his 1994 inaugural presidential address, Mandela listed the key documents which had expressed the ANC's vision of a free South Africa:

> It was that vision that inspired us in 1923 when we adopted the first ever Bill of Rights in this country. That same vision spurred us to put forward the African Claims in 1946 [sic]. It is also the founding principle of the Freedom Charter we adopted as policy in 1955, which in its very first lines, places before South Africa an inclusive basis for citizenship.[1]

Each document reiterated the ANC dream of a free South Africa based upon a democratic political order with universal franchise, equality before the law and a free market economy. The ANC vision of freedom evolved through its successive incarnations. The 1923 Bill of Rights demanded that 'the peoples of African descent . . . have direct representation by members of their own race in all the legislative bodies of the land', but the demand was based upon their status as subjects of His Majesty King George, and upon 'the legal and moral right to claim the application or extension to them of Cecil Rhodes' famous formula of "equal rights for all civilised men south of the Zambesi"'.[2] The 1943 (not 1946) *African Claims* no longer appealed to King George and Rhodes, but to Churchill and Roosevelt's promises in the Atlantic Charter, insisting that the terms '"nations", "states", "peoples" and "men". . . are understood by us to include Africans', and that therefore 'the demands [of black South Africans] for full citizenship rights and direct participation in all the councils of state should be recognised'.[3] The 1955 Freedom Charter repeated the demands for universal franchise and the associated liberal freedoms, but in addition declared that 'The People Shall Share in the Country's Wealth,' and that 'There Shall be Houses, Security and Comfort.'[4] Mandela continued that the values enshrined in these three documents were consolidated by the ANC's Bill of Rights of 1990, and formalised in the 1993 interim constitution (confirmed by the Constitution of the Republic of South Africa Act, 1996).

A century of sacrifice and struggle culminated in the triumph of the ANC's liberal-nationalist dream of freedom in 1994. However, as the ANC's years in government have followed the decades of resistance, its liberal-nationalist vision has relegated competing dreams of freedom to the footnotes of history. Reinhart Koselleck points out that the history of the victors 'is focused on those series of events that, through their own efforts, brought them victory [and] the historian who is on the side of the victor is prone to interpret short-term successes from the perspective of a continuous long-term teleology ex post facto'.[5] Mandela's linking of the iconic ANC dates from 1923 to 1990 exemplifies just such a retrospective teleology. For the historian on the side of the vanquished, however, the challenges are greater, as s/he must explain why history did not unfold as hoped or as planned. These greater challenges prompt Koselleck to hypothesise that '[F]rom the unique gains in experience imposed upon [the vanquished] spring insights of lasting duration and, consequently, of greater explanatory power. If history is made in the short term by the victors, historical gains in knowledge stem in the long run from the vanquished.'[6]

As a preliminary to assessing the 'historical gains in knowledge' to be derived from the vanquished traditions of South Africa's history, a parallel list of their freedom documents can be assembled: the 1926 ICU Manifesto, which demanded not only 'full political, economical, civic and social rights to all citizens who make up the South African nation, irrespective of colour, race or creed', but also 'the complete overthrow of capitalism and the establishment of a Socialistic Commonwealth of all nations and races;[7] the 1928 CPSA Native Republic thesis, which demanded 'an independent Native Republic, as a stage towards a workers' and peasants' government';[8] the 1943 NEUM Ten-Point Programme, which demanded (in addition to the franchise) equal access to education, land restitution, the redistribution of wealth through taxation, and the reform of labour laws;[9] and the 1959 PAC Manifesto, which proclaimed that Pan-Africanism serves 'the material, intellectual and spiritual interests of Africa [and] operates to liberate Africa and to create a socialist social order, original in conception, Africanist in orientation, and creative in content'.[10] For all their differences, these documents – the 1926 to 1959 counter-tradition – share several important qualities. First, they resemble the ANC tradition insofar as they oppose racism unequivocally, and regard the universal franchise and associated liberal freedoms as non-negotiables. Secondly, they all differ from the ANC tradition in their conceptions of nationalism. The ICU and NEUM documents elevate working-class internationalism above nationalism; the CPSA casts national liberation as but the first stage of a journey toward the ultimate destination of 'a workers' and peasants' government'; and the PAC embraces a pan-continental Africanist identity transcending the South African nation. Thirdly, they all oppose capitalism. The ICU seeks 'a Socialistic Commonwealth of all nations and races'; the CPSA (to repeat) 'a workers' and peasants' government'; the NEUM permanent revolution leading to international socialism; and the PAC 'a socialist social order Africanist in orientation'. In relation to Wallerstein's schematic macro-history, the visions of freedom expressed by the ICU, CPSA, NEUM and PAC documents do not satisfy the normative prescriptions of centrist liberalism. By imagining futures beyond nationalism and capitalism, they dreamed of forms of freedom that have – at least for now – proved impossible to realise.

As regards the more strictly literary texts expressing dreams of freedom, certain broad patterns can be identified. The first is that there were many more expressions of hope than of despair. Conceding that some of the texts are difficult to categorise, it is nonetheless clear that the optimistic literary texts out-number the dystopian ones by a ratio of about 3:1. Those texts expressing visions of happier futures include: Schreiner's *Dreams* and Smith's *The Great Southern Revolution* in the 1890s; the Marshalls's *1960 (A Retrospect)* in 1919; Lamont's *South Africa in Mars*, Nicholls's *Bayete!* and Mqhayi's *U-Don Jadu*, Ethelreda Lewis's *Wild Deer*, Kadalie's appropriations of *Bayete!* and 'Invictus', and the appropriations of Shelley, Morris and Swinburne in the CPSA newspapers of the 1920s; the poems, plays and reviews of Taylor in the 1940s; the PAC's appropriation of *Spartacus* in the 1950s; Allighan's *Verwoerd – The End*, Delius's *The Day Natal Took Off* and Head's *When Rain Clouds Gather* in the 1960s; and Ngcobo's *Cross of Gold* and Mqotsi's *The House of Bondage* in the 1970s. Many of these texts dwell at great length upon the suffering to be endured in the short term, but then offer glimpses of a new dawn to follow the long night of oppression. The much shorter list of literary dystopias includes: Flemming's 1924 'And So It Came To Pass'; Holtby's 1933 *Mandoa, Mandoa*; Keppel-Jones's 1947 *When Smuts Goes*; Sowden's 1951 *Tomorrow's Comet*; and Ngubane's *Ushaba* and Schoeman's *Promised Land* in the 1970s.

A second pattern is that the critiques animating these visions of the future are directed as much at the economic system as at the racist political order and its agents. The pre-occupation, even obsession, with money and land extends to utopian and dystopian texts alike. Examples abound: Schreiner and the Marshalls save their bitterest words for the speculators, imperialists and brokers of 'Commercialism'; Lamont frets over the way that protectionism has sabotaged the South African economy; Taylor's literary reviews routinely foreground the exploitation of working-class communities; the most offensive character in Sowden's novel is the capitalist Kennaway Laver; the PAC's enthusiasm for *Spartacus* derives in part from the identification of white South Africa's wealthy with the slave-owners of Rome; Mqotsi's critical anger is aimed at those white politicians and black sell-outs facilitating the appropriation of African land in the Transkei; and the economics of a rural co-operative are at the heart of *When Rain Clouds Gather*. In some instances (like Smith and Lamont), the economic critique is motivated by the desire to make capitalism more efficient, but in the majority of cases, the critique aims at replacing capitalism with a more humane means of producing and distributing material resources.

A third pattern is the concentration of utopian/dystopian productivity at particular moments. By far the highest concentration appeared in the 1920s, with twelve literary texts to add to the manifestos of the ANC, ICU and CPSA. The next moment of intensive thinking about the future was the 1940s, designated with good reason by Mda as 'the golden age of schemers and planners',[11] with the manifestos and programmes of the ANC, NEUM and ANCYL supplemented by Taylor's reviews in *Trek* and *When Smuts Goes*. As to whether any general conclusions can be adduced about the relationship between these utopian texts and their immediate contexts, the parallels between the 1920s and the 1940s are striking. Both decades follow (or partly include) a World War; both are characterised by internal economic and political upheaval; and both coincide with or follow inspiring revolutions and independence struggles on the international stage, pre-eminently the Russian Revolution and Indian independence. Such evidence suggests that it is not at the darkest of times that utopian thought appears (as Winter argues on the basis of his European examples), but rather at moments of rapid political change, which encourage dreamers to imagine the changes in the present continuing and ultimately leading to better futures. By contrast, certain periods of deep reaction in twentieth-century South Africa, notably the 1930s and 1960s, produced silence. The 1960s in particular have been characterised as the decade when anti-apartheid opposition was immobilised, and the absence of literary or political works imagining hopeful futures in this period lends weight to this characterisation.[12]

After the 1940s, individual texts like the Freedom Charter expressed optimistic visions of the future, but the fourth general pattern to note is the one of deepening pessimism from the late 1940s onward. Punctuated by lengthy silences, a line of increasingly grim literary dystopias runs from Keppel-Jones and Sowden to Ngubane and Schoeman. Even those texts expressing some hope are ambiguous: the bloodshed and chaos in Delius's satire *The Day Natal Took Off* is barely leavened by the comic narrator; the most hopeful novel, *When Rain Clouds Gather*, is set outside South Africa; and Ngcobo and Mqotsi kill off their respective struggle heroes, prophesying liberation in the distant future.

Beyond these general patterns lie faint but inconclusive tendencies. For one, there is a tradition of white writers imagining South Africa under a black tyranny (Flemming, Nicholls, Keppel-Jones, Schoeman), but at the same time, there are also texts by white writers reconciled to benevolent black rule – Smith's *The Great Southern Revolution* and Allighan's *Verwoerd – The End*. A second tendency is for the women writers to embrace hope more readily, and this is borne out to an extent in the writings of Schreiner, Lewis, Ngcobo and Head. However, all four oscillate between hope and despair, and in the writings of Holtby and Taylor, the cold stream of critique flows more strongly than the warm stream of utopianism. A third tendency is best expressed as the absence of a pattern or tendency, namely that there is no discernible link between the dream of freedom and the race of the dreamer. There are many examples of individual dreamers of different races sharing the same dream: Schreiner and Mqhayi; Kadalie and Holtby; Roux, Gomas and Nzula; Tabata, Kies and Taylor; Sobukwe, Pogrund and Head. And conversely, of course, there are at least as many examples of individuals of the same race holding to fiercely opposed dreams of freedom.

FUTURE IMPERFECT

Dreaming of freedom may have become largely redundant with the end of apartheid, but the impulse to prophesy the future has flourished since the transition to the new South Africa. Carlos Amato's 2014 compilation in the *Sunday Times* of forty essays by writers from around the country imagining South Africa in 2034 provides a convenient update of how the future is being imagined.[13]

Commemorating the twenty years since the 1994 elections, and looking forward to the next twenty years, the essays fall into roughly three groups. The largest group by some distance sees South Africa plunging into an ever-deteriorating state, with twenty-seven of the essays predicting combinations of environmental degradation, civil war, criminal anarchy, economic meltdown, hyper-exploitation, unchecked police violence, Stalinist tyranny and Chinese-led colonial plunder. Angela Makholwa's 'The wanderers, Joburg/15.30' captures the sense of disillusionment best, as the narrator remembers that 'the first years of the revolution were the closest thing to Utopia that any country has ever experienced', but ends with the ironic observation, 'I know that our country is recovering. I saw the Great Leader building another new mansion in Mpofu Manor – formerly known as Hyde Park.'[14] A variation within this first group are a couple of essays which see South Africa as worse off, but not quite as badly off as the rest of the world. Koos Kombuis describes an authoritarian society, but beyond South Africa's borders, Australia has burnt down and Japan has disappeared; and Sarah Lotz imagines refugees fleeing the destructive consequences of climate change in North America and dying as they try to reach the safety of Durban.

Eight of the essays are difficult to place on the utopian–dystopian spectrum, as they combine elements of nostalgia, despair, resilience and hope. The most interesting essay in this group is Sihle Khumalo's 'Church Square, Pretoria/09.35', which predicts the ANC's apathy, nepotism and corruption causing its electoral defeat in 2024 by the People's Emancipation Party (PEP). The new governing party has renamed Church Square in Pretoria 'Sankara Square, after the visionary father of the Burkina Faso nation', but despite its best efforts, 'South Africa is still a country in transit. A country alive with possibilities and inspiring new ways, but still a mediocre nation with an exceptionally high tolerance level for dubious leadership.'[15] Much easier to pick out are the five essays in the smallest group, which imagine South Africa as a much better nation in 2034. In Kgebetli Moele's 'Diamond City/16.22' and Sindiwe Magona's 'Robben Island/Noon', all the promises of the Mandela presidency are honoured. Moele looks forward to a national community no longer divided by race and language, with the worship of 'profit for personal gain [replaced by] profit for the advancement of society',[16] and Magona anticipates 'All bathing in happiness; United; A Nation Strong!'[17] The narrator of Steven Boykey Sidley's 'Gugulethu/03.00' writes from 'a modest house of modest comfort, here in the same street where there were only shacks and tears so long ago', explaining to his dead father that he has had a child with a white woman: 'for you, Ndabezitha, race was the prison house into which you were forced [but] I am the first to cross this racial divide, and I seek your blessing, and to see this as a victory'.[18] Finally, Richard De Nooy's 'Auckland Park/09.00' echoes Kombuis and Lotz's dystopian visions for the rest of the planet, but differs in its optimistic prophecy for South Africa: Dutch asylum-seekers escaping floods and social unrest in Europe seek refuge and employment in South Africa, which 'has been a peaceful democracy for four decades [with] social welfare, health and education systems among the best in the world [and an] entire economy founded on innovation'.[19]

The forty 'FFWD 2034' essays are strikingly different from the literary and political texts making up the earlier tradition from the 1880s to the 1970s. Most obviously, a dystopian imagination has superseded the tradition of hope, with the 2014 essays outdoing each other in their endless varieties of despair. Certain of the dystopian essays are propelled by a spirit of critique. Foreseeing an impenetrable wall encircling the townships, C. A. Davids in 'D6/08.02' concludes, 'The revolutionaries, it had turned out, were no better than the capitalists, just more intent on iron rule.'[20] And Michiel Heyns in 'Nature's Valley/18.02' describes foreign multinationals ruthlessly monetising every available natural resource on the Garden Route. But many more of the stories fixate upon spectacles of misery, echoing the attempts at morbid humour in Flemming's 'And So It Came To Pass' or in Keppel-Jones's *When Smuts Goes*.

If the impulse to critique survives, the complementary utopian impulse is in poor shape. None of the five utopian stories prophesies futures beyond the limits of the nation and capitalism. Quite simply, no other alternatives are imaginable. The most optimistic model is a well-administered northern European welfare state – the Netherlands or Norway – but with better music and weather. This, however, is precisely why the dreams of freedom of earlier generations deserve renewed attention. For all their many flaws, they combined compelling critiques of capitalism and nationalism with attempts to imagine different and better ways of living. They function as a challenge to the present.

Notes

INTRODUCTION

1. Brutus, *Stubborn*, p. 95.
2. Ibid.
3. Mandela, 'Inaugural'.
4. Ibid.
5. Turok, 'SA'.
6. For a sample of the abundant scholarship in sympathy with Turok's diagnosis, see Justice Malala's *We Have Now Begun Our Descent: How to Stop South Africa Losing its Way* (2015); Hein Marais's *South Africa Pushed to the Limit* (2011), and John Saul and Patrick Bond's *South Africa: The Present as History* (2014).
7. Wallerstein, *The Modern*, p. 217.
8. Ibid. p. 217.
9. Ibid. p. 277. Domenico Losurdo makes a similar argument: 'Having been asserted in countries (Holland, England and the United States) more involved than any others in the slave trade and colonial expansion (overseas in the case of the first two, continentally in that of the third), liberalism spread in the West at a time when it seemed destined by Providence itself to dominate the whole world and wipe out all other cultures' (*Liberalism*, p. 318).
10. On Wallerstein's Eurocentrism, and the counter-histories of struggles for freedom in nineteenth-century West Africa and the Yucatan, see Kazanjian, *The Brink*, pp. 22–6.
11. Ibid. p. 143.
12. Scott, *Domination*, pp. 80–1.
13. Ibid. p. 92.
14. Arendt, *Men*, p. 19.
15. Ibid. p. 22.
16. Ibid. p. 52. Arendt repeated her resistance to confining freedom to the 'inward domain', arguing *contra* that: 'Freedom needed, in addition to mere liberation [from struggling for the necessities of life], the company of men who were in the same state, and it needed a common public space to meet them – a politically organized world, in other words, into which each of the free men could insert himself by word and deed' (*Between*, p. 148).
17. Williams, *Keywords*, pp. 183–8.
18. Jameson, 'The politics', p. 41.
19. Literary utopias and dystopias have been receiving attention in postcolonial literary studies

in recent years. See, for example, Ralph Pordzik's *The Quest for Postcolonial Utopia* (2001), Nicholas Brown's *Utopian Generations: The Political Horizon of Twentieth-Century Literature* (2005), Eric D. Smith's *Globalization, Utopia and Postcolonial Science Fiction* (2012) and Bill Ashcroft's *Utopianism in Postcolonial Literatures* (2017). These studies focus largely on literary fiction, paying little attention to utopian texts outside the main literary genres.
20. Bakhtin and Medvedev, *The Formal*, p. 129.
21. Jameson, *The Political*, p. 79.
22. See Koselleck, *Futures*, pp. 270–5, and Engerman, 'Introduction: histories', pp. 1402–10.
23. Moylan, *Scraps*, p. 111.
24. Bloch, *The Utopian*, p. 11.
25. Bloch, *The Principle*, p. 1368.
26. Jameson, *Archaeologies*, p. 12, xiii.
27. I discuss the post-apartheid elevation of individual leaders as political heroes in 'Anti-apartheid', pp. 88–103.
28. Le Guin, *The Wave*, p. 219.
29. There is much scholarship on religious dreams of freedom. See, for examples, Bengt Sundkler's *Bantu Prophets in South Africa* (1961); Jean Comaroff's *Body of Power, Spirit of Resistance: The Culture and History of a South African People* (1985), Jeff Peires's *The Dead Will Arise: Nongqawuse and the Great Xhosa Cattle-Killing Movement of 1856–7* (1987), Robert Edgar's *Because They Chose the Plan of God: The Story of the Bulhoek Massacre* (1988), Richard Elphick and Rodney Davenport's collection *Christianity in South Africa: A Political, Social, and Cultural History* (1997), and Jennifer Wenzel's *Bulletproof: Afterlives of Anticolonial Prophecy in South Africa and Beyond* (2009).
30. Scenario-planning continues to be a major pre-occupation. See Patrick Bond's discussion of its political role in the 1990s (*Elite*, pp. 53–85).
31. South African utopianism in the fifteen years before 1990 conforms for the most part to the pattern Jameson identifies in the European tradition:

> as one approaches periods of genuine pre-revolutionary ferment, when the system really seems in the process of losing its legitimacy, when the ruling elite is palpably uncertain of itself and full of divisions and self-doubts, when popular demands grow louder and more confident, then what also happens is that those grievances and demands grow more precise in their insistence and urgency. We focus more sharply on very specific wrongs, the dysfunctioning of the system becomes far more tangibly visible at crucial points. But at such a moment the utopian imagination no longer has free play: political thinking and intelligence are trained on very sharply focused issues, they have concrete content, the situation claims us in all its historical uniqueness as a configuration; and the wide-ranging drifts and digressions of political speculation give way to practical programmes. (Jameson, 'The politics', p. 44)

CHAPTER 1

1. Maharaj (ed.), *Reflections*, p. 9.
2. Ibid. pp. 20–1.
3. Ibid. p. 213.
4. Ibid. p. 218.
5. Ibid. p. 214.
6. Ibid. p. 219.
7. Winter, *Dreams*, p. 100.
8. Ibid. pp. 1–2.

9. Ibid. p. 167.
10. There is a vast body of scholarship on the creation of the Union of South Africa, which I summarise in 'Print', pp. 105–27.
11. Flint, *Cecil*, pp. 248–9.
12. Quoted in Gardiner, *Life*, vol. 2, p. 392.
13. Galbraith, 'Cecil', p. 178.
14. On the history of the relationship between Rhodes and the Bond, see Davenport, *The Afrikaner*, pp. 118–23, 127–65; Tamarkin, *Cecil*, pp. 6–25, 290–304; and Giliomee, *The Afrikaners*, pp. 220–7, 239–43.
15. Quoted in Lewsen, *John X.*, p. 98.
16. See Bundy, *The Rise*, pp. 109–33 and Lewis, 'The rise', pp. 1–24.
17. On the Glen Grey Act and its effects, see Bundy, *The Rise*, pp. 134–9 and Ntsebeza, *Democracy*, pp. 64–9.
18. Quoted in Rotberg, *The Founder*, p. 611. Rotberg emphasises that Rhodes's words never amounted to more than a slogan.
19. On the history of the Cape African franchise in the decades before Union, see Trapido, 'African', pp. 79–98, and Parry, '"In a sense"', pp. 377–91.
20. On African opposition to the machinations of Rhodes and the Bond in the 1880s–1890s, see Limb, 'Intermediaries', pp. 54–68 and Odendaal, *The Founders*, pp. 124–57. Odendaal contrasts Jabavu's Imbumba (Union), with its Mfengu support base and mission-educated leadership, and the newer Ingqungqutela (SANC/Congress), with its Rharhabe–Thembu constituency and stronger national orientation.
21. Butler points out that Rhodes's views on South Africa's relationship with Britain fluctuated in the 1890s, as he made several speeches threatening independence from Britain: 'when there were serious conflicts with ministers in London, he was likely to shift from a position of a devoted subject to that of a calculating ally' (Butler et al., *The Liberal*, p. 8).
22. Almost certainly a pseudonym. I have failed to uncover the identity of the author.
23. Smith, *The Great*, pp. 4–5.
24. Ibid. p. 9. The narrator uses the terms 'coloured' and 'African' interchangeably.
25. Ibid. p. 19.
26. Ibid. p. 22.
27. Ibid. pp. 23–4.
28. Ibid. p. 26.
29. Ibid. p. 26.
30. Ibid. p. 27.
31. Ibid. p. 28.
32. Ibid. p. 29.
33. Ibid. p. 31.
34. Ibid. p. 35.
35. Ibid. p. 35.
36. Schreiner to Rhys, February 1888, *Letters Online*.
37. Gill, 'Olive', p. 334. On Schreiner's *Dreams*, see Berkman, *The Healing*, pp. 213–21; Albinski, 'The laws', pp. 55–7; Chrisman, 'Allegory', pp. 126–50; McCracken, 'Stages', pp. 231–42; Burdett, *Olive*, pp. 77–85; and Ong, 'Dream', pp. 711–14.
38. 'Three dreams in a desert' was first published in the *Fortnightly Review* in August 1887.
39. Jay (ed.), *Dreams*, p. 16.
40. Ibid. pp. 16–17.
41. Ibid. p. 18.
42. Ibid. p. 18.
43. Ibid. p. 19.
44. Ibid. p. 19.

45. Ibid. p. 20.
46. Ibid. p. 20.
47. Ibid. p. 20.
48. Ibid. p. 21.
49. First and Scott, *Olive*, p. 185.
50. Blatchford, *Merrie*, p. 206.
51. Schreiner, *The Political*, p. 29.
52. Ibid. pp. 73–4.
53. Schreiner, *An English*, pp. 88–9.
54. Schreiner, *Thoughts*, p. 367.
55. Ibid. p. 369.
56. Schreiner, *The Political*, p. 16.
57. Ibid. p. 35.
58. Schreiner, *An English*, p. 56.
59. Schreiner, *Thoughts*, p. 372.
60. Ibid. p. 375.
61. See Schreiner, *Closer*, p. 25.
62. Schreiner, *The Political*, p. 51.
63. Schreiner, *An English*, p. 66.
64. Ibid. p. 72.
65. Schreiner, *Thoughts*, pp. 369–70.
66. Ibid. p. 370.
67. Schreiner, *Closer*, pp. 46–7.
68. Ibid. p. 48.
69. Ibid. p. 50.
70. Wallerstein, *The Modern*,
71. Ibid. p. 217.
72. Eybers, *Select*, pp. 364, 286.
73. Ibid. p. 528.
74. Thompson, *The Unification*, pp. 225–6.
75. Lamont, *South*, p. 25.
76. Ibid. p. 30.
77. Ibid. p. 31.
78. Ibid. p. 46.
79. Ibid. p. 46.
80. Ibid. p. 101.
81. Ibid. pp. 104–5. Nigel Leask argues that Burns negotiated a tension between 'broadcasting the values of "Caledonian" liberty and Christian righteousness to the denizens of less fortunate lands' (as per Lamont's version of Burns), and 'the fear that the colonial experience would cast [Scots] in the role of tyrants, with colonized people – quite literally – as their slaves' ('"Their Groves"', p. 173).
82. Ibid. p. 115.
83. Marks, 'Natal', p. 179.
84. On his discussions with Smuts and Langenhoven about *Bayete!*, see Nicholls, *South*, p. 93.
85. Nicholls, *South*, p. 6.
86. Ibid. p. 6.
87. The plot structure of *Bayete!* conforms to that of a sub-genre of twentieth-century settler fiction inaugurated by John Buchan's *Prester John* (1910), and repeated with variations in Sarah Gertrude Millin's *The Coming of the Lord* (1928), Ethelreda Lewis's *Wild Deer* (1933), Jack Cope's *The Fair House* (1955) and Laurens van der Post's *Flamingo Feather* (1955).
88. Nicholls, *Bayete!*, pp. 365–6.

89. *Bayete!* exerted an influence long after its first publication, and continued to draw critical reviews. Winifred M. Lunt in a 1936 review captured the paradoxical appeal of *Bayete!* for Kadalie and Msimang: 'Mr Nicholls wrote this book as a solemn warning. To whom? To the white boss to make his domination secure. But in practice it has served rather as an inspiration to members of the Bantu race to tell them what they could do' ('When'). On Heaton's role in segregationist politics in the 1920s, see Marks ('Natal', pp. 179–83), and for a recent discussion of *Bayete!*, see Graham (*State*, pp. 59–67).
90. Flemming (1880–1946) was a prolific farmer-essayist-satirist, who published several collections of his writings: *A Settler's Scribblings on South Africa* (1910), *A Fool on the Veld* (1916), *A Crop of Chaff* (1924), *The Call of the Veld* (1927), *A Bard in the Backveld* (1934) and *The Curious Continent and Other Stories* (1941).
91. Flemming, 'The romance', p. 128.
92. Flemming, *A Crop*, p. 27.
93. Ibid. pp. 27–8.
94. Ibid. pp. 29–30.
95. Ibid. p. 31.
96. Ibid. p. 31.
97. 'Resolutions of the Annual Conference of the African National Congress, May 28–29, 1923', in Karis, Carter and Johns (eds), *From Protest*, vol. 1, p. 297.
98. For introductions to Mqhayi and his writings, see his own short autobiography in Scott (ed.), *Mqhayi*, pp. 5–34 and Opland's introduction to Mqhayi in *Abantu*, pp. 1–28, as well as Scott's bibliographic survey of Mqhayi, *Samuel Edward*. For discussions of *U-Don Jadu*, see Gérard, *Four*, pp. 56–9; Jordan, *Towards*, pp. 109–11; Zotwana, 'Literature', pp. 104–9; and Saule, 'Images', pp. 3, 47, 57–60. I have also drawn upon Peter Kallaway's unpublished chapter on Mqhayi in his forthcoming book on the history of education in South Africa.
99. Mqhayi, *U-Don*, p. 8. The quotations are from the 1951 Lovedale edition of *U-Don Jadu*, and all the translations are by Fundile Majola. Since completing copy-editing, a translation of the 1929 Lovedale edition of *U-Don Jadu* has been published as: *Don Jadu* (Cape Town: Oxford University Press, 2018).
100. Ibid. p. 14.
101. Ibid. p. 61.
102. Ibid. p. 64.
103. Ibid. pp. 61–2.
104. Ibid. p. 61.
105. Ibid. p. 65. On other occasions in the 1920s, Mqhayi was more ambivalent about the British Empire. In his praise poem to the Prince of Wales on the occasion of the state visit in 1925, for example, criticism and praise were delivered in equal measure, with the final stanza juxtaposing the beneficence delivered and the damage inflicted by Britain: '[Britain] hath drained the little rivers and lapped them dry;/ She hath swept away the little nations and wiped them away . . . She sent us the Bible, and barrels of brandy . . . You [Britain] hath sent us Truth, denied us Truth;/ You sent us *ubuntu*; denied us *ubuntu*;/ You gave us light; we live in darkness;/ Benighted at noon-day, we grope in the dark' (see Gérard, *Four*, p. 61 and Jordan, *Towards*, p. 114).
106. Mqhayi, *U-Don*, p. 63.
107. Ibid. p. 66.
108. Ibid. p. 65.
109. Ibid. pp. 67–8.
110. On the Hertzog Bills and the opposition to them, see Roux, *Time*, pp. 286–301 and Dubow, *Racial*, pp. 131–76.
111. Msimang, *The Crisis*, p. 9. On Msimang's response to the Hertzog Bills, see Mkhize, 'Class', pp. 145–55, and Wentzel, *Bulletproof*, pp. 83–6.

112. Msimang, *The Crisis*, p. 9.
113. Ibid. p. 11.
114. Ibid. p. 12.
115. Ibid. pp. 12–13.
116. Kadalie's thoughts on *Bayete!* are discussed in Chapter 2.
117. Msimang, *The Crisis*, p. 13.
118. Ibid. p. 14.
119. Hoernlé's liberalism has been much analysed, with critical discussions by Marxists like George Findlay ('Review') and Martin Legassick ('Race'), and a more sympathetic assessment by MacCrone ('R. F. A. Hoernlé – a memoir'). For the most recent accounts, see Rich (*Hope*, pp. 40–65), Sweet ('R. F. A. Hoernlé') and Kissack and Titlestad ('The antimonies'). An indispensable guide to the roots of Hoernlé's political thought is provided by Nash, 'Colonialism'.
120. Hoernlé, *South*, p. 185.
121. Ibid. p. 185.
122. Ibid. p. 185.
123. Ibid. p. 158.
124. Ibid. pp. 166, 168.
125. Ibid. p. 178.
126. Ibid. pp. 183. Hoernlé's endorsement of 'separation' as a political solution in 1939 repeats the solution he proposed to white South Africa's 'native problem' in a letter to his mother of 11 January 1910. The 1910 letter anticipates precisely the 1939 lecture:

> One inclines more and more to wish that a policy of 'segregation' advocated by certain Transvaal politicians were feasible: the main idea is, to reserve all parts of the country suitable for permanent colonisation by a white race, i.e. the southern coast-belt and the Uplands in the Transvaal, Orange River Colony, and the mountain tracts in Rhodesia (even the Katanga copper district in the Congo is said to be suitable) exclusively for white settlers, while herding the native races into the more tropical parts, which they can stand, but not the whites. A clear separation: the colour line to coincide with a geographical line: within these reservations everything to be done for the 'civilisation' of the native, every encouragement to development, etc. The scheme has the further advantage of reducing the race-mixture (miscegenation, they call it technically) to a minimum, whereas if the races live side-by-side, in the long run it seems inevitable that 'pure' whites and 'pure' blacks will disappear, and a uniform coloured race will result. And that is not a result which one can bring oneself to contemplate with any satisfaction. But the segregation-scheme, though in principle the best solution, would involve the forcible shifting of such large masses of natives from Basutoland to Natal, that it could hardly be carried out without bloodshed. In any case, it would require tremendous immigration of white men, to give decisive power to the policy and to occupy the territories, cleared of blacks, in sufficient numbers to hold them against pressure. (R. F. A. Hoernlé Papers, Unprocessed correspondence, 1905–1919, Wits).

127. Ibid. p. 183.
128. On the reception of the Atlantic Charter in the colonial world, see Moyn, *The Last*, pp. 84–100 and Ibawoh, 'Testing', pp. 842–60; for its reception in South Africa, see Neame, *The Unfolding*, vol. 3, pp. 178–84 and Dubow, *South*, pp. 55–74. More broadly on the new mood in South Africa during and immediately after the Second World War, see the collection edited by Dubow and Jeeves, *South Africa's 1940s: Worlds of Possibilities* (2005), especially the essays by Seekings and Edgar.
129. *African Claims in South Africa* [1943], in Karis and Carter, *From Protest*, vol. 2, p. 209.

130. Ibid. pp. 209–10.
131. Ibid. p. 212.
132. Ibid. p. 214.
133. Ibid. p. 215.
134. Keppel-Jones, *When*, p. 33.
135. Ibid. p. 48.
136. Ibid. p. 60.
137. Ibid. p. 109.
138. Ibid. p.71.
139. Ibid. p. 124.
140. Ibid. p. 129.
141. Ibid. p. 149.
142. Ibid. p. 153.
143. Ibid. pp. 186, 192, 194–5, 202.
144. Keppel-Jones, *Friends*, pp. 171, 179.
145. Ibid. p. 225.
146. Ibid. p. 231.
147. On the first phase of the imposition of apartheid rule, see Posel, *The Making*, pp. 91–149; O'Meara, *Forty*, pp. 17–82; Breckenridge, *The Biometric*, pp. 138–63; and Dubow, *Apartheid*, pp. 1–73. On black resistance to the first wave of apartheid legislation, see Lodge, *Black*, pp. 33–90.
148. Sowden, *Tomorrow's*, p. 235. Sowden was a liberal journalist, novelist and poet, who published fifteen books between 1943 and 1976.
149. Ibid. p. 196.
150. Ibid. p. 302.
151. Matthews, 'Review', p. 37.
152. Matthews, *Freedom*, p. 168.
153. Ibid. p. 169.
154. Ibid. p. 176.
155. Ibid. p. 182.
156. Turok, *Nothing*, p. 60.
157. Ibid. pp. 182–3.
158. Suttner and Cronin, 30 *Years*, p. 262.
159. Ibid. p. 264.
160. Ibid. p. 263.
161. Ibid. p. 264.
162. Ibid. p. 265.
163. Ibid. p. 265.
164. Ibid. pp. 263–6. On the socio-economic clauses in the Freedom Charter, see Archer, 'Economic', pp. 335–52.
165. Luthuli, *Let*, p. 168.
166. Ibid. p. 168.
167. Ibid. p. 169.
168. Luthuli describes the immediate context of the meeting in his autobiography, *Let*, pp. 188–9.
169. Luthuli, 'Freedom is the Apex' [1958], in Karis and Carter, *From Protest*, vol. 3, p. 456.
170. Ibid. p. 457.
171. Ibid. p. 457.
172. Ibid. p. 458.
173. Ibid. p. 462.
174. Luthuli, 'Nobel Prize acceptance speech' [1961], in Karis and Carter, *From Protest*, vol. 3, p. 714.

175. Ibid. p. 715.
176. This claim is made by Paton's biographer, Peter F. Alexander: *Alan*, p. 290. Paton felt a strong affinity with Luthuli – see Paton's tributes to Luthuli in *The Long View*, pp. 201–3, 265–7.
177. Paton, *Cry*, p. 227.
178. Ibid. p. 235.
179. Paton, *The Long*, pp. 60–1.
180. Paton, *Cry*, Author's Note. The sympathetic character Msimangu describes Hoernlé in similar terms as 'the greater fighter for justice ... [T]here was no white man that could speak against him' (p. 43).
181. Paton, *Hope*, p. 54.
182. Ibid. p. 56.
183. Ibid. p. 58.
184. The six-point blueprint first appeared in the Liberal Party magazine, *Contact*, and was subsequently republished as a pamphlet and sold for five cents (Liberal Party of South Africa Papers [UY]). The history of the Liberal Party has received sympathetic scholarly attention: see Robertson, *Liberalism*, pp. 108–21, 162–72, 194–203, 215–25; Irvine, 'The Liberal', pp. 116–35; Vigne, *Liberals*, pp. 19–212; Driver, *Patrick*, pp. 120–69; Everatt, *The Origins*, pp. 123–68; and Cardo, *Opening*, pp. 81–142, 153–85. Apologias for liberalism in the spirit of Paton's *Hope for South Africa* continued to appear in the 1960s, notably Julius Lewin's *Politics and Law in South Africa* (1963) and Leo Marquard's *Liberalism in South Africa* (1965). Since the 1960s, a steady stream of similar publications has continued to flow, broadening beyond the Liberal Party *per se* to address the history of and prospects for liberalism in South Africa: Phyllis Lewsen's article 'The Cape Liberal tradition – myth or reality?' in the journal *Race* (1971); Heribert Adam's *Modernizing Racial Domination: South Africa's Political Dynamics* (1971); R. W. Johnson's *How Long Will South Africa Survive?* (1977); Pierre van den Berghe's collection *The Liberal Dilemma in South Africa* (1979); Paul Rich's *White Power and the Liberal Conscience* (1984); Jeffrey Butler, Richard Elphick and David Welsh's collection *Democratic Liberalism in South Africa* (1987); R. W. Johnson and David Welsh's collection *Ironic Victory: Liberalism in Post-Apartheid South Africa* (1998); and most recently, Eusebius McKaiser's *Mail and Guardian* opinion piece 'A black liberal is not an oxymoron' (16 March 2018). The many critiques of liberalism in South Africa are analysed in subsequent chapters.
185. Paton, *Hope*, p. 58
186. Allighan, *Verwoerd*, pp. 162, 217.
187. Delius, *The Day*, p. 161.
188. Ibid. p. 164.
189. On the period of high apartheid, see O'Meara, *Forty*, pp. 99–167 and Dubow, *Apartheid*, pp. 74–157. For a summary of recent scholarship on high apartheid, see Dubow, 'New', 307–9.
190. For an overview of all the legislation, see Matthews, *Law*, pp. 54–260.
191. These statistics are summarised by Worden, *The Making*, pp. 108–18.
192. Ngubane, *An African*, p. 211.
193. Ibid. p. 205.
194. Ibid. p. 242.
195. Ibid. p. 231.
196. Ibid. p. 238.
197. Ibid. p. 226. Many of Ngubane's concerns in *An African Explains Apartheid*, most notably his anti-Communism, were echoed a decade later in R. W. Johnson's *How Long Will South Africa Survive?* (1977), pp. 295–6, 317. In the same tradition and of the same moment, but less pessimistic, is the final chapter of Herbert Adam's *Modernizing Racial Domination*

(1971), which ends, 'South Africa's political dynamics dialectically strengthens the antagonists of white domination by the very process of their separation and exclusion until the subordinates themselves have accumulated enough power for their own liberation' (p. 183).
198. Ngubane, *Ushaba*, p. 1.
199. Ibid. p. 2.
200. Ibid. p. 5.
201. Ibid. pp. 13–14.
202. Ngubane repeats his argument that Buthelezi is the most important African leader in South Africa, far surpassing the ANC leaders, in *The Conflict of Minds*: 'Buthelezi's leadership translates the Collective Will into action . . . The massive urban and rural endorsement Buthelezi continues to receive are evidence that the Evolving Revolt is now a factor to be reckoned with in the crisis' (p. 284). In 1974, Buthelezi delivered the Alfred and Winifred Hoernlé Memorial Lecture, the first black South African to do so. Entitled 'White and black nationalism, ethnicity and the future of the homelands', Buthelezi argued in the lecture that 'the homelands concept could easily be the formula for the basis of a future South Africa, provided certain conditions were met' (p. 7).
203. Ibid. pp. 230–1.
204. Ibid. p. 75.
205. Ibid. pp. 151–2.
206. Ibid. pp. 276–7.
207. Schoeman wrote two biographies of Schreiner, *Olive Schreiner: A Woman in South Africa, 1855–1881* (1991) and *Only an Anguish to Live Here: Olive Schreiner and the Anglo-Boer War, 1899–1902* (1992).
208. Schoeman, *Promised*, p. 80.
209. Ibid. p. 82
210. Ibid. p. 69.
211. Ibid. p. 76.
212. Ibid. p. 164.
213. In terms that echo Schreiner's experience of her initial reception in metropolitan society, Carla berates George for patronising her: '"I've read and listened to others and heard about other things, even though I've lived my whole life on the farm and spend all day in the yard and vegetable-garden. Who are you to come and look down on me and say that I wouldn't understand"' (pp. 115–16). *Promised Land* anticipates well-known novels of the 1980s: Carla working on the vegetable garden in arid climes precedes J. M. Coetzee's protagonist of *The Life and Times of Michael K* (1983), and the scenario of terrified white people on a remote farm and subject to capricious black rule is repeated in Nadine Gordimer's *July's People* (1983).
214. Schoeman, *Promised*, p. 64.
215. Ibid. p. 118.
216. Ibid. p. 202.
217. Ibid. p. 20. Mandela also named Randolph Vigne of the Liberal Party, but as I have argued, the dreams of the ANC and Liberal Party were very similar.

CHAPTER 2

1. 'I. C. U. Manifesto'.
2. Ibid.
3. The historiography of the ICU is vast and contested: Gitsham and Trembath, *A First*, pp. 122–6; Barnes, *Caliban*, pp. 96–103; Nzula, Potekhin and Zusmanovich, *Forced*,

pp. 206–10; Tyamzashe, 'History of the ICU', Saffrey Collection, AD 1278, Wits; Roux, *Time*, pp. 153–97; Simons and Simons, *Class*, pp. 340–85; Johns, 'Trade', pp. 695–794; Webster, 'Champion', pp. 6–13; Wickins, *The Industrial*; Bonner, 'The decline', pp. 114–20; La Hausse, 'The message', pp. 19–58; Bradford, *A Taste*; Beinart and Bundy, *Hidden*, pp. 270–330; Neame, 'The ICU', pp. 69–82; Mouton, *Voices*, pp. 36–50; Breckenridge, '"We must speak"', pp. 71–108; Drew, *Discordant*, pp. 78–86; Phiri, *I See*, pp. 18–54; Van der Walt, 'Anarchism', pp. 150–4, and 'The first', pp. 237–43; Limb, *The ANC's Early*, pp. 263–72; Collis, 'Anxious', pp. 156–223; Mkhize, 'Empire', pp. 135–49; Neame, *The Congress*, vol. 1, pp. 125–57, 266–314, 387–466, 507–78; Roth, *The Communist*, chapter 4; and Dee, 'Nyasa', pp. 383–406. This is not the place for an extended discussion of the historiography, but it should be emphasised that opinions on the ICU and Kadalie diverge widely, even within the same political organisations. Contrast, for example, the judgments of CPSA members Albert Nzula and Roux: Nzula dismissed Kadalie as 'completely reactionary and a tool of the bourgeoisie' (*Forced*, p. 210), whereas Roux described him as a man of 'great talents. Intelligent, versatile, passionate [with] natural gifts of charm and persuasive oratory' (*Time*, p. 196).
4. In analysing the ICU's dreams of freedom, an important qualification is necessary. In this account, the language of dreaming is English, but it is crucial to register the centrality of translation to the production and dissemination of ICU ideas. Kadalie could not speak the African languages of Southern Africa, so many of his speeches were communicated to his audiences via translators. There were also many speeches by his ICU comrades that were translated from African languages (mainly Xhosa and Sotho) into English by the police informants transcribing them.
5. Kadalie, *My Life*, p. 32.
6. Ibid. p. 32.
7. Ibid. p. 78.
8. Ibid. p. 90.
9. Ibid. p. 140.
10. P. S. Sijadu, 7 January 1930, Native Agitation, Police Reports from 1928 to 1933, 1/ELN vol. 86 file C3 (1) and vol. 87 file C3 (2), WCA. The speeches of Kadalie and his ICU comrades in the Eastern Cape during the 1930–3 labour disputes are held at: Native Agitation, Police Reports from 1928 to 1933, 1/ELN vol. 86 file C3 (1) and vol. 87 file C3 (2), WCA. Another set of ICU speeches from roughly the same period, but covering the whole country, are held at: Native Agitation, Police Reports from 1927 to 1938, JUS 918–25 1/18/26, NASA. My references are to the date of the speech; the date of the record of each speech is either on the same day or within a couple of days of the speech. I accept Beinart and Bundy's arguments for broadly recognising the reliability of the police recordings of ICU speeches (Beinart and Bundy, *Hidden*, pp. 318–19). I am very grateful to Henry Dee for sharing his transcriptions of the ICU speeches held at the NASA in Pretoria.
11. Alex Maduna, 19 January 1930, Native Agitation, Police Reports from 1928 to 1933, 1/ELN vol. 86 file C3 (1) and vol. 87 file C3 (2), WCA.
12. Clements Kadalie, 24 June 1928, Native Agitation, Police Reports from 1928 to 1933, 1/ELN vol. 86 file C3 (1) and vol. 87 file C3 (2), WCA.
13. Keable 'Mote, 27 May 1929, Native Agitation, Police Reports from 1928 to 1933, 1/ELN vol. 86 file C3 (1) and vol. 87 file C3 (2), WCA.
14. Clements Kadalie, 25 May 1930, Native Agitation, Police Reports from 1928 to 1933, 1/ELN vol. 86 file C3 (1) and vol. 87 file C3 (2), WCA.
15. Clements Kadalie, 18 August 1930, Native Agitation, Police Reports from 1928 to 1933, 1/ELN vol. 86 file C3 (1) and vol. 87 file C3 (2), WCA.
16. Clements Kadalie, 10 February 1930, Native Agitation, Police Reports from 1928 to 1933, 1/ELN vol. 86 file C3 (1) and vol. 87 file C3 (2), WCA.

17. Clements Kadalie, 8 September 1930, Native Agitation, Police Reports from 1928 to 1933, 1/ELN vol. 86 file C3 (1) and vol. 87 file C3 (2), WCA.
18. 'Another'.
19. Alex Fifani, 18 August 1930, Native Agitation, Police Reports from 1928 to 1933, 1/ELN vol. 86 file C3 (1) and vol. 87 file C3 (2), WCA.
20. John Mciza, 18 August 1930, Native Agitation, Police Reports from 1928 to 1933, 1/ELN vol. 86 file C3 (1) and vol. 87 file C3 (2), WCA.
21. Dorrington Mqayi, 12 January 1931, Native Agitation, Police Reports from 1928 to 1933, 1/ELN vol. 86 file C3 (1) and vol. 87 file C3 (2), WCA.
22. 'Meetings'.
23. Quoted in Elphick, *Christianity*, p. 359.
24. Clements Kadalie, 'The King versus Clements Kadalie', 29 May 1928, W. M. Ballinger Collection, BC 347/A5/X/3.3, pp. 1–2, UCT.
25. Ibid.
26. Kadalie, *My Life*, p. 213.
27. Clements Kadalie, 6 January 1927, Native Agitation, Police Reports from 1927 to 1938, JUS 918–25 1/18/26, NASA.
28. Clements Kadalie, 29 February 1927, Native Agitation, Police Reports from 1927 to 1938, JUS 918–25 1/18/26, NASA.
29. Clements Kadalie, 18 January 1932, Native Agitation, Police Reports from 1928 to 1933, 1/ELN vol. 86 file C3 (1) and vol. 87 file C3 (2), WCA.
30. Clements Kadalie, 20 July 1930, Native Agitation, Police Reports from 1928 to 1933, 1/ELN vol. 86 file C3 (1) and vol. 87 file C3 (2), WCA.
31. Clements Kadalie, 4 March 1927, Native Agitation, Police Reports from 1927 to 1938, JUS 918–25 1/18/26, NASA.
32. Solomon T. Plaatje, *Native*, p. 262. On the relationship between South Africa's black political leaders and the missionaries in the early twentieth century, see Elphick, *The Equality*, pp. 121–7.
33. The impact of Garveyism in Southern Africa is discussed by Edgar, 'Garveyism'; Hill and Pirio, '"Africa"'; West, 'Seeds'; Higginson, 'Liberating'; and Vinson, 'The Americans', pp. 63–132. On the impact of Garveyism specifically on the ICU, see Bradford, *A Taste*, pp. 77–8, 93–4, 123–7; Hill and Pirio, '"Africa"', pp. 214–22; Campbell, *Songs*, pp. 316–20; and Neame, *The Congress*, vol. 1, pp. 451–63.
34. Kadalie's letter to Ncwana of 20 May 1920 is quoted and discussed in Dee, '"Enemy"'. Dee traces Kadalie and Ncwana's relationship from its convivial beginnings to its acrimonious denouement.
35. On Thaele's political career, see Kemp and Vinson, '"Poking"'.
36. W. D. Cingo, *Kokstad Advertiser*, 30 September 1927, quoted in Edgar, 'Garveyism', p. 37. Cingo's impressions were echoed a decade later in the travel notes of the African American academic Ralph J. Bunche, which recorded that 'South African [blacks] became all excited about Garveyism and the slogan was "the American Negroes are coming to save us". They, too, grasp frantically at any sort of hope of escape' (Edgar, *An African*, p. 134).
37. Ncwana, 'Bolshevism'.
38. Thaele, 'The African Empire'.
39. Ibid.
40. Ernest Wallace, *Matatiele Mail*, 23 December 1925, quoted in Edgar, 'Garveyism', p. 36.
41. See Edgar, 'Garveyism', p. 54.
42. Thaele, 'The African Empire'.
43. Thaele, 'Editorial'.
44. See Van der Walt, 'The first', pp. 237–43. In addition to stressing the internationalism of the ICU, Van der Walt's emphasis on the significance of syndicalism to the ICU adds another necessary dimension to the understanding of the ICU's multiple strands.

45. 'There are some'.
46. Thaele, 'The Laws'.
47. Thaele, 'Beware'.
48. Ibid.
49. Editorial, *The Workers' Herald*, 26 March 1926. The poem was first published in the November 1920 issue of *The Black Man* and initialled 'CK'.
50. 'Advertisement: Garvey's *Africa*' p. 4.
51. 'Advertisement: Percine', p. 6.
52. Thaele, 'The Negro'.
53. Garvey, *Philosophy*, vol. 2, pp. 68, 72.
54. Thaele, 'Editorial'.
55. See Vinson, *The Americans*, pp. 98–9.
56. For Garvey's justification of his dialogue with the Klan, and the reactions of African American radicals at the time, see Bergin, *African American*, pp. 143–73. For an influential critique of Garvey, see George Padmore's identification of Garveyism with fascism (Padmore, *Pan-Africanism*, pp. 96–7). Padmore anchors his analysis in quotations of Garvey's own words: '"We were the first Fascists. We had disciplined men, women and children in training for the liberation of Africa. The black masses saw that in this extreme nationalism lay their only hope, and readily supported it. Mussolini copied fascism from me, but the Negro reactionaries sabotaged it"' (p. 97). For a contrasting view of Garvey, which sees an implicit socialism complicating his pro-capitalist and fascist rhetoric, see Cedric Robinson, who characterises Garveyite ideology as 'incorporating elements of Christianity, socialism, revolutionary nationalism and race solidarity', and argues further that 'Garvey, himself, had strong hostilities towards capitalists on the grande bourgeois scale and often seemed to publicly move towards a tentative commitment to socialism' (Robinson, *Black*, pp. 296, 341).
57. Ncwana, 'Bolshevism'.
58. Thaele, 'The Negro'.
59. Ibid.
60. Thaele was also criticised by moderate and conservative African leaders. For summaries, see Hill and Pirio, '"Africa"', pp. 222–38, and Vinson, *The Americans*, pp. 88–90. Neither chapters mention the later attacks on Thaele in *Umsebenzi*.
61. 'Thaelopirowism'. See also the *Umsebenzi* article likening Thaele's anti-Communism to Kadalie's – 'Then and now'.
62. On the CPSA's relationship with the ICU, see Johns, *Raising*, pp. 168–81; Drew, *Discordant*, pp. 78–86; and Neame, *The Congress*, vol. 1, pp. 296–306, 467–78 and vol. 2, pp. 201–10.
63. 'The Fifth Annual'.
64. Quoted in Johns, *Raising*, p. 170.
65. James La Guma, 'Awake!'
66. Ibid.
67. 'I. C. U. Programme'.
68. Kadalie, *My Life*, pp. 220–1.
69. Kadalie, 'A call', p. 814.
70. Swinburne's volume *Songs before Sunrise* was dedicated to Mazzini's unification of Italy.
71. Edward Roux and Win Roux, *Rebel*, p. 51.
72. Ibid. p. 51.
73. Roux's enthusiasm for Swinburne is discussed in Chapter 3.
74. Eddie Daniels recalls Mandela reciting the poem in his Robben Island prison cell, and also describes teaching the poem to his high-school pupils after he was freed from prison: 'I had always emphasized the last two lines of the poem, substituting "You" for "I". You are the

Master of your Fate: You are the Captain of your Soul. I would tell them that they could use themselves for good or evil. They could be responsible or irresponsible. They were the captains of their souls, they were the masters of their fate' (Daniels, *There*, p. 244). Henley's 'Invictus' also plays a central role in the 2009 Hollywood movie of the same name, and Barack Obama read a stanza of the poem at Mandela's funeral.

75. Quiller-Couch, *The Oxford*, p. 1019.
76. 'Fighting'.
77. Ibid.
78. Clements Kadalie, 24 January 1930, Native Agitation, Police Reports from 1928 to 1933, 1/ELN vol. 86 file C3 (1) and vol. 87 file C3 (2), WCA.
79. Kadalie, *My Life*, p. 206.
80. Ibid. p. 207.
81. Kadalie, 'Manifesto', 9 July 1928, W. M. Ballinger Collection, BC 347/A5/II/1, p. 4, UCT.
82. William Ballinger, 'Winifred Holtby and Africa' (1937), W. M. Ballinger Collection, BC 347/A5/VII/16, UCT. On Ballinger's role in the ICU, see Mouton, *Voices*, pp. 32–56.
83. I have followed M. W. Swanson, the editor of the only compilation of Champion's writings, in determining the publication dates of the three pamphlets (Swanson, *The Views*, p. 47).
84. Champion, *The Truth*, p. 6.
85. Ibid. pp. 9–10.
86. Ibid. p. 10.
87. Ibid. p. 27.
88. Ibid. p. 28.
89. Ibid. p. 28.
90. Champion, *Mehlomadala*, p. 22.
91. Ibid. p. 26.
92. Ibid. p. 29.
93. Ibid. p. 30.
94. Ibid. p. 30.
95. Champion, *Blood*, p. 59.
96. Ibid. p. 59.
97. Ibid. p. 58.
98. Ibid. p. 60.
99. Lewis's career, including her relationship with the ICU, is discussed by Tim Couzens in his Introduction to the reissued edition of her novel *Wild Deer*, and in 'Keeping', pp. 39–52. For recent discussions of Lewis's relationship with the ICU, see Courau ('States', pp. 160–2, 198–200) and Collis ('Anxious', pp. 227–41).
100. Lewis, 'The Book' (31 October 1928).
101. For a summary of recent interpretations of Blake's 'The Little Black Boy', see Bohls, *Romantic*, pp. 59–68.
102. Lewis, 'The Book' (18 March 1927).
103. Lewis, 'The Book' (6 April 1927).
104. Jackson, *Countee*.
105. Lewis, 'The Book' (15 July 1927).
106. Lewis, 'The Book' (15 August 1927).
107. Lewis, *Wild*, p. 269.
108. Ibid. p. 269.
109. Ibid. p. 273.
110. Holtby's relationship with the ICU is described in Brittain, *Testament*, pp. 216–18, 236–50; Shaw, *The Clear*. pp. 168–98; and Reagan, *Winifred*, pp. 103–34.
111. Klenerman, 'Interview', Fanny Klenerman Papers, file 2, A2031/a, Wits.

112. Holtby, *Mandoa*, pp. 78–9.
113. Ibid. p. 89.
114. Ibid. p. 277.
115. Ibid. p. 261. Holtby held Schreiner in the highest regard, singling out for particular praise Schreiner's prescience: 'She could foresee with prophetic clarity the course of social change, so that her writings on feminism and racial questions are almost as relevant today as when she wrote them' ('The writers').
116. Ibid. p. 380.
117. Holtby, 'Jan'.
118. Letter from Winifred Holtby to Margaret Ballinger, 16 August 1935, W. M. Ballinger Collection, BC 347/D1/I/8–1–6, UCT.
119. Holtby, 'An appeal'.
120. Ibid.
121. Letter from Winifred Holtby to William and Margaret Ballinger, 25 December 1934, W. M. Ballinger Collection, BC 347/D1/7–1–14, UCT.
122. Brittain, *Testament*, p. 248.
123. James La Guma and James Gumba, Joint statement to the Economic and Wage Commission (1925), p. 15, P. L. Wickins Collection, BC 657, UCT.
124. William Ballinger, 2 September 1928, Native Agitation, Police Reports from 1927 to 1938, JUS 918–25 1/18/26, NASA.
125. Mmereki Molohlanyi, Interview, 19 April 1984, Institute for Advanced Social Research (henceforth IASR), Share Cropping and Labour Tenancy Oral History Project (1979–85), Interview no. 100, p. 33, Wits.
126. 'Kadalie's'.
127. P. S. Sijadu, 5 January 1930, Native Agitation, Police Reports from 1928 to 1933, 1/ELN vol. 86 file C3 (1) and vol. 87 file C3 (2), WCA.
128. Dorrington Mqayi, 12 January 1931, Native Agitation, Police Reports from 1928 to 1933, 1/ELN vol. 86 file C3 (1) and vol. 87 file C3 (2), WCA.
129. Kadalie, 'The Aristocracy', p. 242.
130. Ibid. p. 242.
131. 'I. C. U. Manifesto'.
132. Kadalie, *My Life*, p. 221.
133. Quoted in Bradford, *A Taste*, p. 81.
134. Limb, *The ANC's*, p. 250.
135. Clements Kadalie, 14 December 1930, Native Agitation, Police Reports from 1928 to 1933, 1/ELN vol. 86 file C3 (1) and vol. 87 file C3 (2), WCA.
136. See Kadalie, *My Life*, p. 39.
137. Rose Sibanyoni, Interview, 4 September 1979, IASR, Share Cropping and Labour Tenancy Oral History Project (1979–85), Interview no. 2, p. 26, Wits.
138. Champion, quoted in Swanson, *The Views*, pp. 4–5.
139. Kadalie, quoted in 'National Secretary's Report'.
140. Kadalie, quoted in 'Chronic'.
141. Scott, *Domination*, p. 92.
142. Ibid. p. 93.
143. On the internationalism of the ICU, see Van der Walt, 'The first', pp. 237–43 and Dee, 'Nyasa', pp. 391–5.
144. Kadalie, 'A call', p. 262.
145. Kadalie, quoted in 'Colour bar'.
146. Kadalie, 'Political', pp. 294, 306.
147. Kadalie, 'The Old', p. 628.
148. Bradford, *A Taste*, p. 143.

149. Such negative assessments correspond with the scholarly consensus that the ICU's material achievements were limited. Phil Bonner, for example, points out that 'its formal achievements were negligible. Labour conditions registered little improvement; wages remained more or less stationary; and a whole new range of discriminatory legislation was placed on the statute books' ('The decline', p. 115).
150. Ramakgelo Dinkebogile, Interview, 28 July 1981, IASR, Share Cropping and Labour Tenancy Oral History Project (1979–85), Interview no. 48, pp. 48–9, Wits.
151. L. H. Mathebula, Interview, 25 November 1981, IASR, Share Cropping and Labour Tenancy Oral History Project (1979–85), Interview no. 224, p. 17, Wits.
152. Ephraim Zondi, Interview, 3 July 1980, IASR, Share Cropping and Labour Tenancy Oral History Project (1979–85), Interview no. 237, p. 9, Wits.
153. Elijah Ngcobo, Interview, 3–4 December 1981, IASR, Share Cropping and Labour Tenancy Oral History Project (1979–85), Interview no. 223, pp. 27, 77, Wits.
154. Lucas Nqandela, Interview, 25 August 1982, IASR, Share Cropping and Labour Tenancy Oral History Project (1979–85), Interview no. 65, pp. 48, 51, Wits.
155. Thabiso Bogopane, Interview, 11 September 1981, IASR, Share Cropping and Labour Tenancy Oral History Project (1979–85), Interview no. 55, p. 25, Wits.
156. Ibid. pp. 25, 28.
157. Rose Sibanyoni, Interview, 4 September 1979, IASR, Share Cropping and Labour Tenancy Oral History Project (1979–85), Interview no. 2, p. 28, Wits.
158. Kas Maine, Interview, 2 July 1980, IASR, Share Cropping and Labour Tenancy Oral History Project (1979–85), Interview no. 30, pp. 30–1, Wits.

CHAPTER 3

1. On the Marxist tradition of utopian thought, see Paden, 'Marx's', pp. 67–91; Webb, *Marx*, pp. 19–35, 85–117; Levitas, *The Concept*, pp. 41–67; Harvey, *Spaces*, pp. 21–52; Lovell, 'Marx's', pp. 629–40; and Fischbach, 'Marx', pp. 117–25.
2. Marx, *Capital*, vol. 1, p. 99 (the Afterword to the 1873 German edition).
3. Engels, 'Socialism', pp. 190, 204.
4. Lenin, *What*, pp. 157–8.
5. Marshall and Marshall, 1960, p. 27.
6. Ibid. p. 71.
7. Ibid. p. 76.
8. Ibid. p. 88.
9. Ibid. p. 90.
10. Ibid. p. 10.
11. Ibid. p. 92.
12. Ibid. p. 12.
13. Ibid. p. 11.
14. Ibid. p. 16.
15. Ibid. p. 92.
16. Ibid. p. 95.
17. Schreiner to Pearson, 6 November 1885, *Letters Online*.
18. Schreiner to Molteno, 1905, *Letters Online*.
19. Schreiner to Carpenter, 17 February 1905, *Letters Online*.
20. Schreiner to the Social Democratic Federation (Cape Town), 3 February 1905, *Letters Online*.
21. Schreiner to Merriman, 2 August 1907, *Letters Online*.
22. Schreiner to Ellis, 21 August 1914, *Letters Online*.

23. Schreiner to Solomon, August 1914, *Letters Online*.
24. Schreiner to Ellis, 1919, *Letters Online*. Although Schreiner praised Marx and Lenin here, in earlier letters she had declared that she preferred John Stuart Mill to Marx (in a letter to Molteno on 24 May 1895, *Letters Online*), and that she '[sympathised] more with the Herbert Spencer school than with the Socialists' (in a letter to Ellis on 29 March 1885, *Letters Online*). The most determined attempt to claim Schreiner as a socialist is the pamphlet by the South African Communist Party (SACP) intellectual, Michael Harmel, commemorating the centenary of Schreiner's birth. Quoting all the passages in Schreiner's writings sympathetic to socialism, and emphasising Schreiner's friendship with Eleanor Marx, Harmel concludes that the task of honouring and revering Schreiner's name belongs 'to the common people of South Africa, in their forward movement for liberation, and to the free South Africa of the future which, tomorrow, we shall build' (*Olive*, p. 12).
25. Schreiner to Molteno, 1 January 1920, *Letters Online*.
26. Schreiner to Smuts, 19 October 1920, *Letters Online*.
27. Ibid.
28. Schreiner to Carpenter, 13 October 1914, *Letters Online*.
29. Olive Schreiner to William Schreiner, 29 July 1916, *Letters Online*.
30. Schreiner, *The Dawn*, p. 42.
31. Histories of the ISL and CPSA include: Roux, *Time*, pp. 198–217, 231–69; Simons and Simons, *Class*, pp. 244–70, 386–415; Johns, *Raising*, pp. 50–162; Mantzaris, 'The promise', pp. 145–73; Grossman, 'Class', pp. 28–161; Kelley, 'The religious', 5–24; Drew, *Discordant*, pp. 46–136; Johanningsmeier, 'Communists', pp. 156–71; Van der Walt, 'Anarchism', 128–75, 492–551; Filatova and Davidson, *The Hidden*, pp. 43–9, 79–140; Neame, *The Congress*, vol. 1, pp. 5–10, 296–306, 467–79, 541–9; vol. 2, pp. 201–10, 312–19; and vol. 3, pp. 31–46; and Roth, *The Communist*, chapters 2–4. For a survey of right-wing histories of the CPSA, see Visser, 'Afrikaner', pp. 306–33, and for an overview of utopianism in CPSA discourse, see Meny-Gibert, 'The nature', pp. 46–92.
32. Cope, *Comrade*, p. 14.
33. See Nzula, 'Letter'. Nzula elaborates further upon the limits of Christianity in his review of the Rev. E. Phillips's *The Bantu are Coming*, which concludes, 'The exploited, the slaves themselves must dispossess the robbers and come into their own. Yes the Bantu are coming and their coming means death to the exploiters and their defender the Church' (Nzula, 'Review').
34. This was a standard pattern wherever Christianity was superseded by socialism. Gareth Stedman Jones argues that from about 1800, '"Socialism" in its different varieties presented itself as the universal replacement for the old religions of the world built upon a new "science"-based cosmology and a new ethical code' ('Religion', p. 172).
35. 'Editorial', *The International*, 11 May 1917.
36. Quoted in Hirson and Williams, *The Delegate*, p. 178.
37. Marx and Engels, *The Manifesto*, p. 81.
38. Quoted in Hirson and Williams, *The Delegate*, 200.
39. Goldman, *My Disillusionment*, p. xvii.
40. Serge, *Memoirs*, p. 155. On sympathetic travellers to the Soviet Union after the Revolution, see David-Fox, *Showcasing*, pp. 28–60.
41. Ibid. p. 160.
42. Jones, 'The black', p. 1194.
43. Quoted in Hirson and William, *The Delegate*, p. 218.
44. Ibid. p. 219.
45. Jones, 'When'. The article title '"When dawn's left hand was in the sky"' is a quotation from Edward Fitzgerald's 1859 translation of *The Rhubáiyát of Omar Khayýam*.
46. Quoted in Hirson and Williams, *The Delegate*, p. 243.

47. See Hirson and Williams, *The Delegate*, 194. On Gumede's conversion to Soviet socialism, see Van Diemel, *In Search*, pp. 96–146; Petersson, '"A man"', pp. 84–5, 93–5; and 'J. T. Gumede'.
48. J. T. Gumede, 'A cry for freedom, liberty, justice and fair play', September 1919, Papers of the Anti-Slavery Society, MSS, Brit. Emp. s. 23, H2/50, folios 55–6, UO.
49. J. T. Gumede, quoted in 'At the Brussels'.
50. J. T. Gumede in 'Proceedings and resolutions of the Non-European Conference' [1927], in Karis, Carter and Johns, *From Protest*, vol. 1, p. 258.
51. Quoted in 'African'.
52. 'Russia'.
53. The successive ISL and CPSA newspapers had the following editors. *The International*: Jones (1915–18); Bunting (1918–19); Jones (1919–20); Andrews (1920–3); Bunting (May 1923–5). *The South African Worker*: Bunting (1925–8); Douglas Wolton (1928–30). *Umsebenzi*: Roux (1930); Douglas and Molly Wolton and Bach (1931); Roux and Molly Wolton (1931–3); Roux and Kotane (1933–5). See Lalu, 'The Communist', pp. 2–30.
54. 'South Africa's'.
55. 'Pirovian Dictatorship' refers to the racist legislation pushed through by the Nazi sympathising cabinet minister Oswald Pirow.
56. Marx, *A Contribution*, p. 244.
57. Webb, *Marx*, p. 25.
58. On Bain and Morris, see Hyslop, *The Notorious*, pp. 65–75, 128–9, 226–7; on Jones and Shelley, see Hirson and Williams, *The Delegate*, p. 189; on Bunting and Browning, see Roux, *S. P. Bunting*, p. 13; and on Roux and Swinburne, see Roux and Roux, *Rebel*, pp. 92–4, 130, 178.
59. See Drew, 'Prisoner', pp. 38–9.
60. 'The Forges'.
61. Ibid.
62. Gilman, 'To Labour'.
63. Gilman, 'Woman'. In addition to these two exhortatory poems, six more of Gilman's poems published under the pseudonym 'Mrs Charlotte Stetson' appeared in *The International*: 'You Must Alter Human Nature' (21 January 1916); 'Survival of the Fittest' (4 February 1916); 'A Man Must Live' (11 February 1916); 'Woman' (18 February 1916); 'To Labour' (25 February 1916); 'The Cart Before the Horse' (3 March 1916); 'To the Single Taxer' (10 March 1916); and 'To the Wise – A Bargain' (15 August 1916).
64. 'I. S. L. Marching'.
65. 'Emancipation'.
66. See 'The Red Flag' in 'A new'.
67. M. H. F., 'Byronic'. The extracts from *Don Juan* are sequenced as follows: Canto 9, stanza 8; Canto 7, stanza 6; Canto 9, stanza 4; Canto 8, stanza 14; Canto 7, stanza 84; and Canto 8, stanza 3.
68. Ibid.
69. 'The workers''. The lines from Byron's 'Lara', Canto 2, stanza 8 appear in *The International* under a poem misattributed to Rudyard Kipling.
70. Hall was a favourite of the editors of *The International*, as others of his poems were also reprinted (unchanged). For example, 'Us, the Hoboes', with its final line 'We shall turn the old world over as a plowman turns the clods,' appeared in *The International* 23 March 1923.
71. 'Nietzsche's'.
72. Ibid.
73. Ibid.
74. The 'tot' system was the payment of farm workers in alcohol instead of cash, and was widely used in the Western Cape.

75. 'Tot'.
76. 'Ndabeni'.
77. Ibid.
78. La Guma, 'Awake'. For a discussion of La Guma's integration of Negritude and Communist ideas in the poem, see Chapter 2, and also Kelley, 'The Third', pp. 106–7.
79. 'Presbyter'.
80. Ibid.
81. Ibid.
82. Ibid.
83. Ibid.
84. 'The higher'.
85. 'May Day hymn'.
86. 'Put in'.
87. 'Great'.
88. Ibid.
89. Ibid.
90. Thompson, *William*, p. 668.
91. Ibid. p. 668.
92. 'Great'.
93. Ibid.
94. Thompson, *William*, pp. 788–9.
95. 'Great'.
96. Ibid.
97. Ibid.
98. For a description of the meeting, see Hyslop, *The Notorious*, pp. 276–7.
99. 'Back'.
100. Gibson, 'National'.
101. Ibid.
102. Marx and Engels, *The German*, p. 461.
103. Jones, *The Iron*.
104. Ibid.
105. Marx and Engels, *The German*, p. 461.
106. Gibson's contributions to *The International* are described by Hirson and Williams as 'an ideas column to help in the re-education of the membership' (*The Delegate*, 149). Several of his signed articles focused on the meaning of freedom: 'Freedom?' (4 May 1917); 'Citizenship first' (18 April 1919); 'Absolute liberty' (18 October 1919). Several more unsigned articles on freedom, in all likelihood also written by Gibson, appeared: 'What the capitalist means by "freedom"' (11 May 1917); 'The land of the free' (7 June 1918); 'Nationalism: freedom's foe' (21 December 1918); and 'Freedom, where art thou?' (21 February 1919).
107. Gibson, 'Freedom'.
108. Ibid.
109. MacKay, 'British'.
110. 'What the capitalist'.
111. Gibson, 'Freedom'.
112. Gibson, 'Citizenship'.
113. Ibid.
114. 'The land'.
115. 'Freedom'.
116. Watson, 'What'.
117. 'Nationalism'.

118. Ibid.
119. Gibson, 'Freedom'.
120. Gibson, 'Absolute'.
121. Ibid.
122. Ibid.
123. 'And this'.
124. See Thompson, *William*, pp. 805–7.
125. Wolton, *Whither*, p. 7.
126. Quoted in Roux, *S. P. Bunting*, p. 58.
127. S. P. Bunting, 'The Moscow'.
128. S. P. Bunting, 'An Open'.
129. Rebecca Bunting, 'Freedom'
130. Ibid.
131. Roux, *S. P. Bunting*, p. 91.
132. The impact and significance of the Native Republic thesis on South African resistance history and politics has been debated ever since 1928. The essential primary documents are introduced and republished in Drew, *South Africa's*, vol. 1, pp. 76–105 and in Davidson et al., *South Africa*, vol. 1, pp. 1–32, 149–32. Sympathetic accounts of the adoption and long-term influence of the Native Republic thesis include: Forman, *A Trumpet*, pp. 75–80; Harmel, *Fifty*, pp. 57–60; B. Bunting, *Moses*, pp. 14–74; Simons and Simons, *Class*, pp. 386–415; Nxumalo, 'Revolutionary', pp. 46–52; and Francis Meli, 'The Comintern and sub-Saharan Africa – an aspect of African history' (1988), pp. 81–115, Brian Bunting Collection, Robben Island Museum and Mayibuye Archive, MCH 07-129-3, UWC. On the occasion of the ninetieth anniversary of the CPSA/SACP, Kgalema Motlanthe repeated the party view that 'the adoption of the Black Republic thesis in 1928 cemented the role of the CPSA in the liberation struggle' ('The history', p. 20). From within the CPSA/SACP tradition, dissenting commentaries include those of Roux, *Time*, pp. 85–100 and 1972, 72–8, 107–24 and First, 'After', p. 97. Critical accounts from the left include Hirson, 'Bukharin', pp. 51–65 and Legassick, *Towards*, pp. 157–82. The most extended attack on the Native Republic thesis from the right is Pike, *A History*, pp. 166–77. Accounts attempting a more detached perspective include: Drew, 'Social', pp. 117–74; Johns, *Raising*, pp. 214–70; Grossman, 'Class', pp. 146–61; Drew, *Discordant*, pp. 94–136; Johanningsmeier, 'Communists', pp. 164–71; and Filatova and Davidson, *The Hidden*, pp. 85–110.
133. Drew, *Discordant*, p. 96.
134. The essential documents related to the New Line are introduced and republished in Drew, *South Africa's*, vol. 1, pp. 108–21 and Davidson et al. (eds), *South Africa*, vol. 1, pp. 3–130.
135. Legassick, *Towards*, p. 181.
136. Drew, *Discordant*, p. 132.
137. Roux, *S. P. Bunting*, p. 60. For Roux, 'Imprecor' (not Inprecor) referred to the *International Press Correspondence/The Communist International*, which exemplified bureaucratic discourse.
138. 'Theses'.
139. Letter from Moses Kotane to Brian Bunting, 15 March 1956, Brian Bunting Collection, Robben Island Museum and Mayibuye Archive, folder 11.3, MCH 07-134-4-2, UWC.
140. Harrison, *Memoirs*, p. 114.
141. Ibid. p. 121.
142. Kotane in Dadoo, *South*, pp 120–1.
143. Roux and Roux, *Rebel*, p. 127.
144. Ibid. p. 100.
145. Ibid. p. 100.
146. Sneguireff, 'Modern', pp. 69–70.

147. Ibid. p. 70.
148. Ibid. pp. 74–6.
149. Roux, *Rebel*, p. 101.
150. Sneguireff, 'Modern', p. 76.
151. Nzula et al., *Forced*, p. 71.
152. Ibid. p. 74.
153. 'Where racial'.
154. Nzula et al., *Forced*, p. 125.
155. Ibid. p. 136.
156. Ibid. p. 183.
157. Roux, 'A South'.
158. Nzula et al., *Forced*, pp. 169, 182, 186.
159. Kotane, 'An engineer'.
160. 'The Communist'.
161. Nzula et al., *Forced*, pp. 131, 206.
162. Gomas, 'Our'.
163. On Bunting's expulsion from the CPSA, see Roux, *S. P. Bunting*, pp. 85–100 and 122–46, and Drew, *Between*, pp. 188–208.
164. 'The right'.
165. 'The fight'.
166. 'Bunting'.
167. Harrison, *Memoirs*, pp. 120–1.
168. Dadoo, *South*, p. 101.
169. Ibid. p. 102.
170. That South African Communists failed to define clearly what they meant by 'the dictatorship of the proletariat' was in no small part due to the fact that the phrase was far from clear in Stalin's own writings. For a discussion of the vague and contradictory content of the term 'the dictatorship of the proletariat' in Stalin's writings, see Robinson, 'Stalin's', pp. 16–21 and Van Ree, *Boundaries*, pp. 208–54.
171. Nzula et al., *Forced*, p. 192.
172. 'Here and there'.
173. 'Where racial'.
174. Stalin, 'Former'.
175. 'Manifesto'.
176. Ibid.

CHAPTER 4

1. Kadalie, *My Life*, pp. 212–13.
2. Ibid. p. 221.
3. 'Germiston'.
4. Gomas, 'The Native'.
5. See Drew, *Discordant*, pp. 188–90.
6. Drew, *South Africa's*, vol. 1, p. 129. For more detail, see Van der Walt, 'Thibedi'.
7. Klenerman, 'Interview', Fanny Klenerman Papers, file 3, A2031/a, Wits.
8. Ibid.
9. See Drew, *Discordant*, pp. 137–65; Hirson, *A History*, pp. 88–105; Hunter, 'Raff'; and R. J. Alexander, *International*, pp. 668–77.
10. Roux, *Time*, p. 312.
11. Ibid. p. 312.

12. On the NEF, see Soudien, *Cape*.
13. On the establishment and early history of the NEUM, see Karis and Carter, *From Protest*, Vol. 2, pp. 71–2, 347–52; Drew, 'Social', pp. 423–517; Hirson, *A History*, pp. 156–79; Hommel, *Capricorn*, pp. 73–106; Fataar, 'Falsification', pp. 1–4; and Kayser, 'Land', pp. 13–19.
14. Negt and Kluge, *Public*, p. 91.
15. *Trek* attracted a wide readership from 1939 until its enforced closure in 1947 (see Sandwith, *World*, pp. 48–85). Dora Taylor was the most prolific literary intellectual within this radical community. Born Dora Jack in Aberdeen in 1899, and orphaned at a young age, Dora completed an MA in English Literature at Aberdeen University before marrying Jim Taylor in 1924, and then moving with him to Cape Town in 1926 after he had taken up a post in the Psychology Department at the university. On Taylor's life and writings, see Sandwith, *World*, pp. 86–128; Rassool, 'The Individual', pp. 395–435; Nash, 'The double', pp. 63–5.
16. There were many more left opposition intellectual-activists of substance, including R. O. Dudley (1924–2009), Alie Fataar (1917–2005), Cissie Gool (1897–1963), Kader Hassim (1934–2011), Hosea Jaffe (1921–2014), Kenneth Jordaan (1924–1988), Helen Kies (1926–2017), Edgar Maurice (1919–1994) and Phyllis Ntantala (1920–2016). I have focused on (Dora) Taylor, Tabata, (Ben) Kies, (Goolam) Gool, Jordan, Mqotsi and Alexander because their writings most illuminate how dreams of freedom could be expressed via literature.
17. The essential primary documents for this period, as well as accounts of the individuals, different parties and affiliated groups, are provided in Drew, *South Africa's*, vol. 2. A selection of articles by NEUM and other anti-Stalinist intellectuals have been republished in Hommel, *Contributions*.
18. Trotsky, *Our Political*.
19. Ibid.
20. Ibid.
21. Ibid.
22. Kies, *The background*, pp. 10–11.
23. 'In the liberal', p. 4.
24. Ibid.
25. Tabata, 'Liberalism', Unity Movement of South Africa (henceforth UMSA)/I. B. Tabata Collection, box 3, BC 925/ A, UCT.
26. Ibid.
27. Quoted in Gool, 'Land', p. 7.
28. Ibid. p. 7
29. Ibid. p. 7.
30. Ibid. p. 7.
31. Ibid. p. 7.
32. Davids, 'The Liberals', p. 14.
33. Ibid. p. 15.
34. Ibid. p. 15.
35. Davids, 'A critical', p. 30.
36. Copies of Numbers 1–177 of *The Bulletin* (with 63 and 69 missing) are held at UMSA/I. B. Tabata Collection, Section E: Publications, BC 925/A, UCT. For a discussion of the internationalism of *The Bulletin*, see Lee, 'The uses', pp. 31–61.
37. *The Bulletin*, 13 October 1943, p. 2.
38. *The Bulletin*, 20 December 1944, p. 1.
39. *The Bulletin*, 7 November 1945, p. 1.
40. Ibid, pp. 1–2.
41. Ibid. p. 2.
42. Gool, 'The Ten', p. 3.

43. Ibid. p. 6.
44. Letter from Tabata to Tstotsi, 4 August 1942, UMSA/I. B. Tabata Collection, box 2, BC 925/A, UCT.
45. Kies, *The Background*, p. 1.
46. Ibid. p. 1.
47. Kies, *The Contribution*, p. 38.
48. Mahabane, Z. R. et al., 'A Declaration', p. 2.
49. *The Bulletin*, 19 May 1945, p. 1.
50. *The Bulletin*, 20 December 1944, p. 2.
51. *The Bulletin*, 29 August 1945, p. 2.
52. Ibid. p. 2.
53. *The Bulletin*, 13 October 1943, p. 1.
54. *The Bulletin*, 23 November 1945, p. 1.
55. Ibid. p. 2.
56. Tabata, 'The boycott', p. 167.
57. Hirson, 'It is time', p. 3. For a recent overview of the Unity Movement's critique of nationalism, see Brown et al., 'The Unity', pp. 77–95.
58. Ibid. p. 149.
59. See Ray, pp. 90–5.
60. A key feature of South Africa's anti-Stalinists was their readiness to question the judgements of Trotsky and his European followers. In addition to Kies and Hirson, both Jaffe and Tabata also wrote critically about Trotsky's analyses of colonial/neo-colonial societies like South Africa. Jaffe interrogated the limits of Trotskyism in relation to the Unity Movement's political record in 'Signposts', pp. 7–15, and in a letter to Neville Alexander, 4 December 1958 (UMSA/I. B. Tabata Collection, box 10, BC 925/A, UCT), Tabata warned his younger comrade to be wary of British Trotskyists.
61. See Tabata's exposition of 'policemen-chiefs' and 'policemen-intellectuals' in 'The boycott', pp. 170–2, 183–7, and *The Awakening*, pp. 81–4.
62. 'Editorial. The National', p. 3.
63. Ibid. p. 3.
64. *The Bulletin*, 6 August 1947, p. 2.
65. 'The turn', p. 4.
66. Ibid. p. 4.
67. Pèon, 'Colonial', p. 2.
68. See *The Bulletin*, 11 February 1948.
69. *The Bulletin*, 2 June 1948, p. 2.
70. Ibid. p. 2.
71. *The Bulletin*, 10 July 1946, p. 2.
72. Hirson, 'It is time', p. 27.
73. Ibid. pp. 29–30.
74. R. E. Viljoen et al., *What*, p. 8.
75. Letter from Tabata to Nkrumah from Nairobi dated 17 April 1964 (UMSA/I. B. Tabata Collection, box 5, BC 925/A, UCT). A second similar letter followed on 20 July 1964 from Cairo (UMSA/I. B. Tabata Collection, box 5, BC 925/A, UCT). For a discussion of Tabata in exile and his negotiations with Nkrumah and other African leaders, see Rassool, 'The individual', pp. 375–7, 389–91, 420.
76. Reprinted in Drew, *South Africa's*, vol. 1, pp. 134–46.
77. Drew, *South Africa's*, vol. 1, pp. 135, 139.
78. Ibid. pp. 142, 144.
79. Ibid. p. 147.
80. Ibid. pp. 147, 149, 150.

80. Ibid. p. 149.
82. Hirson, *A History*, p. 92.
83. Drew, 'The theory', p. 64.
84. Drew, *South Africa's*, vol. 2, p. 306.
85. Ibid. p. 309.
86. Tabata, *The Dynamic*, pp. 131, 124.
87. Ibid. p. 126.
88. Taylor, *Don't*, p. 56.
89. Mqotsi, *House*, pp. 42–3.
90. Ibid. p. 107.
91. Ibid. p. 184.
92. Ibid. p. 185.
93. Ibid. p. 213.
94. Drew, *South Africa's*, vol. 2, pp. 62–3.
95. R. E. Viljoen et al., *What*, p. 5.
96. There is much evidence that the tensions between the AAC and anti-CAD factions of the NEUM bubbled beneath the surface from the beginnings of their alliance. For example, in her diary, Taylor (in Tabata's AAC faction) described Kies (of the Anti-CAD faction) in the following terms: 'the pettiness of that young muck-raker, egoist, spiteful, incapable of maturity' (unpublished diary, entry: 24 November 1949, Dora Taylor Collection, folder A. 2, BC 1422, UCT). Taylor and Kies's shared literary-political sympathies failed to bridge the factional divide.
97. Drew, *South Africa's*, vol. 2, p. 334.
98. Ibid. p. 334.
99. Ibid. p. 334.
100. Trotsky, *Literature*, pp. 45–6.
101. Ibid. p. 198.
102. Ibid. pp. 48, 51.
103. Ibid. p. 199.
104. Trotsky, *On Literature*, p. 176.
105. Ibid. p. 118.
106. Trotsky, *Literature*, pp. 207–8.
107. Taylor, 'Poets', p. 13.
108. Taylor, 'Review: R. M. Fox', p. 15.
109. Taylor, 'Poetry past', p. 86.
110. Taylor, unpublished diary, entry: added in 1976, Dora Taylor Collection, folder A. 2. BC 1422, UCT. Taylor's dating of her first encounters in Cape Town with Marxist (and Trotskyist) thought may have been earlier than 1935 because her article 'Poetry past and present' published in *The Critic* in the same year already demonstrates a close knowledge of Trotsky's *Literature and Revolution*.
111. Unpublished poem, Dora Taylor Collection, folder E. 3, BC 1422, UCT.
112. Ibid.
113. Taylor, 'They'.
114. Ibid.
115. Ibid.
116. Taylor, 'Olive, II'.
117. Taylor, 'Olive, III'.
118. Taylor, 'Olive IV'.
119. Ibid.
120. Ibid.
121. For a bibliography of Taylor's output, see Sandwith, 'Dora', pp. 81–4.

122. Taylor, unpublished diary, entry: November 1948, Dora Taylor Collection, folder A. 2, BC 1422, UCT.
123. Taylor and Tabata's relationship is described by Rassool, 'The individual', pp. 395–435. Rassool's account is challenged by Hassim, 'Rebuttal'.
124. Taylor, unpublished diary, entry: May 1949, Dora Taylor Collection, folder A. 2, BC 1422, UCT.
125. On the centrality of history to NEUM politics, see Nasson, 'The Unity', pp. 189–211.
126. Taylor, unpublished diary, entry: added in 1976, Dora Taylor Collection, folder A. 2, BC 1422, UCT.
127. Tabata, 'The future of industry in South Africa' (1942), UMSA/I. B. Tabata Collection, box 6, BC 925/A, UCT.
128. Ibid.
129. For examples of three such stories, see Tabata, *The Dynamic*, pp. 22–8.
130. Ibid. p. 25.
131. Ibid. p. 25.
132. The political and aesthetic differences between Tabata and Jordan are fictionalised in Deirdre Levinson's novel *Five Years: An Experience of South Africa* (1966) In chapter 8, the protagonist (a young white woman, the first-person narrator) argues with the Tabata-character (French) about the literary achievements of the Jordan-character (Boris), with Tabata/French denigrating Boris/Jordan's skills as a novelist: '"[His novel, *The Wrath of the Ancestors*] is written by a man on the side of backwardness," said French. As for its artistic merit, he's simply copied Hardy's technique"' (Levinson, *Five*, p. 82).
133. Letter from Tabata to Jordan, 12 October 1944, UMSA/I. B. Tabata Collection, box 2, BC 925/A, UCT.
134. Jordan, *Towards*, p. ix.
135. Ibid. p. x.
136. Ibid. p. 101.
137. Ibid. p. 104.
138. Kies, 'The swan'.
139. Kies, 'Art'.
140. Kies, 'First'.
141. Letter from Neville Alexander to Dora Taylor, 23 November 1958, UMSA/I. B. Tabata Collection, box 9, BC 925/A, UCT. Alexander recollects his experiences in Cape Town and Germany in the 1950s in Busch, Busch and Press, *Interviews*, pp. 36–68.
142. Letter from Neville Alexander to Dora Taylor, 23 November 1958, UMSA/I. B. Tabata Collection, box 9, BC 925/A, UCT.
143. 'The Good Woman', p. 9.
144. Thomas, 'Review: *The Good*, p. 9.
145. Ibid. p. 9.
146. The play is reprinted in Drew, *South Africa's*, vol. 1, pp. 174–6. Other plays by Taylor performed for the Spartacus Club include *Bitter Waters*, an adaptation of Ignazio Silone's *Fontamara*, and *The Peasants*, which Taylor describes in her diary as 'a poor effort of mine, praised unduly by Miss Goodlatte, our finest old member ... who was then giving classes attended by [Tabata] and [Jane] Gool and the other Africans in the group. That is how they learned their Marxism' (unpublished diary, entry: added in 1976, Dora Taylor Collection, folder A. 2, BC 1422, UCT).
147. Taylor, unpublished poems, Dora Taylor Collection, folder E. 3, BC 1422, UCT.
148. Ibid.
149. Letter from Dora Taylor to I. B. Tabata, 25 January 1952, UMSA/I. B. Tabata Collection, box 9, BC 925/A, UCT.
150. Taylor, 'Review: Silone's'.

151. Ibid.
152. Taylor, 'Review: John'.
153. Taylor, 'Review: Erskine'.
154. Taylor, 'Review: André'.
155. See Taylor, unpublished diary, entry: 15 July 1949, Dora Taylor Collection, folder A. 2, BC 1422, UCT.
156. Goolam Gool, 'Presidential address to the AAC on 17 December 1951', Goolam and Halima Gool Collection, box 4, BC 1141, UCT.
157. Clough's 'Say Not the Struggle Nought Availeth' had earlier been reprinted without accompanying commentary in *The International* (19 May 1916).
158. Gool, 'Presidential address to the AAC on 17 December 1951', Goolam and Halima Gool Collection, box 4, BC 1141, UCT.
159. Ibid.
160. Sihlali, 'Presidential address delivered at the 32nd annual conference of the Cape African Teachers Association in Queenstown, 24th-27th June, 1953', UMSA/I. B. Tabata Collection, box 4, BC 925/A, UCT.
161. Kies, 'Looking'.
162. Ibid.
163. Kies, '"For"'.
164. On the state repression of NEUM and APDUSA activists in the early 1960s, see Kayser, 'Land', pp. 103–4, 140–4.
165. Alexander, 'Non-collaboration', pp. 187–8.
166. The fiercest criticisms have come from CPSA/SACP supporters. For a selection from across the decades, see by Mary Simons, 'Organised', pp. 223–8; Jack and Ray Simons, *Class*, pp. 541–6 and 598–601; and Pallo Jordan, 'Waiting', pp. 12–21. For a literary version of the criticism that the NEUM leadership betrayed its collective character, see Frank Anthony's autobiographical novel *The Journey: The Revolutionary Anguish of Comrade B.*, which describes a recently released Robben Island prisoner's journey to meet a Tabata-like political leader in exile in Zimbabwe.
167. Letter from Tabata to Mqotsi, 24 May 1961, UMSA/I. B. Tabata Collection, box 10, BC 925/A, UCT.
168. 'Speech delivered by Mr Mqotsi at the meeting of HUC member held from 19th to 26th April 1966 in Lusaka, Zambia', Livingstone Mqotsi Collection, box 27, UFH. Papers relating to the Tabata/Mqotsi split are also contained in Neville Alexander Collection, folder D 3.1, BC 1538, UCT.

CHAPTER 5

1. 'Ghana conference', p. 58.
2. Sobukwe, 'My idea', p. 48.
3. The *Kokstad Advertiser*, 30 September 1927, quoted in Edgar, 'Garveyism', p. 37.
4. There is no scholarly consensus as to the extent or durability of Garveyism's influence in South Africa since the 1920s. Vinson argues that '[Garveyism's] pan-Africanist race-conscious ideals would remain important to successive African political groupings, such as the ANC Youth League of the 1940s and the Pan-Africanist Congress of the 1950s' ('Providential', p. 131). But other scholars have suggested that the next generation of Africanists forged their ideas with limited reliance on Garveyism. Edgar and Msumza, for example, note, 'Also curiously absent from Lembede's writings is any mention of Marcus Garvey' (*Freedom*, p. 23), and Saunders describes a rupture separating the different generations of Pan-Africanists in Cape Town:

But by the early 1930s the second phase of Pan-African activity in Cape Town had come to an end: the Garvey movement, along with the ICU, had become virtually defunct, mainly because their exaggerated promises were not fulfilled. Thaele, who broke with the ANC, soon lost influence, and the newspapers that had spread Pan-African ideas all ceased publication. It was to be three decades before a new form of Pan-Africanism came to life in Cape Town. ('Pan-Africanism', p. 295)

5. For historical accounts describing the formation of the ANCYL, see Gerhart, *Black Power*, pp. 45–84; Lodge, *Black Politics*, pp. 20–8; Halisi, *Black Political*, pp. 59–66; and Glaser, *The ANC*, pp. 11–51. Also informative are the biographies of key individuals: by Pogrund on Sobukwe, *How Can*, pp. 23–9; by Edgar and Msumza on Lembede, *Freedom*, pp. 13–29; by Edgar and Msumza on Mda, *Africa's Cause*, pp. 29–54; by Sampson, *Mandela*, pp. 39–42, 48–54; by Elinor Sisulu on Walter and Albertina Sisulu, *Walter*, pp. 73–5, 89–2; and by Callinicos on Tambo, *Oliver*, pp. 147–8, 151–6, 161–4.
6. Dr W. F. Nokwe, *African Advocate*, August/September 1947, in Edgar and Msumza, *Freedom*, p. 172.
7. 'Basic policy of Congress Youth League', Manifesto issued by the National Executive of the ANCYL, 1948, in Karis and Carter, *From Protest*, vol. 2, p. 328.
8. Ibid.
9. Mda interview by Gerhart, 1 January 1970, Gerhart Collection A, box 1, A 2422, Wits.
10. Lembede, *Ilanga lase Natal*, 24 February 1945, in Edgar and Msumza, *Freedom*, p. 86.
11. Lembede, *Inkundla ya Bantu*, May 1946, in Edgar and Msumza, *Freedom*, p. 93.
12. Mda interview by Gerhart, 1 January 1970, Gerhart Collection A, box 1, A 2422, Wits.
13. There is no record, for example, of Mda and Lembede having read Nancy Cunard and George Padmore's *The White Man's Duty: An Analysis of the Colonial Question in Light of the Atlantic Charter* (1943), which argued that it was the white man's duty to de-colonise, to meet the growing demands of the colonised for sovereignty and equality. Padmore's dream was to transform the British Empire into a 'Socialist Commonwealth': '*The organisation of the economies of all Colonial territories should be made for the benefit of all the peoples there under their own direction and control* [italics in original]. Furthermore, we would like to see the collaboration and co-operation of all the lands which now comprise the British Empire on a Federal basis, evolving towards a Socialist Commonwealth' (Cunard and Padmore, *The White*, p. 19).
14. 'Congress Youth League Manifesto', issued by the Provisional Committee of the Congress Youth League, March 1944, in Karis and Carter, *From Protest*, vol. 2, p. 303.
15. 'Policy of the Congress Youth League', *Inkundla ya Bantu*, May 1946 and 'African Nationalism and the New African masses', *Ilanga lase Natal*, 21 June 1947, in Edgar and Msumza, *Freedom*, pp. 92, 97.
16. 'Why General Smuts' proposals will be rejected', *African Advocate*, July 1947; 'Last message of late A. M. Lembede, M.A. LL.B', *African Advocate*, August/September 1947, in Edgar and Msumza, *Freedom*, pp. 99, 101.
17. Lembede, *Bantu World*, 30 June 1945, in Edgar and Msumza, *Freedom*, p. 88.
18. Lembede, 'The conception', p. 40.
19. Diederichs, *Die Kommunisme*, pp. 115, 117 (my translation).
20. Lembede, 'The conception', p. 40.
21. Diederichs, *Die Kommunisme*, p. 40 (my translation).
22. Ibid.
23. 'Some basic principles of African nationalism', *Ilanga lase Natal*, 24 February 1945, in Edgar and Msumza, *Freedom*, p. 85.
24. My translation. Lembede, 'African nationalism and the new African masses', *Ilanga lase Natal*, 21 June 1947, in Edgar and Msumza, *Freedom*, p. 98.

25. Mda interview by Gerhart, 1 January 1970, Gerhart Collection A, box 1, A 2422, Wits.
26. Ibid.
27. 'Hitler's new convert', *Inkululeko*, 9 September 1944, in Edgar and Msumza, *Freedom*, p. 116.
28. 'Mr Lembede replies', *Inkululeko*, 23 September 1944, in Edgar and Msumza, *Freedom*, p. 117.
29. Letter from A. P. Mda to G. M. Pitje, 24 August 1948, in Karis and Carter, *From Protest*, vol. 2, p. 321.
30. Mda interview by Gerhart, 1 January 1970, Gerhart Collection A, box 1, A 2422, Wits.
31. Lakaje interview by Gerhart, 2 February 1970, Gerhart Collection A, box 1, A 2422, Wits. In *The Possessed*, the poseur Stefan Trofimovitch 'firmly and loudly declared that boots were of less consequence than Pushkin; of much less indeed' (Dostoevsky, *The Possessed*, p. 18).
31. Lembede, 'The conception', p. 12. Lembede also alluded to Wordsworth in an article on the ICU and ANC in *Ilanga lase Natal* (26 October 1946), when he adapted the sonnet 'London, 1802', replacing Milton (the individual prophet) with the ICU (the collective trade union), and declaring, 'ICU you shouldst be living at this hour, Africa has need of thee' (in Edgar and Msumza, *Freedom*, p. 126).
33. Lembede, 'The conception', pp. 18, 20. Translation from Gezelle, *Poems*, p. 103.
34. Ibid. p. 32.
35. Ibid. p. 50.
36. Lembede, 'An African Academy of the Sciences', *Inkundla ya Bantu*, August 1947, in Edgar and Msumza, *Freedom*, p. 147.
37. Lembede, 'Book review of *Nje-Nempela* by B. Wallet Vilikazi', *Teachers' Quarterly Review*, September 1946, in Edgar and Msumza, *Freedom*, p. 145.
38. Ibid. p. 145.
39. 'Basic policy of Congress Youth League'. Manifesto issued by the National Executive of the ANC Youth League, 1948, in Karis and Carter, *From Protest*, vol. 2, p. 326.
40. 'Congress Youth League Manifesto' (1944), in Karis and Carter, *From Protest*, vol. 2, p. 306.
41. 'The Congress Youth League', *Bantu World*, 18 January 1947, in Edgar and Msumza, *Freedom*, p. 75.
42. '"Programme of Action": statement of policy adopted at the ANC Annual Conference, 17 December 1949', in Karis and Carter, *From Protest*, vol. 2, p. 337.
43. 'The Freedom Charter adopted at the Congress of the People at Kliptown, Johannesburg on 25 and 26 June 1955', in Drew, *South Africa's Radical, Vol. 2*, p. 121.
44. Leballo interview by Gerhart, 11 September 1968, Wits, Gerhart Collection A, box 1, A 2422, Wits.
45. Gerhart, 'Gail', p. 61.
46. Mda interview by Gerhart, 1 January 1970, Gerhart Collection A, box 1, A 2422, Wits.
47. '1960 P. A. C. campaign', p. 5.
48. Ibid. p. 6.
49. Ibid. p. 6.
50. Sobukwe, 'Facing', p. 17.
51. Ibid. p. 18.
52. Gerhart, 'Gail', p. 63.
53. Transcript of the trial *Regina v Sobukwe and 22 Others*, quoted in Lodge, *Black Politics*, p. 205.
54. 'Future of the Africanist Movement', *The Africanist*, January 1959, in Karis and Carter, *From Protest*, vol. 3, p. 506.
55. Ibid. p. 513.

56. 'Manifesto of the Africanist Movement', April 1959, in Karis and Carter, *From Protest*, vol. 3, p. 523.
57. Ibid. p. 523.
58. Raboroko, 'Congress', pp. 25–6.
59. Rodda, 'The Africanists', pp. 23–4.
60. Dyantyi, 'The Africanists', pp. 22–3.
61. 'Address on behalf of the graduating class at Fort Hare College, 21 October 1949', in Karis and Carter, *From Protest*, vol. 2, p. 334.
62. Mda, 'Comment on the 1949 Programme of African Nationalism' (1954), p. 8, Gerhart Collection B, document 80, A 2422, Wits. Since completing copy-editing, Mda's scattered writings have been gathered together and published as: Robert Edgar and Luyanda ka Msumza (eds), *Africa's Cause Must Triumph: The Collected Writings of A. P. Mda* (Cape Town: HSRC Press, 2018).
63. Leballo, 'The nature of the struggle today', *The Africanist*, December 1957, in Karis and Carter, *From Protest*, vol. 3, p. 502.
64. Mda, 'Some targets', pp. 10, 11. The essay has recently been republished in Edgar and Msumza, *Africa's Cause*, pp. 329–32.
65. Mda, 'Some targets', p. 10.
66. Ibid. p. 10.
67. Ibid. p. 10.
68. Ibid. p. 11.
69. Ibid. p. 11.
70. On the popularity of Macaulay's poem in PAC circles, see Pogrund, *How Can*, pp. 190–1.
71. Sobukwe, 'Facing', p. 18.
72. Ibid. Fast, *My Glorious*, p. 178. Fast's historical novel, published during the war that established the state of Israel, endorses Zionist ideology. Sobukwe never refers to the novel's ideology in relation to contemporary Middle Eastern politics, and never refers to the fate of Palestinians.
73. Sobukwe, 'Facing', p. 18.
74. The line functions as a mantra in the novel, repeated several times: Fast, *My Glorious*, pp. 60, 116, 152, 173.
75. Letter from Sobukwe to Pogrund, 20 April 1966, Sobukwe Papers, A 2618, Wits. Since completing copy-editing, Sobukwe's Robben Island correspondence with Pogrund and Marquard has been published as: Derek Hook (ed.), *Lick Your Wounds: The Prison Correspondence of Robert Sobukwe* (Johannesburg: Wits University Press, 2019).
76. Letter from Sobukwe to Pogrund, 1 June 1966, Sobukwe Papers, A 2618, Wits. Sobukwe also refers to *My Glorious Brothers* fondly in a letter from Robben Island to Nell Marquard of 5 June 1968, Sobukwe Papers, A 2618, Wits.
77. Letter from Sobukwe to Pogrund, 5 February 1969, Sobukwe Papers, A 2618, Wits.
78. Z. B. Molete interview by Gerhart, July 1970, Gerhart Collection A, box 2, A 2422, Wits.
79. 'Tell the Senate', p. 17. Fast, *Spartacus*, pp. 170–1. The extract in *The Africanist* leaves out a few lines from the passage in the novel, but faithfully reproduces the sequence of the argument.
80. 'Freedom for its own sake?', p. 4
81. '1960 P. A. C. campaign', p. 6.
82. Ibid. The lines are inaccurately transcribed. Scott's original reads: 'Breathes there the man, with soul so dead,/ Who never to himself hath said,/ This is my own, my native land!'
83. 'Extremely valuable', p. 9
84. For descriptions of all the Poqo attacks, see Maaba, 'The PAC's war', pp. 264–83.
85. On the first decade of the PAC's history, see Gerhart, *Black Power*, pp. 173–256 Lodge,

Black Politics, pp. 201–30, 241–55, 305–17; Leeman, Lesotho, pp. 97–101, 110–13; Maaba, 'The PAC's war', pp. 257–98; Mathabatha, 'The PAC', pp. 299–318; Plaatje, 'The PAC's internal', pp. 669–702, and 'The PAC', pp. 703–48; Lodge, Sharpeville, pp. 193–213; and Kondlo, In the Twilight, pp. 49–155.
86. On the ANC attitude to the PAC, see Tloome's 1958 article 'Exit' and Sisulu's 1959 article, 'Congress'.
87. On the NEUM attitude to the PAC, see Tabata and Jane Gool's 1960 pamphlet, 'The Pan African'.
88. On the SACP attitude to the PAC, see Yusuf Dadoo's 1962 article, 'Why the united'.
89. Mafeje, 'The role', p. 211.
90. The Mbashe Bridge attack is described in Maaba, 'The PAC war', pp. 281–2.
91. Mafeje, 'The role', p. 217.
92. Ibid. p. 219.
93. Ibid. p. 211.
94. Ibid. p. 211.
95. Rive, Emergency, pp. 162–3.
96. Ibid. pp. 163–4.
97. Ibid. pp. 121, 226.
98. Ibid. p. 217.
99. Abrahams, A Night, pp. 60–1.
100. Ibid. p. 61.
101. Ibid. pp. 251–2.
102. La Guma, In the Fog, p. 101.
103. Field, Alex, p. 186.
104. Sobukwe reviewed Guybon B. Sinxo's Isakhono somfazi namanye amabalana in 1957; W. K. Tamsanqa's Buzani Kubawo in 1958; and C. A. W. Sigila's Ndalikhenketha elasentla, E. S. M. Dlova's Umvuzo wesoono and E. W. M. Mesatywa's Izaci Namaqhalo esiXhosa in 1959.
105. Sobukwe, 'Review: Witness', pp. 230–1.
106. Sobukwe, 'Review: E. S. M. Dlova', p. 101.
107. Ibid. p. 102.
108. Dyantyi, 'The Africanists', pp. 86–7.
109. Pogrund discusses Sobukwe's reading on Robben Island in How Can, pp. 228–35. In rough chronological order, the literary works Sobukwe read on Robben Island and mentioned in his letters to Pogrund and Marquard were: in 1963, George Orwell's 1984 (1948), Eugene Burdick and William Lederer's The Ugly American (1958); in 1964, Brendan Behan's memoir Borstal Boy (1958), plays by Behan, John Osborne, Arnold Wesker and Ibsen, Eugene O'Neill's The Hairy Ape (1922), Ah Wilderness (1924) and All God's Chillun Got Wings (1933), Arthur Koestler's The Sleepwalkers (1959), and Hesketh Pearson's Smith of Smiths (1934); in 1965, Shakespeare's Hamlet, C. P. Snow's Time of Hope (1949), The Light and the Dark (1947) and The Affair (1959), short stories by Somerset Maugham, J. B. Priestley's The Good Companions (1929), Angel Pavement (1930), Midnight on the Desert (1937), Let the People Sing (1939) and Bright Day (1946), and Morris West's The Shoes of the Fishermen (1963); in 1966, Wole Soyinka's The Lion and the Jewel (1962), H. G. Wells's The History of Mr Polly (1910), James Hilton's Goodbye Mr Chips (1934), Carson McCullers's The Heart is a Lonely Hunter (1940), C. P. Snow's The Masters (1951), Sophocles' Oedipus in Gilbert Murray's 1911 translation, a James Bond novel by Ian Fleming, and works by Laurens van der Post; in 1967, novels by G. K. Chesterton, Afrikaans poetry by Jan Rabie and Hennie Aucamp and short stories by James Thurber and Ernest Hemingway; in 1968, P. G. Wodehouse's Ice in the Bedroom (1961) and several Jeeves and Wooster novels, Mayakovsky: Poems (1965), C. P. Snow's The New Men (1954), Sheridan's The Rivals (1775) and Irving Wallace's The Man (1964); and in 1969, John Betjeman's High and Low

(1966). Spliced in throughout Sobukwe's Robben Island letters are quotations from and references to literary favourites from his pre-prison reading, notably Shaw, Galsworthy, Koestler, Goldsmith, Shelley, Pope, Gray, Wordsworth, Coleridge, Mqhayi, Modisane, Mphahlele, De la Mare, Roy Campbell, Keats, Spenser, Robert Frost, Tennyson, Conrad and Faulkner. He also refers to his own efforts at poetry, and to the draft of a novel he was working on set in Graaf Reinet (Sobukwe to Pogrund, 27 September 1967, in Pogrund, *How Can*, pp. 277–8).

110. Sobukwe to Pogrund, 15 November 1966, Sobukwe Papers, A 2618, Wits.
111. Sobukwe to Marquard, 5 October 1966, Sobukwe Papers, A 2618, Wits.
112. Sobukwe to Marquard, 16 October 1968, Sobukwe Papers, A 2618, Wits.
113. Sobukwe's view of Paton was inconsistent. In one letter to Pogrund, he claimed to 'admire intensely' Paton's *Cry, the Beloved Country* (1948), and suggested that although black South African writers like Mphahlele and Modisane had also attempted to write a 'great story about African existence', they had failed to match Paton: 'none in my view comes anywhere near the power and insight which Paton displayed' (quoted in Pogrund, *How Can*, pp. 250–1). In a later letter, however, Sobukwe wrote, 'Do you know that at Fort Hare we loathed *Cry, the Beloved Country*[?] The Rev. Nxumalo typified for us the "Uncle Tom" mentality we abhorred. In other words, none of us could have ever had such a character as a hero. And yet he is a typical missionary school product' (Sobukwe to Pogrund, 29 June 1966, Sobukwe Papers, A 2618, Wits.
114. Sobukwe to Marquard, 29 April 1965, Sobukwe Papers, A 2618, Wits.
115. Marquard, 'The meaning', p. 59.
116. Ibid. pp. 69–70.
117. Sobukwe to Marquard, 21 November 1965, Sobukwe Papers, A 2618, Wits.
118. Ibid.
119. Sobukwe to Marquard, 3 January 1966, Sobukwe Papers, A 2618, Wits.
120. Sobukwe to Marquard, 2 July 1968, Sobukwe Papers, A 2618, Wits.
121. See Desai, *Reading*, pp. 23–5. Sobukwe shared Dingake's fondness for Polonius's advice to Laertes, referring to the speech in a letter to Pogrund (1 June 1966, Sobukwe Papers, A 2618, Wits). On the inflated claims made on behalf of Venkatrathnam's Robben Island 'Shakespeare Bible', see Dickson, *Worlds*, pp. 300–9.
122. Sobukwe to Marquard, 30 August 1967; 27 March 1968; 27 November 1963; and 6 March 1969, Sobukwe Papers, A 2618, Wits.
123. Sobukwe to Marquard, 10 June 1965; 7 September 1965; 21 November 1965; 21 November 1965; 16 January 1966; and 7 August 1968, Sobukwe Papers, A 2618, Wits.
124. Sobukwe to Marquard, 6 March 1969, Sobukwe Papers, A 2618, Wits.
125. Sobukwe to Marquard, 21 November 1965, Sobukwe Papers, A 2618, Wits.
126. Ibid.
127. Sobukwe to Marquard, 16 January 1966, Sobukwe Papers, A 2618, Wits.
128. Sobukwe to Pogrund, 12 June 1968, Sobukwe Papers, A 2618, Wits.
129. Sobukwe to Marquard, 3 January 1966, Sobukwe Papers, A 2618, Wits.
130. Sobukwe to Pogrund, 4 August 1965, Sobukwe Papers, A 2618, Wits.
131. Sobukwe to Pogrund, 26 June 1968, Sobukwe Papers, A 2618, Wits. In the letter to Marquard, following the long Mayakovsky quotation, Sobukwe declares, 'I know [these lines] will thrill you,' 5 June 1968, Sobukwe Papers, A 2618, Wits.
132. Nyaose, 'Essay: information on questionnaire on 21 March 1960', Sobukwe Papers, A 2618–Ck12, Wits.
133. Nyaose interview by Gerhart, 4 December 1969, Gerhart Collection A, box 1, A 2422, Wits.
134. Nyaose, 'The Party Dictator', in Gerhart Collection B, item 608, A 2422, Wits. Leballo had been given the label 'the great dictator' two years earlier in an interview in *Drum* by

Stanley Motjuwadi ('The great'). For an overview of Leballo's controversial political career, see Bolnick, 'Potlako'.
135. Ibid.
136. Ngcobo, 'My life', p. 136. The pervasiveness of the PAC's patriarchal culture is revealed in Sobukwe's unguarded observations in a 1970 interview with Gail Gerhart in which he complained, 'we were up against a situation that has always existed in South Africa, namely that the masses will automatically follow a leader or organization that they have loyalty to, without thinking about the wisdom or weakness of particular policies they are told to support. This is particularly true of the women. Oh, the women!' ('Gail', p. 61). Later in the interview, Sobukwe paid tribute to individual woman activists – Ellen Molapo and Lucy Mvubelo – but repeated his assessment that 'in general we knew that women were more conservative politically than men' ('Gail', p. 77).
137. Ngcobo, Cross, p. 25.
138. Ibid. p. 263.
139. Ibid. p. 56.
140. Ibid. p. 87.
141. Ibid. p. 219.
142. Sobukwe, 'Opening address' (1959), in Karis and Carter, From Protest, vol. 3, p. 514.
143. Ibid. p. 286.
144. Head to Sobukwe, 6 January 1972. Sobukwe Papers, A 2618, Wits. Two further indicators of Head's high regard for Sobukwe are her hagiographic portrait in the short story, 'The Coming of the Christ Child', and her letter to Randolph Vigne on the death of Sobukwe, in which she confessed,

> Robert Sobukwe died. I loved the man deeply and since his death been looking over some things he wrote. He worried about the very thing you mention but like a question. A planned economy and democracy have not yet succeeded, he wrote, in any country that has tried the experiment so far. Can we not secure the two in South Africa[?] Do we not guarantee the highest when we guarantee human rights? I knew he was a rich and creative man, but looking over his papers it never struck before that he was also so idealistic. The light went out for me with his death. For days and days I cried simply because he was the only man I loved and trusted. (Vigne (ed.), A Gesture, pp. 219–20)

On Head's relationship with Sobukwe and the PAC, see Eilersen, Bessie, pp. 43–9, 218–23.
145. Head, When, p. 10.
146. Ibid. p. 80.
147. Ibid. p. 122.
148. Ibid. p. 47. See also pp. 62–4.
149. Ibid. p. 31.
150. Ibid. p. 156.
151. Ibid. p. 166.
152. Ibid, p. 145.
153. Ibid. p. 180.
154. Gerhart, Black, p. 250.

CONCLUSION

1. Mandela, 'Inaugural'.
2. 'Resolutions of the annual conference of the African National Congress, May 28–29, 1923', in Karis and Carter (eds), From Protest, vol. 1, p. 297.

3. *African Claims in South Africa* [1943], in Karis and Carter (eds), *From Protest*, vol. 2, pp. 212, 215.
4. Suttner and Cronin, *30 Years*, pp. 263–6.
5. Koselleck, *The Practice*, p. 76.
6. Ibid. p. 76.
7. 'I. C. U. Manifesto'.
8. Drew, *Discordant*, p. 96.
9. Gool, 'The Ten', p. 3.
10. 'Manifesto of the Africanist Movement' [April 1959], in Karis and Carter (eds), *From Protest*, vol. 3, p. 523.
11. Mda interview by Gerhart, 1 January 1970, Gerhart Collection A, box 1, A 2422, Wits.
12. See Friedman, 'The sounds', pp. 236–50, for an interrogation of this characterisation of the 1960s.
13. On post-apartheid dystopian fiction beyond my concluding snapshot here, see Titlestad ('Future', pp. 30–41), and on African postcolonial speculative fiction, see Eatough ('African', pp. 237–57).
14. Amato, 'FFWD', p. 27.
15. Ibid. p. 10.
16. Ibid. p. 22.
17. Ibid. p. 25. Moele's playful tone suggests self-awareness, a quality absent in Magona's earnest tribute.
18. Ibid. p. 27.
19. Ibid. p. 30.
20. Ibid. p. 8.

Bibliography

ARCHIVAL SOURCES

National Archives of South Africa, Pretoria (NASA)

Native Agitation. Police Reports from 1927 to 1938. JUS 918–25 1/18/26.

University of Cape Town Special Collections (UCT)

Neville Alexander Collection, BC 1538.
W. M. Ballinger Collection, BC 347.
Lionel Forman Collection, BC 455.
Goolam and Halima Gool Collection, BC 1141.
Dora Taylor Collection, BC 1422.
Unity Movement of South Africa (UMSA)/I. B. Tabata Collection, BC 925/ A.
P. L. Wickins Collection, BC 657.

University of Fort Hare (UFH)

Livingstone Mqotsi Collection.

University of Oxford Bodleian Library Special Collections (UO)

Papers of the Anti-Slavery Society, MSS, Brit. Emp. s. 23.

University of the Western Cape (UWC)

Brian Bunting Collection, Robben Island Museum and Mayibuye Archive, MCH 07–129–3.

University of Witwatersrand Historical Papers (Wits)

Fanny Klenerman Papers, A 2031/a.
Gail Gerhart Collection, A 2422.
R. F. A. Hoernlé Papers, Special Collections.
Institute for Advanced Social Research (IASR), Share Cropping and Labour Tenancy Oral History Project (1979–85). Interviews transcribed and translated into English. Aa. 1–326.

Saffrey Collection, AD 1178.
Robert Mangaliso Sobukwe Papers, A 2618.

University of York Borthwick Institute (UY)

Liberal Party of South Africa Papers.

Western Cape Archives (WCA)

Native Agitation, Police Reports from 1928 to 1933, 1/ELN vol. 86 file C3 (1) and vol. 87 file C3 (2).

PUBLISHED SOURCES

'1960 P. A. C. campaign under review', *Mafube (The Dawn of Freedom)*, 1 May 1961.
Abrahams, Peter, *A Night of Their Own* (London: Faber and Faber, 1965).
Adam, Heribert, *Modernizing Racial Domination: South Africa's Racial Dynamics* (Berkeley: University of California Press, 1971).
Adi, Hakim, *Pan-Africanism and Communism: The Communist International, Africa and the Diaspora, 1919–39* (Trenton, NJ: Africa World Press, 2013).
'Advertisement: Garvey's *Africa for the Africans*', *The Workers' Herald*, 26 March 1926.
'Advertisement: Percine', *The Workers' Herald*, 26 March 1926.
'African National Congress welcomes Gumede: a new Jerusalem', *The South African Worker*, 2 March 1928.
Albinski, Nan Bowman, '"The laws of justice, of nature, and of right": Victorian feminist utopias', in Libby Falk Jones and Sarah Webster Goodwin (eds), *Feminism, Utopia, and Narrative* (Knoxville: The University of Tennessee Press, 1990), pp. 51–68.
Alexander, Neville, 'Non-collaboration in the Western Cape', in Wilmot G. James and Mary Simons (eds), *The Angry Divide: Social and Economic History of the Western Cape* (Cape Town: David Philip, 1989), pp. 180–91.
Alexander, Peter F., *Alan Paton: A Biography* (Oxford: Oxford University Press, 1994).
Alexander, R. J., *International Trotskyism, 1929–1985: A Documented Analysis of the Movement* (Durham, NC: Duke University Press, 1991).
Allighan, Garry, *Verwoerd, The End: A Look-Back from the Future* (London: T. V. Boardman, 1961).
Amato, Carlos (ed.), 'FFWD >> SA 2034', *Sunday Times*, Lifestyle Magazine, 27 April 2014.
'And this is capitalist civilisation', *The International*, 11 May 1923.
'Another outburst by Kadalie. Intemperate speeches at Bloemfontein', *Natal Advertiser*, 24 February 1926.
'An appeal to the sons of Africa', *The Black Man*, December 1920.
Archer, Sean, 'Economic means and political ends in the Freedom Charter', in Butler, Elphick and Welsh, pp. 335–52.
Arendt, Hannah, *Between Past and Future* (New York: The Viking Press, 1961).
—, *Men in Dark Times* (New York: Harcourt Brace Jovanovich, 1968).
'At the Brussels Congress of Oppressed and Enslaved Peoples: a South African delegate denounces imperialism', *The South African Worker*, 1 April 1927.
'Back to William Morris', *The International*, 14 July 1916.
Bakhtin, M. M. and P. N. Medvedev, *The Formal Method in Literary Scholarship* [1928], in Pam Morris (ed.), *The Bakhtin Reader* (London: Edward Arnold, 1994).
Barnes, Leonard, *Caliban in Africa* (London: Victor Gollancz, 1930).

Beinart, William and Colin Bundy, *Hidden Struggles in Rural South Africa: Politics and Popular Movements in the Transkei and Eastern Cape, 1890–1930* (London: James Currey, 1987).
Benson, Mary, *The African Patriots* (London: Faber and Faber, 1963).
Bergin, Cathy (ed.), *African American Anti-Colonial Thought 1917–1937* (Edinburgh: Edinburgh University Press, 2016).
Berkman, Joyce, *The Healing Imagination of Olive Schreiner: Beyond South African Colonialism* (Amherst: University of Massachusetts Press, 1989).
Blatchford, Robert, *Merrie England* (London: The Clarion Office, 1895).
Bloch, Ernst, *The Utopian Function of Art and Literature: Selected Essays*, trans. Jack Zipes and Frank Mecklenburg (Cambridge, MA: MIT Press, 1988).
—, *The Principle of Hope. Vol. 3*, trans. Neville Plaice, Stephen Plaice and Paul Knight (Cambridge, MA: MIT Press, 1995).
Bohls, Elizabeth A., *Romantic Literature and Postcolonial Studies* (Edinburgh: Edinburgh University Press, 2013).
Bolnick, Joel, 'Potlako Leballo – the man who hurried to meet his destiny', *The Journal of Modern African Studies*, 29, 3 (1991), pp. 413–42.
Bond, Patrick, *Elite Transition: From Apartheid to Neoliberalism in South Africa* (London: Pluto Press, 2000).
Bonner, Phil, 'The decline and fall of the ICU – a case of self-destruction?', in Edward Webster (ed.), *Essays in South African Labour History* (Johannesburg: Ravan, 1978), pp. 114–20.
Bradford, Helen, *A Taste of Freedom: The ICU in Rural South Africa, 1924–1930* (New Haven, CT: Yale University Press, 1987).
Breckenridge, Keith, '"We must speak for ourselves": the rise and fall of a public sphere on the South African gold mines, 1920–1931', *Comparative Studies in Society and History*, 40, 1 (1998), pp. 71–108.
—, *The Biometric State: The Global Politics of Identification and Surveillance in South Africa, 1850 to the Present* (Cambridge: Cambridge University Press, 2014).
Brittain, Vera, *Testament of Friendship: The Story of Winifred Holtby* (London: Virago, [1940] 1980).
Brown, Basil et al., 'The Unity Movement and the National Question', in Edward Webster and Karen Pampallis (eds), *The Unresolved National Question: Left Thought under Apartheid* (Johannesburg: Wits University Press, 2017), pp. 77–95.
Brutus, Dennis, *Stubborn Hope: Selected Poems of South Africa and a Wider World* (London: Heinemann, 1978).
Bundy, Colin, *The Rise and Fall of the South African Peasantry* (London: Heinemann, 1979).
Bunting, Brian, *Moses Kotane: South African Revolutionary* (London: Inkululeko Publications, 1975).
Bunting, Rebecca, 'Freedom; echoes form [sic] the Comintern Congress', *The South African Worker*, 30 November 1928.
Bunting, S. P., 'The Moscow Congress; down to brass tacks', *The International*, 19 January 1923.
—, 'An Open Letter', *The International*, 23 March 1923.
'Bunting and the Trotskyites form a counter-revolutionary alliance', *Umsebenzi*, 22 October 1932.
Burdett, Carolyn, *Olive Schreiner and the Progress of Feminism: Evolution, Gender, Empire* (Basingstoke: Palgrave, 2001).
Busch, Brigitta, Lucijan Busch and Karen Press, *Interviews with Neville Alexander: The Power of Languages against the Language of Power* (Pietermaritzburg: University of KwaZulu-Natal Press, 2014).
Bush, Barbara, *Imperialism, Race and Resistance: Africa and Britain, 1919–1945* (London and New York: Routledge, 1999).
Buthelezi, M. Gatsha, 'White and black nationalism, ethnicity and the future of the homelands',

The Alfred and Winifred Hoernlé Memorial Lecture 1974 (Pietermaritzburg: The Natal Witness, 1974).
Butler, Jeffrey, Richard Elphick and David Welsh (eds), *The Liberal Party and South Africa, 1895–1902* (Oxford: Clarendon Press, 1963).
—, *Democratic Liberalism in South Africa* (Cape Town: David Philip, 1987).
Callinicos, Luli, *Oliver Tambo: Beyond the Ngele Mountains*, 2nd edn (Cape Town: David Philip, 2015).
Campbell, James, *Songs of Zion: The African Methodist Episcopal Church in the United States and South Africa* (New York: Oxford University Press, 1995).
Cardo, Michael, *Opening Men's Eyes: Peter Brown and the Liberal Struggle for South Africa* (Cape Town: Jonathan Ball Publishers, 2014).
Champion, A. W. G., *The Truth about the ICU* (Durban: The African Workers' Club, 1927).
—, *Mehlomadala: My Experiences in the I. C. U.* (Durban: Crown Printing Press, 1929).
—, *Blood and Tears* (Durban: The African Workers' Club, 1930).
Chrisman, Laura, 'Allegory, feminist thought and the *Dreams* of Olive Schreiner', in Tony Brown (ed.), *Edward Carpenter and Late Victorian Radicalism* (London: Frank Cass, 1990), pp. 126–50.
'Chronic constipation', *The Workers' Herald*, 11 May 1927.
Cobley, Alan Gregor, '"Far from home": the origins and significance of the Afro-Caribbean community in South Africa to 1930', *Journal of Southern African Studies*, 18, 2 (1992), pp. 349–70.
'Colour bar and segregation. Speeches at native demonstration. White supporters' threats of strikes and revolt', *The Star*, 1 February 1926.
'The Communist Party points the way to freedom: ANC leaders have no programme of struggle', *Umsebenzi*, 7 April 1934.
Cope, R. K., *Comrade Bill: The Life and Times of W. H. Andrews, Workers' Leader* (Cape Town: Stewart and Co., 1949).
Couzens, Tim, 'Introduction', in Ethelreda Lewis, *Wild Deer* (Cape Town: David Philip, 1984), pp. v–xxxii.
—, 'Keeping the runway clear', *English Academy Review*, 4 (1987), pp. 39–52.
Cunard, Nancy and George Padmore, *The White Man's Burden: An Analysis of the Colonial Question in the Light of the Atlantic Charter* (London: W. H. Allen, 1943).
Dadoo, Yusuf M., 'Why the united front failed: disruptive role of the PAC', *New Age*, 29 March 1962.
—, *South African Communists Speak, 1915–1981* (London: Inkululeko Publications, 1981).
Daniels, Eddie, *There and Back: Robben Island 1964–1979* (Bellville: Mayibuye Books UWC, 1998).
Davenport, T. R. H., *The Afrikaner Bond: The History of a South African Political Party, 1880–1911* (London: Oxford University Press, 1966).
David-Fox, Michael, *Showcasing the Great Experiment: Cultural Diplomacy and Western Visitors to the Soviet Union, 1921–1941* (New York: Oxford University Press, 2011).
Davids, Arthur, 'A critical appraisal of I. B. Tabata's Book *The All African Convention or the Awakening of a People*', *Discussion*, 1, 2 (1951), pp. 1–32.
—, 'The Liberals and the democratic movement', *The Citizen*, 7 October 1957.
Davidson, Apollon, 'Delegate from Transvaal', in M. Cachin, G. Dimitrov and J. Reed (eds), *Lenin's Comrades-in-Arms* (Moscow: Progress Publishers, 1969), pp. 54–71.
—, Irina Filatova, Valentin Gorodnov and Sheridan Johns (eds), *South Africa and the Communist International: A Documentary History. Vol. 1: Socialist Pilgrims to Bolshevik Footsoldiers, 1919–1930* (London: Frank Cass, 2003).
—, *South Africa and the Communist International: A Documentary History. Volume 2: Bolshevik Footsoldiers to Victims of Bolshevisation, 1931–1939* (London: Frank Cass, 2003).
Dee, Henry (written as Henry Mitchell), '"Enemy of the African workers": General Agent S. M.

Bennett Ncwana', *The Journalist*, 93 (2017) <http://www.thejournalist.org.za/academic-papers/enemy-of-the-african-workers-general-agent-sm-bennett-ncwana> [downloaded 10 June 2018].

—, 'Nyasa leaders, Christianity and African internationalism in 1920s Johannesburg', *South African Historical Journal*, 70, 2 (2018), pp. 383–406.

Delius, Anthony, *The Day Natal Took Off* (London: Pall Mall Press, 1963).

Derrick, Jonathan, *Africa's 'Agitators': Militant Anti-Colonialism in Africa and the West, 1918–1939* (London: Hurst, 2008).

Desai, Ashwin, *Reading Revolution: Shakespeare on Robben Island* (Pretoria: Unisa Press, 2012).

Dickson, Andrew, *Worlds Elsewhere: Journeys around Shakespeare's Globe* (London: Penguin, 2015).

Diederichs, Nicolaas, *Die Kommunisme: Sy Teorie en Taktiek* (Bloemfontein: Nasionale Pers, 1938).

Dostoevsky, Fyodor, *The Possessed*, trans. Constance Garnett (London: William Heinemann, [1914] 1951).

Drew, Allison, *South Africa's Radical Tradition: A Documentary History. Vol. 1: 1907–1950* (Cape Town: UCT Press, 1996).

—, 'The theory and practice of the agrarian question in South African socialism, 1928–60', in Henry Bernstein (ed.), *The Agrarian Question in South Africa* (London: Frank Cass, 1996), pp. 53–92.

—, *South Africa's Radical Tradition: A Documentary History. Vol. 2: 1907–1950* (Cape Town: UCT Press, 1997).

—, *Discordant Comrades: Identities and Loyalties on the South African Left* (Aldershot: Ashgate, 2000).

—, 'Prisoner number 3566: an interview with Joseph Leon Glazer', *Socialist History*, 22 (2002), pp. 32–55.

—, *Between Empire and Revolution: A Life of Sidney Bunting, 1873–1936* (London: Pickering and Chatto, 2007).

Driver, C. J., *Patrick Duncan: South African and Pan-African* (London: Heinemann, 1980).

Dubow, Saul, *Racial Segregation and the Origins of Apartheid in South Africa, 1919–36* (Basingstoke: Macmillan, 1989).

—, *South Africa's Struggle for Human Rights* (Auckland Park: Jacana, 2012).

—, *Apartheid, 1948–1994* (Oxford: Oxford University Press, 2014).

—, 'New approaches to high apartheid and anti-apartheid', *South African Historical Journal*, 69, 2 (2017), pp. 304–29.

— and Alan Jeeves (eds), *South Africa's 1940s: Worlds of Possibilities* (Cape Town: Double Storey Books, 2005).

Dyantyi, B., 'The Africanists: fireworks – or false alarm?' *Drum*, April 1960, pp. 21–3, 86–7.

Eatough, Matthew, 'African science fiction and the planning imagination', *The Cambridge Journal of Postcolonial Literary Inquiry*, 4, 2 (2017), pp. 237–57.

Edgar, Robert R. (ed.), *An African American in South Africa: The Travel Notes of Ralph J. Bunche, 28 September 1937–1 January 1938* (Athens: Ohio University Press, 1992).

— and Luyanda ka Msumza (eds), *Freedom in our Lifetime: The Collected Writings of Anton Muziwakhe Lembede* (Athens: Ohio University Press, 1996).

—, *Africa's Cause Must Triumph: The Collected Writings of A. P. Mda* (Cape Town: BestRed, 2018).

Edgar, Robert, 'Garveyism in Africa: Dr Wellington and the American Movement in the Transkei', *Ufahamu: A Journal of African Studies*, 6, 3, (1976), pp. 31–57.

'Editorial', *The International*, 11 May 1917.

'Editorial. The National Question and its relation to South Africa', *Discussion*, 1, 6 (1952), pp. 1–8.

'Editorial', *The Workers' Herald*, 26 March 1926.

Eilersen, Gillian Stead, *Bessie Head: Thunder behind her Ears. Her Life and Writing* (Portsmouth: Heinemann, 1995).
Elphick, Richard, *Christianity in South Africa: A Political, Social and Cultural History* (Oxford: James Currey, 1997).
—, *The Equality of Believers: Protestant Missionaries and the Racial Politics of South Africa* (Scottsville: University of KwaZulu-Natal Press, 2012).
'Emancipation', *The International*, 23 July 1919.
Engels, Friedrich, 'Socialism, utopian and scientific [1880]', in W. O. Henderson (ed.), *Engels: Selected Writings* (Harmondsworth: Penguin, 1967), pp. 185–225.
Engerman, David, 'Introduction: histories of the futures and the future of history', *American Historical Review*, 117, 5 (2012), pp. 1402–10.
Everatt, David, *The Origins of Non-Racialism: White Opposition to Apartheid in the 1950s* (Johannesburg: Wits University Press, 2009).
'Extremely valuable manuscripts', *The Africanist*, January/February 1960.
Eybers, G. W., *Select Constitutional Documents Illustrating South African History, 1795–1910* (London: George Routledge and Sons, 1918).
Fast, Howard, *Spartacus* (Aylesbury: Panther, [1951] 1962).
—, *My Glorious Brothers* (Napierville: Sourcebooks, [1948] 2011).
Fataar, Ali, 'Falsification of history: the role of the Unity Movement in liberation' (Cape Town: unpublished article, 1999).
Field, Roger, *Alex La Guma: A Literary and Political Biography* (Woodbridge: James Currey, 2010).
'The Fifth Annual Conference of the ICU', *The Workers' Herald*, 15 May 1925.
'The fight against the right danger: expulsions from the party. Resolution of the Political Bureau C.P.S.A.', *Umsebenzi*, 4 September 1931.
'Fighting the ban', *The Workers' Herald*, 15 June 1927.
Filatova, Irina and Apollon Davidson, *The Hidden Thread: Russia and South Africa in the Soviet Era* (Roggebaai: Jonathan Ball, 2013).
Findlay, George, 'Review: South African Native Policy and the Liberal Spirit', *Race Relations*, 7, 2 (1940), pp. 32–4.
First, Ruth, 'After Soweto: a response', *Review of African Political Economy*, 11 (1978), pp. 93–100.
— and Ann Scott, *Olive Schreiner: A Biography* (London: The Women's Press, [1980] 1989).
Fischbach, Franck, 'Marx and utopia', in S. Chrostowska and James Ingram (eds), *Political Uses of Utopia: New Marxist, Anarchist, and Radical Democratic Perspectives* (New York: Columbia University Press, 2017), pp. 117–25.
Flemming, Leonard, 'The romance of a new South African farm', *Journal of the Royal African Society*, 21, 82 (Jan. 1922), pp. 115–28.
—, *A Crop of Chaff* (Pietermaritzburg: Natal Witness, 1924).
Flint, John E., *Cecil Rhodes* (Boston. MA: Little, Brown, 1974).
'The Forges of the Nations', *The International*, 13 April 1917.
Forman, Lionel, *A Trumpet from the Rooftops: Selected Writings*, ed. Sadie Forman and André Odendaal (London: Zed Press, 1992).
'Freedom for its own sake?', *Mafube (The Dawn of Freedom)*, 1 May 1961.
'Freedom, where art thou?' *The International*, 21 February 1919.
Friedman, Steven, 'The sounds of silence: structural change and collective action in the fight against apartheid', *South African Historical Journal*, 69, 2 (2017), pp. 236–50.
Galbraith, John S., 'Cecil Rhodes and his "cosmic dreams": a reassessment', *Journal of Imperial and Commonwealth History*, 1, 2 (1973), pp. 173–89.
Gardiner, Alfred George, *The Life of Sir William Harcourt*, 2 vols (London: Constable, 1923).
Garvey, Amy Jacques (ed.), *Philosophy and Opinions of Marcus Garvey or Africa for the Africans*. Two volumes in one (London: Frank Cass, [1923] 1967).

Gérard, Alert S., *Four African Literatures: Xhosa, Sotho, Zulu, Amharic* (Berkeley: University of California Press, 1971).
Gerhart, Gail, *Black Power in South Africa: The Evolution of an Ideology* (Berkeley: University of California Press, 1978).
—, 'Gail Gerhart interviews Robert Mangaliso Sobukwe (1970)', *Psychology in Society*, 50 (2016), pp. 53–85.
'Germiston: Communist Party enters the field with a native candidate', *Umsebenzi*, 1 October 1932.
Gezelle, Guido, *Poems of Guido Gezelle*, ed. Paul Vincent (London: UCL Press, 1999).
'Ghana conference brings a new vision of a happy Africa', *Drum*, July 1958, pp. 40–3.
Gibson, J. M., 'Freedom', *The International*, 4 May 1917.
—, 'Absolute liberty', *The International*, 18 October 1919.
—, 'Citizenship first', *The International*, 18 April 1919.
—, 'National guilds', *The International*, 18 July 1919.
Giliomee, Hermann, *The Afrikaners: Biography of a People* (London: Hurst and Co., 2011).
Gill, Clare, 'Olive Schreiner, T. Fisher Unwin and the rise of the short fiction collection in Britain', *English Literature in Transition, 1880–1920*, 55, 3 (2012), pp. 315–38.
Gilman, Charlotte Perkins [pseud. Mrs Charlotte Stetson], 'To Labour', *The International*, 25 February 1916.
—, 'Woman', *The International*, 18 February 1916.
Gitsham, Ernest and James F. Trembath, *A First Account of Labour Organisation in South Africa* (Durban: E. P. and Commercial Printing, 1926).
Glaser, Clive, *The ANC Youth League* (Auckland Park: Jacana, 2012).
Goldman, Emma, *My Disillusionment in Russia* (London: William Heinemann, 1923).
Gomas, John, '"Good boy" attack on Reds: attempt to bar Communist speakers', *Umsebenzi*, 6 June 1930.
—, '"Our "Trotskyists"'', *Umsebenzi*, 12 September 1930.
—, 'The Native Representation Bill', *Umsebenzi*, 25 April 1936.
'The Good Woman of Setzuan', *The Citizen*, 4 April 1958.
Gool, Goolam, 'The Ten Point Programme: a review of ten years' (Lady Frere: SOYA, 1953).
—, 'Land and the national question' (Cape Town: n. p., 1954).
Graham, Lucy, *State of Peril: Race and Rape in South African Literature* (New York: Oxford University Press, 2012).
'Great expectations', *The International*, 12 April 1918.
Halisi, C. R. D., *Black Political Thought in the Making of South Africa* (Bloomington: Indiana University Press, 1999).
Hall, William Covington, 'Us, the hoboes', *The International*, 23 March 1923.
Harmel, Michael (pseud. A. Lerumo), *Fifty Fighting Years: The South African Communist Party, 1921–1971* (London: Inkululeko Publications, 1971).
—, *Olive Schreiner: 1855–1955* (Johannesburg: New Age Press, n. d.).
Harrison, Wilfrid H., *Memoirs of a Socialist in South Africa, 1903–1947* (self-published, 1947).
Harvey, David, *Spaces of Hope* (Edinburgh: Edinburgh University Press, 2000).
Hassim, Kader, 'Rebuttal of Ciraj Rassool's denigration of I. B. Tabata', *APDUSA Views*, Special Issue, April 2010.
Head, Bessie, *When Rain Clouds Gather* (Oxford: Heinemann, [1969] 1987).
'Here and there: South Africa and the Soviet Union – a contrast', *Umsebenzi*, 2 November 1932.
Higginson, John, 'Liberating the captives: independent Watchtower as an avatar of colonial revolt in Southern Africa and Katanga, 1908–41', *Journal of Social History*, 26, 1 (Fall 1992), pp. 55–80.
'The higher imperialism', *The International*, 10 December 1915.
Hill, Robert A. and Gregory A. Pirio, '"Africa for the Africans": the Garvey Movement in South

Africa, 1920–1940', in Shula Marks and Stanley Trapido (eds), *The Politics of Race, Class and Nationalism in Comparative Perspective in South Africa* (London: Longmans, 1987), pp. 209–53

Hirson, Baruch [pseud. R. Mettler], 'It is time to awake: a critique of *The Awakening of the People* by I. B. Tabata' (Cape Town: self-published, 1957).

—, 'Bukharin, Bunting and the "Native Republic" slogan', *Searchlight South Africa*, 1, 3 (1989), pp. 51–72.

—, *A History of the Left in South Africa: Writings of Baruch Hirson* (London: I. B. Tauris, 2005).

— and Gwyn A. Williams, *The Delegate for Africa: David Ivon Jones, 1883–1924* (London: Core Publications, 1995).

Hoernlé, R. F. A., *South African Native Policy and the Liberal Spirit: Being the Phelps-Stokes Lectures Delivered before the University of Cape Town, May 1939* (Cape Town: University of Cape Town, 1939).

Hommel, Maurice (ed.), *Capricorn Blues: The Struggle for Human Rights in South Africa* (Toronto: Culturama, 1981).

—, *Contributions of Non-European Peoples to World Civilisation* (Braamfontein: Skotaville, 1989).

Holtby, Winifred, 'An appeal for books', *The Workers' Herald*, 15 June 1927.

—, 'The writers of South Africa: an illuminating survey. Olive Schreiner the first and greatest', *The Bookman*, September 1929.

—, 'Jan Christiaan Smuts', *Time and Tide*, 27 October 1934.

—, *Mandoa, Mandoa: A Comedy of Irrelevance* (London: Virago, [1933] 1982).

Hunter, Ian, 'Raff Lee and the pioneer Trotskyists of Johannesburg', *Revolutionary History*, (2009) <http://www.revolutionaryhistory.co.uk/index.php/169-articles/articles-of-rh0404/4479-raff-lee-and-the-pioneer-trotskyists-of-johannesburg> [accessed 18 August 2017].

Hyslop, Jonathan, *The Notorious Syndicalist: J. T. Bain – A Scottish Rebel in Colonial South Africa* (Johannesburg: Jacana, 2004).

Ibawoh, Bonny, 'Testing the Atlantic Charter: linking anticolonialism, self-determination, and universal human rights', *The International Journal of Human Rights*, 18, 7–8 (2014), pp. 842–60.

'I. C. U. Manifesto. Pass Laws to be challenged. Struggle for freedom. Minimum wage for African workers demanded', *The Workers' Herald*, 12 January 1927.

'I. C. U. Programme for 1928', *The Workers' Herald*, 12 May 1928.

'In the liberal camp', *The Torch*, 19 January 1948.

Irvine, Douglas, 'The Liberal Party, 1953–1968', in Butler, Elphick and Welsh, pp. 116–35.

'I. S. L. Marching Song', *The International*, 11 June 1919.

Jackson, Major (ed.), *Countee Cullen: Collected Poems* (New York: The Library of America, 2013). Kindle edition.

Jaffe, Hosea, 'Signposts of the history of the Unity Movement: two lectures', Cape Town: UCT History Department, 1992.

James, C. L. R., *A History of Negro Revolt* (New York: Haskell House Publishing, [1938] 1969).

Jameson, Fredric, *The Political Unconscious: Narrative as a Socially Symbolic Act* (London: Methuen, 1981).

—, 'The politics of utopia', *New Left Review*, 25 (2004), pp. 35–54.

—, *Archaeologies of the Future: The Desire Called Utopia and Other Science Fictions* (London: Verso, 2005).

Jay, Elizabeth (ed.), *Dreams by Olive Schreiner: Three Works* (Birmingham: The University of Birmingham Press, 2003).

Johanningsmeier, Edward, 'Communists and black freedom movements in South Africa and the U. S.: 1919–1950', *Journal of Southern African Studies*, 30, 1 (2004), pp. 155–80.

Johns, Sheridan W., 'Trade union, political pressure group or mass movement. The Industrial and Commercial Workers' Union of Africa', in R. I. Rothberg and A. A. Mazrui (eds), *Protest and Power in Black Africa* (New York: Oxford University Press, 1970), pp. 695–754.

—, *Raising the Red Flag: The International Socialist League and the Communist Party of South Africa, 1914–1932* (Bellville: Mayibuye Books, 1995).
Johnson, David, 'Print culture and imagining the Union of South Africa', in Caroline Davis and David Johnson (eds), *The Book in Africa: Critical Debates* (Basingstoke: Palgrave Macmillan, 2015), pp. 105–27.
—, 'Anti-apartheid people's histories and post-apartheid nationalist biographies', in Aziz Choudry and Salim Vally (eds), *Reflection on Knowledge, Learning and Social Movements: History's Schools* (London: Routledge, 2018), pp. 88–103.
Johnson, R. W., *How Long Will South Africa Survive?* (London: Macmillan, 1977).
Jones, David Ivon, 'The Iron Heel: Is it propaganda?', *The International*, 10 January 1919.
—, '"When dawn's left hand was in the sky"', *The International*, 16 November 1922.
—, 'The black question', in John Riddell (ed.), *To the Masses: Proceedings of the Third Congress of the Communist International, 1921* (Leiden: Brill, [1921] 2015), pp. 1193–6.
Jordan, A. C., *Towards African Literature: The Emergence of Literary Form in Xhosa* (Berkeley: University of California Press, 1973).
Jordan, Pallo, 'Waiting for October: revisiting the national question', in Allan Zinn (ed.), *Non-Racialism in South Africa: The Life and Times of Neville Alexander* (Stellenbosch: SUN Media, 2016), pp. 1–30.
'J. T. Gumede', '"I have seen the new Jerusalem"', *Sechaba*, December 1982, pp. 20–7.
Kadalie, Clements, 'A call from Macedonia', *The Messenger*, September 1923, pp. 813–14, 822.
—, 'The aristocracy of white labor in South Africa', *The Messenger*, August 1924, pp. 242–3, 262.
—, 'Political storms in Africa', *The Messenger*, August 1925, pp. 294, 306.
—, 'The growth of African trade unionism', *The Messenger*, September 1927, pp. 271, 282.
—, 'The old and the new Africa', *Labour Monthly*, 9, 10 (1927), pp. 624–31.
—, *My Life and the ICU: The Autobiography of a Black Trade Unionist in South Africa* (London: Frank Cass, 1970).
'Kadalie's lapse', *Umteteli wa Bantu*, 24 January 1925.
Karis, Thomas and Gwendolyn M. Carter (eds), *From Protest to Challenge: A Documentary History of African Politics in South Africa. Vol. 2 Hope and Challenge, 1935–1952* (Stanford: Hoover Institution Press, 1973).
Karis, Thomas, Gwendolyn Carter and Sheridan Johns (eds), *From Protest to Challenge: A Documentary History of African Politics in South Africa. Vol. 1 Protest and Hope, 1882–1934* (Stanford: Stanford University Press, 1972).
—, *From Protest to Challenge: A Documentary History of African Politics in South Africa. Vol. 3 Challenge and Violence, 1953–1964* (Stanford: Hoover Institution Press, 1977).
Kazanjian, David, *The Brink of Freedom: Improvising Life in the Nineteenth-Century Atlantic World* (Durham, NC: Duke University Press, 2016).
Keach, William, 'Introduction' to Leon Trotsky, *Literature and Revolution*, trans. Rose Strunksy (New York: Haymarket Books, 2005).
Keegan, Tim, *Facing the Storm: Portraits of Black Lives in Rural South Africa* (Cape Town: David Philip, 1985).
Kelley, Robin D. G., 'The Third International and the struggle for national liberation in South Africa', *Ufahamu: A Journal of African Studies*, 15, 1–2 (1986), pp. 99–120.
—, 'The religious odyssey of African radicals: notes on the Communist Party of South Africa, 1921–1934', *Radical History Review*, 51 (1991), pp. 5–24.
Kemp, A. and R. T. Vinson, '"Poking holes in the sky". Professor James Thaele, American negroes and modernity on segregationist South Africa', *African Studies Review*, 43, 1 (2000), pp. 141–59.
Keppel-Jones, Arthur, *When Smuts Goes: A History of South Africa from 1952 to 2010 First Published in 2015* (Cape Town: The African Bookman, 1947).

—, *Friends or Foes? A Point of View and a Programme for Racial Harmony in South Africa* (Pietermaritzburg: Shuter and Shooter, 1950).
Kies, Ben [pseud. I. N. Fandum], 'Art for art's sake', *The Sun*, 25 April 1941.
—, [pseud. I. N. Fandum], 'First person very singular', *The Sun*, 23 May 1941.
—, [pseud. I. N. Fandum], '"For whom the bell tolls"', *The Sun*, 18 July 1941.
—, [pseud. I. N. Fandum], 'Looking ahead', *The Sun*, 10 January 1941.
—, [pseud. I. N. Fandum], 'The swan song of Jim Crow', *The Sun*, 6 June 1941.
—, *The Background of Segregation: Address Delivered to the National Anti-CAD Conference*, 29 May 1943 (Wynberg: Anti-CAD Committee, 1943).
—, *The Contribution of the Non-European Peoples to World Civilisation* (Cape Town: Teachers' League of South Africa, 1953).
Kissack, Mike and Michael Titlestad, 'The antimonies of a liberal identity: reason, emotion and volition in the work of R. F. A. Hoernlé and W. M. Macmillan', *South African Historical Journal*, 60 (2008), pp. 41–59.
Kondlo, Kwandiwe, *In the Twilight of the Revolution: The Pan Africanist Congress of Azania (South Africa), 1959–1994* (Basel: Basler Afrika Bibliographien, 2009).
Koselleck, Reinhart, *Futures Past: On the Semantics of Historical Time*, trans. Keith Tribe (Cambridge, MA: MIT Press, 1985).
—, *The Practice of Conceptual History: Timing History, Spacing Concepts*, trans. Todd Samuel Presner (Stanford: Stanford University Press, 2002).
Kotane, Moses, 'An engineer in Soviet Russia', *Umsebenzi*, 25 July 1930.
La Guma, Alex, *In the Fog of the Season's End* (Nairobi: Heinemann, 1972)
La Guma, James, 'Awake! Africa!', *The Workers' Herald*, 15 June 1925; *The South African Worker*, 13 April 1928.
La Hausse, Paul, 'The message of the warriors: the ICU, the labouring poor and the making of a popular political culture in Durban, 1925–30', in Phil Bonner (ed.), *Holding their Ground: Class, Locality and Culture in Nineteenth- and Twentieth-Century South Africa* (Braamfontein: Ravan Press, 1989), pp. 19–58.
Lalu, Premesh, 'The Communist Party press and the creation of the South African working class, 1921–36' (Cape Town: University of Cape Town Centre for African Studies, 1993).
Lamont, Archibald, *South Africa in Mars* (London: Grant Richards, 1923).
'The land of the free', *The International*, 7 June 1918.
Leask, Nigel, '"Their Groves o' Sweet Myrtles": Robert Burns and the Scottish colonial experience', in Murray Pittock (ed.), *Robert Burns in Global Culture* (Lanham, MD: Bucknell University Press, 2011), pp. 172–88.
Lee, Christopher Joon-Hai, 'The uses of the comparative imagination: South African history and world history in the political consciousness and strategy of the South African left, 1943–1959', *Radical History Review*, 92 (2005), pp. 31–61.
Leeman, Bernard, *Lesotho and the Struggle for Azania: Africanist Political Movements in Lesotho and Azania* (London: University of Azania, 1985).
Legassick, Martin, 'Race, industrialization and social change in South Africa: the case of R. F. A. Hoernlé', *African Affairs*, 75, 299 (1976), pp. 224–39.
—, *Towards Socialist Democracy* (Scottsville: University of Kwazulu Natal Press, 2007).
Le Guin, Ursula, *The Wave in the Mind: Talks and Essays on the Writer, the Reader and the Imagination* (Boston, MA: Shambhala, 2004).
Lenin, V. I., *What Is To Be Done?* (Moscow: Progress Publishers, [1902] 1947).
Levinson, Deirdre, *Five Years: An Experience of South Africa* (London: Andre Deutsch, 1966).
Levitas, Ruth, *The Concept of Utopia* (Oxford: Peter Lang, [1990] 2011).
Lewis, Ethelreda (pseud. 'Reader'), 'The Book Shelf', *The Workers' Herald*, 18 March 1927.
—, 'The Book Shelf', *The Workers' Herald*, 6 April 1927.
—, 'The Book Shelf', *The Workers' Herald*, 15 July 1927.

—, 'The Book Shelf', *The Workers' Herald*, 15 August 1927.
—, 'The Book Shelf', *The Workers' Herald*, 31 October 1928.
—, *Wild Deer* (Cape Town: David Philip, [1933] 1984).
Lewis, Jack, 'The rise and fall of the South African peasantry: a critique and reassessment', *Journal of Southern African Studies*, 11, 1 (1984), pp. 1–24.
Lewsen, Phyllis, *John X. Merriman: Paradoxical South African Statesman* (New Haven, CT and London: Yale University Press, 1982).
Limb, Peter, 'Intermediaries of class, nation, and gender in the African response to colonialism in South Africa, 1890s-1920s', in Peter Limb, Norman Etherington and Peter Midgely (eds), *Grappling with the Beast: Indigenous Southern African Responses to Colonialism, 1840–1930* (Leiden: Brill, 2010), pp. 47–85.
—, *The ANC's Early Years: Nation, Class and Place in South Africa before 1940* (Pretoria: Unisa Press, 2012).
Lodge, Tom, *Black Politics in South Africa since 1945* (Johannesburg: Ravan Press, 1983).
—, *Sharpeville: An Apartheid Massacre and its Consequences* (Oxford: Oxford University Press, 2011).
Losurdo, Domenico, *Liberalism: A Counter-History*, trans. Gregory Elliott (London: Verso, 2011).
Lovell, David, 'Marx's utopian legacy', *The European Legacy*, 9, 5 (2004), pp. 629–40.
Lunt, Winifred M., 'When Mayibuye comes true. A general strike that could not fail', *Umvikeli-Thebe*, February 1936.
Luthuli, Albert, *Let My People Go: An Autobiography* (London: Fontana, [1962] 1982).
Maaba, Brown Bavusile, 'The PAC's war against the state, 1960–1963', in Magubane et al., vol. 1, pp. 257–98.
McCracken, Scott, 'Stages of sand and blood: the performance of gendered subjectivity in Olive Schreiner's colonial allegories', *Women's Writing*, 3, 3 (1996), pp. 231–42.
MacCrone, I. D., 'R. F. A. Hoernlé – a memoir', in R. F. A. Hoernlé, *Race and Reason: Being Mainly a Selection of Contributions to the Race Problem in South Africa* (Johannesburg: Witwatersrand University Press, 1945), pp. vii–xxxvi.
MacKay, Charles, 'British Freedom', *The International*, 14 July 1916.
Mafeje, Archie, 'The role of the bard in a contemporary African community', *Journal of African Languages*, 6, 3 (1967), pp. 193–223.
Magubane, Bernard et al. (eds), *The Road to Democracy in South Africa. 1960–1970*, 2 vols (Johannesburg: South African Democracy Education Trust, 2004).
Mahabane, Z. R., G. H. Gool and E. C. Roberts, 'A Declaration to the Nations of the World' (Cape Town: Non-European Unity Committee, 1945).
Maharaj, Mac (ed.), *Reflections in Prison* (Cape Town: Zebra Press, 2001).
Mandela, Nelson, 'Inaugural Address as President of South Africa' (1994), <https://blackpast.org/1994–nelson-mandela-s-inaugural-address-president-south-africa-o> [accessed 17 June 2016].
'Manifesto of Communist Party of South Africa to the workers and poor farmers', *Umsebenzi*, 26 June 1931.
Mantzaris, Evangelos, 'The promise of the impossible revolution: the Cape Town Industrial Socialist League, 1918–1921', *Studies in the History of Cape Town*, 4 (1981), pp. 145–73.
Marks, Shula, 'Natal, the Zulu royal family and the ideology of segregation', *Journal of Southern African Studies*, 4, 2 (1978), pp. 172–94.
Marquard, Nell, 'The meaning of the graveyard scene in Hamlet', *Theoria: A Journal of Social and Political Theory*, 7 (1955), pp, 59–70.
Marshall, James and Margaret Scott Marshall, *1960 (A Retrospect)* (Los Angeles: J. F. Rowny Press, 1919).
Marx, Karl, *A Contribution to the Critique of Hegel's Philosophy of Right*, in Lucio Colletti (ed.), *Early Writings* (Harmondsworth: Penguin, [1844] 1975), pp. 243–57.

—, *Capital: Volume 1*, trans. Ben Fowkes (Harmondsworth: Penguin, [1867] 1976).
— and Frederick Engels, *The Manifesto of the Communist Party*, in David Fernbach (ed.), *Karl Marx. The Revolutions of 1848* (Harmondsworth: Penguin, [1848] 1973), pp. 62–98.
—, *The German Ideology*, in *Marx and Engels Collected Works*, vol. 5 (London: Lawrence and Wishart, [1846] 2010), pp. 19–584.
Mathabatha, Brown Bavusile, 'The PAC and Poqo in Pretoria, 1958–1964', in Magubane et al., vol. 1, pp. 299–318.
Matthews, Anthony S., *Law, Order and Liberty in South Africa* (Berkeley: University of California Press, 1972).
Matthews, Z. K., 'Review: R. F. A. Hoernlé's *South African Native Policy and the Liberal Spirit*', *Race Relations*, 7, 2 (1940), pp. 34–7.
—, *Freedom for My People* (Cape Town: David Philip, 1983).
'May Day hymn', *The International*, 28 April 1916.
Mda, A. P. (pseud. Sandile), 'Some targets to be aimed at in art and literature', *The Africanist*, January-February 1956.
'Meetings, Good Friday and Easter Monday', *The Workers' Herald*, 11 May 1927.
M. H. F., 'Byronic Reveries', *The International*, 3 March 1916.
Motjuwadi, Stanley, 'The great dictator', *Drum*, February 1964, pp. 10–12.
Motlanthe, Kgalema, 'The history of the SACP is the history of us all!' *African Communist*, 184 (2011), pp. 18–23.
Mouton, F. A., *Voices in the Desert: Margaret and William Ballinger. A Biography* (Pretoria: Benedic Books, 1997).
Moylan, Tom, *Scraps of the Untainted Sky: Science Fiction, Utopia, Dystopia* (Boulder: Westview, 2000).
Moyn, Samuel, *The Last Utopia: Human Rights in History* (Cambridge, MA: Belknap Press, 2010).
Mqhayi, Samuel Edward Krune, *U-Don Jadu* (Alice: The Lovedale Press, [1929] 1951).
Mqotsi, Livingstone, *House of Bondage* (London: Karnak House, 1990).
Msimang, Henry Selby, *The Crisis* (Johannesburg: n.p., 1936).
Nash, Andrew, 'The double lives of South African Marxism', in Peter Vale, Lawrence Hamilton and Estelle Prinsloo (eds), *Intellectual Traditions in South Africa: Ideas, Individuals and Institutions* (Pietermaritzburg: University of Kwazulu-Natal Press, 2014), pp. 51–72.
Nasson, Bill, 'The Unity Movement: its legacy in historical consciousness', *Radical History Review*, 46/7 (1990), pp. 189–211.
'National Secretary's Report for 1925', *The Workers' Herald*, 28 April 1925.
'Nationalism: freedom's foe', *The International*, 21 December 1918.
Ncwana, Bennet, 'Bolshevism', *The Black Man*, November 1920.
'Ndabeni', *Umsebenzi*, 18 April 1930.
Neame, Sylvia (pseud. Theresa Zania), 'The ICU reaches its peak – and begins to break up', *African Communist*, 123 (1990), pp. 68–82.
—, *The Congress Movement: The Unfolding of the Congress Alliance 1912–1961*, vols 1–3, (Cape Town: HRSC Press, 2015).
Negt, Oscar and Alexander Kluge, *Public Sphere and Experience: Toward an Analysis of the Bourgeois and Proletarian Public Sphere*, trans. P. Labanyi, J. Owen Daniel and A. Oksiloff (Minneapolis: University of Minnesota Press, 1993).
'A new labour hymn', *The International*, 1 October 1915.
Ngcobo, Lauretta, *Cross of Gold* (London: Longman, 1981).
—, 'My life and my writing', in Lauretta Ngcobo (ed.), *Let it be Told: Black Women Writers in Britain* (London: Virago, 1988), pp. 133–43.
Ngubane, Jordan K., *An African Explains Apartheid* (New York: Praeger, 1963).
—, *The Conflict of Minds* (New York: Books in Focus, 1979).
—, *Ushaba: The Hurtle to Blood River* (Washington, DC: Three Continents Press, [1974] 1979).

Nicholls, George Heaton, *Bayete! Hail to the King* (London: George Allen and Unwin, 1923).
—, *South Africa in my Time* (London: George Allen and Unwin, 1961).
—, *The Native Bills and Native Views on the Native Bills*, ed. Gary Baines (Durban: Killie Campbell Africana Library, 1995).
'Nietzsche's Superman: Might is Right', *The South African Worker*, 9 April 1927.
Ntsebeza, Lungisile, *Democracy Compromised: The Chiefs and the Politics of the Land in South Africa* (Leiden: Brill, 2005).
Nxumalo, Jabulani (pseud. Comrade Mzala), 'Revolutionary theory on the national question in South Africa', in Maria van Diepen (ed.), *The National Question in South Africa* (London: Zed, 1988), pp. 30–55.
Nzula, Albert, 'Letter', *South African Worker*, 24 September 1928.
—, 'Review of Rev. E. Phillips' *The Bantu are Coming*', *Umsebenzi*, 12 September 1930.
—, I. I. Potekhin and A. Z. Zusmanovich, *Forced Labour in Colonial Africa*, ed. Robin Cohen, trans. Hugh Jenkins (London: Zed Press, [1933] 1979).
Odendaal, André, *The Founders: The Origins of the ANC and the Struggle for Democracy in South Africa* (Auckland Park: Jacana, 2012).
O'Meara, Dan, *Forty Lost Years: The Apartheid State and the Politics of the National Party, 1948–94* (Randburg: Ravan Press, 1996).
Ong, Jade Munslow, 'Dream time and anti-imperialism in the writings of Olive Schreiner', *Journal of Postcolonial Writing*, 50, 6 (2014), pp. 704–16.
Opland, Jeff (ed.), *Abantu Besizwe: Historical and Biographical Writings, 1902–1944* (Johannesburg: Wits University Press, 2009).
'The PAC's internal underground activities, 1960–80', in Magubane et al. (eds), *The Road*, vol. 2, pp. 669–702.
Paden, Roger, 'Marx's critique of utopian socialists', *Utopia Studies*, 13, 2 (2002), pp. 67–91.
Padmore, George, *The Life and Struggles of Negro Toilers* (London: R. I. L. U. Magazine for the International Trade Union Committee of Negro Workers, 1931).
—, *Pan-Africanism or Communism? The Coming Struggle for Africa* (London: Dobson Books, 1956).
Parry, Richard, '"In a sense citizens, but not altogether citizens . . .": Rhodes, race, and the ideology of segregation at the Cape in the late nineteenth century', *Canadian Journal of African Studies*, 17, 3 (1983), pp. 377–91.
Paton, Alan, *Hope for South Africa* (London: Pall Mall Press, 1958).
—, ed. Edward Callan, *The Long View* (London: The Pall Mall Press, 1968).
—, *Cry, the Beloved Country* (Harmondsworth: Penguin, [1948] 1987).
Pèon, 'Colonial liberation: the colonial merchant class', *The Torch*, 27 January 1953.
Petersson, Fredrik, '"A man of the world": encounters and articulations of anti-imperialism as cosmopolitanism', *Issues in Communism*, 10 (2016), pp. 84–111.
Phiri, *I See You: Life of Clements Kadalie, the Man in South Africa, Malawi, Zimbabwe and Namibia should not Forget* (Blantyre: College Publishing, 2000).
Pike, Henry R., *A History of Communism in South Africa* (Johannesburg: Christian Mission International of South Africa, 1985).
Plaatje, Solomon T., *Native Life in South Africa* (London: Longmans, [1916] 1987).
Plaatje, Thami ka, 'The PAC in exile', in Magubane et al. (eds), *The Road*, vol. 2, pp. 703–48.
Pogrund, Benjamin, *How Can Man Die Better? The Life of Robert Sobukwe* (Johannesburg: Jonathan Ball, 1990).
Posel, Deborah, *The Making of Apartheid, 1948–1961* (Oxford: Clarendon, 1991).
'Presbyter is only priest writ large: nationalism shows the cloven hoof', *The International*, 18 January 1918.
'Put in the sickles and reap!' *The South African Worker*, 22 May 1930.
Quiller-Couch, Arthur, *The Oxford Book of English Verse 1250–1900* (Oxford: Clarendon Press, [1901] 1918).

Raboroko, Peter Nkutsofu, 'Congress and the Africanists: (1) The Africanist case', *Africa South*, 4, 3 (1960), pp. 24–32.
Ray, Sibnarayan, *In Freedom's Quest: Life of M. N. Roy, Vol. 1: 1887–1922* (Calcutta: Minerva, 1998).
Reagan, Lisa, *Winifred Holtby's Social Vision: 'Members One of Another'* (London: Pickering and Chatto, 2012).
'Review: *The Good Woman of Setzuan*', *The Citizen*, 4 April 1958.
Rich, Paul, *Hope and Despair: English-Speaking Intellectuals and South African Politics, 1876–1976* (London: British Academic Press, 1993).
'The right wing danger: Comrade Bunting "makes the best of it"', *Umsebenzi*, 30 January 1931.
Rive, Richard, *Emergency* (London: Collier-Macmillan, [1964] 1970).
Robertson, Janet, *Liberalism in South Africa, 1948–1963* (Oxford: Clarendon Press, 1971).
Robinson, Cedric J., *Black Marxism: The Making of the Black Radical Tradition* (London: Zed Books, 1983).
Robinson, Gerard Tanquary, 'Stalin's vision of utopia: the future Communist society', *Proceedings of the American Philosophical Society*, 99, 1 (1955), pp. 11–21.
Rodda, Peter, 'The Africanists cut loose', *Africa South*, 3, 4 (1959), pp. 23–6.
Rotberg, Robert I., *The Founder: Cecil Rhodes and the Pursuit of Power* (New York: Oxford University Press, 1988).
Roth, Mia, *The Communist Party in South Africa: Racism, Eurocentricity and Moscow, 1921–1950* (Johannesburg: Partridge Publishing, 2016). Kindle edition.
Roux, Edward, '"A South African republic": what does it mean? "Clear Hoggenheimer out!"', *Umsebenzi*, 15 December 1934.
—, *S. P. Bunting: A Political Biography* (Cape Town: The African Bookman, 1944).
—, *Time Longer Than Rope* (Madison: The University of Wisconsin Press, [1948] 1964).
— and Win Roux, *Rebel Pity* (Harmondsworth: Penguin, 1972).
'Russia today: reception to Comrade La Guma', *The South African Worker*, 20 March 1928.
Sampson, Anthony, *Mandela: The Authorised Biography* (London: HarperPress, 1999).
Sandwith, Corinne, 'Dora Taylor: a bibliography', *English in Africa*, 29, 2 (2002), pp. 81–4.
—, *World of Letters: Reading Communities and Cultural Debates in Early Apartheid South Africa* (Pietermaritzburg: UKZN Press, 2014).
Saunders, Chris, 'Pan-Africanism: the Cape Town case', *Journal of Asian and African Studies*, 47, 3 (2012), pp. 291–300.
Schoeman, Karel, *Promised Land*, trans. Marion V. Friedmann (London: Futura, [1972] 1979).
Schreiner, Olive, *The Political Situation* (London: T. Fisher Unwin, 1896).
—, *An English South African's View of the Situation* (London: Hodder and Stoughton, 1899).
—, *Closer Union* (London: A. C. Fifield, 1909).
—, *Thoughts on South Africa* (London: T. Fisher Unwin, 1923).
—, *The Olive Schreiner Letters Online*, 2012, <https://www.oliveschreiner.org> [accessed 10–30 June 2016].
—, *The Dawn of Civilisation*, ed. Liz Stanley (Edinburgh: X Press, [1921] 2018).
Scott, James C., *Domination and the Arts of Resistance: Hidden Transcripts* (New Haven, CT: Yale University Press, 1990).
Scott, Patricia E. (ed.), *Mqhayi in Translation* (Grahamstown: Department of African Languages: Rhodes University, 1976).
—, *Samuel Edward Krune Mqhayi, 1875–1945: A Bibliographic Survey* (Grahamstown: Department of African Languages: Rhodes University, 1976).
Serge, Victor, *Memoirs of a Revolutionary* (New York: New York Review of Books, [1951] (2012).
Shaw, Marion, *The Clear Stream: The Life of Winifred Holtby* (London: Virago, 1999).
Simons, Jack and Ray Simons, *Class and Colour in South Africa 1850–1950* (Harmondsworth: Penguin, 1969).

Simons, Mary, 'Organised coloured political movements', in H. W. van der Merwe and C. J. Groenewald (eds), *Occupational and Social Change among Coloured People in South Africa* (Cape Town: Juta and Co., 1976), pp. 202–37.
Sisulu, Elinor, *Walter and Albertina Sisulu: In our Lifetime* (London: Abacus, 2003).
Sisulu, Walter, 'Congress and the Africanists', *Africa South*, 3, 4 (1959), pp. 27–34.
Smith, Jaapie Ahmet De Villiers, *The Great Southern Revolution: A Chapter in the History of the United States of South Africa, 1894–1934* (Cape Town: Darter Bros and Walton, 1893).
Sneguireff, I. L. (1937), 'Modern economic and social terminology in the Zulu, Xoosa [sic] and Suto [sic)] languages', *Africana: Transactions of the Section of African Languages* (Moscow: Academy of Science of the USSR, 1937), pp. 69–76.
Sobukwe, Robert Mangaliso, 'Review: Guybon B. Sinxo, *Isakhono somfazi namanye amabalana*', *African Studies*, 16, 3 (1957), pp. 193–4.
—, 'Review: Witness K. Tamsanqa, *Buzani Kubawo*', *African Studies*, 17, 4 (1958), pp. 230–2.
—, 'My idea of Africa in 1973', *Drum*, November 1959, pp. 48–9.
—, 'Review: C. A. W. Sigila, *Ndalikhenketha elasentla (A long journey up-country)*', *African Studies*, 18, 1 (1959), p. 34.
—, 'Review: E. S. M. Dlova, *Umvuzo wesoono*', *African Studies*, 18, 2 (1959), pp. 101–2.
—, 'Review: E. W. M. Mesatywa, *Izaci Namaqhalo esiXhosa*', *African Studies*, 18, 2 (1959), pp. 100–2.
—, 'Facing fearful odds: opening address to Basuto Congress Party, 1957', *The Commentator*, August 1968, pp. 16–19.
Soudien, Crain, *Cape Radicals: Intellectual and Political Thought of the New Era Fellowship, 1930s-1960s* (Johannesburg: Wits University Press, 2019).
Sowden, Lewis, *Tomorrow's Comet* (London: Robert Hale, 1951).
'South Africa's new constitution', *Umsebenzi*, 7 April 1934.
Stalin, Joseph, 'Former "backward races" marching to socialism', *Umsebenzi*, 7 November 1930.
Stedman Jones, Gareth, 'Religion and the origins of socialism', in Ira Katznelson and Gareth Stedman Jones (eds), *Religion and the Political Imagination* (Cambridge: Cambridge University Press, 2010), pp. 171–89.
Suttner, Raymond and Jeremy Cronin, *Thirty Years of the Freedom Charter* (Johannesburg: Ravan, 1986).
Swanson, M. W. (ed.), *The Views of Mahlathi: Writings of A. W. G. Champion. A Black South African* (Pietermaritzburg: University of Natal Press, 1982).
Sweet, William, 'R. F. A. Hoernlé and idealist liberalism in South Africa', *South African Journal of Philosophy*, 29, 2 (2010), pp. 178–94.
Tabata, I. B. (pseud. Mpumelelo Tembo), 'The boycott as a weapon of struggle' [1952], in Maurice Hommel (ed.), *Contributions of the Non-European Peoples to World Civilisation* (Braamfontein: Skotaville, 1989), pp. 165–200.
—, *The Dynamic of Revolution in South Africa: Speeches and Writings of I. B. Tabata*, ed. Dora Taylor (London: Resistance Books, [1969] 2014).
— and Jane Gool, 'The Pan African Congress venture in retrospect' (Cape Town: Non-European Unity Movement, September 1960).
Tamarkin, Mordechai, *Cecil Rhodes and the Cape Afrikaners: The Imperial Colossus and the Colonial Parish Pump* (London: Frank Cass, 1996).
Taylor, Dora, 'Poetry past and present', *The Critic* 3, 2 (1935), pp. 75–85.
—, 'Review: André Malraux's *Storm of Shanghai* and *Days of Contempt*', *Trek*, 4 July 1941.
—, 'Review: Erskine Caldwell's *Tobacco Road*', *Trek*, 20 June 1941.
—, 'Review: Ignazio Silone's *Fontamara* and *Bread and Wine*', *Trek*, 23 May 1941.
—, 'Review: John Steinbeck's *Grapes of Wrath*', *Trek*, 9 May 1941.
—, 'Review: R. M. Fox's *Green Banners*', *Trek*, 10 October 1941.
—, 'Olive Schreiner – a challenge to today, II', *Trek*, 13 February 1942.

—, 'Olive Schreiner – a challenge to today, III', *Trek*, 27 February 1942.
—, 'Olive Schreiner – a challenge to today, IV', *Trek*, 13 March 1942.
—, 'They speak of Africa III', *Trek*, 19 June 1942.
—, 'Poets in crisis', *Trek*, 2 June 1944.
—, *Don't Tread on my Dreams* (Cape Town: Penguin Global, 2008).
'Tell the Senate that . . . ', *The Africanist*, January 1959.
Thaele, James, 'The African Empire', *The African World*, 3 May 1925.
—, 'Beware of the wolves in sheepskins', *The African World*, 27 June 1925.
—, 'Editorial', *The African World*, 23 May 1925.
—, 'The laws of psychology the only key to race problem', *The African World*, 8 August 1925.
—, 'The Negro Labor Congress and radical Soviet propaganda', *The African World*, 26 September 1925.
'Thaelopirowism', *Umsebenzi*, 20 June 1930.
'Then and now. Communists and good boys, 1926–1930', *Umsebenzi*, 13 June 1930.
'There are some men upon this earth', *The Black Man*, September 1920.
'Theses of the Twelfth Plenum', *Umsebenzi*, 24 February 1933.
Thomas, Albert, 'Review: *The Good Woman of Setzuan*', *The Citizen*, 12 May 1958.
Thompson, E. P., *William Morris: Romantic to Revolutionary* (London: Merlin Press, [1955] 1977).
Thompson, L. M., *The Unification of South Africa, 1902–1910* (Oxford: Clarendon, 1960).
Titlestad, Michael, 'Future tense: the problem of South African apocalyptic fiction', *English Studies in Africa*, 58, 1 (2015), pp. 30–41.
Tloome, Dan, 'Exit the Africans', *Fighting Talk*, August-December, 1958.
'Tot System in the North', *The South African Worker*, 18 April 1930.
Trapido, Stanley, 'African divisional politics in the Cape Colony, 1884–1910', *The Journal of African History*, 9, 1 (1968), pp 79–98.
Trotsky, Leon, *Our Political Tasks* (1904) <https://www.marxists.org/archive/trotsky/1904/tasks> [accessed 2 December 2017].
—, 'The Lessons of the Great Year' (1917). <http://www.marxistsfr.org/archive/trotsky/1918/ourrevo/ch07.htm> [accessed 20 December 2017].
—, *On Literature and Revolution*, ed. Paul N. Siegel (New York: Pathfinder Press, 1970).
—, *Literature and Revolution*, ed. Lindsey German, trans. Rose Strunsky (London: RedWords, [1923] 1991).
'The turn of the tide', *The Torch*, 9 January 1950.
Turok, Ben, *Nothing but the Truth: Behind the ANC's Struggle Politics* (Johannesburg: Jonathan Ball, 2003).
—, 'SA is at a turning point – pessimism is a problem', *Daily Maverick* (25 May 2018), <https://www.dailymaverick.co.za/article/2018-05-25-sa-is-at-a-turning-point-pessimism-is-a-problem> [accessed 10 June 2018].
Van der Walt, Lucien, 'The first globalisation and transnational labour activism in Southern Africa: white labourism, the IWW, and the ICU, 1904–1934', *African Studies*, 66, 2–3 (2007), pp. 223–51.
—, 'Anarchism and syndicalism in an African port city: the revolutionary traditions of Cape Town's multiracial working class, 1904–31', *Labor History*, 52, 2 (2011), pp. 137–71.
—, 'Thibedi, T. W. (1888–1960)', in H. L. Gates and E. Akyeampong (eds), *Dictionary of African Biography* (Oxford: Oxford University Press, 2012), pp. 13–14.
Van Diemel, R., *In Search of 'Freedom, Fair Play and Justice': Josiah Tshangana Gumede, 1867–1947. A Biography* (Cape Town: self-published, 2011).
Van Ree, Erik, *Boundaries of Utopia: Imagining Communism from Plato to Stalin* (London: Routledge, 2015).
Vigne, Randolph (ed.), *A Gesture of Belonging: Letters from Bessie Head, 1965–79* (Portsmouth: Heinemann, 1991).

—, *Liberals against Apartheid: A History of the Liberal Party of South Africa, 1953–68* (Basingstoke: Macmillan, 1997).
Viljoen, R. E., S. A. Jayiya, C. M. Kobus and B. M. Kies, *What has Happened in the Non-European Unity Movement?* (Cape Town: International Printers, 1959).
Vinson, Robert Trent, 'Sea kaffirs: "American negroes" and the gospel of Garveyism in early twentieth-century Cape Town', *Journal of African History*, 47 (2006), pp. 281–303.
—, 'Providential design: American negroes and Garveyism in South Africa', in Michael O. West, William G. Martin and Fanon Che Wilkins (eds), *From Toussaint to Tupac: The Black International since the Age of Revolution* (Chapel Hill: University of North Carolina Press, 2009), pp. 130–54.
—, *The Americans Are Coming! Dreams of African American Liberation in Segregationist South Africa* (Athens: Ohio University Press, 2012).
Visser, Wessel, 'Afrikaner anti-communist history production in South African historiography', in Hans Erik Stolten (ed.), *History Making and Present Day Politics: The Meaning of Collective Memory in South Africa* (Uppsala: Nordiska Afrikaininstutet), pp. 306–33.
Wallerstein, Immanuel, *The Modern World System. Vol. 4. Centrist Liberalism Triumphant, 1789–1914* (Berkeley: University of California Press, 2011).
Watson, Blanche, 'What is freedom?' *The International*, 20 July 1923.
Webb, Duncan, *Marx, Marxism and Utopia* (Aldershot: Ashgate, 2000).
Webster, Eddie, 'Champion, the ICU and the predicament of African trade unions', *South African Labour Bulletin*, 1, 6 (1974), pp. 6–13.
Wentzel, Jennifer, *Bulletproof: Afterlives of Anticolonial Prophecy in South Africa and Beyond* (Chicago: University of Chicago Press, 2009).
West, Michael O., 'Seeds are sown: the Garvey Movement in Zimbabwe in the interwar years', *International Journal of African Historical Studies*, 35, 2–3 (2003), pp. 335–62.
'What the capitalist means by "freedom"', *The International*, 11 May 1917.
'Where racial strife is no more. Workers of all races and colours unite to build up their own country. What South Africa can learn from the Soviet Union', *Umsebenzi*, 10 November 1933.
Wickins, P. L., *The Industrial and Commercial Workers' Union of Africa* (Cape Town: Oxford University Press, 1978).
Williams, Raymond, *Keywords: A Vocabulary of Culture and Society* (London: Fontana, 1983).
Winter, Jay, *Dreams of Peace and Freedom: Utopian Moments in the Twentieth Century* (New Haven, CT: Yale University Press, 2006).
Wolton, Douglas, *Whither, South Africa?* (London: Lawrence and Wishart, 1947).
Worden, Nigel, *The Making of Modern South Africa: Conquest, Segregation and Apartheid* (Oxford: Blackwells, 1994).
'The workers' challenge', *The International*, 20 June 1919.

THESES

Collis, Victoria J., 'Anxious records: race, imperial belonging, and the black literary imagination, 1900–1946', PhD, New York: Columbia University, 2013.
Courau, Rogier Philippe, 'States of nomadism, conditions of diaspora: studies in writing between South Africa and the United States, 1913–1936', PhD, Pietermaritzburg: University of Kwazulu-Natal, 2008.
Drew, Allison, 'Social mobilisation and racial capitalism in South Africa, 1928–1960', PhD, Los Angeles: University of California, 1991.
Grossman, Jonathan, 'Class relations and the policies of the Communist Party of South Africa, 1921–1950', PhD, Coventry: University of Warwick, 1985.

Kayser, Robin, '"Land and liberty!" The Non-European Unity Movement and the land question, 1933–1976', MA, Cape Town: University of Cape Town, 2002.

Lembede, Anton Muziwakhe, 'The conception of God as expounded by or as it emerges from the writings of great philosophers – from Descartes to the present day', MA, Pretoria: University of South Africa, 1945.

Meny-Gibert, Sarah, 'The nature and function of utopianism in the Communist Party of South Africa, 1921–1950', MA, Johannesburg: University of Witwatersrand, 2007.

Mkhize, Khwezi, 'Empire unbound – imperial citizenship, race and diaspora in the making of South Africa', PhD, Philadelphia: University of Pennsylvania, 2015.

Mkhize, Sibongiseni Mthokozisi, 'Class consciousness, non-racialism and political pragmatism: a political biography of Henry Selby Msimang, 1886–1982', PhD, Johannesburg: University of Witwatersrand, 2015.

Nash, Andrew, 'Colonialism and philosophy: R. F. Alfred Hoernlé in South Africa, 1908–11', MA, Stellenbosch: University of Stellenbosch, 1985.

Rassool, Ciraj, 'The individual, auto/biography and history in South Africa', PhD, Cape Town: University of the Western Cape, 2004.

Saule, Needile, 'Images in some of the literary works of S. E. K. Mqhayi', PhD, Tshwane: UNISA, 1996.

Van der Walt, Lucien, 'Anarchism and syndicalism in South Africa, 1904–21: re-thinking the history of labour and the left', PhD, Johannesburg: University of the Witwatersrand, 2007.

Zotwana, Sydney Zanemvula, 'Literature between two worlds. The first fifty years of the Xhosa novel and poetry', PhD, Cape Town: University of Cape Town.

Index

Note: Page numbers in italics denote illustrations.

1960 (Marshall and Marshall), 72–3, 160

AAC *see* All African Convention
abolitionism, 57; *see also* slavery
Abrahams, Peter, 148, 149–50, 155
Africa for the Africans (Garvey), 49, 134
African Claims in South Africa (ANC), 27–8, 32, 39, 111, 158
African Explains Apartheid, An (Ngubane), 36, 37
African National Congress (ANC)
   as agent of freedom, 1–2
   allies of, 40, 114
   Communist influence on, 50
   criticisms of, 65, 116, 140
   dreams of freedom, 41, 140–1, 158
   liberalism, 2, 40
   opponents of, 107, 132–3
   response to Atlantic Charter, 27–8
   suppression of, 35, 147
   see also African Claims in South Africa; Bill of Rights; Freedom Charter
African National Congress Youth League (ANCYL), 4, 134–6, 138, 140, 160, 188n
African People's Democratic Union of Southern Africa (APDUSA), 121, 132, 188n
African People's Organisation (APO), 107, 114, 116

African World, The, 46, 49
Africanism *see* Pan-Africanism
Africanist, The, 134, 142–6
Afrikaner Bond, 10–11, 13
Alexander, Neville, 107, 127–8, 131
All African Convention (AAC), 106–7, 121, 130
allegories, 13–14, 43, 75, 150
Allighan, Garry, 35, 39, 160, 161
Amato, Carlos, 161
America *see* United States of America
Amery, Leo, 78
ANC *see* African National Congress
ANCYL *see* African National Congress Youth League
'And So It Came To Pass' (Flemming), 20–1, 24, 30, 160, 163
Andrews, W. H., 75, 100, 180n
Anti-CAD Movement, 106–7, 116, 121
anti-colonial movements, 8, 27, 47–8, 112–16, 118, 136, 144; *see also* resistance
anti-Stalinism
   critique of anti-colonial nationalism, 112–17
   critique of Atlantic Charter, 110–11
   critique of liberalism, 108–10
   land ownership, 117–21
   literature as critique, 121–8
   reasons for failure, 131–2
   utopias, 128–31

see also Non-European Unity Movement; Stalin, Joseph; Trotsky, Leon
apartheid
　critiques of, 5, 120, 148, 155
　high apartheid period, 35–6, 39–40, 133, 161
　legislation, 9, 30–1, 35–6, 151
　struggle against, 2, 3, 8, 131–2, 147–9
　see also racism: racist legislation; racism: state; segregationism
APDUSA *see* African People's Democratic Union of Southern Africa
APO *see* African People's Organisation
Arendt, Hannah, 4, 39, 164n
assimilation, 26, 30; *see also* segregationism
Atlantic Charter, 9, 27–8, 110–11, 136, 158
'Awake! Africa!' (James La Guma), 51, 58, 86
Awakening of a People, The (Tabata), 107, 114, 124

Bach, Lazar, 95, 96, 180n
Bain, J. T., 84, 90
Ballinger, Margaret, 59, 61, 62
Ballinger, William, 55–6, 57, 59, 62, 63
Bantustans
　policy, 35–6
　legislation, 30–1, 36, 119
Basotho Congress Party (BCP), 141, 144
Bayete! (Nicholls), 19–20, 24, 25, 53, 55–6, 58, 123–4, 160
BCP *see* Basotho Congress Party
Berkeley, George, 138
Bernard Shaw, George *see* Shaw, George Bernard
Bill of Rights (ANC), 21–2, 24, 27–8, 32, 103, 158
Black Man, The, 46–8
Blake, William, 58
Bloch, Ernst, 5, 161
Blood and Tears (Champion), 57–8
Bloom, Harry, 143
Blueprint for South Africa (Liberal Party), 34
Bogopane, Thabiso, 69
Bonner, Phil, 178n
Bradford, Helen, 68, 157
Brecht, Bertolt, 127–9
British Empire *see* colonialism; imperialism

Brittain, Vera, 62
Brutus, Dennis, 1–2
Bulletin, The, 107, 110, 113–16, 145
Bunche, Ralph J., 174n
Bunting, Sidney, 75, 84, 93–6, 100, 101, 180n
Bunyan, John, 45, 49
Buthelezi, Mangosuthu, 37, 172n
Buthelezi, Wellington, 47
Byron, George Gordon, 85

Caldwell, Erskine, 130
capitalism
　apartheid state's reliance on, 131
　critiques of, 2–3, 51–3, 64–5, 68, 72–3, 77–8, 91–3, 103, 111, 160, 163
　economic exploitation, 3, 86–8, 91–3, 97–8, 108, 110, 112–21
　freedom from, 101, 159–60
　Garveyite relationship with, 135, 175n
　opposition to, 3, 51–3, 112–13
　positive attitudes to, 40, 49–50, 68
　relationship to imperialism, 10–11, 118
　relationship to liberalism, 2, 19, 110
Chamber of Mines, 29, 99, 110
Champion, A. W. G., 4, 56–8, 65, 68
Chernyshevsky, Nikolay, 71
Christianity
　Communists' use of biblical tropes, 76–9, 84
　critiques of, 43–4, 64, 83–4
　education, 42, 75–6
　and Garveyism, 46–7
　ICU's use of biblical tropes, 42–3, 45–6, 54, 57, 58
　ideal of equality, 42–4, 46
　influence on Communists, 75–6
　Lembede's faith, 137–9
　missionaries, 42, 44, 78
　shared values with ICU, 42, 44–6, 56–7
　support for white domination, 43–4, 64
Cingo, W. D., 46–7
Clough, A. H., 130
colonialism
　critiques of, 5, 141
　justifications for, 10
　and liberalism, 164n
　white economic interests, 10–11
　white land grabs, 44, 46, 146, 160

colonialism (*cont.*)
    see also anti-colonial movements; divide-and-rule; imperialism; India: British Empire; pre-colonial African society
Comintern
    Congresses, 77, 93–4, 114
    leadership, 93–4
    relationship with CPSA, 94–101
    see also Imprecor discourse
Communism
    Christianity and, 75–6
    critiques of, 49–50
    influence on the ANC, 50
    influence on the ICU, 51–3
    suitability for South African context, 79
    suppression of, 30, 35, 128, 151
    unsuitability for South African context, 36, 135
    utopianism, 83–4, 92, 108
    see also Comintern; Communist Party of South Africa; Imprecor discourse; International Socialist League; Lenin, V. I.; Marx, Karl; Marxism; South African Communist Party; Stalin, Joseph; Trotsky, Leon
Communist International *see* Comintern
Communist Party of South Africa (CPSA)
    attitudes to Christianity, 75–6, 80, 81, 82, 83
    critique of capitalism, 91–3, 103
    critique of nationalism, 86–7, 91–2
    dictatorship of the proletariat, 101–2, 183n
    dreams of freedom, 4, 71, 91–3, 103, 159–60
    literary influences, 84–91
    Native Republic thesis, 94–5, 111, 118, 135, 159, 182n
    New Line, 95, 99, 182n
    opposition to, 50, 107, 111
    relationship with Comintern, 94–101
    relationship with ICU, 51–3
    two-stage theory *see* Native Republic thesis
    see also Communism; *International, The*; socialism; South African Communist Party; *South African Worker, The*; *Umsebenzi*
Congress of the People, 31–2

continentalism *see* Pan-Africanism
CPSA *see* Communist Party of South Africa
Crisis, The (Msimang), 25
Cross of Gold (Ngcobo), 155, 160
Cry, the Beloved Country (Paton), 33–4, 38, 193n
Cullen, Countee, 59

Dalinyebo, Sabata, 148
Daniels, Eddie, 8–9, 39, 175n
Davids, Arthur, 110
Davids, C. A., 163
Day Natal Took Off, The (Delius), 35, 160, 161
De Nooy, Richard, 162–3
Delius, Anthony, 35, 39, 160, 161
Dhlomo, H. I. E., 143, 146
Diederichs, Nicolaas, 136–7, 138
Dinkebogile, Ramakgelo, 68
divide-and-rule, 55, 98, 113, 141
Dlova, E. S. M., 151
Donne, John, 131
Dreams (Schreiner), 13–15, 75, 160
Drew, Allison, 95, 118
Drum, 133, 142, 151
Du Toit, S. J., 10
Durban strikes, 35
dystopias, 5, 9, 38, 40, 160–3; *see also* utopias

'Emancipation' (anon.), 85, 86
Emergency (Rive), 148–9
empire *see* colonialism; imperialism; India: British Empire
Engels, Friedrich, 71, 90, 92, 103
equality
    centrality to dreams of freedom, 2, 8, 39, 101–2, 155
    as Christian ideal, 42–4, 46
    economic, 4, 17, 32, 36, 41, 63–5, 91, 117–21
    education, 112, 159
    franchise, 4, 11, 17, 18, 22, 24–5, 112, 158–9
    gender, 1, 4, 14, 17, 23, 61, 73, 85
    racial, 4, 18, 21–2, 146

farming

black farmers' loss of land, 32–3, 43, 65, 73, 121
  economic hardship, 93, 102–3, 118–19, 130
  exploitation of black labour, 11, 51, 53, 67–8, 86–7, 97, 102, 121
  white ownership, 10–11, 69–70, 79, 102, 121
  see also land ownership
fascism, 27, 98, 100, 113, 136–8, 175n
Fast, Howard, 144–5, 146, 150
feminism see equality: gender
Fifani, Alex, 43
Flemming, Leonard, 20–1, 24, 30, 38, 160, 161, 163
Forced Labour in Colonial Africa (Nzula, Potekhin and Zusmanovich), 97–8, 99, 101–2
Fourier, Charles, 71, 90–1
franchise
  as essential for freedom, 4, 8, 17, 39, 41, 112, 158–9
  failure to achieve universal, 18, 30
  legislation limiting, 11, 24
  see also equality: franchise
freedom, definitions of, 1–4, 8
Freedom Charter, 5, 31–2, 34, 39, 140, 146, 150, 158, 161
French Revolution, 8, 108, 112, 136; see also Jacobinism
Friends or Foes (Keppel-Jones), 30

Gandhi, Mohandas K., 20, 47, 116–17
Garvey, Marcus, 46–50, 53, 100, 134, 175n
Garveyism, 42, 46–53, 134–5, 174n, 188–9n
Gerhart, Gail, 145, 157
Germany, 4, 45, 61, 75, 113, 127–8
Gezelle, Guido, 136–7, 138
Ghana, 33, 117
Gibson, J. M., 90, 91–2, 181n
Gilman, Francis Perkins, 85, 180n
Glass, Frank, 100, 105
Glazer, Henry, 84
Glen Grey Act, 9, 11
Goldman, Emma, 77
Gomas, John, 50, 51, 76, 100, 104, 106, 161
Gool, Cissie, 106, 184n
Gool, Goolam, 106, 107, 109–12, 130
Gordon, Max, 105

Graaf, De Villiers, 34
Great Southern Revolution, The (Smith), 11–13, 160, 161
Green, William, 50
Gumede, Josiah, 78–9, 84, 96

Hall, William Covington, 85–6, 180n
Hamlet (Shakespeare), 7, 152–3
Harmel, Michael, 179n
Harrison, Wilfrid, 96, 101
Head, Bessie, 134, 155–7, 160, 161, 194n
Hemingway, Ernest, 131
Henley, William Ernest, 53–5, 160
Hertzog, J. B. M., 44, 50, 64, 66, 99
Hertzog Bills, 9, 24–7, 44, 64
Heyns, Michiel, 163
Hirson, Baruch, 107, 114–15, 117, 118
historical materialism, 71, 97, 121–4, 126–8; see also Marxism
Hitler, Adolf, 9, 137–8; see also fascism
Hoernlé, R. F. Alfred, 25–7, 30, 31, 34, 35, 39, 109, 169n
Hofmeyr, Jan Hendrik, 10–11, 13
Holtby, Winifred, 59, 60–3, 160, 161, 177n
Hope for South Africa (Paton), 34
House of Bondage (Mqotsi), 119–20, 132, 160

ICU see Industrial and Commercial Workers' Union
imperialism
  ambitions in South Africa, 9–10, 15
  critiques of empire, 15–16, 78–9, 84, 168n
  cultural, 48
  economic exploitation, 97–8, 102–3, 110
  endurance of ideology, 24
  freedom from, 101–3
  in India, 19, 92, 116, 136
  sympathetic attitudes toward empire, 19, 22, 24, 27, 29, 78, 168n
  see also anti-colonial movements; colonialism
Imprecor discourse, 95–7, 103, 182n
In the Fog of the Season's End (Alex La Guma), 149, 150
Independent Industrial and Commercial Workers' Union (IICU), 54

India
   British Empire, 19, 92, 116, 136
   independence struggle, 20, 48, 91–2, 112, 114, 116–17, 161
Indian community in South Africa, 1, 149–50
Indonesia, 114, 115–16, 136
Industrial and Commercial Workers' Union (ICU)
   appeal to pre-colonial Africa, 63–4
   campaigns for quotidian freedoms, 65
   Christianity, 42–6
   Communism, 51–3
   critique of capitalism, 51–3, 64–5
   critique of nationalism, 66–8
   dreams of freedom, 3–4, 41–2, 63, 66–7, 104, 159
   economic hardship of members, 64–5
   failures, 68–9
   Garveyism, 46–50, 174n
   manifesto, 41
   political uses of literature, 53–8
   publications, 58–60
   victories, 69–70
   see also Kadalie, Clements; *Workers' Herald, The*
inequality see equality
Institute of Race Relations (IRR), 25, 109
International, The, 51, 76–7, 79, 84–6, 88–92
International Socialist League (ISL), 71, 75–6, 84, 87, 91, 101
internationalism, 4, 48, 50, 66–8, 112, 114, 118, 159; see also trans-national community of resistance
'Invictus' (Henley), 53–5, 160
IRR see Institute of Race Relations
Italy, 53, 88, 113, 175n

Jabavu, D. D. T., 99
Jabavu, John Tengo, 11
Jacobinism, 108, 111, 129; see also French Revolution
Jaffe, Hosea, 107, 121, 184n, 185n
Jameson, Fredric, 4, 5, 165n
Jameson Raid, 10, 15
Jones, David Ivon, 75–8, 84, 90–1, 95–6, 103, 180n
Jordaan, Kenneth, 107, 121, 184n
Jordan, A. C., 107, 125–6, 151, 187n

Kadalie, Clements
   Christianity, 42–6, 54, 64
   Communism, 52–3
   dreams of freedom, 4, 41–2, 63, 66, 70, 104, 161
   economic conditions of black Africans, 64–5
   education, 42, 54
   Garveyism, 46–7, 52–3
   internationalism, 66–8
   literary tastes and influences, 53–6, 58, 160, 168n
   others' views of, 68–70, 117, 173n
   Pan-Africanism, 49, 55
   poetry, 49, 53
   relationship with ICU, 55–6, 57
   rhetoric, 66
   trans-national community of resistance, 66–8, 136
   see also Industrial and Commercial Workers' Union
Kant, Immanuel, 138
Keats, John, 143, 146, 193n
Keppel-Jones, Arthur, 28–30, 38, 40, 160, 161, 163
Kgosana, Philip, 147
Khumalo, Charles, 65
Khumalo, Sihle, 162
Kies, Ben
   critique of Atlantic Charter, 110–11
   critique of divide-and-rule, 112–13
   critique of nationalism, 115
   dreams of freedom, 161
   land ownership, 121
   literary criticism, 126–7
   political use of literature, 127, 130–1
   publications, 107, 126–7
   role in political organisations, 106–7, 186n
   trans-national community of resistance 131, 136
   Trotskyism, 108, 126
   utopias, 130–1
Klenerman, Fanny, 60, 105
Kombuis, Koos, 162
Koselleck, Reinhart, 5, 159
Kotane, Moses, 76, 96, 99
Kruger, Paul, 18–19, 137

La Guma, Alex, 148, 149–50, 155
La Guma, James, 51, 58–9, 63, 76, 86, 94–5, 106
Lamont, Archibald, 18–19, 24, 30, 39, 103, 160
land ownership
  'agrarian problem', 117–19
  communal in pre-colonial Africa, 79, 135
  racist legislation restricting, 11, 18, 24, 121
  redistribution of land, 102, 103, 119–20, 146
  restoration of rights, 4, 28, 32, 34, 36, 112, 120–1, 159
  white land grabs, 44, 46, 146, 160
  see also farming
Langenhoven, C. J., 20
Le Guin, Ursula, 5–6
Leballo, P. K., 40, 134, 140, 143, 154
Legassick, Martin, 95
Lembede, Muziwakhe Anton, 4, 134–40, 157
Lenin, V. I., 51, 71–2, 84, 94, 97, 100, 114–15, 118, 123–5
Lenin Club, 105–6
Levinson, Deirdre, 187n
Lewis, Ethelreda, 58–62, 160, 161
liberal nationalism *see* nationalism: liberal
Liberal Party, 8–9, 34, 36, 40, 171n, 172n
liberalism, 2–3, 108–11, 19, 159, 164n; *see also* Liberal Party; nationalism: liberal
literature
  African American, 58–9, 62
  African-language, 4, 37, 126, 148, 150–1, 153
  allegorical, 13–14, 43, 75, 150
  as critique, 5, 121–8, 154–7
  dystopian, 5, 9, 38, 40, 160–3
  Holtby on, 61–3
  Jordan on, 126
  Kies on, 126–7, 130–1
  Lembede on, 138–9
  Mda on, 143
  oral traditions, 4, 126, 148, 151, 153
  political uses of, 53–8, 125, 127, 130–1, 143, 145–6, 151, 153–4
  Sobukwe on, 143–4, 150–4
  Taylor on, 122–5, 129–30
  Trotsky on, 121–3, 124, 126–9

utopian, 4–5, 11–13, 21–4, 46, 72, 128–31, 143, 154–7, 160–3
London, Jack, 90–1
Lopes, Manuel, 100
Losurdo, Domenico, 164n
Lotz, Sarah, 162
Lunt, Winifred M., 168n
Luthuli, Albert, 3–4, 32–4, 39
Luxemburg, Rosa, 4

Macaulay, Thomas Babington, 144, 146, 150
McCrae, John, 53
MacKay, Charles, 91
McKay, Claude, 130
Maduna, Alex, 42
Madzunya, Josias, 141
Mafube (*The Dawn of Freedom*), 141, 145–6
Magona, Sindiwe, 162
Maharaj, Mac, 8
Maine, Kas, 70
Majeke, Nosipho *see* Taylor, Dora
Makabeni, Gana, 76, 95
Makholwa, Angela, 162
Malraux, André, 130
'Man with the Hoe, The' (Markham), 87
Mandela, Nelson, 1–2, 8–9, 39–40, 54, 134, 140, 149, 158–9, 175n
Mandoa, Mandoa (Holtby), 60–1, 62, 160
Matanzima, Kaiser, 148
Markham, Edwin, 87
Marks, J. B., 76
Marquard, Leo, 151
Marquard, Nell, 151–2
Marshall, James and Margaret Scott, 72–3, 75, 160
Marx, Karl
  critique of British apologists for free trade, 91
  critique of religion, 82–4, 136–7
  German Ideology, The, 90–1
  influence on ICU constitution, 52
  influence on Tabata, 125
  interconnectedness of the economic and political, 52
  on utopian socialism, 90–1
Marxism
  'cold' and 'warm' streams, 5
  critique of liberalism, 109

Marxism (*cont.*)
　critiques of, 136–7
　dreams of freedom inspired by, 71–2, 103
　Marxist International League, 105–6
　language, 51, 76, 84, 96–7, 115
　proletarian political control, 93
　relationship with African socialism, 135
　understanding of history, 87
　see also Communism; historical materialism
Mathebula, L. H., 68
Matthews, Z. K., 31–4, 39
Mbutumu, Melikhaya, 148, 150
Mciza, John, 43
Mda, Solomzi Ashby Peter ('A. P.'), 134–5, 136, 137–8, 140, 143, 160
Mehlomadala (Champion), 57
Merriman, John X., 10, 74
Messenger, The, 53, 67
'Might is Right' (Hall), 85–6
Milner's kindergarten, 6
mining, 10–11, 42, 67, 110
missionaries, 42, 44, 78
Moele, Kgebetli, 162
Mofutsanyana, Edwin, 76, 95, 137
Molete, Z. B., 145
Molohlanyi, Mmereki, 63
monopolism, 15, 17, 19
Moore, Barrington, 3
Morris, William, 84, 87–90, 93, 160
'Mote, Keable, 43
Mpama, Josephine, 76
Mqayi, Dorrington, 43–4, 63–4
Mqhayi, S. E. K., 21–4, 30, 35, 39, 103, 134–5, 146, 153–4, 160, 161, 165n, 168n
Mqotsi, Livingstone, 107, 119–20, 131–2, 160, 161
Msimang, H. Selby, 25–7, 39, 99
My Glorious Brothers (Fast), 144–5, 191n

National Party, 28, 30–1, 123, 133; *see also* apartheid
nationalism
　African *see* Pan-Africanism
　Afrikaner, 29, 30, 37, 39, 86
　anti-colonial, 112–17
　critiques of, 66–8, 86–7, 91–2, 112–17, 140–2, 163
　liberal, 2–3, 40, 41, 48, 50, 63, 68, 159
　ultra-nationalism, 136–7
Native Bills *see* Glen Grey Act; Hertzog Bills
Native Republic thesis, 94–5, 98, 100, 102–3, 111, 118, 135, 159, 182n
Nazism *see* fascism
Ncwana, Samuel Michael (S. M.) Bennett, 46–7, 50
'Ndabeni' (anon.), 86
Nehru, Jawaharlal, 116–17
NEUM *see* Non-European Unity Movement
New Line, 95, 99, 182n; *see also* Communist Party of South Africa
Ngcobo, A. B., 154
Ngcobo, Elijah, 68
Ngcobo, Lauretta, 134, 154–5, 160, 161
Ngedlane, Josiah, 97
Ngubane, Jordan K., 36–8, 40, 137, 160, 161, 172n
Nicholls, George Heaton, 19–20, 24, 25, 39, 53, 55–6, 123–4, 160, 161
Night of Their Own, A (Abrahams), 149–50
Nje-Nempela (Vilikazi), 139
Nkrumah, Kwame, 116, 117, 132, 142, 185n
Non-European Unity Movement (NEUM)
　conflict with Congress parties, 121, 135, 148–9
　criticisms of, 131, 188n
　critique of anti-colonial nationalism, 112–17
　critique of liberalism, 108–12
　critique of private property, 117–21
　dreams of freedom, 3, 159–60
　Ghanaian independence, 117
　history of, 107, 121
　internationalism, 159
　literary culture of, 121–31
　publications, 107, 109
　Ten-Point Programme, 111–12, 114, 120–1, 136, 159
Nqandela, Lucas, 68–9
Nyaose, J. D., 154
Nzula, Albert, 4, 76, 97–8, 99, 100, 101–2, 161, 173n, 179n

Okafor, Amanke, 146
Orage, A. R., 90
Owen, Robert, 71, 90

PAC *see* Pan-Africanist Congress
Padmore, George, 142, 175n, 189n
Palmer, Mabel, 59
Pan-Africanism
  dreams of freedom, 134, 155
  Garveyism, 47–8, 134–5, 188n
  literature, 49
  in post-apartheid South Africa, 157
  as response to European nationalism, 141
Pan-Africanist Congress (PAC)
  anti-Communism, 142
  campaigns by, 147–8, 150, 155, 157
  Christianity, 143
  criticisms of, 148–50, 154–7
  critique of capitalism, 135
  critique of liberalism, 140–2
  critique of nationalism, 140–2
  dreams of freedom, 3–4, 40, 140–1
  genesis, 140–1
  literary culture, 143–7, 154–7, 160
  manifesto, 142, 159
  publications of, 142, 144, 145–7
  relationship to Afrikaner nationalism, 136–8
  suppression of, 35, 133
  see also Pan-Africanism; Poqo; Sobukwe, Robert Mangaliso
Parallelism, 26; *see also* assimilation; segregationism
'Party Dictator, The' (Nyaose), 154
Pass Laws, 32, 41, 44, 65–6, 98–9, 147
Paton, Alan, 33–5, 38, 39, 152, 193n
Pilgrim's Progress, The (Bunyan), 45, 49
Pirow, Oswald, 50, 81–3, 83, 86, 87, 88, 98, 180n
Plaatje, Sol, 46, 78
Pogrund, Benjamin, 144–5, 151, 153–4, 161
Popular Front, 95, 99, 106
Poqo, 133, 147–50; *see also* Pan-Africanist Congress
Potekhin, Ivan, 97
pre-colonial African society, 63–4, 79, 97, 135, 155
Programme of Action, 140
Promised Land, The (Schoeman), 38–9, 160

Raboroko, Peter, 142
racism
  freedom from, 8, 101, 112, 159

racist ideology, 4, 10, 124
racist legislation, 8, 9, 11, 18, 24–5, 28, 41, 57, 65, 78, 103
racist myths, 48
state, 3, 8–9, 84, 98, 131, 148
white working-class, 98
see also apartheid
Rehabilitation Scheme, 118–19
resistance
  African American, 59, 134, 175n
  historical precursors, 3, 45, 144–5
  Indian, 20, 112, 161
  lack of in oppressed societies, 5–6
  liberal-nationalist, 3
  peaceful, 20, 26
  utopianism and, 5–6, 42, 140
  violent, 26
  vocabulary of, 97
  see also anti-colonial movements; transnational community of resistance
'Return, The' (Taylor), 119, 129
Rheinnalt-Jones, J. D., 109
Rhodes, Cecil John, 10–11, 15–17, 18, 22, 28, 72–3, 158
Rive, Richard, 148, 150
Robben Island, 8–9, 133, 124–5, 151, 153, 175n, 192n, 193n
Robeson, Paul, 59, 61
Roux, Edward
  cartoons, 80, 81, 82, 83, 88
  critique of capitalism, 98–9
  dreams of freedom, 4, 161
  as historian of CPSA, 106
  literary tastes and influences, 84, 87–8
  memories of Kadalie, 53, 173n
  use of biblical imagery, 79–84
  use of language, 95–7
  visit to Moscow, 94
Roy, M. N., 114–15
Russia
  absence of racial discrimination, 102
  critiques of Soviet Union, 77, 105
  Czarist Russia likened to South Africa, 97–8
  literature, 121
  Schreiner's interest in, 73–5
Russian Revolution, 8, 25, 27, 51, 71–9, 89, 93–4, 101–2, 112, 136, 161

SACP *see* South African Communist Party
Saint-Simon, Henri de, 71, 90
Schoeman, Karel, 38–9, 40, 160, 161, 172n
Schreiner, Olive
   acceptance of racially mixed polity, 73
   allegories, 13–14, 17, 75
   anti-imperialism, 15–16, 124, 160
   anti-monopolism, 15, 17, 19, 32, 160
   attitude toward capitalism, 17, 72
   attitude toward Marxism, 179n
   Dreams, 13–15, 75, 160
   dreams of freedom, 3–4, 14–15, 17–18, 39, 161
   feminism, 14, 177n
   fictionalised representations of, 20, 38
   interest in Russia, 73–5
   journalism, 14–17, 72
   letters, 73–5
   others' views of, 60–1, 124
   Story of an African Farm, The, 38
Scott, J. (cartoonist), 66, 67, 68, 69
Scott, James C., 3, 66
Scott, Walter, 146
segregationism
   critiques of, 5, 26, 30
   policies, 50, 64, 66, 120
   protests against, 106–7
   segregationist literature, 19–20, 24, 35, 58–60, 73
   as system of oppression, 112, 140
   see also apartheid; Hertzog, J. B. M.; separate development
Seme, Pixley K., 99
separate development, 35–6, 120; *see also* apartheid; segregationism
Serge, Victor, 77, 93
Shakespeare, William, 125, 130, 143, 146, 152–3, 193n
Sharpeville massacre, 9, 35, 37, 147–50, 154
Shaw, George Bernard, 25–6, 125, 143, 146, 153–4, 193n
Shelley, Percy Bysshe, 84, 87, 160, 193n
Sibanyoni, Rose, 65, 69–70
Sidley, Steven Boykey, 162
Sihlali, Leo, 107, 130
Sijadu, P. S., 42, 63–4
Silone, Ignazio, 129, 187n
Sinclair, Upton, 84, 90
Sinxo, Guybon B., 150–1

Sisulu, Walter, 134, 140, 149
slave mentality, 32, 48, 125, 147
slavery, 25, 45–6, 57–8, 59, 91, 110, 145
Smith, Jaapie Ahmet De Villiers, 11–12, 17, 72, 160, 161
Smuts, Jan Christiaan, 19–20, 25–6, 61, 74, 110–11, 137
Sneguireff, I. L., 97
Snow, C. P., 153, 192n
Sobukwe, Robert Mangaliso
   critique of ANC leadership, 140
   dreams of freedom, 4, 133, 140, 161
   imprisonment, 133, 151
   influence on later generations, 155, 157
   literary tastes and influences, 143–5, 150–4, 192n, 193n
   literary works, 146–7
   Pan-Africanism, 134, 141–2
   patriarchal views, 194n
   political use of literature, 143, 151, 153–4
   relationship with Bessie Head, 155–6, 194n
   see also Pan-Africanist Congress
socialism
   communalism of pre-colonial African society, 79, 135
   dreams of freedom, 4, 72–5, 91–8, 101–3, 104, 108
   enemies of, 98–100
   internationalism, 114, 159
   opposition to nationalism, 68, 114
   organisations in South Africa, 105–6
   political uses of literature, 84–91, 122, 129
   relationship to national liberation, 95, 111, 142
   scientific, 92
   in United States, 91–2
   utopian, 71, 83–4, 90–1
   see also Communism; International Socialist League
Sotho (language), 97, 173n
South Africa in Mars (Lamont), 18–19, 24, 103, 160
South African Communist Party (SACP), 40, 132, 148, 179n; *see also* Communism; Communist Party of South Africa

South African Native National Congress (SANNC), 11, 92
South African Native Policy and the Liberal Spirit (Hoernlé), 25–6, 31
South African Worker, The, 79, 80, 82, 86, 87, 88, 100
Sowden, Lewis, 31, 34, 40, 160, 161, 170n
Soyinka, Wole, 153–4
Spartacus (Fast), 7, 144–5, 160
Spartacus Club, 106, 123, 129
Spenser, Edmund, 127, 193n
Spinoza, Baruch, 138
Stalin, Joseph, 9, 84, 102–3, 118, 123, 139, 183n; *see also* anti-Stalinism
Stedman Jones, Gareth, 179n
Steinbeck, John, 129–30
Story of an African Farm, The (Schreiner), 38
Sunter, Clem, 6
Swinburne, Algernon, 53, 84, 87–8, 160, 175n

Tabata, I. B.
 critique of liberalism, 109–10
 dream of freedom, 4, 40, 161
 formation of APDUSA, 121
 internationalism, 112, 114
 land ownership, 118–19, 121
 leadership of AAC, 106, 121
 meeting with Nkrumah, 117, 132
 political use of literature, 125, 130, 151
 publications, 107, 118–19, 124
 relationship with Jordan, 187n
 relationship with Mqotsi, 131–2
Tambo, Oliver, 134, 140
Tamsanqa, K., 151
Taylor, Dora, 4, 107, 119, 122–5, 127–30, 160, 161, 184n, 186n, 187n
Ten-Point Programme *see* Non-European Unity Movement: Ten-Point Programme
Thaele, James Saul Mokete, 46–50, 134; *see also* Garveyism
Thibedi, William, 76, 95, 104–5, 117
Thomas, Albert, 128–9
Thompson, E. P., 89
Thompson, Francis, 138–9
Thomson, John, 138–9

Tomorrow's Comet (Sowden), 31, 160
'Tot System in the North' (anon.), 86
trade unionism, 42, 52, 55–7, 62–3, 66, 95, 100, 105–6; *see also* Industrial and Commercial Workers' Union
trans-national community of resistance, 25, 47–8, 66–8, 112–14, 131, 136, 161; *see also* anti-colonial movements; internationalism; Pan-Africanism; resistance
Trek, 107, 124, 160
Trotsky, Leon
 analysis of South Africa, 114–15, 118
 critiques of, 100, 185n
 early writings, 108
 on literature and art, 121–3, 124, 126–9
 Trotskyism in South Africa, 104–9, 111–12, 117–18, 125, 185n
 Trotskyist publications, 105
 see also anti-Stalinism
Truth About the I. C. U., The (Champion), 56–7
Turok, Ben, 2, 32

U-Don Jadu (Mqhayi), 21–4, 103, 160
UMSA *see* Unity Movement of South Africa
Umsebenzi, 50, 79, 81, 83, 96–9, 100, 102–3, 104
Union of South Africa, 9–10, 18
United Party, 29, 34
United States of America
 African American culture, 53, 59, 62
 African American literature, 58–9, 62
 African American resistance, 59, 134, 175n
 denial of workers' rights, 91–2
 as economic model, 49–50
 imperialism, 91, 113
 slavery, 58, 164n
Unity Movement of South Africa (UMSA), 121
Ushaba (Ngubane), 36–8, 160
USSR *see* Russia; Russian Revolution
utopianism
 Communist critiques of, 83–4, 92, 108
 major and minor utopias, 9, 31, 35
 in resistance groups, 5–6, 42, 140
 utopian socialism, 71, 83–4, 90–1

utopias
  allegorical, 13–14
  contexts for utopian texts, 5–6, 160–1
  as critique of present, 5, 46, 161
  genres, 4
  literature as utopia, 4–5, 128–31
  optimism, 21–4, 46, 72–3, 160, 162–3
  satirical, 11–13
  see also dystopias

Verwoerd, H. F., 137, 140
Verwoerd – The End (Allighan), 35, 160, 161
Vilikazi, B. W., 139
Visser, A. G., 137
voting rights *see* franchise

Wallace, Ernest, 47
Wallerstein, Immanuel, 2–3, 17, 159
When Rain Clouds Gather (Head), 156–7, 160, 161
When Smuts Goes (Keppel-Jones), 28–30, 160, 163
Whittier, John Greenleaf, 57–8
Wild Deer (Lewis), 58, 59–60, 160, 167n

Williams, Raymond, 4
Winter, Jay, 9, 31, 35, 40, 161
Wolton, Douglas, 93, 95, 96, 180n
Wolton, Molly, 95, 96, 180n
Wordsworth, William, 138, 190n, 193n
Workers' Herald, The, 46, 49, 51–2, 54, 58–9, 62, 66–69, 86; *see also* Industrial and Commercial Workers' Union

Xhosa
  land ownership, 120
  language, 47, 81, 97, 173n
  law, 23
  literary representations of, 151
  literature, 126, 151
  nation, 22–4
  prophets, 64
Xuma, A. B., 27, 135, 136

Yeats, W. B., 119

Zola, Emile, 113
Zulu literature and language, 37, 97
Zuma, Jacob, 2
Zusmanovich, Aleksander, 97

EU representative:
Easy Access System Europe
Mustamäe tee 50, 10621 Tallinn, Estonia
Gpsr.requests@easproject.com